DATE DUE

Understanding Diverse Families

Understanding Diverse Families

WHAT PRACTITIONERS NEED TO KNOW

Barbara F. Okun

Foreword by Carol M. Anderson

THE GUILFORD PRESS
New York / London

©1996 The Guilford Press
A Division of Guilford Publications, Inc.
72 Spring Street, New York, NY 10012

Printed in the United States of America

This book is printed on acid-free paper.

Last digit is print number: 9   8   7   6   5   4   3   2   1

Library of Congress cataloging-in-publication data is
available from the publisher.

ISBN 1-57230-056-6

For Doug,
with love, respect, and admiration

Foreword

Family diversity deserves far more attention than it gets. Today, there are more single-parent and reconstituted families than families with two biological parents. There also are an increasing number of grandparents raising children, marriages and families across the boundaries of race and ethnicity, families based on adoption rather than biological parenthood, and even more singles living alone. Although, clearly, traditional families are now the minority family form in this country, we continue to act as if they are not only the gold standard against which all other families should be judged, but as if this family form is absolutely essential for the healthy growth and development of children. Unfortunately, at the very times when diverse types of families are ever more prevalent, governmental policies, the radical right, the culture in general, and even the literature of the family field consistently operate to marginalize and pathologize alternative families.

We look at the disappearance of the traditional family and the emergence of these new patterns of family life, and bemoan the fact that the family, long seen as the building block of society, the cornerstone of the culture, is crumbling, becoming fragmented, lacking in direction and structure. We not only hold families responsible for the problems of their members, but also for the ills of the culture.

Many have responded to their anxieties about a changing world with an increasing emphasis on the need to return to "family values," an unfortunate shorthand phrase that has become associated with decreased tolerance for difference and diversity. Fear of the changes that are occurring has spurred a movement that attempts to turn back the clock to a time that never was. This move to become more constrictive in our definition of a healthy family would have families stay together regardless of the experiences their members have with one another, be it garden-variety marital unhappiness, infidelity, or even persistent and severe family violence. But it isn't possible to eliminate alternatives, even for those who desperately wish to do so. The time we live in is a time of options and choices. We can't put the genie back in the bottle, any more than we can return to a nonindustrial, rural culture, or "undiscover" that the world is round.

We live in a culture in which there are fewer rules, more choices, greater pressure to achieve, and less support from our religious and secular communities for the family unit. How much have we helped families to make their way with fewer maps, fewer universal rules to tell them how to behave and who to be? How much have we helped parents find ways to nurture their children and give them the right values and ways of being in the world? Certainly there is a frightening loss of predictability and stability in the world, but we are a product of our times, our technology, our media, and the pace of our culture. Our security cannot be restored by returning to the past. Families today may be struggling unsuccessfully in part because of the pressure to maintain a structure that no longer works for many people. Perhaps the culture is contributing to making it hard for families to survive, particularly since it has been so slow to recognize the problems of today's families and accept alternative solutions.

What is the problem with not recognizing and accepting the changes occurring in families? At a time when so many families are in trouble, consumed more by the struggle to survive rather than provide their members with a "haven in a heartless world," at a time when the family as we have known it (or at least idealized it) seems to be disintegrating, the failure to address these changes makes it less likely that society will provide the support families need. It also makes it less likely that we will be aware of the strengths of these new family forms and what they can offer to us.

The divergent families depicted in this book do not represent life at the center of society, but rather life on the edges, where families are less steeped in tradition. These families have less to lose by questioning the way things are. Alternative models of families, families thriving on the margins of the culture, present us with new and ever more creative ways of living. On the edges, there is less investment in the way things used to be, less commitment to the status quo, more awareness of the advantages of new ways. Living outside the mainstream culture may be evidence of courage rather than pathology. For those strong and willing enough to cross the boundaries of traditions, perhaps only dimly aware of the trouble they are bargaining for, isn't it in the best interests of children, the culture, and the future to provide them with support? They may well have something to teach us about the possibilities and about ourselves.

Those supporting "family values" would have us believe that there is a cost for diversity, and perhaps there is. On the other hand, there is also a cost for not recognizing and supporting the diversity among us. Rather than marginalizing the alternative families that are emerging, we must begin to recognize their courage, support their strengths, help them to perform their internal tasks, and allow them to become a part of the glue that preserves the values and solidarity of our communities.

The examples of diverse family types that Dr. Okun writes about are not only underrepresented in the literature of psychology and family therapy, but pathologized by it. Additionally, our training programs largely ignore the relevance of diversity, the impact of racial, ethnic, and gender identity on development and functioning, and its centrality to the process of therapy. In fact, we act as if we can put aside the ongoing stress of racism and discrimination because it is a social issue, not the stuff of therapeutic encounters. We are also largely silent on the impact of adoption, except to acknowledge that adopted teens are likely to act out and adopted adults who don't want to search for their birthparents cannot possibly find true mental health.

We assume that children without fathers are children who are deprived, that single-parent families and "broken homes" are an unfortunate and regrettable fact of life, but are certainly not strong and capable of producing healthy children. We assume that having a two-parent, opposite-sex, same-race, right-generation family is always better. Maybe it is, all things being equal. But of course they never are.

It is hard and relentless work raising children, a job that could easily employ two if not a half dozen adults, but isn't a loving grand-parent or single-parent home better for children than years of witnessing and experiencing abuse? Better than experiencing multiple foster-home placements with no sense of permanency? Better than being warehoused in an orphanage?

And for those who assume an intact marriage is better at all costs, is it indicative of some lack of ability to commit if a woman leaves an abusive relationship? Is it good for a child to have a role model of a mother who allows herself to be abused? What has been the cost of family preservation in cases such as these? How many abused and murdered women and children does it take to stimulate the development of supportive policies that allow protection and life outside the "traditional family"?

Too often our assumptions about what constitutes a healthy family remain unexamined, because *well-adjusted* single-parent, grand-parent, multiracial, homosexual, or other diverse families are not part of the clinical populations that we see. We never come to grips with the baggage of our privilege, the impact of the intensity of racism faced by minorities on a daily basis, the insensitivity we have to the needs and priorities of those who are different from ourselves. Yet we assume we can help those who are different without thought for our own prejudices, or even recognition that we have them; without needing to acknowledge that others "not like us" may have a different set of values, priorities, or sense of self. How would we know if our theories and interventions are relevant to their world if we have not examinied it and our own? Without attention to these issues, we may well be missing what is most important to others; we are very likely to impose our ideas about normality and pathology on others inappropriately. It is essential that we become aware of and challenge our core assumptions about family health, reality, and the nature of relationships. The unexamined assumption is not worth having.

This book is a celebration of diversity and an invitation to tolerance. It is not a naive celebration, but one that fully acknowledges the many new forms families have taken and the problems inherent in the new paths they are traveling. By telling us the stories of divergent families, Dr. Okun challenges the grand illusion of the traditional family and the belief that we can return to it. In fact, Dr. Okun challenges our very definition of family. She raises our consciousness about those family forms that are underrepresented in the literature yet prevalent in our world. She attempts to help us understand the context of family functioning. In conducting over 200 interviews, she learned something about the optimism and awareness of these courageous and resilient families who challenge the mainstream culture.

What do the divers families she writes about have to say to us? One central message is the intense need we all have for family, and the lengths we go to to create them for ourselves when we don't have them. These families also help us see the truth about ourselves, our assumptions, biases, values, and our tolerance—or lack thereof.

At a very pragmatic level, in this world of managed care, most of us no longer have the luxury of choosing not to work with certain subgroups. We can no longer afford to eliminate whole categories of clients, nor should we be allowed to. There should be no therapists who say they know nothing about other cultures, gays, adoption, or biracial families. Nor should we be allowed to assume that the same techniques, same theories, and same methods work with all families, regardless of their different experiences, tasks, and problems. The therapy we all must do today demands insight into our own cultural assumptions and awareness of our own cultural blocks to understanding. We must learn to engage and move those who differ from us, those with whom we do not have a common language, a common set of values, or common assumptions. We must learn appropriate strategies of intervention for a variety of families and family experiences.

At a more profound level, Dr. Okun's book begins to prepare us for the needs of tomorrow's families and tomorrow's world by challenging our tolerance for diversity. It is not a book that will please the radical right. It will certainly challenge those who have not given up the dream of returning to the fantasy world of Ozzie and Harriet or the Cleavers. She provides no pat formulas for fitting these families into old templates. She helps us understand families not in the mainstream and gives us pragmatic techniques for helping them. More importantly, she helps us see that it may well be these families who can show us new ways to help all families survive.

Since we cannot return to the way we never were, the essence of the crisis for the family in our time is the need to shift from one traditional family structure to a variety of new forms of family life, all of which must preserve what we value and need most. The family must continue to address our personal and spiritual needs, nurture our relationships and ties, transmit to our children the values of the culture in which we are embedded, and give us a sense of belonging and mutual responsibility to something greater than ourselves, the larger community.

Carol M. Anderson, Ph.D.
University of Pittsburgh

Acknowledgments

I am indebted to the many people who shared their lives so openly over the years: students, clients, colleagues, and interviewees. They have allowed me to learn about the realities of diversity, to feel both the pain and the gratification that comes from authenticity and consistency between one's self-identity and life style choices. The only way I know how to thank them is by spreading their messages, through teaching and writing, in order to help others broaden their own clinical views and practices.

In particular, I want to acknowledge the substantive contributions of particular graduate students: Kevin Kelly and Christine Frizzell, with regard to adoption; Lucia Matthew's wonderful literature review and personal experiences about transracial adoption; Todd Kates and Kendra Bryant's work on homosexuality; Suzanne St. Onge's presentation on biracial identity; and the comprehensive presentations on the history of racism by Jane Pertillar and Deborah Young-Ware, as well as Deborah and her husband's model of biracial couple development. My graduate assistant of two years, Donna Greenberg, contributed enormously to the study of grandparent families as well as the tedious task of reference checking.

To all of the students, colleagues, and friends who sent interviewees my way, I extend heartfelt appreciation. This work has been a collaborative project, requiring the input, encouragement, and support of many.

Contents

Introduction

I n this era of managed health care, neither clinicians nor clients have free range of choice about those with whom they can work. Therefore, regardless of our particular discipline, ethical responsibility requires us to learn how to be effective with diverse populations.

This book is intended to confront myths and stereotypes about what we consider "normal" and what constitutes a "family." It aims to update traditional definitions of "normal families," to fill a gap in professional knowledge, and to highlight the invaluable contributions of people with diverse life experiences to our theories and practice. This book looks at healthy families with creative family structures and practices, and it expands our notions of families and how they work. The book is also intended to help expose clinicians, both entry-level and experienced, to an appreciation of the powerful influences of gender, class, ethnicity, race, geography, and multiple social systems on individuals and their families. I believe that this ecological understanding is essential to effective assessment and treatment.

This book is intended for practitioners who want to understand family types with whom they have little or no clinical or personal experience. It is also intended for graduate students and trainees in counseling and clinical psychology, social work, psychiatric nursing, family therapy, and psychiatry who have had introductory coursework in personality and family therapy theory. People who are considering adopting or entering a gay, lesbian, and/or biracial relationship may also benefit from this book, as may grandparents raising grandchildren and parents concerned about disclosure to their children conceived by advanced reproductive technologies such as sperm donation.

WHAT IS A "NORMAL FAMILY" TODAY?

In the past few decades, there has been a significant shift in the nature and composition of families. In the 1950s and 1960s, a family con-

sisted typically of heterosexual parents in a long-term marriage raising their biological children. Since then, divorce, remarriage, intermarriage, and different kinds of adoption have become much more
prevalent along with openly gay and lesbian relationships, comingling
of races, and women's changing roles. The idea of a single, normative
type of family, even if it ever did exist, no longer applies. The U.S.
Bureau of the Census ("Single Parent Households Rise," 1994) indicates that so-called normative two-parent family comprises less than
one-half of our families today. Many of the data we've relied on to
help us understand "normal families" are out of date.

There is no evidence that abuse, pathology, violence, and incest
are more prevalent in one particular form of family than another. Such
problems cut across class, ethnicity, race, and types of family. What
is noteworthy in the mental health literature is a growing awareness
and increasingly open discussion of the impact of deindustrialization,
racism, sexism, poverty, urban crime, violence, and other sociocultural ills on individuals and families of every persuasion. There is even
acknowledgment that the yearning for the traditional "Ozzie and Harriet" family is nothing more than nostalgia for a life style that was far
from representing the norm.

Traditional family therapy theories were based on the research
and clinical study of conventional families, primarily a narrow band
of White, middle-class urbanites who lived in a very different sociocultural context than many of today's families. Studies of the "normalcy" of alternative family structures are quite recent (see Walsh, 1993).
Attention to family diversity can be largely credited to the courageous
determination of theorists and therapists who are feminist, gay and
lesbian, and/or of color. In the past decade, they have successfully
confronted the biases of the mainstream mental health professions and
have challenged traditional theoretical and clinical assumptions. These
efforts are supported by the work of contemporary developmental psychologists, who are introducing us to notions of variant normative paths
of development, which require us to reassess and modify our concepts
of "normal" and "deviant."

OVERVIEW OF THE BOOK

In this book, readers can learn about adoptive families from the perspective of birth mothers, adoptive parents, and adoptees; about gay
and lesbian families from the perspective of their offspring, siblings,
and parents; about youngsters raised from birth by never-married parents, and the special tribulations of these single parents; and about

couples who break racial and ethnic taboos by marrying outside their groups and hear their offspring talk about growing up "different." Through hearing all these voices, we can gain new appreciation for the resilience, courage, and strengths of those who dare to be different. If clinicians learn more about the particular psychological issues associated with family differences, they can alter their own internal paradigms and bring a supportive nonjudgmental demeanor to their contacts with different kinds of families or individuals in diverse families.

This book provides an in-depth focus on three variant normative types of families: adoptive, gay and lesbian, and multiracial (including transracial adoption). Adoptive, gay and lesbian, and multiracial families were selected because they are increasingly visible and yet they have the least amount of exposure in the literature. In addition to these three family types, there is briefer coverage of three other family types: single parents by choice, grandparent families, and families by reproductive technology. The latter are more recent, fewer in number, and little studied. This book is based on a review of the relevant literature to the extent it exists and is supplemented by my own ongoing phenomenological research, which I will describe shortly.

Chapter 1 provides an overview of diverse families in context with a rationale for the ecological perspective that will be used. Chapters 2 through 10 examine in depth the three different family formats that were the focus of this study: adoptive, gay and lesbian, and multiracial. There are three chapters for each family format: the first providing an overview of the literature and the family format in historical and contemporary sociocultural context, the second presenting psychological issues from a developmental perspective, and the third discussing clinical implications. Throughout, the voices of interviewees and clinical vignettes are presented to illustrate the integration of ecological, intergenerational, current, developmental, and other facets of family life in assessment and intervention. The book is organized to begin the discussion of each family format from a historical and developmental ecological perspective. The purpose is to highlight the impact of historical, political, and sociocultural variables on psychological issues over the life span of the family. This conceptual framework leads to discussion of clinical issues and implications for assessment and intervention. Chapter 11 discusses three emerging family types that do not as yet have the literature and numbers to warrant in-depth focus: single parents by choice, grandparent families, and families by artificial reproductive technology.

In organizing this book, I had to make some arbitrary choices. I decided to include transracial adopters and adoptees in the multiraciality section and biracial gay and lesbian couples in the gay and lesbian section. This reflects my subjective view of salience at the time of manuscript preparation. With regard to language, I have received much conflicting feedback about correct terminology. Both the professional literature and the popular media utilize varied terms, depending upon whether the context is political, conceptual, and/or clinical. My intent is to be inclusive and nonoffensive.

ABOUT THE STUDY

For the past 3 years, I have been conducting an ongoing phenomenological study of members of the above-mentioned family types. This is a nonclinical sample. I have been particularly interested in nonclinical populations for three reasons: (1) Most studies about diverse families are based on clinical populations and, therefore, are not representative of people who do not consider themselves troubled; (2) many of the biases reflected in the literature stem from overgeneralization of data from clinical populations with little attention to the wide range and extent of intragroup differences; and (3) I have sufficient access to clinical cases through colleagues, supervisees, and my own clinical practice.

This study was begun to expand my own knowledge base to inform my teaching and clinical practice. The idea for a book came after I began the study and realized that I wanted to share the richness of my learning. I learned from the literature, from my interviewees, and from my own clients that they experience the same developmental crises that conventional families do, but they experience these crises differently. Due to the very fact of their being less accepted by society than members of traditional families, members of variant family types have difficulty trying to obtain unbiased advice, information, and counsel. They may need help handling the pressures of prejudice and discrimination against those with different life styles and viewpoints.

The study upon which the book is based began 3 years ago, when I sought out interviewees who were directly or indirectly associated with adoptive, gay and lesbian, multiracial, and/or single-parent-by-choice families. I wanted to talk to birth mothers, adoptees, and adoptive parents; gay and lesbians and their families of origin, spouses, and children; biracial couples and their families of origin and children; single parents by choice and their children; and grandparents and the grandchildren they are rearing. I asked students, colleagues, friends, clients, and participants in workshops and conferences to steer subjects my way. What was at first a gradual response to my requests for interviewees has proved overwhelming; after two years, I had to put potential subjects on hold.

As of this writing, I have conducted 187 interviews. Some of these have been individual interviews, but most have been with couples and families. About 40 have been telephone interviews, conducted in order to reach distant members of a subject family. The telephone interviews averaged 1 hour, whereas the personal interviews ranged from 2 to 3 hours. While a majority of the personal interviews took place in Boston, the subjects did not necessarily reside in Boston. Many were visiting friends or family or passing through on business or vacation.

The study sample consists of 12 birth mothers, 14 pairs of adoptive parents, and 31 adoptees; 12 lesbian couples; 14 gay male couples; 10 single gay men; 12 single lesbians; 4 siblings of gays or lesbians and 18 parents of gays or lesbians; 22 biracial couples; 16 transracial adoptive parents; 9 parents or siblings of biracial and transracial adoptive couples and 14 children of biracial and transracial adoptive families; 12 single mothers by choice, 2 single fathers by choice, and 8 adolescent or young adult offspring of single parents by choice; 11 grandparents as parents and 7 adults raised in grandparent families; and 8 sperm donors and 4 couples who have used artifical reproductive technology.

The interview format was open and nondirective. After a description of my purpose for the interview, to learn about variant normative family structures, the interviewee was encouraged to "tell your story," and to "tell me what you think is important for me to learn." I participated as a collaborative guide, and I had only to ask few questions; people were eager to talk and to participate in dialogue. They often answered my questions before I even asked them! I was awed by the strength and resilence I found, and touched by people's open sharing.

The people who speak in this book have requested anonymity in order to be able to speak openly and freely. I respect these requests and, in my writing, use composite as well as direct anecdotes. I disguise the identity and specific geographical location of all subjects. These interviewees are primarily middle class, at least in their current family systems; many were raised, however, in blue-collar families. Several of the gay and lesbian interviewees consider themselves still to be blue collar. Several adoptive parents, biracial couples, and most of the single parents by choice describe themselves as "professional" or "upper middle class." None of the interviewees felt that they were discriminated against because of their class; many were surprised that their class status did not protect them more from societal disapproval. I recognize and acknowledge that my interviewees are more representative of the middle class than lower or upper classes. I also make no attempts to generalize from this informal study with a limited sample. There are indeed methodological flaws in a study such as this, particularly in terms of sampling and inevitable interviewer bias. My retelling their story makes me a co-constructor.

These interviewees were all eager volunteers whose major motivation was to help others understand and appreciate that they are just as healthy and worthy as those who have made more traditional choices. My objective is to share my learning by describing the psychological issues with which marginalized groups contend and by stating my respect for their successful survival and coping capacities. In addition, I present an overview of significant literature as a framework for my interviews and discussion of clinical implications. I sincerely hope that this book brings a greater understanding of these healthy and courageous families.

ONE

Diverse Families
in Context

Myths abound about adoptive, gay and lesbian, and multiracial families, and their viability, health, and normality. Whereas a few decades ago they were not recognized as "true families," today, due to changes in cultural values, and a subsequent reduction of social stigma, these families are increasingly prevalent and visible.

No longer in the minority, diverse families may be more typical today than the traditional nuclear family (Gottfried & Gottfried, 1994). As therapists, and members of society in general, variant families offer us the opportunity to broaden our perspectives, to revisit our presumptions and assumptions of "normalcy" and "pathology," and to appreciate more fully the effects of dominant sociocultural constructs on our lives and work. Understanding these families also enables us to develop respect for others' self-determination and unique approaches to living.

In order to appreciate, understand, and be of help to these families, clinicians need a broader grasp of the particular psychological issues associated with their differences. These issues cannot be considered outside of historical and sociocultural contexts. For, just as there are intergenerational influences within a family system, so these influences exist within larger social systems.

As clinicians, we need to take into account the multivariate nature of children's development in all kinds of family structures from a neutral, rather than a biased negative or positive, viewpoint. Just as a child who is not a "good fit" in his or her family may become the identified patient, scapegoat, or lightening rod for family distress, the family that is not a "good fit" in a larger sociocultural context may serve the same function as the focus of the frustrations of the community. An ecological perspective can enable clinicians to be active advocates for client families across individual, family, and larger social system spheres.

Although clinical strategies and techniques utilized with more conventional families may not differ with variant families, therapists' listening can become more attuned to how these individuals and families cope with the reactions and prohibitions society has against those who dare to challenge authority and traditional mores. If therapists understand that people are embedded in a social context, their perception of clinical priorities and emphases can't help but be affected. Active advocacy and empowerment become higher priorities within the clinician's armamentarium.

Ralph, a 45-year-old African American, is married to Tina, a 41-year-old Caucasian. They have two children, Bobby, age 11, and Lianne, age 8. Ralph also has a 24-year-old daughter, Martha, from a previous marriage to his African American high school sweetheart. Martha has been in a lesbian relationship with Torrie, 36, for 4 years. Torrie, a single Caucasian woman, adopted a baby, Grace, in Central America 7 years ago.

All of these family members live in the Washington, DC, area and they spend a lot of time together. Martha lived with her mother for the 2 years between Ralph's divorce and his marriage to Tina. Shortly after the marriage, because of the tensions and conflicts between mother and daughter, Martha chose to live with Ralph and Tina. While this family experiences the same disappointments, stresses, and strains as any middle-class American family, they describe themselves as "happy and lucky." Ralph and Tina acknowledge that the first couple of years of their marriage were difficult, particularly because they had little time alone as a couple before Martha moved in with them. But they learned to talk openly with each other and to work collaboratively to make decisions and solve problems. They say that they feel lucky to be healthy; to have healthy, easy children; to have loving, supportive families; and, particularly in these hard economic times, to love their chosen professions. They talk passionately about their family, friends, and work. There is tremendous energy in this family; they are vibrant, and they thrive on activities with extended family and friends.

As school teachers in city elementary schools and in the liberal suburban community in which they reside, they have not been faced with much racial intolerance or lack of acceptance. Occasionally, when they go into the city for an evening, they hear snide remarks, but they do not let it bother them. The children are in integrated schools and play with both African American and Caucasian children. Although Ralph and Tina's families of origin do not have much occasion to interact with each other, Ralph and Tina maintain warm relations with both, alternating holiday trips.

Ralph and Tina are more accepting of Martha's lesbianism than her biological mother is. However, Ralph reports that coming to terms with Martha's lesbianism, which emerged while she was in college, was the most difficult challenge he ever faced in his family life, more so than his divorce. Without Tina, he doesn't know if he would have become aware of and confronted his homophobia. He believes that his upbringing in a Southern Baptist community is the reason his homophobia was more intense than Tina's. During Martha's college years when she was exploring her sexual orientation, Tina was her confidant and the connecting link between father and daughter. Today, he kids around about being a "grampa" at the same time he's a "daddy." He is proud of his African American heritage and has consciously fostered biracial pride in his and Tina's children. Both Ralph and Tina claim that they are equally comfortable with friends and colleagues of both races.

Martha, currently in graduate social work school, and Torrie, a nurse, are active in a lesbian community and belong to a lesbian parenting group. While Torrie is definitely the primary parent, Martha's involvement is increasing as she becomes more secure in her adult lesbian identity.

Does this family sound like a fictitious invention? It isn't. In our complex, varied society, this family represents the dramatic changes that have occurred in the composition and structure of family form in the past 25 years. This family is one of the most relaxed, enjoyable families I've ever spent time with. Laughingly they report that they do have their moments of tension and conflict. But they are able to engage actively in discussion, to problem solve together, and they never lose sight of their basic loyalty and commitment to each other and to their core value of family.

How are they able to withstand the presumably devastating effects of racism, homophobia, and divorce? They have had to work hard throughout their lives to achieve what they have, but both Ralph and Tina believe that the support and acceptance they received from significant others (for Ralph, his parents, and for Tina, her grandmother and a particular elementary school teacher) allowed them to develop sufficient self-esteem to view problems and difficulties as challenges rather than catastrophes. They have developed a nurturing family system that seems to foster resiliency in its members.

WHAT IS A NORMAL FAMILY?

Is the above family "normal"? That depends, of course, on how you define the term "normal." Statistically, they clearly are not the norm, given that they are biracial and that lesbianism and adoption are part of the family system. Although multiculturalism is on the rise in our society, multicultural families are still treated as a minority by a threatened, shrinking, White, middle-class, dominant culture. Torrie, originally a single parent by choice, is also not the statistical norm.

In terms of religious norms, there are many organized religions that would find this family "sinful" and "immoral." Legally, lesbian relationships are not acknowledged or recognized, and there are some states where biracial marriages are discouraged and where they would not be given recognition or status as a family. Socioculturally, this family might be viewed by the dominant culture as pathological because it violates mainstream notions of how a family is to be composed and how it is supposed to function. Within subgroups of a particular culture, however, they may be considered normal, for example, in biracial or gay and lesbian communities, or transracial adoption groups. If one considers normalcy from a biological perspective, they would be deemed normal in that, regardless of their race, ethnicity, class, and sexual orientation, they live and function as do other human beings.

According to traditional psychological, theoretical norms based on patriarchal, White, middle-class individuals and nuclear families, this family would be considered at "high risk" for psychological disturbance. Until recently, adoption, single parenting, intermarriage, and homosexuality have been discussed in abnormal psychology courses! Although these are no longer viewed as "pathological" family types, many people in our society, including many mental health professionals, still have ingrained biases that lead them to expect individual and family dysfunction from people who differ from convention. If conformance to traditional models is viewed as the norm, than any questioning or challenge is considered deviant.

Our current medical-based models label (in the form of diagnosing) what is "normal" and "healthy" and what is "abnormal" and "sick." These labels enable and support expectations about which people and families will become sick and which won't, and are the basis of the criteria for defining and determining health. Thus, a self-fulfilling prophecy is likely to occur. If we expect, for example, an adopted child to have learning difficulties in school, the expectation itself can create perceptions of behavior that we label as "learning disabled," and the responses to these "learning disabled" behaviors reinforce any difficulties the child may have. Labeling theory is predicated on the notion that labels reflect cultural values and expectations. Over and over, we see that once we give something a label, a new category exists to be filled.

Within the mental health professions, we are still struggling with concepts of "normal" and "pathological," as well as with whether we believe psychological development to be linear or circular, monolithic or multiplistic, influenced more by biology or environment. The conventional theoretical views about human development and psychological functioning are now being challenged earnestly by contemporary theorists (see Rutter & Rutter, 1993) and practitioners who appreciate the multifaceted complexity of human behavior and development. The culture-specific psychological stage theories of human development may be constrictive when applied to diverse populations.

Demographic changes within the mental health professions have reflected societal demographic changes. These have created a context for change agents, namely increased numbers of women, people of color, and gays and lesbians who are already in the field and currently entering it. Change is also resulting from the differing needs of a more diversified client population. These shifting demographics challenge the field to acknowledge and incorporate into theory and practice the effects of gender, class, ethnicity, sexual orientation, and race on individual and family development, and on general psychological functioning and well-being. They challenge us to incorporate reciprocally influencing interactions among individuals, families, and larger social institutions in our clinical assessment and treatment. To do this, individual human development and behavior need to be considered from a contextual perspective: The individual is embedded within a family that, in turn, is embedded within a culturally diverse society. Not only will psychological stresses emanating from any one context affect the individual's functioning in other contexts, but personality is shaped by the family and larger social context, by gender, race, class, and ethnicity.

Contextual consideration enables us to reformulate the concept of "normal" with regard to psychological functioning. The concept of "normal" is neither phenomenological nor objective; it is a social construction (see Gergen, 1985). Without understanding context, we cannot make meaning of people's concerns and behaviors. Without understanding clients' meaning and its implications, we cannot help people to understand what part of their difficulties can be attributed to intrapsychic, to interpersonal, and to larger social system variables. How these difficulties are approached depends on their contextual nature.

Our demographics have begun to shift toward a more multicultural society, due to increased immigration and intermarriage. The civil rights, women's, and gay liberation movements have challenged the assumptions about roles, functions, and the family structure of the traditional White, male, middle-class dominant culture. In this context, conventional views of what is a "normal family" require reconsideration.

Traditionally, a family has been defined as an intact, biologically related system of two heterosexual parents in which the father is the sole or primary economic provider and the mother the sole or primary caretaker. The father is supposed to provide for the basic physical needs of family members, such as food, clothing, and shelter; the mother is supposed to monitor and supervise children's daily activities, provide protection, and teach children how to behave according to the rules of society. She also traditionally manages the domestic chores of the household and the family's social interactions with extended family and the community. Both parents are supposed to teach children right from wrong, respect for the rights of others, and societal values. The parents are supposed to act complementarily, while at the same time meeting each other's needs for emotional and sexual relationship. This definition of family was socially constructed and assumed to be the best way to raise children.

A recent U.S. Bureau of the Census report ("Single Parent Households Rise," 1994) notes that today less than 50% of American children are being raised in two-parent heterosexual families. The remaining 50% include the increasing number of children being raised by their grandparents, single parents by choice, families who have adopted, and lesbian and gay families, many of whom are not recognized legally as constituting a family. Interfaith and multiracial families might be counted in both groups, depending on whether they are two-parent married families.

As people become more open about their personal lives, clinicians are learning from adult offspring that many of those intact families considered to represent our ideal, typical American family concealed serious problems, such as physical, sexual, substance, and emotional abuses. Secrecy, not normalcy and/or health, characterized these families more than we care to acknowledge. The traditional idea of family no longer fits well with the reality of today's families if it ever did. Far-reaching societal changes over the past 40 years have had an impact.

Social Changes

The seeds for great social change were planted during World War II, when people were uprooted and exposed to members of different classes, races, and cultures; to different value systems; and to different geographical locations. This exposure resulted in the loosening of geographical family ties and changed the functions of the family. The family no longer worked together as in the earlier agrarian and beginning industrial societies. Increased mobility led to psychological as well as geographical separation. This psychological separation from family and community connectedness fostered further value change. An increase of consumerism enhanced materialistic values; individualism enhanced individual entitlement, and there were other dramatic value shifts. People began to marry "others," those from different backgrounds. Or they formed new relationship formats, such as single people living alone or with a partner of the same or opposite sex, dual-career families with or without children, single parents, stepfamilies, communal groups, and so forth.

The first major challenge to the conventional social construction of family came about with the post-World War II increase in divorce. This resulted in more single-parent families and more reconstituted or blended families from remarriages. This challenge was not easily tolerated by mainstream society; people who did divorce were considered "failures," "sick," or "immoral." Because of this stigma, many people chose to remain in unhappy marriages, even though this created tense, confusing family environments for many children. The prevailing view among mental health professionals, was (and still is, to a large extent) that children from divorced families would be particularly vulnerable to psychological difficulties. A further post-World War II challenge was an increase in interfaith and interracial marriages. The children of these marriages were also considered to be at risk for psychological problems, and their parents were considered "rebellious" or "foolhardy" to attempt to cross racial, religious, and ethnic barriers. Other changes and challenges followed, including nonconformance in sexual orientation.

Today's Families

In the past 25 years, we have seen the steady increase of varied family types. As women have entered the work force, and as two incomes have become necessary for most families, couples have postponed marriage and childbearing. This has heightened incidences of infertility, creating an international market for adoption. As new ethnic minorities have diversified our demographics and value systems, there have been more opportunities for intermarriage. More and more single professional and managerial women are choosing to bear children without the "benefit" of marriage.

Our notions of family need to be reassessed and broadened. Does a family, for example, have to have biological ties? May it be a committed group of people who care about each other? Must it be heterosexual? of one race or culture? Does it require two parents? Does the primary parent have to be female? Is the critical factor in outcome family structure or adults' generative capacities to focus on children's needs and development? The seminal work of McGoldrick, Pearce, and Giordano (1982); McGoldrick (1993); and Walsh (1993) lays the groundwork for reconsidering assumptions about normal families.

As we learn about more cases of sexual, physical, and emotional abuse; of alcoholism and other substance abuse; of neglect, exploitation, and other horrors, we have to ask ourselves why these serious problems exist in so-called normal family structures if that is the "only" or "right" way for families to be.

It becomes obvious that what makes a family work is not biology, legality, or cultural dominance, but, rather, commitment, caring, and the capacity to value others' needs and welfare as much as one's own. These conditions foster adaptable and flexible responsiveness to inevitable developmental and systems change. It also becomes obvious that we need social policies that provide individuals, couples, and families with opportunities for survival and growth. Until we provide everyone—across class, race, and geography—with quality education, employment, health care, and child and family supports, we are going to have troubled families who are unable to care for each other and to sustain commitment. These troubles will be manifested in disabling tensions; conflict; substance abuse; physical, emotional, and sexual abuses; abandonment; neglect; increased crime and random violence; and physical and mental illnesses.

As we learn about different relationship rules and roles from clients who have been reared and socialized in different ethnic groups, we can recognize different family values and formats. And, we can learn that different family types share some overarching values and objectives such as safety; mutual respect and caring; nurturing; raising healthy, productive children; and developing and maintaining effective relationships within a loyal, committed organization of kin. The White, middle-class assumptions we have about how a family should be comprised and how it should function do not hold up as the only "right" way for families.

There are many families who, despite their nondominant status in our society, have resilience, strengths, and levels of commitment far beyond our conventional "Leave It to Beaver" model. We need to learn from them how they have created their families and maintained their strengths in the face of cultural devaluation. The more than 200 people whom I have interviewed for this book represent a nonclinical population belonging to alternative family types. They are living proof that being different has the potential for strength and resilience as well as unhappiness and illness. They challenge our presumption that being different is a sure path to pathology. Furthermore, most of them do not view themselves as experiencing undue differences or stresses. The overall theme of their perceptions appears to be pride in their identities and in their courage to create and develop a family structure that, while it differs from convention, works for them.

EXAMINING ASSUMPTIONS
ABOUT MENTAL HEALTH AND FAMILY

Some children from divorced families, adopted children, gay and lesbian youth, single parents, or multiracial people can and do experience psychological difficulties. But these may be related more to societal prejudice and oppression than to some inherent pathological condition or type of family structure. The alienation and discomfort that derives from being different, from being ignored and devalued cannot be underestimated. If we do not acknowledge the fluidity of human development within sociocultural contexts, we perpetuate the development of psychological distress. We need to examine and reassess our theoretical and clinical assumptions in accordance with sociocultural changes. This does not mean that we should abandon our traditional heritages. Continuing to redefine and refine basic assumptions and concepts is part of the profession's traditional heritage. Our paradigms can then continue to evolve, rather than becoming static and outdated.

Data from developmental psychology indicate multiple, multifaceted paths of development for individuals and families. The data from social psychology and sociology confirm the damaging impact of biased, constrictive sociocultural institutions on human beings. The effects of poverty, unemployment, inaccessibility to adequate health care, and unequal educational opportunities, to name a few, add to institutionalized sexism, racism, heterosexism, and classism. These critical factors have a significant impact on the psychological and physical well-being of individuals, couples, and families. Divorced families not adversely affected by economic reverses do not have the same difficulties as divorced families whose economic circumstances are drastically reduced. Interracial and gay and lesbian couples and families who can choose tolerant communities and fields of work that allow economic self-sufficiency are less likely to be as overwhelmed by discrimination as are those without these resources.

Mental health professionals today are working with an increasingly diverse client population. More varied clients are requesting services as the overall population becomes more diversified. Managed health care has spawned limited panels of providers. So, clients may not have the option of choosing clinicians of their own gender, sexual orientation, race, or ethnicity. Clinicians, of necessity, must become more aware of the effects of their own socialization and training on their assumptions. They need to reassess and revise their paradigms in order to adapt to the reality of changing treatment contexts — managed, brief, and with a more diverse client population.

As previously noted, since the 1970s traditional theories of human development and psychotherapy have been challenged by women and feminists, and now by multiculturalist, gay, and lesbian theorists and practitioners. Feminist therapists have shown us how applying male standards to female development and functioning has pathologized women. These challenges result in the continuous questioning of the assumptions of traditional models. For example, the theories of women's development as differing from male development (Gilligan, 1982; J. B. Miller, 1976) have paved the way for feminist family therapy theorists (Boyd-Franklin, 1989; Goodrich, Rampage, Ellman, & Halstead, 1988; Laird, 1988, 1989; Luepnitz, 1988; Mirkin, 1994; Walters, Carter, Papp, & Silverstein, 1988) to challenge patriarchal family theories. We are learning to value different family types and styles, rather than expecting all families to fit into a universal, traditional model of family composition and functioning.

Let me give an example of traditional family therapy theory that does not always apply. Many of the multigenerational family theorists, such as Bowen and Framo, explicitly state that people need to be connected to their family of origin in order to develop and maintain satisfactory relationships in their current family system. Current relationship difficulties are thought to emanate from unresolved family-of-origin relationship difficulties. This appears to be based on two assumptions: that "blood is thicker than water," and that family members mean well, despite behaviors that may be harmful and destructive to others in the family. The implication is that parents who have cut themselves off from their families of origin will perpetuate troubled relationships with their children. This may be a nice ideal, but for many of the people I interviewed for this book and with whom I have worked for the past 30 years, it isn't so. They are able to develop and engage in gratifying and effective relationships in adulthood because of a successful divorce from the toxic relationships of their family of origin. Gays, for example, have created families by a conscious affinity so as to provide caretaking for AIDS victims isolated and ostracized by their own biological families (Nuland, 1994). This may not fit in with our Norman Rockwell image of the American family, but, for many, that ideal was, unfortunately, just an image. So, we can't assume that connection to one's family of origin is a requisite for adult relationship functioning. There are too many varying circumstances.

Other assumptions that need to be questioned include the following: biological relationships are better than chosen relationships; two opposite-gender parents are required for effective childrearing; the primary caregiver must be the mother; there must be one primary caregiver; the stigma attributed to alternative life styles will be psychologically crippling; psychopathology emanates from within people and families, regardless of contexts.

Questioning the assumptions of our psychological theories leads to questioning the assumptions of our clinical work. Just as the family therapy movement challenged the prevailing assumptions of individual psychological theory and therapy, we now must question the assumptions of family therapy theory and practice (as has been eloquently done by Luepnitz, 1988; Roberts, 1993; and the authors in Mirkin's [1994] volume). If we understand that individuals and their families must be viewed within the contexts of gender, class, race, and sexual orientation and that families must be viewed within the contexts of other ecological systems (geographical location, religion, as well as political, economic, educational, health, legal, judicial, welfare, kinship, and friend systems to name some), we can reformulate and expand our notions of clinical interventions. Our roles and functions become more multifaceted.

AN ECOLOGICAL PERSPECTIVE OF CLINICAL PRACTICE

Over the years, it has become clear to me that there is no one model of clinical practice that is effective in all situations. As I have shifted my paradigms from the traditional ones in which I was trained and socialized, I have attempted to retain those aspects of theory and practice that have proven over time to be viable. I continue to value relational models, in particular object relations (see Scharff & Scharff, 1987; Slipp, 1984) and the Stone Center model (see J. B. Miller, 1976; Jordan, Kaplan, Miller, Stiver, & Surrey, 1991) based on empathic attachment, as well as the integrative tenets of constructivist cognitive theory. Family systems theories have taught me to appreciate the importance of organizational structures and interactional patterns. I have learned to nest these models within the following larger ecological framework: (1) psychosociobehavioral consideration of the individual within the contexts of family of origin and current family systems; (2) consideration of families within larger sociocultural, political, and economic contexts; and (3) consideration of (1) and (2) as shaping and being shaped by gender, ethnicity, class, sexual orientation, and race. I try to differentiate among individual, group, and universal issues in order to have a better understanding of each client.

The ecological perspective (see Bronfenbrenner, 1979; Keeney & Sprenkle, 1982) is particularly relevant for clients who have been marginalized in our society, such as the families discussed in this book.

Because cultural norms, values, and expectations contribute to the problems for which people seek therapy, we need to understand the unique experiences and coping styles of clients whose cultural assumptions and experiences differ from our own, and the effects of these differences on their lives.

Each clinical situation, then, must be assessed from its own circumstances. What is the treatment context? What kinds of services are accessible and available? This assessment process is inclusive, in that it acknowledges the possibilities of mutually influencing individual pathology, family dysfunction, and societal oppression. There can be simultaneous or intermittent multiple interventions, such as the use of medications, support groups, individual therapy, couple therapy, family therapy, social advocacy, and psychoeducation. Treatment can be intermittent, spread out over time and modalities, or intensely focused in a brief time period.

In this framework, the primary therapist becomes the case manager, the coordinator or orchestrator. A major objective of the overall treatment is the empowerment of the individuals and family to make informed decisions and choices. This requires strategies that will enable them to seek information, and to identify and utilize resources. In order to achieve this, therapists must quickly develop an active, collaborative, supportive, and empathic relationship with individuals and their families. They must demonstrate their empathic understanding of each family's unique experiences and circumstances. Validating these experiences and realities is critical to the therapeutic process. We can begin by reframing clients' concerns from an ecological perspective. For example, we can acknowledge the reality of societal oppression and the impact of this on psychological development. We can help people learn to understand, value, and take pride in their differences and nonconformance with the dominant culture. We can help them to become aware of how they have internalized sociocultural values that lead them to consider themselves "bad" or "sick" because they are different.

Collaboration

From my experiences as part of a family therapy team behind the mirror, I have become more aware of how each of us is influenced in our perceptions by our own lenses. Others' inputs are invaluable in providing effective treatment. Thus, it has become clear to me that we can no longer practice autonomously. In order to maximize quality of services within a cost-effective context, we need to move away from our conventional, solo, independent practices (whether in private practice or in the privacy of our own office within a larger delivery system) toward collaboration. This can be very threatening to independent practitioners' power and status. Many do not take well to questioning and possible disagreement by others once they have completed their required periods of supervision. While I, too, have difficulties with the way utilization review is being conducted in current managed health-care systems, I value the theory of consultation, of checks and balances.

Case management, then, becomes a significant component of service delivery. The primary therapist becomes responsible for coordinating the utilization of pertinent resources from all of the relevant contexts. Because these contexts influence each other, the primary therapist needs to reframe the clients' presenting concerns within these contexts and coordinate the information processing and inputs of all the providers. As a case manager, an objective is to facilitate collaborative interactions among resources, between providers and clients, as well as among clients.

As clinicians, our thinking and actual work becomes open to others' reactions. Although in my private practice I do not have a one-way mirror, I often use audio tapes (as do my collaborators) so that we can not only aid clients in their growth, but also so we can ensure that we are all working toward the same objectives. Thus, I will listen to a client's sessions with another therapist or a psychopharmacologist, just as other providers will listen to tapes of my sessions. This does take more time, but it helps to focus treatment and is well worth the time investment. In addition, it provides an enriching learning opportunity for me in that I receive "live" consultation.

CASE EXAMPLE

Jennifer, a 52-year-old biracial elementary school teacher, was referred by the school psychologist in her building a few months after she was put on administrative leave for "conduct unbecoming a teacher." The agreement she had signed with her superintendent for reinstatement required psychological treatment. Jennifer didn't have a clue as to what this "unbecoming" behavior was; the incidents she recited seemed far too benign for such extreme action. She believed that the new African American female principal in her building was threatened by her outspokenness and the fact that she was the only staff member "of color," and was using a few unsubstantiated parents' complaints as a way of "getting rid of her." She could not understand why her colleagues and the large group of parents of her pupils from the past 12 years remained silent and had not come to her support.

Jennifer's husband, Ralph, an African American secondary school principal in another district, had insisted on Jennifer's using the services of his attorney friend and both he and the attorney had discouraged Jennifer from resisting the imposition of this leave. Her 27-year-old son, Greg, who lived at home, and her 29-year-old daughter, Kerry, who lived in another city, were split: Greg wanted her to fight and Kerry wanted her to let it go. By the time I saw Jennifer, she had not been working for 3 months and was showing clear signs of depression: inability to sleep, weight loss, agitation, social isolation, and disorientation.

In a family session with her husband and son, other difficulties emerged. Ralph's obesity and recent absorption in a religious cult had drawn him further away from his family. This had developed over the past 5 years, since Ralph's change of career from higher education teaching to secondary school administration. The couple had little contact with each other outside of that required by living in the same household. Each was completely absorbed in his or her own career, which made it clear why Jennifer was experiencing such a severe grief reaction, cut off from her major source of self-esteem and gratification.

Ralph was upset by his wife's evident distress and kept urging her to look for a job in another district and to "get with it." He was impatient with her. Greg, a college graduate, was not working and exhibited his own signs of depression. With this new structuring of the family brought on by Jennifer's being at home, mother and son were becoming close buddies while Dad drifted further and further away. Jennifer reported that Ralph was furious at Greg for not finding a job and that she always had been the placater between him and the children. Ralph could not tell me why he had urged Jennifer to sign the agreement with her school district (in which she literally gave away all of her rights to dispute the charges against her).

As a therapist, what struck me the most was my feeling that there were secrets lurking in the background, that everyone was wearing a mask so that the others could not get too close to what was really going on. The legal documents I had requested to see just did not make sense. Jennifer appeared to be unusually naive, lacking any awareness of what was going on in her family or anywhere else, as well as lacking sensitivity to interpersonal cues and the need for self-protection. No one in this family seemed to have any real knowledge of who anyone else in the family was. In the first few sessions, family members insisted that race was not an issue, even though Ralph and Greg made reference to Jennifer's and Kerry's "light skin."

After several sessions with Jennifer, and then with different combinations of the family (including Kerry when she was home for a visit), I referred Jennifer for a pharmacological consultation. The woman psychiatrist to whom I referred her felt that, while Jennifer might benefit from some medication, we should hold off and see how a few more sessions of active therapy would progress. She would be reassessed in 1 month. We both agreed that Jennifer's lifelong theme was "keeping her head buried in the sand." Having my clinical impressions confirmed was enormously helpful.

As I developed credibility with Jennifer, I was able to urge her to consult another attorney. I was concerned that, if she was not reinstated, she might not receive references enabling her to obtain a job in another district. I also could not understand the legalities of the situation; it seemed to me that she was being grossly mistreated. Within 24 hours, the activist attorney to whom I had referred Jennifer had met with the superintendent and the school committee and had arranged for Jennifer's reassignment to another school in the district for the following school year. From this process, I learned enough about the incidents that had caused this administrative leave that I was able to work with Jennifer on her insensitivity to others' cues and her impulsive responses. I was able to show her how her behaviors were perceived by others and to teach her to question her assumptions about what something means or doesn't mean. The incidents were unsubstantiated and, by themselves, did not warrant such reactions as she received. There clearly was something else going on here, but whatever it was, Jennifer certainly contributed to it by her thoughtless remarks to parents and colleagues. I was also able to help Jennifer understand that, in this era of cutbacks, her colleagues were frightened and their avoidance of outright support for her against their principal was due to their own vulnerabilities (although she did receive some private letters and phone calls).

As Jennifer began to regain some self-esteem, Ralph began to attend couple sessions. He agreed to attend a support group for compulsive eaters in order to lose weight (I had urged him to have a physical examination, which, not surprisingly, indicated severe hypertension). The couple began to talk about racial issues for the first time. They acknowledged how they had become isolated from an African American community and identity and how lonely they each felt. Reviewing their genograms, they began to talk to each other for the first time about their feelings regarding race, life style, hopes, and dreams. Jennifer felt terribly betrayed by the African American principal who she believed (probably with accuracy) was "out to get her," and this had caused her to pull away from participating in Ralph's few work functions that included interracial groups. Ralph had interpreted her pulling away as pulling away from him, not realizing that it had to do with her distrust of others. We designed some new social activities for them to initiate as a couple with both African American and Caucasian couples. I had an individual session with Ralph to check out a hunch: that his reason for not wanting Jennifer to resist the job action was due to his fear of publicity, which might expose secrets in his life. My hunch proved correct, and Ralph, after disclosing adulterous relationships with White women, one of which resulted in his losing a former job, acknowledged that he did not want to disrupt his marriage and that he was going to work hard to build a bridge with Jennifer.

At the end of the 2nd month of therapy, Greg requested an individual session. He revealed his homosexuality and told me that he was terrified of complete ostracism by his parents if they were ever to find out. I referred him to an African American gay therapist and my colleague and I agreed that Greg would also benefit from participation in an interracial gay group. The African American gay therapist confirmed the validity of Greg's fears about his parents' likely reaction to his homosexuality and became very helpful to him. One month after these referrals, Greg was making enough progress that he was able to find a job. That was a major accomplishment, although we were still aiming for him to be able to live away from home.

One of my goals of therapy with Jennifer and Ralph became the building of a family climate where eventually Ralph could be more open with Jennifer, where Jennifer could learn to open her eyes without fear, and where Greg would be able to be open and honest with his parents. Without my interactions with the consulting psychiatrist, who later prescribed antidepressant medication for Ralph; with the gay therapist treating Greg; and with the attorney representing Jennifer, I might never have enabled this family to progress as far as they did in the course of a few months. My consideration of the educational/work, legal, medical, gay, African American, and White suburban contexts enabled me to understand the multifaceted variables contributing to their psychological identities and functioning. An added benefit of this collaborative therapeutic process was the family's stated appreciation of the efforts of the several professionals working with them. The family trusted me and that carried over to their reactions to the other providers. They knew we operated as a team and that reinforced our effectiveness. Against this background, I was able to engage Jennifer in deeper introspection as to the development of her "see no evil, hear no evil," isolating defenses.

Currently, I am seeing Jennifer and Ralph every 6 weeks. Jennifer has just begun teaching in a new school, and, at the suggestion of her attorney, I will be available to help her keep her eyes open and not repeat some of the mistakes she made in the past. I use these sessions to check on how they are doing as a couple, to see how Ralph is taking care of himself. Before each session, I check in with the treating psychiatrist and Greg's therapist, and together we plan for the next 6 weeks.

In total, I have had 16 sessions with members of this family. I have probably had a dozen telephone conversations with other treaters. Although it is always uncomfortable for me to have information that is not known to all family members, such as Greg's homosexuality and Ralph's secrets concerning adultery, that is my problem. Unless and until this family is able to deal with this information, I do not feel I have the right to force disclosure. If I did not have this information, I would still be in the dark and unable to be of effective assistance.

This case example illustrates the utilization of active empowerment techniques, consultation with collaborators, acknowledgment and understanding of the sociocultural contexts in which this family is embedded, and continuous reassessment and redefinition of objectives. I doubt that Ralph and Jennifer will ever have a truly intimate marriage. But I think they can enjoy a mutually respectful, congenial friendship. When the day arrives that Greg feels secure enough in his identity development to disclose his homosexuality, I hope that his parents are able to accept and embrace him as a beloved son. If and when that day comes, I trust that they will reconnect with me and allow me the privilege of helping them work through that process of acceptance and redefinition of their family identity.

The above case example illustrates the necessity of sensitivity to and understanding of the racial, class, gender, and sexual orientation contexts of clients and their families. In addition, it illustrates the effective employment of multiple service providers, each of whom offers an important component to broader-based treatment.

TWO

About Adoption:
The Participants in Context

Adoption is a complex process and experience. There are three sets of participants in every adoption: the birth family, the adoptive family, and the adoptees. Members of this adoption triangle may share some feelings and experiences but they also differ in what and how they experience adoption. Each individual brings to adoption a unique set of biological and psychological propensities and characteristics.

The purpose of this chapter is to describe the changing nature and process of adoption, to highlight salient issues, and to provide information that will differentiate misconceptions from reality. Clinicians are subject to the same biases and distortions about the participants and the process of adoption as is the general public, and sensitization to psychological and societal variables will enable them to be more aware and helpful to the increasing number of people affected by and involved with adoption. Anderson, Piantanida, and Anderson (1993) conceptualize four different configurations of adoptive families: (1) infertile single adults or couples who adopt healthy, same-race infants; (2) adults who would prefer to adopt healthy, same-race infants but, due to limited resources, adopt special needs and/or transracial infants or children; (3) adults who are willing to adopt special needs children but who instead are matched with a basically healthy, young child; and (4) adults who choose to adopt children with more extreme disabilities or handicaps. Although most of the literature focuses on traditional healthy infant adoptions, some attention will be paid in these chapters to special needs and older child adoptions. Transracial adoptions are discussed in Chapters 8, 9, and 10.

Some of the more prevalent misconceptions about adoption shared by mental health professionals and the general public are as follows:

Myth: Most children are adopted in infancy.

Fact: Less than half of adopted children are newborns.

Myth: Adoptees are scarred for life by being separated from birth mothers.

Fact: Certainly most adoptees are affected by being abandoned by and separated from birth mothers, but there is no evidence that they will be scarred for life or would have fared better with their birth mothers.

Myth: Birth mothers are relieved after relinquishing a baby and are able to forget and put it in the past.

Fact: Few birth mothers forget their relinquished child, but most can come to terms with this loss by progressing through a mourning and grieving process.

Myth: Birth mothers do not forget their children and cannot achieve inner peace until they have reconnected with them.

Fact: Whether or not a birth mother needs to reconnect with her relinquished child in order to achieve inner peace depends on the circumstances of her life and her individual psychological state pre- and postrelinquishment.

Myth: Adoptees who do not want to search for their birth mothers are emotionally disturbed because of their denial of the reality of their adoption.

Fact: Adoptees who do not want to search for their birth mothers may be perfectly content with themselves and their lives.

Myth: Adoptive parents can never really feel the same way about adopted children as they would about biological children.

Fact: Adoptive parents, like all parents, can love all their children equivalently, but value and appreciate them differently as individuals.

Myth: The quality of adoptive parenting is more important than the adoptees' genetic endowment.

Fact: Current research indicates that nature and nurture both influence human development.

Myth: Infertile couples who adopt are likely to become fertile.

Fact: Given today's variety of medical infertility treatment, most infertile couples who adopt have exhausted all possibilities for biological conception; there are fewer infertile couples today likely to become fertile after adoption than in previous years before the availability of infertility treatment.

Myth: There are always more psychological problems in adoptive than in biological families.

Fact: Adoptive families, because of their previous experiences with social workers, may come to the attention of mental health workers more often than traditional families who have never experienced acknowledging problems and talking to others about them.

Myth: Adoptees who search for their birth parents are dissatisfied with their adoptive parents.

Fact: Many adoptees who search for their birth parents do so to fill a gap of knowledge and understanding that has little to do with their feelings about their adoptive parents.

Myth: Open adoptions are dangerous because the birth parents will reclaim the child.

Fact: Despite media attention to a few dramatic cases, open adoption has been found to enhance closure and peace of mind for all adoption participants.

Myth: Closed adoptions always cause psychological problems.

Fact: There are advantages and disadvantages to both open and closed adoptions at extreme ends of the continuum; the best process seems to be an individually tailored, semi-open process.

Certainly, there is some validity, some of the time, to these beliefs about adoption. But overgeneralization leads to the biased assumption that everyone has the same experiences and outcomes. We lose sight of the reality that, while the individuals involved in any aspect of adoption share some parts of the adoption process, each may respond differently to shared experiences. In addition, there are nonshared environmental influences, that is, each individual's particular relationships, events, and experiences. So there are many different perceptions and experiences within groups of birth parents, adoptive parents, and adoptees, just as there are different tasks and issues for each of these groups.

These misconceptions are derived, in part, from a larger, societal denigration of adoption as a second-best route to parenthood. This devaluing suggests inferior heredity of adoptees and inferiority or badness of parents who cannot or choose not to produce their own biological children. Suspicion of nonbiological family formats produces an ignorant mythology and lack of sensitivity toward adoptive families. There is a presumption that children are biological, and in public places parents often hear comments by strangers such as, "He doesn't look anything like you," or, "Where did she get her red hair?" These comments can trigger uneasy feelings about adoption by both the children and parents, depending on how they have worked through these issues.

Mental health workers have traditionally relied on a psychopathological model, which focuses on parents' resolution of infertility as a prerequisite for adoption readiness. This model also creates expectations of parental ambivalence, which not only leads to a denial of differences but fosters the likelihood of the adoptee's "adoption" syndrome. This syndrome is manifested in the adoptee's inability to integrate "good" and "bad" internal parental images. In a review of adoption and mental health literature, Wegar (1996) highlights the need for mental health workers to go beyond a psychopathological model and consider cultural components when assessing and addressing the needs of any individuals who hold a stigmatized social status.

Adoption is not an easy decision for many couples to make because adoptive parents are viewed by society as "second best"; there is little, if any, support. One study (Miall, 1987) of 71 involuntarily childless women aged 25–45 years found most subjects believing that society's view was that the biological tie is necessary for bonding and parental love, that adopted children are inferior because of their unknown genetic past, and that adoptive parents can never be "real parents." As Rosenberg (1992, p. 51) states, "Adoptive parents thus suffer from the trauma of being deprived of bearing their own children and from the handicap of a social norm that presumes bloodline to be an inviolate and preferable tie."

By the same token, this constricted societal view puts enormous pressures on the so-called "normal" family to be "perfect," to "succeed" without problems. This can lead to destructive denial and repression. There are many couples with biological children who cannot or choose not to provide adequate levels of physical and emotional care. Abuse, neglect, and deprivation run rampant in families across socioeconomic and ethnic lines. Because affluent families are often more successful at hiding their problems and avoiding the attention of authorities, society tends to view troubled families as belonging to minority or "other" groups, who do not have the resources to avoid detection and labeling. My point is, as stated in Chapter 1, that society's devaluation of adoption can cause problems by expectation and self-fulfilling prophecy.

Whether or not adoption is socially acceptable, in reality the newborn adoption of healthy children is becoming even more difficult. For example, while comprehensive medical insurance may defray most expenses for childbirth as well as costly fertilization procedures, adoptive parents are forced to bear the cost of adoption, which could exceed $25,000. (There are, however, subsidies available for families who adopt special needs children.) Adoptive parents may not be eligible for parental leave, may have a waiting period for health coverage for the adoptee, and may incur further legal fees if the adoption is ever questioned by a birth parent who changes his or her mind. These financial burdens, in addition to the lack of societal support, discourage many middle-class families from even considering adoption.

THE PARTICIPANTS

George, 52, was surprised at how uncomfortable he was when his daughter and son-in-law, who had struggled with infertility for years, phoned to tell him that they were adopting a 4-day-old baby boy the very next day. While pretending to be joyful for his children, he could not still the internal voices predicting doom about unknown genetic heritage and subsequent years of pain and struggle. What if the birth mother changes her mind? or if the birth father suddenly comes back to claim the baby?

Jan, 39, returned home shaking with anger from her school conference with her 11-year-old son, Bobby's, teacher. How could this have happened in the 1990s in what was considered to be a top-notch school system? Yes, Bobby seemed to have difficulty reading and he fooled around a lot as a way of avoiding reading aloud and being corrected by the teacher in front of the other kids. But he was a kind, lovable boy, and Jan could not understand how his teacher could have said what he did about him. In the midst of reporting Bobby's standardized verbal and arithmetic test scores, Mr. Flynn had commented, "We expect these kinds of learning and behavioral difficulties with adopted children."

Shawn, 19, decided to go for vocational counseling. A sophomore in college, he was unhappy in the engineering curriculum, didn't really know what he wanted to do, and felt generally confused. When the counselor learned that he had been adopted at the age of 3, she told him that searching for his birth parents was more important than changing majors, that his difficulties stemmed from having been adopted and not knowing what his real heritage was.

Tammy, 41, winced when her best friend, Gail, confided that she had given up a baby for adoption when she was a junior in high school. Gail wanted to know what Tammy thought about Gail's registering with a search agency so that her son, who would now be 26, could find her if he wanted. Tammy had never told Gail that she too had given up a child for adoption; she was in college at the time. Tammy was comfortable with the closed adoption process, and Gail was yearning for more openness.

Each of the above is a participant in the adoption triangle: the birth parents, the adoptive parents, and the adoptees. Adoption obviously means different things to each of these participants, who are inextricably linked together from the moment of adoption. This link may be visible or invisible, acknowledged or denied, but it can never be erased.

Recent media attention to high profile cases heightens conflict among birth parents' rights versus adoptees' rights versus adopted parents' rights. This has been further complicated by recent attention to birth fathers' rights. Our legal system, as seen in the Baby Jessica case, pits the bonds of biology against the bonds of psychology, intensifying the competing needs and interests of all three parties of the adoption triangle.

In the same week in 1993, there were three highly publicized cases: (1) The Baby Jessica case made front page news with the return of a child, who had been raised for her 2½ years by adoptive parents, to her biological parents; (2) there was the Mays case in Florida, where a 13-year-old girl won the right to remain with her adopted parent and not be required to have visitation with her biological parents (there was a mysterious switch at birth of two babies that was not discovered for years); and (3) the Vermont Baby Pete case, where a sensitive judge made a Solomon-like ruling: The adopted parents and the birth father would share legal custody of the 8-month-old child and the biological father would have visitation rights, while the adopted parents retain physical custody. And then there was the 1994 decision by the Illinois Supreme Court that ordered that a 3½-year-old boy, Baby Richard, adopted at 4 days, be given to his biological parents after the biological father, who subsequently married the biological mother, stated that the mother had falsely told him the baby had died. He claimed that he was unable to assert his paternal rights. In 1995, the United States Supreme Court denied appeals by both the adoptive parents and the court-appointed guardian, ensuring the child's return to biological parents he has never met.

One consequence of this media attention has been that public opinion is beginning to influence the judicial systems (which differ from state to state) to begin to consider the rights of children in their own best interests, not as pawns or possessions of either set of parents. Another consequence, however, has been the undermining of confidence in the adoption system, particularly among prospective or recent adoptive parents whose customary fear of reclaiming by birth parents is becoming more realistic. More recent developments in these cases suggest that the predicted disastrous outcomes for Baby Jessica and Kimberly Mays have not, in fact, occurred. Jessica is reported to be thriving in her new home, and Kimberly was recently returned to her biological parents for a "visit of undetermined length." Custody was later given to her biological parents with visitation rights for her adoptive father. In the spring of 1996, she ran away from all her "parents," claiming she needed relief from the publicity and ensuing pressures. Surely, these disruptions have created their own troubling ramifications.

Before discussing adoption controversies, I will describe the changing nature and process of adoption that has occurred in the past few decades. Adult clients in the adoption triangle, who were adopted in infancy or childhood under the traditional closed model, may present different adoption issues than clients who experienced adoption in a more open model. Clinicians need to understand the specific context in which clients experienced the adoption triangle. In Chapter 3, we will listen to the voices of members of the adoption triangle as they experience different aspects of the adaptive process. In Chapter 4, we will discuss treatment issues pertaining to helping the members of the adoption triangle navigate their ways through this lifelong adjustment.

OPEN VERSUS CLOSED ADOPTION

Traditional or closed adoption was the predominant form of adoption until the 1970s. Of course there have always been informal adoptions (without official recording or legal sanction). In most of these cases, extended family, close friends, or neighbors "took in" a troubled or orphaned child to raise as one of their family. For some, the informal adoptee may have been treated like an indentured servant, but in other cases, the child was treated the same as the family's biological children. In some close-knit communities, such as among African Americans, informal adoption continues. Today, we have expanded adoption policies with varying degrees of openness. The changes in these policies clearly reflect the changing mores and values in our larger society.

Traditional Closed Adoption

For the dominant White culture, formal adoption, legislated in each state by adoption laws, was managed by social service agencies and most commonly involved newborns. This process, now termed "closed adoption," depended on secrecy. The adoptive parents often experienced anxiety, tension, and some shame, having to endure a lengthy (sometimes lasting several years) process of intense and often intrusive evaluation after registering with one or more agencies. Many report that the process felt adversarial, as if the social workers were looking for "secrets" to rule them out. Their financial, personal, family, educational, and occupational backgrounds, social standing, and home life were carefully scrutinized. The objective of the agency social worker was to select the "best suited" parents from a large applicant pool. The "best suited" parents were those who matched the ethnicity and characteristics of the adopted baby and who fit the social worker's concepts of ideal parents. It was a tense, competitive situation and only an estimated 3% of applicants were successful in actually achieving adoption (Feigelman & Silverman, 1983). The applicants were completely at the mercy of the social worker's power to decide who gets a baby. If and when selected, the prospective parents were given minimal information about the birth parents and the circumstances of the pregnancy and birth. They were not supposed to have any awareness or understanding of the birth mothers as people with feelings. They were supposed to pretend that their new babies were the same as if they had given birth to them. This fits into the societal beliefs that biological families are better and that it is dangerous to be different.

At the same time, birth parents, often unmarried teenagers, were routed by clergy, teachers, and health professionals into homes for unwed mothers to await delivery. These homes were outside the communities in which the birth mothers lived, in order to protect their families' reputations. Unmarried females were not supposed to be sexual, and becoming pregnant was evidence of sexuality and a source of great shame for the entire family. These birth mothers were counseled by their social workers to give up their babies for adoption because "that is what is best for the baby." They were also told that after the delivery, they could resume their normal lives and everything would go on as if this "mistake" had never occurred. The birth mothers (until recently, the birth father was ignored) were likewise not given any information about the adoptive family. This gave them the chance to continue their lives as if they had never "sinned" by having an illegitimate baby, which was seen as a stigma to be covered up and forgotten. It was not uncommon for these birth mothers, such as Tammy, to keep their secret forever, even from their subsequent husbands and children. Feelings about pregnancy and delivery were supposed to evaporate within days or weeks of the birth. While they might have fleeting thoughts tinged with sadness and curiosity about their child on subsequent birthdays or holidays, they could reassure themselves with the satisfaction of knowing that their "surrender" was best for the child.

For the "unwanted" babies, the notion was that without adoption, they would be subject to neglect and abuse or orphanage upbringing. They were to be grateful for having two carefully screened parents who had to be highly motivated in order to endure the lengthy wait and screening.

The goal of traditional adoption policy was to replicate the traditional, nuclear biological family wherein children "belong" to their parents. This newly structured family pretended it was no different from biological families. The children were told they were "special and chosen," the adopted parents felt some kind of resolution to their infertility problems, and everyone lived "happily ever after."

Traditional adoption was supposed to meet the needs of childless adults and homeless children. Closed adoption attempted to create a complete substitution of the adoptive family for the biological family in every way. All actual contact with or knowledge of the biological family by both adoptive parents and adopted children was completely severed in order for the adoptee to develop primary emotional attachments exclusively with the adoptive family. With sealed records, the adopted family was ensured that the biological family could never assert claims to the child's affection, care, or control. In the 1940s and 1950s, many adoptive families kept the adoption a secret from neighbors, the school, and the community, even if they were open with their immediate family system.

As seen in Jan's experience with her adoptive son's teacher, the devaluing by the larger society of "different" families such as adopted families could produce its own set of problems: Over time, the burdens of secrecy and hiding could influence the characters and personalities of both the adoptive parents and the adoptees. This was often manifested in school-related and familial behavioral problems. We are now aware that societal oppression and being devalued and made to feel inferior can by themselves result in negative psychological effects.

Advocates of closed adoption, however, still believe that this secretive process is in the best interests of all members of the adoption triangle. The belief is that closed adoption finalizes the relinquishment and facilitates the mourning process in the biological mother. Biological mothers are thought to depend on the protection afforded by secrecy. Adoptive parents are thought to be more secure in their bonding with their child because they do not have to fear having their child reclaimed. Adopted children are thought to need only the secure attachment to their current families.

In order to understand these beliefs, it is important to remember that, through the 1960s, psychological theory emphasized the influences of environment on child development over the influences of biology. Childhood experiences of secure attachment and parental recognition and appreciation at critical developmental junctures—as well as from later environmental influences, such as teachers and peers—were thought to underlie self-esteem, the key to success and happiness. We did not know then what we know now about the long-range aftereffects of nutritional deprivation, substance and physical abuse experienced prenatally or in early infancy, and the lack of adequate prenatal medical care. There is some speculation among child developmental theorists today that the emotional state of the pregnant mother influences the baby *in utero,* that the seeds for later psychological functioning are formed prior to birth. And there is compelling evidence from separated twin studies (Wright, 1995) that genetic determination influences the effects of environment on child development.

It was in the late 1960s, when major sociocultural upheaval led to the acknowledgment, valuing, and exploration of feelings, that the adoption reform movement began, in a similar fashion to other civil rights movements. Adoptees began to acknowledge their feelings about being different and feeling disconnected from their biological heritages. Birth parents began to acknowledge their pain and refused any longer to keep silent and pretend that they did not have feelings about having given birth and relinquished a child.

Transitions in Policy

In the past 20 years, as women's and family roles have changed and awareness of individual rights has heightened, there have been many pressures from activist adoptees and birth parents as well as from social service and mental health professionals to revise the traditional adoption policies and to release and open up adoption information. Several factors influence this transition.

Firstly, there has been a decrease in availability of healthy infants for adoption. This is in part due to legal abortion and better contraception as well as to an increase in society's acceptance of single parenting and more varied, flexible adoptive processes. Ironically, during this same period, later marriages, delayed childbearing, and a rise in sexually transmitted disease have combined to produce an increase in infertility, resulting in an increased demand for healthy, White babies.

Secondly, state and federal legislatures have become less insistent about the need for a total, lifelong severance of the relationship between the adoptee and his or her biological parents. This may be attributable to an increasing belief in biological influences on personality and temperament as well as the importance of medical history. As discussed by Weyrauch, Katz, and Olsen (1994, pp. 957–958), legislation and judicial activity in the 1970s began to be enacted which allowed adoptees 18 years and older the right to know who their natural parents were and to have some information about their roots. There was much controversy among adoption workers about these new laws and decisions, which paved the way for the development of what is now termed "open adoption."

Thirdly, the media's popularization of adoptive children's identity issues has increased the search for reunion. Popular movies and books romanticize the search for roots and reunion—all with a "live happily ever after" ending. Many true stories have been published, pulling at everyone's heartstrings.

Fourthly, mental health professionals, who had been noting a disproportionate number of adopted children and families in their client population, began to express the view that many adoptees were experiencing psychological problems as a result of the secrecy and anonymity surrounding their biological parents. This was thought to disrupt the adopted child's capacity for trusting, intimate relations. In fact, in recent years, mental health workers began to grasp and understand the unique problems experienced by all members of the adoption triangle:

- Adopted youth seem to suffer different types of self-image and identity formation issues than do biological youth.
- Birth mothers who deny and repress this milestone event in their past often experience later negative consequences if they have not successfully come to terms with the loss of their child.
- Adoptive parents seem to need to work through and resolve the loss of their fertility in order to experience effective adoptive parenting.

Open Adoption

Open adoption is a process in which the birth parents and the adoptive parents meet and exchange identifying information. The type and amounts of information exchanged vary, and we need to understand these variances before drawing conclusions about the viability of open adoption.

Demick and Wapner (1988) summarize four types:

1. Semi-open adoption, in which the biological parents meet the adoptive family. Usually, there is no identifying information shared and only one face-to-face meeting. There is no further sharing of information between the two families.
2. Restricted open adoption, in which the adoptive family shares pictures and information regarding the child's development with the biological parents; this information may be sent periodically for a specified time following the placement of the child. Often the adoption agency acts as a liaison between the two sets of parents.
3. Fully open adoption, in which the adoptive family and the biological parents meet face to face and share information directly,

rather than through a liaison. This sharing of information is usually set by a contract made at the beginning of the adoptive procedure.

4. Continuing open adoption, in which the birth parents and the adoptive parents establish a plan for continuing contact with one another and the child over the course of the child's development.

The plans for contact are negotiated by both sets of parents. Increasingly, in open adoption, biological parents actively participate in the selection of adoptive parents. They may do this privately, through an advertisement or word of mouth. More often, they utilize the services of a lawyer or other type of broker for private adoption or a private or community agency that subscribes to an open adoption model. The birth parents may screen prospective adoptive parents by studying the scrapbooks of pictures and memorabilia they submit to communicate to birth parents who they are, including their interests, values, and life style, as part of the application process. They may meet or interview by telephone. In most cases, the "match" is brokered through the mediator or agency. But the decision is made by the birth parent(s), perhaps in conjunction with an advisor such as a social worker or lawyer; this is quite different from the traditional model where the agency social worker made the decision. Most states still require a social worker to assess and approve parents for "fitness" but not to match.

Prospective parents may be given a couple of weeks' notice that they have been "matched." There are some agencies today that require adoptive parents, after having their own infant for a few months, to take into their homes and host another birth mother through her pregnancy and delivery. Sometimes the adoptive parents attend the delivery of their infant or wait nearby as the delivery is occurring. Sometimes they arrive after the delivery. Depending on the laws in the state where the birth occurs, adoptive parents remain at the adoption location for a specified period during which the birth mother may change her mind.

It is not uncommon for birth mothers to change their minds immediately before or right after delivery. Thus, many adoptive parents report that they have had three or four matches that did not work out prior to an actual adoption. Needless to say, it is a trying, anxious time for all participants. Most adoptive parents report that after one failed match, they temper their expectations to protect themselves from further disappointment. They do not feel totally secure until finalization of the adoption process, the length of time for which differs according to state.

Grace and Alfred were notified of their first match 3 weeks before the baby's birth. Very excited, they purchased a layette and baby furniture, told their family and friends about the impending birth, and even participated in two baby showers. When the baby was born, they were just leaving the house to go to the airport, when they received a phone call from the social worker saying that the birth mother's mother had persuaded her to keep the baby. Crushed, Grace and Alfred closed the door to the nursery and avoided further discussion with friends and family. Three months later, when they were informed of another match, they were so cautious and skeptical that they did not even tell their parents until they returned home with a 5-day-old baby. Grace reports that the first, failed match was like a death in the family, and she doesn't know how she could have endured another failed match.

Evaluation of the Types of Adoption

There is much disagreement among members of the adoption triangle and adoption experts as to how much openness there should be. Some fear that too much openness will be confusing for adoptees, others want as much openness as possible, and still others favor a balanced approach, but disagree about how much and what kinds of information should be shared. Should, for example, mutual consent be required for release of information?

There is little research or anecdotal material that is unbiased. Many writers have personal reasons for seeking certain outcome data, being adopted or adoptive or birth parents themselves. This may increase the subjectivity of the interviews and questionnaires used in studies. Some studies look at clinical populations of adoptees and then generalize the findings to nonclinical adoptees. Sampling difficulties arise from the need and desire for privacy; thus, research samples may be comprised of a self-selected group. A sample does not necessarily represent the larger population of birth mothers, adoptive parents, and adoptees. Also, many studies do not control for the age of the child at adoption or on how many previous placements the adoptee may have had. Finally, open adoption has not been in existence long enough to conduct valid outcome studies.

The 12 birth mothers, 14 pairs of adoptive parents, and 31 adoptees (separate from the transracial adoption interviews) that I met with support the findings of Sachdev (1991), who followed 300 members of the adoption triangle and adoption agency workers for a period of 3 years. This study is significant in terms of the size of its sample and the long-term follow-through. Sachdev found persistent but unsubstantiated fears and suspicions among the adoption triangle about each others' motives for wanting information. However, as with my interviewees, this study also indicated, contrary to prevailing thought, that each member of the adoption triangle does, in fact, have sensitivity and concern for the others' interests and welfare. Many of the birth mothers continued their search for a reunion with their relinquished child, but were reluctant to take the initiative, for fear of disrupting the child's and the adoptive parents' lives. Adoptees reported their belief that the birth mother's right to remain anonymous was more important than their need to know her identity. It is important to note the fact that people have both desire for information as well as fears and concern about family disruption. Thus, we cannot assume that searchers will disregard the needs and interests of the other members of the adoption triangle.

Recently, a client whose deceased sister had relinquished an infant 25 years ago, showed me a touching letter from the niece she never knew existed. The young woman had traced her biological heritage through her adoptive parents to a cousin of her biological mother, who sent the letter on to the biological mother's sister. I was struck by the respect, sensitivity, and yearning of the letter writer. While she did not reveal much about herself, she carefully opened the door for information and contact. My client was in a state of shock, not having known about the birth of this child. Receiving this letter rekindled unfinished business around her troubling, abusive family history. The biological mother's violent suicide had resulted in the necessity for the surviving sister to assume responsibility for another child, 5 years old at the time, left orphaned by the suicide. The biological aunt was torn by her feelings of wanting to be fair to this newly found niece, but not wanting to have to contend with her tumultuous feelings about her sister. She did not know how to respond to the letter. Her husband and adopted niece were pressuring my client to respond immediately with open arms. They were excited by the drama of the situation. With my encouragement to take her time, she was able, within several weeks, to write back, showing the letter writer the same considerate respect as had been shown to her. Carefully, contact was established via letters and phone calls, and a future private meeting between aunt and niece was planned. My client had written her new niece that her biological mother was dead, but needed time and help to formulate how she would disclose the circumstances of this death. Despite the painful neediness of both parties, consideration for each other was paramount in both players' minds.

Many experts believe that an open adoption can benefit the adopted child and the birth parent as well as the adoptive parents (Chapman, Dorner, Silber, & Winterberg, 1987; McRoy, Grotevant, &

White, 1988; Sorosky, Baran, & Pannor, 1976). In open adoption, the adopted child sees the birth parent as a real person, not as a fantasy, and has knowledge of his or her genealogical history. Likewise, the birth parent has no fears and no unknowns about the child's welfare. The birth parent knows if her child is happy and well cared for. This offsets the birth parent's pain about seeing the child and knowing that she cannot have this child. Open adoption requires a broader model of parenting for adoptive parents in that, from the beginning, they are sharing, to some degree, psychological bonds. The openness and authenticity that comes with open adoption can enrich the feelings of security and emotional connection for all members of the adoption triangle in that the adoption story is honest and open for discussion at all times.

A semi-open adoption is seen by some experts (McRoy et al., 1988) as being the best arrangement for the adoption triangle. The birth parents and adoptive parents can share some pictures or letters at intervals, perhaps on the adoptee's birthday and/or at Hanukkah or Christmas. The adoptive parents do not have to worry about intrusions by the birth parent, but they serve as the link between the birth parent and the adoptee. The birth parent is able to know how the relinquished child is faring. The adoptee also can know about his or her genealogy and can communicate with the birth parent through the adoptive parents.

McRoy et al. (1988) cite the following reasons for favoring semi-open adoption: (1) a strong bond between adoptive parents and child will develop with no birth parent interference; (2) information on birth parents helps the adoptee form his or her identity, and there is no role confusion; (3) the adoptee can understand the reasons for placement; (4) without a birth parent coming in and out, the family can have stable boundaries; (5) if the adoptee wants more information, the adoptive parent can easily acquire it; and (6) the birth parent has security in knowing about the child and has pictures of the child.

My interviewees, with two exceptions, were all in favor of this balanced open model. Even those who adopted traditionally 25–50 years ago reported that secrecy and the unknown were always hovering like shadows in the background and that it was sometimes difficult to know what part those shadows played, if any, in the normal ups and downs of family life. However, they were uneasy about too much openness, fearing that it would prevent the birth mothers from getting on with their lives and would allow the adoptees to play the two sets of parents off against each other, as often occurs in divorced families.

One of the interviewees' major reasons for favoring more open-

ness is a reflection of media attention to current research, which focuses today more on biological influence than on environmentalism
for understanding child development. It is increasingly hypothesized
that temperament is influenced by neurotransmitters and stress hor-
mones (Kagan, 1984; Plomin, 1993; Rutter & Rutter, 1993; Scarr,
1993). It seems safe to say that we are tending toward a biosocial theory of personality, which consists of the interrelationship of biology,
family experience and circumstances, and larger environmental influences. We are paying more attention to the equivalence and interaction of subjective individual, interpersonal, and cultural influences
on one's experiences. It no longer seems possible to consider any one
of these variables outside of a context that includes the other two.

However, the ideal objectives of a semi-open adoption may be
easier to state than implement. For newborn adoptions, it seems to
me that the birth mother is the person who has the power to determine how much contact there will be. It is unlikely that adoptive parents will want more contact than birth parents, and infants are not
old enough to state their preferences. Some people arrange flexible contracts for contact with a renegotiation clause. This allows them to reconsider later how much contact is advisable for all parties, depending
on the circumstances of their lives.

The two adoption triangles I interviewed who were not satisfied
with their open adoption contract felt that geography was an important factor. In one of these cases, the adoptive parents and the birth
mother lived in the same small southwestern city. The adoptive mother,
whose adopted son was age 3 at the time of the interview, thought
she saw the birth mother "lurking around" the playground and
preschool center several times, but she was never sure. The birth
mother, on the other hand, found that she was often preoccupied,
knowing that she could see her son so easily, and she thought that
if she were perhaps to relocate, she would have an easier time deciding what she wanted to do with her life. Although the birth mother
denied seeking contact outside the terms of the agreement, she did acknowledge her preoccupation, and she articulated feelings about "unfinished business." Before agreeing to talk with me, she had decided
to get some professional help and was just in the process of making
these arrangements when we talked.

The other dissatisfied couple found themselves frustrated because
the birth mother, who lived 1 hour away in another community, kept
breaking dates to visit with the 5-year-old daughter. The birth mother
was seen as being "flighty" and "irresponsible," and the adoptive parents were dismayed by trying to explain to their daughter why Mama
Sue never came when she said she would. The birth mother's mother,

the biological grandmother, who also had visitation rights, suggested to the adoptive parents that they seek a renegotiation of the contract that had been agreed to at the time of the adoption in the office of the brokering lawyer. In this case, the birth mother was unavailable to me, but her mother did talk to me, expressing great appreciation for the home the adoptive parents provided and the loving care her granddaughter was receiving. She felt that her daughter's ambivalence about the little girl was keeping the birth mother stuck in "immature adolescent behavior" and that the adoptive family was being held hostage to the birth mother's whims.

PUBLIC VERSUS PRIVATE ADOPTION

Up until the 1970s, traditional adoption was usually managed by social service agencies adhering to a state's regulatory legislation. Although private adoption through doctors and lawyers, usually for a fee, has always existed, the nonprofit adoption agencies with religious or community affiliation dominated adoption placements. And because the "right fit" meant similar ethnicity, people tended to work with agencies representing their own religion and race.

The shortage of adoptable White infants that began in the late 1960s and early 1970s has led to a proliferation of private parties and private, often unregulated, agencies brokering adoptions for what are often astounding fees. This, in turn, has challenged the practices and beliefs of the local, traditional adoption agencies who, as we will see, have turned more of their attention to special needs and older-children adoptions.

Many adoptive parents wish to avoid the lengthy, intrusive, and often humiliating process of agency screening, and they attempt to seek out babies privately—perhaps through advertisement, word of mouth, or physicians and lawyers. The state mandated screening is often less thorough and rigorous than the screening that community and religious agencies conduct.

Along with this loss of regulated agencies' dominance has come abuse and corruption within the adoption system. Some unscrupulous agencies have been known to abscond with enormous "down payments" by desperate adoptive parents. Some pregnant teenagers have reported being lured by private brokers who mislead them with threats and promises. Other, older birth mothers may become pregnant in order to earn financial remuneration from the adoption fees. The adoptive parents are so vulnerable that they are likely to try anything to get a baby. Those who are affluent are particularly likely targets for adoption brokers. One has only to keep up with the media to learn of "baby selling" and other questionable practices.

The problem for prospective adoptive parents is how to select an honest broker, particularly in the private sector. It is important that people check out all resources, ask lots of questions, interview past clients, and attend open informational meetings for prospective adoptive parents. There is an increase of nontraditional adoptions—transracial, intercultural, and special needs to name a few—and prospective adopters need to consider all options carefully and check out thoroughly all the people and agencies involved in the process. Clinicians working with prospective adoptive parents need to know about available resources and to help their clients collect and assess information.

One advantage of the community agencies is their long years of experience and their nonprofit nature. They are not in the adoption business for the money, but to make what they believe to be the most desirable placements. Yes, one may be assigned to a troublesome case worker, but there are other people in the agency and established agency policies that may afford some protection against an individual's unsatisfactory participation. On the other hand, the private agencies and brokers may be more expedient and less rigid. And the supply and demand and the length of the estimated waiting period will all influence prospective parents' decisions. It seems that affluent people are more likely to utilize the services of private brokers, whereas less affluent people, already at a disadvantage for adopting newborns, will utilize religious and community agencies.

BIRTH PARENTS AND ADOPTIVE PARENTS

Who Are the Birth Parents?

The majority of birth mothers who relinquish newborns are teenagers or college-age youth. While today a large majority of this age group are keeping their babies, many find they are unable to provide for the infants. For these birth parents, adoption can mean a way of ensuring secure families for children they are unprepared to rear—often by virtue of age and economic status. The meaning of relinquishment and the process of the decision to relinquish is likely to depend on the age and circumstances of the birth mother. Was it a decision she thoughtfully came to on her own? Was it imposed on her by others? Did she feel she had any options?

In recent years, another group of birth mothers is emerging. These are older, often married, women who already have biological children.

They may become pregnant accidentally or outside of their marriage (particularly if they are separated or divorced), and they can neither afford economically to rear another child nor consider abortion. So, they choose to relinquish their baby, sometimes for financial gain as well as in the best interests of the child. Whether or how these women explain this to their children varies. One birth mother, who was divorced when she conceived her fourth child, arranged with her former husband to leave the other children with him for the last 4 months of her pregnancy so she could relocate for delivery and relinquishment. She decided that she never wanted her children to know about this pregnancy and relinquishment, and her ex-husband deferred to her wishes.

Another group of birth parents is those whose parental rights have been terminated involuntarily by court action because they have abused, neglected, or abandoned their children. This is a complicated group, and they are likely to feel angry and deprived as well as relieved and released. They may insist on contact with their children and the adoptive parents, or they may insist on no contact. Or, in some cases, the courts prohibit them from any contact. Obviously, adoptive parents are going to have different feelings about parents who have been negligent or abusive than they might about birth parents who have never parented, having relinquished at birth.

A more recent variable is the rights of birth fathers. Most states now also require the birth father to sign a relinquishment release, following the 1972 *Stanley v. Illinois* decision by the United States Supreme Court, which recognized and gave birth fathers rights as well as responsibilities. Prior to this decision, fathers who were not married to the mothers of their children could neither exercise their rights nor assume paternal responsibilities even if they wanted to. Often, however, the birth father cannot be identified or found and, after a legally mandated period of time, wherein newspaper ads are placed, the courts can decide to proceed with relinquishment with just the birth mother's signature. In Massachusetts, for example, hundreds of petitions are filed in the Probate Court each year to terminate the parental rights of unknown fathers in order to free their children for adoption. In most cases, the father does not step forward as that could involve assuming financial responsibility for the child. DNA procedures can verify the identity of birth fathers, as seen in the Vermont Baby Pete case.

Historically, "the fathers of children relinquished for adoption have been invisible and, until recently, largely ignored" (Deykin, Patti, & Ryan, 1988, p. 240). It would not be surprising, due to socialization influences, if many men considered an unwanted pregnancy to be the "woman's problem." Father–child attachment has been viewed by our culture as being less profound or important than that of mother–child.

Two of the couples I interviewed reported that they had given up a jointly conceived child prior to their later marriage. They were both in their late teens at the time of pregnancy and in the middle of high school. Getting married and having a baby then was not feasible, and neither couple felt they could consider abortion, due to their religious beliefs. Their parents were not supportive of their leaving school to get married and have a child at that time. The birth mothers and fathers were in agreement, although they went back and forth during the pregnancies. They would have liked things to have been different so that they could have married and kept their babies, but the job market was tight even for high school graduates and they just didn't see how they could manage. Listening to these two couples reflect back on their youth was very touching. They held hands and cried as they relived the torment of the decision making.

Now, years later, these two couples have developed stable marriages; one has two biological children, the other, one. They do not plan to tell their children of the existence of another sibling until their children are grown. Both birth mothers report feelings of sadness, but feel comfortable with their decision to relinquish and feel that being able to share the responsibility and sadness with their spouses eases their psychological burden. The birth fathers "don't think about it much," except when the birth mothers remind them of the firstborn's birthday. None of these adults think there are any negative effects on their current relationships or family functioning. The two couples describe themselves as satisfied with their lives and committed to their families. Interestingly, these two couples have no desire to search for their relinquished children, but would not be adverse to being "found." They both happened to have worked with very reliable community adoption agencies and feel confident that the families selected for their babies were the "right kind."

Who Are the Adoptive Parents?

The majority of adoptive parents choose adoption as a resolution to a long, painful process of attempting to cope and come to terms with infertility. Some others may be fertile couples who, emphasizing social and humanitarian reasons, wish to provide a home for a needy child in our overpopulated world or who wish to choose the sex of their child. The experience of adoption differs for these preferential adoptive parents. They have not had the same frustrating and demeaning experiences as infertile couples, and they are less apt to feel defensive and humiliated by the process of submitting to the agency personnel's evaluation process. In general, preferential adoptive parents tend to be older, wealthier, more liberal, and less involved with their extended family. Frequently, they already have biological children (Feigelman & Silverman, 1983). They also, perhaps because they have more confidence in their parenting abilities, are more likely than traditional adoptive parents to consider older, minority, or handicapped children.

When Birth Parents and Adoptive Parents Conflict

When birth and adoptive parents become embroiled in conflict over whose child it is and who is the better parent for the child, everyone in the adoption triangle is likely to lose. There is no psychological evidence whatsoever to indicate that biological parents are necessarily the best parents for a child, and it is naive to assume that because one has given birth to a child that automatically means that one can be a loving, caring parent. Likewise, there is no evidence to indicate that attachment depends on biological relationship, although certainly a biological parent who keeps her child has continuity in developing attachment. There is also no evidence that infants and children can only have bonding with one set of parents. Consistent secure attachment between an infant and at least one caretaker is what we are seeking. We do know that effective parenting requires commitment, a capacity to put a child's needs ahead of one's own, and physical and emotional nurturing skills.

Birth parents are responsible for providing a biological heritage and prenatal caring. As stated earlier, we now know that prenatal care can influence personality and temperament and that learning disabilities and other medical disorders may be at least partially attributed to prenatal and birthing experiences. A birth parent's decision to relinquish a child has to be one of the most heartwrenching decisions anyone can make. Most birth parents make a decision based on what they believe will be best for their baby, given their current circumstances.

Adoptive parents are often more highly motivated and committed to becoming parents than those who easily conceive and deliver their offspring; adoptive parents cannot take for granted their capacity to become parents. They are a select group simply for having endured and passed at least a minimal level of screening by a social services agency. They experience the same joys, frustrations, and hurts in their parenting experiences as do any parents, in addition to the special ones associated with adoption. And they, too, usually base their decisions on what is best for the child. In those cases where birth parents are pitted against adoptive parents, or birth fathers later decide they want the child, it seems to me that what is independently assessed by impartial child development specialists selected by the court to be in the best psychological interests of the child should be the primary criterion.

Acknowledgment of the different nature of parenting rights of birth and adoptive parents and consideration of the particular circumstances of any particular case should contribute to the next most important criterion, fairness. Fairness can be based on equivalence of the value of biological and psychological bonding. If the 50 states had similar waiting periods for final relinquishment decisions, there might be less confusion and opportunity for abuse of what is meant to be a humanitarian adoption process. Unfortunately, there is a built-in conflict, in that babies usually are ready to leave the hospital after 24 hours and, if relinquishment is going to occur, that is probably the best time for it to occur for all three members of the adoption triangle. If the birth mother finds herself unable to go through with a relinquishment after delivery, or if the birth father decides he wants the baby, then adoption is either eliminated as an option or postponed. And it is unclear what effects weeks or months with the birth parent might have on a later adoption process.

My point is that each participant in the adoption triangle has needs, interests, and rights and that the overarching concern must be what is best for the child. I think that the judge in the Vermont Baby Pete case, who worked out a compromise solution of shared connectedness and involvement, has set a remarkable example for compassionate understanding of all parties. I wish that the Baby Jessica case judge had been able to come to a similar type of decision so that we could have had a both–and rather than an either–or ruling.

NEWBORN VERSUS OLDER CHILD ADOPTION

Although there is no current collection of adoption data by any federal source, it is estimated by Barth and Berry (1988) that approximately 50% of adoptions involve older children, special needs children, or sibling groups. The term "special needs" refers to children who are "hard to place."

Much of how a newborn adoption works out may depend on the genetic predisposition and prenatal and delivery experience of the adoptee, the psychological characters of the adoptive parents and the birth parents, the quality and nature of the marital relationship of the adoptive parents as well as the support or lack of support within their community, and what kinds of life events occur. When there are problems, it is often difficult to know what can be attributed to the adoption itself and what can be attributed to the same kind of family problems as occur in so-called typical family systems, or even what can be attributed to the impact of societal attitudes toward adoption and adopted families. Although a 1994 study financed by the National Institute of Mental Health (Benson, Sharma, & Roehlkepratain, 1994) found that most children adopted as infants, regardless of race, adjusted well in later life, there is much controversy within the mental health profession about the credibility of empirical research in this area as well as about the reliability of clinical anecdotal material.

Two of the most difficult cases I have ever treated were adopted families. Coincidentally, the adoptive fathers in both families were prominent physicians and the mothers, traditional housewives. Yes, it was certainly true that in both families the adopted adolescents were experiencing severe difficulties—suicidality, runaway, and substance abuse. But in both families it became clear to me and my cotherapist that the parents suffered severe psychological disturbances and that, even if the children had been their biological children, it was likely there would have been serious problems. I'm not saying that adoption was not a contributing factor to or a convenient couple "explanation" for these problems. However, what I marveled at was that these couples passed what was supposed to have been an intense screening process more than once!

As social norms regarding families changed, public agencies began to change their definition of acceptable adoptive families. For example, rules requiring couples to prove their infertility and meet stringent age and income requirements were relaxed. Singles, couples with biological children, and older couples became acceptable parents to formerly unplaceable children. Foster families, who previously had been discouraged or prohibited from adopting children placed with them, were now actually encouraged to adopt them by the agencies supervising the foster care.

This 1970s and 1980s era of "permanency planning" was a professional revolution in the child welfare system that developed out of the child advocacy movement, growing concerns about children's rights (part of the many civil rights movements), and long-term research on children in foster care. These children had been in multiple placements and really belonged to no one. A significant human resource was not being attended to. The permanency planning movement was also influenced by data that indicated cost savings and better educational and psychological outcomes for even the most difficult children in permanent placements as opposed to multiple temporary foster placements. The Adoption Assistance and Child Welfare Act of 1980 funded the provision of permanent homes for children who have been abused or neglected. If a child (3 years or older) could not be returned to his biological family within a specified period of time, planning for adoption was begun. This put pressure on both the social workers and foster parents to meet the states' mandates for permanent placement. Both national and state governments are attempting legislation to make adoption more affordable and socially acceptable. To this end, a series of pro-adoption bills was introduced in mid-1995 to Congress to provide a tax credit to defray adoption expenses and to provide sick leave benefits for federal workers who adopt. Several states are considering legislation that would make it impossible for fathers to prevent an adoption if they have abandoned either the birth mother who is carrying the child or the child after birth. Searching for missing fathers not only slows the adoption process, but also adds to the cost.

Older children, in general, seem to have a less satisfactory adoption adjustment than do newborns. While Berry and Barth (1989) report that up to 10% of older children adoptions do not last, many of those that do last are troubled and receiving services. The term "disruption" is used for those adoptions in which the child is removed from the home prior to legalization of the adoption. The term "dissolution" refers to the removal of the child following legalization of the adoption. These children often have endured several disrupted foster care or adoption placements and may also have suffered severe deprivation, abuse, or illness.

Because adoption policies have been based on newborn adoption, there has not been enough attention given to the special preparation and support services required for older children and special needs adoptions. There is often a disparity in expectations, in that the parents believe that a nurturing environment will enable the child to become someone who can provide what they expect. Parents need additional, special parenting skills in order to raise adopted children who have experienced trauma and disappointments in attachment. Only recently have mental health professionals realized the lifelong impact of early trauma and begun to understand the effects of attachment and separation disruptions on later interpersonal relationships.

Thus, some children who have been too damaged by their early experiences may not be the most suitable candidates for adoption. Yet, because of the pressures for permanent placement, they may be unwisely placed. At the same time, some agencies do not provide adequate preparation and support for the necessary transition between foster care and adoption; they may not disclose full information about the child's past experiences and difficulties. And, after adoption, necessary follow-up and support services are not in place.

Most of the research (Barth, Berry, Carson, Goodfield, & Feinberg, 1986; Barth, Berry, Yoshikami, Goodfield, & Carson, 1988;

Berry & Barth, 1989; Groze, 1986; Rosenthal, Schmidt, & Connor, 1988; Schmidt, Rosenthal, & Bombeck, 1988) has attempted to determine those factors that distinguish failed from successful adoptions of older children. Significant findings include the following:

- As the age of the child increases so does the incidence of disruption.
- Multiple preadoptive or previous adoptive placements are associated with disrupted adoption.
- A greater severity of abuse history is correlated with an increased susceptibility to adoption disruption.
- Disparity between the adoptive family's socioeconomic and educational status and the older adoptee's background heighten susceptibility to disruption.
- A marriage of less than 3 years' duration presented a greater risk for disruption than longer marriages.

Lest the picture for older child adoption appear to be all grim, Ward (1980) points to some advantages of older child adoption: the potential of an older child is better known, and physical, emotional, and intellectual abilities and deficits are likely to be apparent. Thus, a better parent–child match may be possible in the case of older children. Also, older children, while having special and sometimes difficult to meet needs, do not require the same kind of intense parenting that infants do, and this may be a better choice for some families.

Parents who adopt older children report a slower, more gradual progress in bonding than do parents who adopt an infant. It may be that those older children who have had close relationships previously will bond more quickly than those who have not. It is not surprising that older children will be more cautious in developing trust and faith in new caretakers. It may also be that the parents experience some ambivalence as they confront the discrepancies between their expectations or fantasies and the real person of the child who comes to them with a formed personality and temperament.

Often, in the case of older child adoption, a period of visitation or a "trial period" precedes the actual adoption. Carefully planned visitations can be seen as tentative explorations for both the adoptive family and the child. However, it is important to be aware of the pressure and anxiety for all parties, particularly for the child who is being considered for adoption. Hopefully, the social or case worker will be able to facilitate the development of a relationship between the child and prospective parents.

It is not unusual for a typical adoption of an older child to proceed through a "honeymoon" period and a testing period before the actual, gradual adjustment to the adoption. During the honeymoon period, the child is apt to be unnaturally well behaved, afraid to make any demands or rock the boat. A very young child may expect to be returned to his or her former environment and believe he or she is just visiting. This child may also cry for the previous caretaker. As the child begins to feel more secure, the honeymoon period ends, and a time of hostility, aggression, and limit testing may begin. Both consciously and unconsciously, the child may challenge the adoptive parents to prove they are going to keep him or her. Older children need time to develop a trust in their adoptive parents' willingness and ability to be permanent parents. They also need patience, tolerance, and assistance in understanding and accepting the factors that made it impossible for their previous caretakers to remain caretakers.

Adoptive parents of older children fall into instant, new parenting roles, and they lack role models and support. Even if they have experienced parenthood with their biological children, this kind of parenting requires different and new rules and roles.

The Allens, an academic couple in a large midwestern university with two biological children, decided to adopt an 11-year-old boy whom Ms. Allen had met through volunteer community service. This child had been found severely abused and neglected at the age of 3 and had been through several foster placements. His biological mother had been a prostitute and substance abuser before disappearing altogether, and it was unclear who the father might have been. The Allens, retaining some of their ideals from their graduate student days in the 1960s, were determined to make this work. They were aware of all of the pitfalls regarding this type of risky adoption. Their own children, Deb, 9, and Matt, 14, at the time of the adoption, were part of the decision making and the visitation process.

After Jay came to live with them, there was a brief honeymoon period. The next 5 years were very turbulent, with many antisocial behaviors at school. But throughout all of this, Jay was particularly considerate and protective of Deb and guarded, but not hostile, with Matt. The Professors Allen often found themselves literally exhausted with frustration, wondering what they had gotten themselves into. But, as she said, "We knew it would be rough, we knew that we would often question our capacity to hang in there, but we also knew that we owed it to all three children and to our own sense of family to ride it through, no matter how rocky it would be."

Living in a university town, there were more support resources than perhaps would have been available in another locale, such as academic tutoring, athletic coaching, and supportive role models for Jay. What particularly frustrated the Allens was the lack of social service support and the feeling that the case worker, when he did come around, was hostile to them and blamed them for "this placement being in jeopardy." When Jay was 16, his parents decided to get him out of the university high school and into a vocational training program. They acknowledge that they held off on that too long, not wanting to take Jay away from the same school that Deb, Matt, and the children of their friends attended. They wanted Jay to have the same opportunities as other children.

In retrospect, they admit that their expectations were unreasonable in that they truly believed that in the "right environment," Jay would be able to take advantage of educational opportunities. In a telephone interview, Jay, now 19, reports that the family's constancy was what made it work. He particularly credits his dad for being "fair" and "straight. . . . You knew when he was mad and you knew when everything was OK. You knew what the rules were and what the consequences were for breaking the rules." Jay felt the major problem he faced was not being able to trust that they would keep him, especially because he knew from the beginning that he wasn't as "smart" as Deb and Matt.

Contrary to the newborn adoptive family, which begins the family life cycle with closeness and moves toward individuation, the older child adoptive family begins with distance and moves slowly toward developmentally appropriate closeness. But there is not the continuity of attachment that serves as a foundation in newborn adoption.

The two older child adoption dissolutions that I have been involved with in recent years can be in part attributed to the rigidity and unrealistic nature of the parents' dreams and expectations. In one case, an upper-middle-class, suburban family expected a troubled 10-year-old girl to become the instant "princess" of the family, an adored younger sister of their 13-year-old, only child son. They were unable to come to terms with the reality of absorbing a child who had spent 10 years on the streets into their family, and they were unable and unwilling to take the time to learn. This adoption had been a private one with minimal screening and preparation.

In the other case, the child was much more psychologically handicapped than previously thought, and after 3 years of valiant efforts on the part of family members and social service workers, all parties agreed that this was not going to work out for anyone and that it was in everyone's best interests to let go without blame and recrimination. My role in this case was very much like that of a divorce consultant, to meet with the family and individual members to facilitate a "constructive divorce."

Difficult older adopted children may need a different kind of parenting than do newborns or older children who have not experienced trauma and neglect. It may be that for difficult children, parents need to think of themselves more as "consultants" or "surrogates" and, therefore, may need to reconceptualize family roles and rules. This kind of parenting would provide consistent, fair caretaking with less, if any, expectations for emotional gratification from the child. It would be more of a teaching, mentoring relationship.

*   *   *

Adoption may start out as a "second-best" kind of family, but it certainly does not have to end up that way. Adopted families are different from biological families but they are by no means inferior or likely to be "sicker." There are many adoptive families who feel enriched by the experience of adoption in that they have learned to value difference, adaptiveness, and psychological bonding. There is no evidence that there are more disturbed adoptive families than disturbed biological families, and not all adoptive families with problem children would be considered to be problem families. In fact, for adoptive families, there may be some very clear-cut reasons for children to have problems that have nothing to do with the adoptive parents or family structure, whereas the same may not be so for biological families.

Adoption is an alternative way of forming a family system. It is an opportunity to form enriching attachments in a very special way. If we are aware of and prepared for some of the complexities associated with adoption, we are less likely to be disrupted by them. Adoption remains one of the most viable options for the large number of children unable to be raised or cared for by their birth families. Recent attempts by government to make adoption less difficult and more acceptable will hopefully encourage more middle-class and working-class adoptions.

THREE

Adapting to Adoption
over the Life Span

"I don't think I ever really appreciated or understood what it was like for my mother and for the woman who bore me until, after 3 years of infertility treatments, I finally became pregnant and delivered my twins. . . . We were prepared to adopt, ourselves, when the last *in vitro* worked. I found myself buffeted by powerful feelings, dreaming that I was a young teenager unexpectedly pregnant [the birth story], or that I was reliving my mom's inability to have children and deciding to adopt. . . . "—Marian, 32

Each member of the adoption triangle confronts the same developmental issues and life cycle tasks as do nonadoptive parents and children. In addition, they face unique emotional vulnerabilities and stresses associated with the process and experience of adoption.

In this chapter, I will describe the common developmental and interactional tasks each party of the adoption triangle faces. The voices of my interviewees will be intertwined with these descriptions. While there is much variation in the way people perceive, experience, and respond to these tasks, it is also important to recognize that each party of the triangle influences and is in turn influenced by the perceptions, experiences, and responses of the other two parties. Each, as so eloquently depicted by Rosenberg (1992), must deal with loss, sometimes associated with anger; attachment and separation, confounded by the knowledge of genealogical discontinuity; and identity formation and consolidation.

BIRTH PARENTS

The first task of birth parents is to acknowledge pregnancy and then to decide whether or not to terminate the pregnancy by abortion. This may be a decision that the pregnant woman makes herself, with the birth father, or with her parents. In many situations, the pregnant woman does not even inform the birth father of the pregnancy.

For those who decide to continue the pregnancy, they must then decide what they will do with the baby. As discussed in Chapter 2, there are three groups of birth parents: the young and unmarried, who are unprepared to rear their children; an emerging group of older women with other children, who choose to carry through with an unwanted pregnancy and to relinquish for adoption; and parents who are ordered by court action to terminate their parental rights on account of abuse, neglect, or abandonment.

Relinquishment

The sexual revolution has expanded the single woman's options: if she chooses to continue her pregnancy, she can decide to raise the baby herself or with her parents without the stigma of earlier decades. Today, it is often possible for pregnant high school students to continue their education at high school pre- and postdelivery. Some urban schools even arrange for infant care so that the mothers can complete their studies.

Many of the women I interviewed did not have the advantage of this kind of enlightenment. During the 1940s, 1950s, and early 1960s, unmarried pregnancy was a source of shame in the dominant White, middle-class culture. Hence, the secrecy. My African American and Cape Verdean interviewees and clients reported that their families and communities were tolerant and accepting of unmarried pregnancy, and shame and secrecy were not issues for them. Attitudes toward these social issues are indeed culture specific.

> Jean, now 46, is a successful corporate lawyer in a midwestern city. She recalls for me her girlhood in a suburban community where she attended a Catholic girls' school. A junior in high school, she went "too far" with a boy from a neighboring Catholic boys' school with whom she had attended a school dance. Actually, she to this day does not believe they had actual intercourse, but were engaged in heavy petting while unclothed. So, when she missed her next period, it never occurred to her that she could be pregnant because she really was a "good girl." Three months later, her mother noticed that she "was putting on weight." Only then did Jean realize what might have happened. Terrified, she kept her secret to herself, crying herself to sleep at night. Finally after a week of this terror, she told her mother.
> The reaction was immediate: Her mother was outraged at her for

putting her family in this position, and Jean was kept home in bed "sick" for a couple of days while her parents made their plans. Without any discussion, Jean was whisked off to a distant cousin's house in the Southwest. She babysat for the children of the family, helped with the housework, and waited out her "confinement." Jean's mother told the school and all of her and Jean's friends and relatives that Jean had contracted "mono" and that the doctor advised her to go away to a "better climate" for a few months. The school principal sent Jean her lessons so that she could keep up with her class. Jean was visited by the social worker from the regional Catholic Charities, who explained to her why she needed to put her baby up for adoption. Jean never considered any options. She was trying very hard to be a "good girl," to win back her mother's goodwill by making up for all the hurt she had caused. Jean says now that she just assumed and internalized that she was a "bad girl" and that "God was punishing her." The pregnancy was relatively easy, but the delivery was traumatic in that the doctors and nurses were not empathic about her pain and she was given minimal medication. She believes she remembers, as she was going under anesthesia, a nurse in the delivery room saying, "It serves her right; she should suffer."

Jean never saw her baby. She signed the papers without reading them and returned to her cousin's for a few weeks' recovery before returning home. When she returned to school, she received all the attention due a convalescent, and life went on as if there had been no interruption. At home, the pregnancy was never mentioned. It was as if those months had been a dream.

Martha, now a 31-year-old financial consultant, became pregnant when she was 18. A freshman at a women's college in the Northeast, Martha realized what had happened within weeks of conception. She was fond of her boyfriend, the birth father, but she had no desire to commit to a permanent relationship. In fact, she broke up with him shortly thereafter and never told him of her pregnancy. Martha remembers phoning her mother, to whom she was and is very close. Her mother urged her to get an abortion, and Martha went back and forth for several more weeks. Although not opposed to abortion philosophically or politically, Martha found it personally distasteful. She was curious about the birthing experience and managed to put off making a decision until it was too late. (In retrospect, Martha realizes that was her decision—to let the timing make it for her.) Finally, she told her mother that she wanted to leave college at the semester break, return home and attend a local college for a semester, have the baby, and then decide the next step. Martha's mother was very supportive of whatever Martha wanted. She made it clear that she could not take responsibility for raising the baby, but that she wanted what was best for "her baby, Martha." She also wanted Martha at home so that she could oversee her medical care. Martha did not tell her ex-boyfriend but she did tell her close and college friends why she was leaving school. They were supportive and excited for her.

She lived at home without any difficulties. Her friends from college and high school visited and asked her to participate in their activities as if nothing had changed. In her final trimester, her physician, a family friend, told her that he had a patient who seemed unable to conceive after the birth of her first child. He talked at great length to Martha about this patient, what a wonderful mother she was to her 3-year-old son, how badly she wanted more children, and he described a warm family with comfortable means. Martha says she realized immediately that this was what she needed to do for the baby and for herself, but she found herself reluctant to commit. She does not feel she was pressured by her doctor or her parents; they provided her with lots of information and carefully, but gently, pointed out what the consequences might be for her if she chose to keep the baby. She had a positive birth experience, held her baby for 2 days, and then told her doctor that he could give the baby to his patient. Martha had no identifying information about the adoptive family other than what her doctor mentioned at the beginning, and it is her understanding that the adoptive family had no specific information about her. The doctor knew the medical histories of both mothers and had some understanding of their family backgrounds.

Martha's circumstances were quite different from Jean's. The 16-year span between their pregnancies meant that social changes allowed Martha to be more open with her family and friends and to take more responsibility for decision making. Her preparation for relinquishment was more conscious. While it is true that she did not first choose to relinquish, then seek out a private or agency adoption, she did not experience the isolation and loneliness during her pregnancy and birth that Jean did. Martha was always with friends and family, whereas Jean had been "sent away." Martha actively fantasized about her baby during pregnancy, forming an attachment along the way. She told herself that if her circumstances were different, if she were older, had wealthier parents, was in love with "the right person," she would keep the baby and raise it herself. Jean did not allow herself to think about what was happening to her and worked very hard to avoid fantasizing or thinking about the baby. Jean complied with the authority figures in her life. Martha came to believe that a specific adoptive family could provide better care than she could.

Two recent birth mothers found themselves pitted against their mothers in terms of their decision making.

Elaine, now age 17, wanted desperately to have an abortion when she became pregnant 2 years ago, but her Irish Catholic mother refused to allow it and said that she could not remain at home if she did. Elaine was not sure who the birth father was and really didn't care. She was angry at her mother for "making her go through this disgusting thing" and rebelled by staying out late, drinking, and taking drugs despite her physician's and her mother's admonitions. Elaine delivered in her 7th month (it is hard to say whether her prenatal life style had anything to do with the premature delivery), and her mother, who was mourning her abandonment by her husband of 20 years, was "in seventh heaven." She continued to control Elaine's life as much as she could, and she took over all of the baby care. After 2 months, Elaine found herself resenting her mother's possessiveness of the baby. Elaine was unwilling herself to take responsibility for the child care even though she belonged to a community teenage mothers' support group that provided infant care. She insisted that her baby daughter would be better off with an adopted family, and, after much legal and social services intervention, she succeeded in having the baby placed with an out-of-state family. Elaine believes that what she did was best for the baby even though it caused a major rupture in her relationship with her mother. She had felt the baby was caught in a tug of war and that she needed to do this in order to get herself out of the struggle. Her mother, when interviewed, was devastated by the loss of the baby to whom she had become very attached. She felt this was "another chance" for her. Yet, her sadness was also tinged with relief in that she, too, felt this would be the best for the baby.

Lisa, 19, has been involved in an interracial relationship for 2 years. Her lover, a Latino drug dealer, has fathered several children with different women. When Lisa, who was raised by a divorced mother, became pregnant, her mother, grandmother, and maternal aunt put a lot of pressure on her to have an abortion. Lisa, relishing her new-found power, refused. She felt sure that, in the end, her mother would "rescue her" as usual and that everything would be like it always had: Lisa would get into some kind of difficulty, there would be a lot of screaming and fighting, but finally a love-in would ensue and everything would calm down until the next episode. But Lisa's mother, still in her late 30s, had received some effective psychotherapy and was beginning to develop her own career and personal life. She recognized that she had been overinvolved with her only child and that Lisa was irresponsible and too dependent. Throughout the pregnancy, she was supportive but much more distant than in the past. After the delivery, when Lisa and her boyfriend found the infant care overwhelming, Lisa's mother offered suggestions, but never once volunteered to take the baby. In fact, she did not allow herself to become attached to the baby. When the baby was 3 months old, Lisa and her boyfriend decided that their life style was not conducive to raising a child. There had been so many articles in the paper about the shortage of infants for adoption that they easily became disposed to pursuing that option. Within a week, their son was placed out of state. Neither Lisa, her boyfriend, nor her mother wanted to know anything more about the adoptive family other than that they would provide security and caring.

Elaine and Lisa acknowledge that it was difficult for them to let go of their babies, for whom they had cared for several months. They were both able to talk about the pleasures of mothering as well as the frustrations, and they both reported a strong sense of physical as well as emotional loss. It is likely that having named and actually lived with the baby for a few months, on the one hand, highlighted the practical necessities of relinquishment while, on the other hand, made the separation that much more heartwrenching. But they both also reported feeling relieved and liberated, able now to put their pregnancy, delivery, and brief attempt to provide mothering behind them and to get on with their lives. Both young girls appear to utilize a defensive style of "I won't care" and "I'm tough" to mask their pain. One grandmother was more open about her attachment and separation pain, and the other had defended herself by distance and "keeping very busy." In these two cases, the birth mothers chose closed adoption, most likely part of their defensive need to get it over with quickly and to shut the door.

Mary, a graduate student age 22, knew from the time she found out about her pregnancy that she would deliver the baby and give it up for adoption. She remembers her paternal aunt's struggles first with infertility and then with adoption, and she told herself when she was a youngster that, if she ever became pregnant out of wedlock, she would have the baby and allow some needy couple to adopt. Her parents and relatives were supportive of her decision but did not become involved. So, in her 4th month of pregnancy, Mary began to research open adoption possibilities. She signed with a private agency that afforded her the opportunity to relocate and live until delivery with a family who had recently adopted an infant through them. She feels she "lucked out" with the family she was assigned to in the South, although she found the humid climate hard during the final trimester. However, she used those months to study scrapbooks of prospective adoptive parents' lives and even had three couples fly out for personal interviews. The first two she rejected because she found them too "driven" and "tense." The third couple, rural schoolteachers, fit her fantasies of a relaxed life style. After several weeks of reflection, aided by her host family, she allowed the agency to notify this couple of a "match." She spoke to them by telephone, bringing them up-to-date on her condition, and asked them to come in just before delivery to be with her. They arrived 2 days before her due date and were with her at the hospital during and immediately after delivery. Mary held her son for several hours, kissed him good-bye, and with tears handed him over to his new parents. They agreed to have contact twice a year. Mary feels very bonded with her host family and still keeps in contact with them. She says that the experience of living with them enabled her to appreciate the benefits of adoption; she imagines the same loving environment for her baby and feels a sense of gratification that she was able to contribute to the formation of a family.

Postrelinquishment

Most of the research on birth mothers' experiences is based on volunteer samples of predominantly unmarried, White women. They appear to be mostly middle class or higher. Birth mothers who do retain their privacy and, therefore, who are not included in research samples, may or may not have similar experiences. The research (Deykin, Campbell, & Patti, 1984; Gediman & Brown, 1989; Pannor, Baran, & Sorosky, 1978; Roles, 1989; Rynearson, 1982) indicates that the most critical factors contributing to the birth mothers' decision to relinquish include recognition of their psychological and financial inability to parent effectively, their parental and religious influences, and their overriding desire for the child to have a "normal" family. There is no reason to question these findings. The literature also suggests that most birth mothers think about the relinquished baby throughout their lives and that they consider relinquishment an extremely stressful event in their life. The themes of loss, guilt, grief, and mourning and their negative effects on birth mothers' subsequent marriage and parenting is strongly suggested.

But can we assume that all birth mothers experience lifelong guilt and grief resulting in psychological impairment? Several of the birth mothers I interviewed honestly believed that they did what was best for them and the baby at the time, that perhaps if circumstances had been different, they would have chosen differently, and that the effects of illegitimate pregnancy and relinquishment on their later life were growth enhancing rather than harmful.

Virginia, age 51, was 15 when she relinquished her newborn for adoption. She finished high school, attended nursing school, married a doctor, and stayed home to raise three children. Her husband knew about the previous birth and relinquishment before they married. She did not tell her children until they became adults (two are now married with children of their own). Virginia believes that this experience has sensitized her to different life choices and styles and helped her to be tolerant and accepting of others as well as to appreciate her own good fortune. She remembers the baby on his birthday and at other holiday times, but she feels certain that he had a much better life in an adoptive family than she could possibly have given him. She says that she would be amenable to a reunion if he initiated it and wanted it, but she is very satisfied with her life as it is, and, while she admits to curiosity, she wants only what is best for all of her children.

Margery, age 46, gave up a baby for adoption when she was 16. She was married for a couple of years in her mid-20s, and has lived alone for 20 years. The only times she thinks of her baby (she never was told the gender) is when her best friend's children have milestone events, such as a graduation, confirmation, or special birthday. She does not think about the baby, has never had any desire to have children, and is not at all interested in reunion. When she reads about Concerned United Birthparents and other activist national organizations devoted to search and reunion, she finds herself wondering at the intensity of those birth mothers who are "obsessed" with finding their birth child. She asks if there is something "wrong" with her? She feels "alienated" from the activist birth mothers. She does not deny her generative needs; indeed, she takes great delight in being a kind of "Auntie Mame" to her nieces and nephews and to her best friend's children, her godchildren.

Marianne, age 28, was 19 when she and her boyfriend, Joe, relinquished their baby. Now married, these birth parents have a son, Joey, currently 6. They will be unable to have more children due to Marianne's emergency hysterectomy 2 months after her son's birth. Marianne and Joe agree that their marriage and subsequent childbirth were a direct result of the confusion and pain they felt after relinquishing their first child. Joe had been the force behind the decision to relinquish as he felt it was critical that he retain his scholarship and finish his schooling in order to be able to provide for a family. Now Marianne feels they did the right thing then. The only time she has angry feelings about this decision is when Joe is what she considers "neglectful" of their son, when he goes out with the guys and is not available to parent actively. Joe admits to fantasizing about finding the relinquished son so that Joey does not have to grow up as an only child (Joe had six siblings and is used to big families). Marianne thinks about searching for assurance that her first child is alive and well. But recently Joe and Marianne have sought counseling to discuss the possibility of adopting another child so that they can "complete" their family. They think that this would bring them "full circle" and that they would be better adoptive parents having been sensitized personally to the benefits of adoption.

Marianne and Joe's experience fits the findings of Deykin et al. (1988), who found significant gender differences in birth parent experiences, with birth mothers wanting to search for assurance about the child's welfare and birth fathers having a more instrumental objective, wanting to retrieve the lost child.

There are no rules or rituals to help birth parents come to terms with relinquishment. Because relinquishment lacks the same finality as death, there may be conscious or unconscious hopes for reunion and reconnection. And we really don't know, although we can always speculate, why some birth mothers experience lifelong negative effects and others seem to find ways to come to terms with this loss. How much the different experiences of the short- and long-term effects of relinquishment have to do with an individual's life circumstances and psychological makeup is another avenue for consideration.

Search and Reunion

Most of the research indicates that a significant majority of birth mothers desire information about their relinquished children but do not want to hurt the adoptive parents or the adopted children (Pannor et al., 1978; Sachdev, 1989, 1991, 1992; Silverman, Campbell, & Patti, 1988). It is unclear from the data how many of these birth mothers are also seeking reunion. It is in this area that there is the most polarization, in that activist groups insist reunion is "psychologically necessary" for the well-being of all members of the adoption triangle and consider a more moderate view to be "rationalization or denial of the psychological realities of adoption." So who are the birth mothers who search? Some are influenced by stories in the media.

> Sarah, age 41, never thought of searching until she learned from a friend of a recent reunion with a relinquished daughter. Sarah had never told this particular friend that she had relinquished a child, and she had not known that her friend had. After listening to the dramatic excitement of the reunion process for several months, Sarah asked her husband how he would feel about her searching. He was very supportive, and Sarah registered with two national organizations that serve as contact points for searching adoptees. Sarah is intrigued by the possibilities of reunion and curious about her offspring. She does not think she would have seriously considered this option if it had "not hit so close to home."

> Sandra, age 38, has no interest in being "found" at this time. She is concerned about everyone's rights in the adoption triangle and believes that the birth mother's consent should be required before identifying information about them is released. She has been in contact

with the agency with which she worked 22 years ago and has been assured that no identifying information would ever be released in her state without her permission. Descriptive information can be released at the discretion of the agency.

Some research (Deykin et al., 1984) suggests that birth mothers who felt external pressures influenced their decision to relinquish were more likely to search than those who felt they were the primary decision makers. More recent relinquishing mothers can choose a closed, semi-open, or open adoption model and have more societal support for their decision making than did relinquishing mothers a couple of decades ago, so there may be less need for recent birth mothers to search than there was when adoption was shrouded in a cloak of secrecy. Sachdev (1989, 1991, 1992), as previously mentioned, found that birth mothers' reasons for not initiating search involved dilemmas about their moral and legal rights or uncertainty of how to search, but mostly concern for the adoptive parents and the adoptive child. They do not want to be a disruptive force in the adoptive family's life.

Now that search and reunion is so possible and available, the decision-making process about search and reunion is as important as was the decision to relinquish. Thus, birth mothers who relinquished prior to the opening up of the adoption process now have the psychological task of deciding whether or not to search or to be found. For some, it is a chance to reconsider and to achieve some opportunity for closure of unfinished business whether or not the outcome is search and reunion. An adjunctive decision is how open the birth mother chooses to be now with her current family and friends about her earlier relinquishment. What was once considered to be sinful and a stigma is now much more empathically accepted.

However, it seems important to respect whatever choices different birth parents make. Those who want to search should be encouraged and supported as long as they are considerate of the needs and desires of the adoptee and adoptive parents. Those who do not wish to search or be found should be supported in their choice for privacy.

While there are similar themes and while we are more aware of the kinds of psychological pain relinquishment can cause over the years for birth parents, we need to keep in mind that not everyone has the same needs or experiences, and we cannot assume that all birth parents suffer lifelong guilt and distress.

Postreunion

The nature of the relationship between birth mothers and adoptees depends on the needs and wishes of all three parties of the adoption triangle. It may range from the development of a close mother–child bond to a one-time meeting and then no further contact. The literature (Sachdev, 1992; Silverman, Campbell, & Patti, 1988) suggests that, in most cases, some kind of friendly contact is maintained, whether it be an occasional telephone call, letter, visitation, or more continuous friendship.

Some of the birth mothers to whom I spoke reported disappointment that the adoptee did not want more contact, that he or she seemed satisfied with meeting once and having questions answered. Two of these birth mothers continue to attempt contacts with their offspring and seem to be engaged in a pursuer–distancer dynamic, where the more they attempt to become part of their child's life, the more the child avoids any kind of contact. Some birth mothers were relieved to have minimal contact, feeling that the knowledge of their child's welfare was sufficient. One woman reported that she was "put off" by the life style of her son and afraid that she would grow to dislike him if contact were to continue. Some developed a friendship that included the adoptee in the birth mothers' current family affairs. Two birth fathers with whom I talked about their postreunion experience reported feeling curious about their daughters, but uneasy about further contact after the initial reunion meeting. They both said that it would be "awkward" with their current families, although one had revealed the existence of an older child to his family.

The fairy tale, "lived happily ever after" ending is not necessarily what happens in real life, nor should it necessarily be the goal. Both adoptees and birth parents have to come to terms with the discrepancies between their fantasies and the realities that emerge when an actual reunion occurs. So much depends on the circumstances of each party's history and current life. Clinicians can be particularly helpful with planning for reunions and postreunion processing.

ADOPTEES

There is more research on the impact of adoption on the adopted child than on the other two parties of the adoption triangle. Being adopted adds a complexity to the normal developmental issues of attachment, loss, and identity formation because the individual must come to terms with and integrate two families: the adoptive family and the birth family, which he or she most likely does not know much about. Research consistently shows that the themes of loss, identity formation, and an imaginary or real search for the birth parents seem to be prevalent issues throughout the lives of adoptees.

The developmental tasks and issues for adoptees have been comprehensively described (Brodzinsky, 1990; Brodzinsky & Schechter, 1990; Brodzinsky, Schechter, & Henig, 1992; McRoy, Grotevant, & Zurcher, 1988; Partridge, 1991; Rosenberg, 1992). Their work is based primarily on those adopted in infancy. There is much overlap in their descriptive models, and the following is an integrated composite of their work. It is important to note that the voices of interviewees are retrospective reflections of adult adoptees.

Infancy and Childhood

During infancy, the critical psychological tasks revolve around attachment and bonding to the primary caretaker, usually the adoptive mother. This will depend on (1) the circumstances of the baby's conception, gestation, birth, and relinquishment; (2) the birth parents' genetic vulnerabilities; and (3) the kinds of stresses the birth mother experiences throughout her pregnancy and delivery. In recent years, much attention has been given to the impact of mothers' behaviors and emotions during pregnancy on the baby's psychological and physical well-being. It is suspected that the seeds for later learning disabilities and emotional difficulties may at least in part be attributed to *in utero* experiences. As stated by Rosenberg (1992, p. 93), "the most reasonable inference would be that the circumstances of the pregnancy and relinquishing mother make it more difficult for her to provide a positive physical and emotional prenatal environment for her baby and place these babies at greater risk."

Individual, family, and societal circumstances will also determine how and when relinquishment occurs. Because babies are born with varying temperaments, which will affect how they cope with the separation from the birth mother and adapt to the adoptive parents, there is bound to be much variation among adoptive families. If placement is prolonged or there are several placements prior to the adoption, the infant's capacity to bond and develop trust may be disturbed. Thus, the development of secure attachment between adoptee and adoptive parents depends on all parties' temperaments as well as the circumstances and environmental context of the adoption. The "fit" is also impacted by the adoptive parents' expectations. This is also true in biological families, but the genetic discontinuity of adoption may exacerbate the potential for matching difficulties, due to heightened anxieties of the adoptive parents about the unknown heritage of the adoptee. The research findings agree that how the adoptive parents deal with their losses underlying adoption and how the infant experiences the loss of the birth mother will be major determinants of the nature of the "fit" between the adoptee and the adoptive parents.

During the toddler and preschool years, children develop a verbal sense of who they are. They begin to ask questions, and to explore their environment. It is during this phase of development that many parents tell children the "adoption story," emphasizing the happiness the chosen adopted child brought into the adoptive parents' lives. The purpose of the adoption story is to answer children's questions about how they were born in the context of a loving and protective family environment, to make them feel special. This sets up most young children to have positive, warm feelings about being adopted. It may even become the ritualized bedtime story. Rosenberg (1992) suggests that preschool age children are really unable to grasp the meaning of being adopted, but this story sets the stage for later comprehension.

> Jim, a graduate student age 33, remembers his adoption story: Once upon a time, there was a young girl who was in love with a handsome soldier. They hoped to get married after the "war." The soldier went off to fight and the lovely young girl found out she was going to have a baby. She was very happy about this because she loved the soldier and knew she would love his baby. However, he was moving around the world so fast that she was never able to find him again. So she had her baby and because she was young and poor, she loved the baby so very much that she wanted the baby to have a wonderful home with a mommy and daddy who would love him and be able to take care of him. Through a friend, the social worker, she found the best mommy and daddy for him and that's how he came to live in this house with this mommy and daddy. "And isn't he a lucky boy to have two mommies and two daddies who love him so much."

Jim remembers snuggling on either parent's lap, hearing this story night after night. Throughout his elementary school years, he would tell himself this story whenever he felt any kind of anxiety. It was like his security blanket and always resulted in warm, fuzzy feelings of being enveloped in love.

School Years

This stage of child development includes the emergence of more operational thinking, causality, and logical planning. It is a time for children to master and understand the world they live in. The two major psychological tasks of this phase are development of (1) self-concept (how they see themselves) and (2) self-esteem (how much they like what they see).

It is during this period that children may first come to realize that they are different from other children. They may struggle with what it means to be adopted, becoming confused by strange feelings of loss and oddness. Although these feelings may certainly complicate the adoptee's development of self-concept and self-esteem, they are normal developmental adjustments for adoptees. Now the child is capable of inferring the flip side of the beloved "adoption story": In order to have been chosen, one had to have been given away. What was so bad about him that his own mother would give him away? If she really is so unlovable, why would her adoptive parents love her? These feelings account for many of the behavioral changes that professionals have noted in elementary-school-age adoptees: increased anger, aggression, oppositional behavior, uncommunicativeness, depression, and self-image problems. If school and mental health personnel do not understand these behaviors to be normal aspects of adoptee development, they may be viewed pathologically. Thus, we can see why Jan was confronted with the school's self-fulfilling expectation that her child's behavioral problems were consistent with adoptee status.

Most children, biological as well as adopted, develop what Freud termed the "family romance fantasy." When a child experiences natural conflict with his or her parents (perhaps not getting what he or she wants when he or she wants it), the child imagines that he or she was secretly adopted and conjures up another set of loving, all-permissive parents who will come and rescue the child from this painful situation. These imagined parents would never be so "mean" as the parents who are raising the child. For adopted children, the reality is that there *are* two sets of parents. Whereas in biological children this fantasy usually ends in adolescence when the child can see bad and good in the same individual, for adoptees defensive splitting may occur and be maintained, making the birth parents all good and the adoptive parents all bad. Adopted children are likely to maintain their internal representations (mental images) of the birth parents through fantasies, thoughts, and feelings. These internal fantasies may accompany them throughout life, being relied on particularly in times of stress. They are fueled by the slight possibility that the adopted child and birth parent will be reunited some day.

> Lenore, age 28, remembers her fantasy world. She had always felt "different" and as if something was missing. She had been told about her adoption, and she had minimal information about her birth parents. So she was free to develop her own story. She loves her adoptive parents and knows they love her and they were very good to her. As an adult (currently a social worker), she now realizes that they were not as affectionate and outgoing as she needed and she always felt constrained, as if she had to be careful and hold back her own spontaneity. In her fantasy life, her parents were warm, loving, open, and full of life. Her secret world served as a soothing mechanism

whenever she was disappointed by friends or other circumstances in her life. It was not until 2 years ago, when she searched for and met with her birth parents, facing the discrepancy between her own production of who they were and the reality, that she gave up her lifelong "internal movie."

If adoption is considered to be a family secret, the fantasies of the adoptee could become more elaborate and the splitting more intense. If there are ensuing behavioral problems at school as well as at home, the responses of the parents and the school will strongly influence the course of these difficulties. More so than biological children, adopted children are trying to feel loved, wanted, and good enough, whether testing through acting-out behavior or trying to be "the perfect child," better than a biological child might have naturally been.

Kathy, age 28, remembers telling herself over and over as a child, "Careful, careful, don't step on a crack or you'll break your mother's back." Adopted by a prominent, affluent couple, she has always felt lucky and grateful to have been chosen by them and to be the recipient of such a rich life style. She never disobeyed parents or teachers, and devoted much of her life to being "the perfect child."

The facts that are given to the child about his or her birth parents when told about the adoption become critical factors in identity formation. Adoptees will wonder how it reflects on them that the birth parents were too young to raise a child, were not married, or were poor. They question how much they really belong to the adoptive family and what would happen to them if the adoptive parents were to divorce or die. The use of fantasy as in the family romance and the questioning of the adoption circumstances indicate that a search for the birth parents has begun mentally. The literature suggests that all adoptees take part, to some degree, in this type of search, the beginning of the child's identity formation process (Brodzinsky et al., 1992; Rosenberg & Horner, 1991). Although many adults do not recall these fantasies from childhood, even their fleeting thoughts indicate some energy devoted to wondering about their birth parents.

Adolescence

This is seen as the most critical stage of development for adoptees, due to the primary task of identity formation accompanied by the beginning of independence and separation from one's family. In order to achieve these tasks, the adoptee also needs to process feelings and fantasies about the birth parents and adoption, working through the family romance fantasy. So, the adoptee has two families to separate from, one about which he has little or no knowledge. This can be a very confusing stage of life for adoptees, and they may experience feelings of shame and low self-esteem, having already experienced a real loss of parents, which may have made them particularly vulnerable to further losses. Working through the feelings of pending separation and independence from their family can take longer for adoptees than for nonadopted teenagers because of this already existing vulnerability to loss.

> Tom, age 19, had been one of the most popular kids in his high school class of 42 kids. He had been adopted at birth and grew up in a rural community 50 miles away from a metropolitan area, where his adoptive father commuted to work. But his home and community life were protective and because his adoptive family was the number one family, he always felt good about himself and his life. He never thought much about his adoption and still does not think that is an issue. Tom had great difficulty going away to college (in the same city his dad works in). It was his first time sleeping away from home except on visits to his grandparents' farm in another state. During freshman orientation week, he met a girl with whom he "fell in love." This eased the transition for him, although he still was homesick and unsure of himself. After 2 months, this girl broke off their relationship, finding Tom too "needy and possessive."

It was at this point, experiencing this major loss, that Tom "fell apart" and was referred to the university counseling center by the resident director of his dorm. The raw pain and anguish that Tom experienced from this rejection and abandonment created a major crisis for him, much more intense than usually seen in the counseling center.

During adolescence, the adoptee's genealogical concerns may become more intense because of developing physical characteristics and emerging sexuality. Adoptees realize they do not know anything about their birth family history, and they have no birth parents to compare themselves to physically (Sorosky et al., 1978). These factors feed into the identity crisis questions of "Who am I?" and "Who will I become?"

The sexual identification of the adoptee can be complicated, because they need to integrate their identification with the adoptive parents and the facts and fantasies about the birth parents. The adoptee knows that the birth parents were sexually active and irresponsible about birth control (or at least that something went wrong with the birth control). There exists both a wish and a fear to be like the birth parents, and part of the identification formation is separating and acknowledging what the wishes and fears are.

So it is not unusual for an adoptee to identify with the birth parents by acting out sexually. This is also a way of testing the limits of the adoptive parents. It a female adoptee becomes pregnant, she may keep the baby in order somehow to fix the "mistake" of her adoption. She may give the baby up for adoption and thereby forgive the birth mother, or she may abort the baby in order to differentiate herself from the birth mother. A male adoptee may also try to identify with birth parents by sexually acting out. If someone becomes pregnant by him, he may also try to influence the keeping of the baby, giving it up, or aborting it, based on his own issues.

The lack of a biological tie and identity confusion may increase the adolescent adoptee's desire to meet birth parents. Although many clinicians do not recommend that adolescent adoptees search for their birth parents at this time, believing they are too immature to handle an actual presence of two sets of parents in their lives, clinicians can acknowledge the real need of adoptees to know as much information as possible about the reasons for their adoption, their genealogical history, and the circumstances of their conception.

Continuing the imaginary search can help adoptees to work through their feelings about these identity and loss issues. An important point made by Hoffman-Riem (1990) is that adolescent adoptees search for the knowledge of their own origin regardless of the relational quality achieved with their adoptive parents. Thus, the search for birth parents is not only a desire in problematic families, but is a need felt by adoptees in all kinds of family relationships.

Often, emotionally secure adoptive parents are the ones to raise the possibility of search to their adopted children. They want to be supportive and helpful from the outset, not seen as a barrier to what's best for their children. There also seem to be some gender differences with regard to the intensity of thoughts and fantasies about searching, in that females seem to be more highly represented in the wanting to search group than males. This very well could be attributed to female needs for connection (Gilligan, 1982; J. B. Miller, 1976) as well as with their gender identification with the birth mother.

> Lou, age 19, remembers being surprised a year ago when his adoptive mother suggested that he consider searching for his birth mother. She was willing to give him the name of the social worker and the adoption agency, and she had researched search organizations and had a whole folder of information for him. Lou was interested in finding out his genealogical history, but he was not particularly interest-

ed in establishing a relationship with his birth parents. He appreciated his mother's support and encouragement but did not feel the time was right, because he was concentrating on deciding what to major in at college. He thought he would wait a year or two to begin his search. He did think, based on a biology course he was taking in his freshman year, that it was important to know his medical history before he could think about having a family of his own.

Young Adulthood

During one's 20s and 30s, the focus is on the formation and main-tenance of intimate relationships as well as on career, life style, and family options and decisions. There are special issues for adoptees: They may feel that because their birth mothers could not commit to them, how could anyone else?; they may insist on excessive indepen-dence because of the isolation they felt as adopted children or they may fear falling in love with someone who might turn out to be a blood relative.

Several adoptees in their 20s and 30s reported particular feelings of affiliation and closeness to other adoptees. One 32-year-old wom-an was delighted upon learning that a coworker of the same age had been adopted the same month from the same midwestern agency. When my interviewee learned that her coworker had visited the agency, she decided that the next time she was in that city, she would do likewise. Another woman interviewee in her late 30s commented that she was always surprised at the shared affinity she experienced with other adop-tees: "We have so much in common, growing up feeling different and not quite fitting in."

The decision to search and whether or not to have a reunion is most common during early adulthood. Some adoptees, like Lou, just want information, such as medical data; some want to establish a rela-tionship and extend (not necessarily replace) their nuclear family; and some may want to search for their own self-understanding and sense of completeness. Still others may view a search as an adventure. For adoptees who have not worked through their issues of loss and aban-donment, intimate relationships can be difficult, and the search and reunion process may offer them the hope of resolving some of their confusion so that they can develop the capacity to sustain intimate rela-tionships.

Laura, age 24, was puzzled by her inability to stay in relationships for long. She would become very involved with the man she was dat-ing, feel excited and secure, and then some point would come when she would find herself to be uneasy and distancing. She always

managed to sabotage the relationship indirectly, and then she felt victimized and hurt when she no longer was pursued. An article she read
about search and reunion motivated her to register with an organization that served as a connection between birth mothers and adoptees. It took less than a year for her to find her birth mother, who
had registered and wanted to be found. Laura says she can't put into
words the relief and closure she felt upon meeting her birth mother,
although she has no desire to have a close relationship with her. In
the past year, there have been a couple of phone calls and the exchange of birthday and holiday cards. Laura found her birth mother
nice enough, but just not anyone she could really relate to, being very
different in class, values, interests, and life style. But some nagging
piece of unfinished business seems to be resolved, and Laura reports
that she feels now she has both feet in the "here and now" rather
than having one dragging in some mysterious past. The relationship
Laura is now in with a coworker has lasted longer than any prior
relationship, and she claims to feel more settled and at peace with
it than she ever has.

We don't know much about the differences between searchers and
nonsearchers, although some studies suggest that there are significant
differences in the two groups' measures of self-esteem, identity, family self, physical self, and self-satisfaction (Aumend & Barrett, 1984;
Sohol & Cardiff, 1983). In addition, searchers appear to be more likely
to have experienced strained adoptive family relationships, a traumatic
adoption revelation, knowledge of negative circumstances surrounding birth and adoption, or stressful life events. However, we need to
be careful not to overgeneralize. For many searchers, the desire for
reunion is in no way a reflection of their relationships with their adoptive
parents. In fact, adoptees and adoptive parents are so sensitive to the
prevailing societal belief that only dissatisfied, unhappy adoptees want
to search, that it's hard for them to believe that searching does not
necessarily indicate dissatisfaction with the adoptive family.

For the achievement of lasting intimate relationships, people must
have a strong sense of identity. At one extreme, only short periods
of attachment may be possible for the adoptee because she or he does
not want to set her- or himself up for significant loss. At the other
extreme, adopted individuals may become overattached in relationships and any interpretation of rejection becomes a magnified problem.

Ellen, age 33, is a classic example of the latter. Currently a physician, she is still living at home with her widowed adoptive mother,
who is in her mid-70s, and suffering from numerous health problems.
Ellen has had fiercely intense, passionate relationships, usually with
a classmate or coworker. She totally subsumes herself to the current

lover, and becomes possessive, clingy, and demanding. When he tries to disentangle, she pursues more vigorously until eventually he has to cut her off very strongly. At each of these rejection/abandonment points, Ellen has suffered a psychological crisis involving suicidality and total incapacity. Twice, she has been hospitalized, and more recently she has been heavily medicated. Ellen, to date, refuses to see the connection to her adoption and continues to obsess over the latest lover.

Pregnancy and the birth of a child may have unique importance for the adoptee. On the one hand, there may be anxiety about the pregnancy and the future health of the child, because the adoptee is unaware of her genealogical background. These concerns may prove to be the impetus for an informational search for the birth parents. The pregnancy may also provoke a search because the adoptee may want to share the experience with the biological grandparents. Another unique quality of an adoptee's pregnancy is that the baby will be the first biological relative the adoptee has ever known. The baby will be the first person to look like the adoptee, or at least have the potential to. A genetic bond will exist that has never been experienced by an adopted individual. That is a profound emotional experience for the adoptee.

Midlife

In their 40s and 50s, adoptees are faced with the reality that their birth parents, if still alive, will likely die soon. Thus, this time of life may be seen as the last chance to search and establish a relationship. But at midlife, this may or may not be a strong need. Often the adoptee has established a gratifying family, career, and close friend network, so the need for the birth family relationship is not as strong as it may have been in earlier years. Or, if an adoptive parent dies, it may be the first time the adoptee sees an opportunity to search without hurting or being disloyal to the adoptive family. There may arise medical reasons for an adoptee to search in midlife.

Rob, age 44, had very high cholesterol and other health problems that were of concern to his doctor and his wife. They both suggested he try to learn his family history. Rob's widowed adoptive mother was willing to assist and gave Rob the information he needed in order to get the court sealed records of his adoption. It took Rob several months to begin this process as he really was disinclined to do so. However, his style was always one of dragging his feet, so his wife knew how to cajole and keep up the pressure until he finally began to search. Eventually, he traced his maternal aunt and through her was able to get at least the medical history of his maternal relatives. When he met his birth mother, he was unmoved and puzzled by her vagueness about who his birth father had been. Checking things out with his maternal aunt only added to the confusion. But the information he did receive about cardiovascular disease in his birth mother's family enabled his physician to have a better understanding of how to treat Rob's high cholesterol and blood pressure. It also got through Rob's defenses so that he began to take better care of himself, modifying his diet and beginning an exercise regimen.

Late Adulthood

During this stage of life, final considerations are given to a search if these issues have not previously been resolved. One is able to view the adoption within the larger context of one's whole life. But the necessary losses, which occur with more frequency during this stage of life, may be experienced with particular intensity, given adoptees' lifelong vulnerability to loss. How one has perceived, interpreted, and resolved earlier life issues will affect how one copes at this later stage of life. And, of course, the circumstances of one's life—health, relationships, life style—are as important as one's psychological state.

While everyone has continuous identity and loss issues to deal with across the life span, there seem to be particular recurring themes throughout an adoptee's life of loss, identity formation, and the question of the search for the biological parents. These themes are interdependent. And each one has to be worked through and then reworked by the adoptee in each developmental stage. Even those adoptees who have searched and established relationships with their birth families may find themselves reworking these relationships as they progress through the life cycle. All adults continuously renegotiate their relationships with their families of origin as they become more immersed in their current families through that newer family life cycle.

Adoptees vary in how long it takes them to sort out their particular issues, if they are able to, and will, therefore, have varying degrees of adjustment. The amount of adjustment appears to be related mostly to the adoptee's personality, how open a subject adoption has been in the family, and the circumstances pertaining to the particular developmental stage. The adoptee must repeatedly come to terms with what it means to be adopted throughout the different stages of childhood, adolescence, and adulthood. This may be wholly conscious at one end of the continuum, wholly unconscious at the other end, or a mixture somewhere in between and that may also vary across the life span.

ADOPTIVE PARENTS

The majority of adoptive parents are those who have experienced primary or secondary infertility. By primary infertility, I mean those who have never been able to conceive or carry a pregnancy to full term. By secondary infertility, I mean those who may have been successful once or twice in delivering a child but later are unsuccessful.

Infertility

Currently, it is estimated that one out of six couples will experience infertility. This may be attributable to couples waiting longer than used to be customary to begin attempts to conceive, to changing sexual practices, or to environmental conditions. Whatever the reasons, most people do not know they have a problem with fertility until they have tried to conceive for several months or years. (The general rule of thumb is not to become concerned until having tried for 1 year.)

When a couple begins to realize they have a fertility problem, they are likely to feel a sense of shame that they can't achieve what everyone else seems to easily enough. They may also feel shock that their bodies are not wholly under their control. For some, it may be their first disappointment that money or influence cannot necessarily fix. Added to the shame is the trauma of the medical procedures necessary to assess the status of one's infertility and the emotional difficulties of undergoing today's high tech methods of facilitating pregnancy. This trauma includes continuous, intrusive assaults on one's own and one's partner's bodies, attacking emotional and sexual self-esteem. Naturally, this affects the couple's sexual relationship as well as their relationships with others who have or are able to have children. It is indeed a trying, isolating time in a couple's life and one for which society provides little support. It is also a financially costly time, and less affluent couples are often limited in their fertility options.

Infertility is a major lifelong loss that couples must come to terms with in order to make appropriate decisions about whether or not and how to become parents. After the shock of finding out they are that one in six, that it really is happening, couples experience a great deal of anger, resentment, and despair before they are able to achieve resolution. It is during this period of despair that feelings of guilt and inadequacy can be manifested in irritability, anger, or blaming. There is a loss of one's self-ideal and one's body-image security. Each member of the couple must reconsider the meaning or importance of becoming a parent. It is likely that women experience the psychological pain of infertility in a different way from men.

Daniluk, in her 1994 presentation to the American Psychological

Association Conference on Women's Health, cites the emotions that infertile women experience once they stop hoping and trying to get pregnant: sense of futility and hopelessness; sense of physical, emotional, and spiritual depletion; profound sense of loss and grief; sense of emptiness—missed experience; sense of exclusion—being different; desire for closure; sense of needing to redefine self and the future; need for acceptance and support from significant others; sense of relief at taking back their lives. Women may confuse reproduction with competency to parent, whereas men may confuse fertility with sexual adequacy. That may be why so many men are reluctant and resistant to being examined medically.

Decision to Adopt

If couples are unsuccessful with fertility procedures or if they decide that their tolerance limits have been reached, they may choose to remain childless or to attempt alternative conceptions such as surrogacy or artificial insemination, or they may choose to adopt. Adoption is visible, whereas one may successfully cover up other methods of becoming a parent. In other words, adoption announces to the world that the parents are unable to bear natural children, whereas if a woman becomes pregnant by alternative means, no one needs to know about it. So couples who are considering adoption need to consider their feelings about the stigma of adoptive parent status.

Adoption Process

Once the decision to adopt is made, couples need to gather information in order to learn what their adoption options are. Even if they adopt privately, they are, as explained in Chapter 2, subject to some kind of public review and, perhaps, disappointments about failed matches or rejection by birth parents. On the other hand, although most adoptive parents do not know when they may receive a baby, they usually have a long time to prepare themselves to give up their fantasy of a birth child and to adapt to the notion of adoption.

Beginning Adoptive Family

When a child arrives, the adoptive family begins its life cycle. The literature suggests that bonding is quicker with infants than with older children. Many adoptive parents report feeling instantly that the baby is theirs as soon as it is placed in their arms, particularly if it is within hours or days of birth. There is definitive research by Kirk (1981, 1984) showing that those adoptive parents who are able to acknowledge the differences between the biological and adoptive routes to becoming parents are better able to develop empathy for the adopted child's unique experiences, and they better communicate to their adopted children the special circumstances in which their child entered the family. There is further research by Brodzinsky (1990) that indicates that parents who overemphasize this distinction may have difficulty forming secure attachments. Recent research by Bohman, McRoy, and Grotevant (1992) suggests differences in the ways mothers and fathers adapt to adoptive parenting. For example, mothers wonder more frequently whether the birth mother is thinking about the child than do fathers. This may be related to mothers' greater involvement in caregiving.

It is not uncommon for adoptive parents to experience "kidnapping guilt," feeling sadness for the birth mother around the loss of the child, and guilt that they have benefited through another's misfortune. They may deal with this guilt by developing negative images of the birth parents in order to justify their having the child and being able to provide a better life for him or her. So we see that adoptive parents have their own "family romance" stories, somewhat different from the ones that children develop. Adoptive parents' stories may be based on whatever information has been given to them about the birth parents. It may be embellished by their own ingrained attitudes about relinquishing parents. If some of the information given to them has been negative, they may feel a need to withhold it from their children in order to protect them. Or they may distort and reframe it in order to feel more comfortable themselves.

Sonia and Will, in their mid-30s, were notified 2 days after the birth of their adoptive child that they were matched. Having been on an agency waiting list for 18 months, enduring two failed matches, they did not let this news fully penetrate for several hours. Then, they rushed around buying equipment and arranging their schedules so they could fly to get their baby. Two weeks later, when they returned home, they were delighted, although exhausted. Sonia reports that it took her longer to feel comfortable with the baby than she would have expected. He was fussy throughout the night, and she was uncomfortable with her own feelings of distress. She found herself unprepared emotionally, ruminating about the birth mother. She also found herself dreaming about breastfeeding, feeling sorry that she could not share this with her friends. Fortunately, Sonia had supportive family and friends. After about 2 months, she really felt relaxed and bonded. She commented on the feelings of jealousy she had toward Will, who seemed relaxed and comfortable with the baby from the beginning. Talking to him and friends, asking others about their coping with fussy infants, and acknowledging her feelings and confusion to herself and others enabled her to work through what she had expected to be a rapturous, easy time and had found to be troublesome and awkward.

In addition to individual differences, amount and type of preparation as well as spousal and family or friend support seem to facilitate parental adjustment. Until the Family and Medical Leave Act went into effect in July 1993, adoptive parents did not receive the same maternity and paternity leaves as were available to biological parents, and this certainly strained adoptive parents' physical and emotional adaptation to parenting. In addition, most adoptive families do not receive health coverage until the placement is finalized. This differs from state to state.

The parents of the adoptive parents may have more influence on the course of the adoption process than previously considered. If there are unresolved conflicts between the adopters and their parents, the adopters may feel that their parents are disappointed in them, which further adds to their own feelings of loss and failure. They may feel that their parents value their biological grandchildren more than their adopted grandchildren, and this may rekindle earlier sibling rivalry issues.

It should be noted that Sonia's experience is similar to that of many birth mothers. Obviously, there is a wide range of attachment experiences in both adoptive and biological families, and the temperament and disposition of the baby influences the parents' experience and development of self-esteem as parents, just as the parents' behaviors and attitudes influence the baby's psychological development.

Preschool Years

The major issue for adoptive parents during the preschool years is what, when, and how to tell their children about their adoptive status. In the 1930s, adoption was considered a secret and not revealed to children. In the 1940s, they were told that they were "special" and "chosen." In the 1950s and 1960s, adoptive parents were told to begin telling their children as soon as they became verbal. One adoptive mother says she called each of her adopted sons "my adopted darling" from the beginning, so they would understand the differences. Since the 1970s, research on cognitive development suggests that preschool children really are not able to comprehend what adoption means and is all about. This means that adoptive parents need to be careful in how they present the information so that young children do not distort it in a way that would be harmful to them later.

Although there is disagreement among experts as to whether preschoolers should be told about their adoption, I am in favor of natural, frequent references to the special difference of adoption. A frame for differences being positive rather than negative can have long range beneficial results. Obviously, it is important for parents to tailor their disclosure to their preschooler's concrete thinking. It is not unusual, for example, for preschoolers to note their friends' mothers' pregnancies. This will usually result in questions about where they came from. What a wonderful opportunity for parents to begin to explain to explain the circumstances of birth and adoption. It is during these years that the adoption story begins to be formulated.

School Age

From about age 6 or 7, adopted children may wonder about the permanency of their adoption and, utilizing their family romance fantasy, have both fears and desires for return to the birth family. There may be verbal and behavioral testing of limits, which may explain adopted children's overrepresentation in mental health facilities. How the parents and school respond to the child's insecurities, how empathic and clear their communication is, may be affected by how the adoptive parents themselves have resolved their disappointments about their infertility, as well as the reality of who their child is and how knowledgeable and empathic school personnel are to the distinctive vulnerabilities of adopted children. The mutual influence cycle of the adopted child, adoptive parents, and the school will determine the course or resolution of difficulties. Issues of who to tell outside the family, for example, will reflect the parents' feelings, and the adoptees' self-concept and comfort levels.

Adolescence and Young Adulthood

As the adolescent grapples with issues of identity, sexuality, and separation, parents are struggling with their own midlife identity issues revolving around their marital functioning, their own self-esteem, their roles and relationships, their sexuality and aging. Because adoptees may experience more intense identity and separation issues than do biological offspring, adoptive parents may also experience overreactions to their own unresolved issues as well as to their adolescent's struggles. Adolescents who conform to their parents' values and expectations are likely to experience less dissonance than those who do not. The power of biology and heredity, the "bad seed" myth, may be the parents' rationalization about their disappointments and feelings of powerlessness.

Sexuality may be a particular issue in adoptive families due to the adolescent's capacity to reproduce and his or her stronger likelihood of replicating a birth parent's experience than may be so for biological children. Adolescence is the time when parents and children have to come to terms with the results of years of influential guiding and shaping. Parents who have not created the type of family environment where youngsters are valued for who they are and allowed to internalize family values rather than resentfully comply to them are likely to experience turbulent power struggles, intensified by adoption vulnerabilities. The adoptive parents' biggest fear centers around the potential psychological or physical loss of the adopted children as these children gain independence and the likelihood of search and reunion increases.

> The Strongs, graduates of Ivy League colleges, have always been disappointed in their adopted son's academic performance. Deciding that he suffered from learning disabilities, they had provided extensive tutoring and support services throughout his years of school. They had a strong need to be "perfect parents" and had worked very hard to achieve this. By the time their son was a junior in high school, he was still in a lower track and was acting out with alcohol abuse and increasing temper tantrums. It was difficult for Betty and Don Strong to accept that all their efforts did not bear the results they thought desirable, and their self-esteem as parents was sorely challenged.
>
> At one particular crisis point, the high school counselor referred them to a parents' group. Wanting to make every effort, they accepted this recommendation even though it felt like failure to them. In the group, they learned that biological parents also experienced disappointments. It was difficult for them to learn and then acknowledge to themselves, their family, and friends, as well as to their son, that "going to college was not a prerequisite for success." But because of their genuine concern and caring, they slowly came to realize that college is not for everyone and that there are many ways to get along in life. By the time their son became a senior, he was in a mechanical drawing program at the regional vocational/technical high school, and the family was able to regain the feelings of closeness that they had previously experienced. "Everyone changed a little and we've become much more tolerant and accepting," stated Betty as she put her arms around her husband and son who were sitting on either side of her on the couch.

Later Life

Parents of adoptees may have to adapt to search and reunion efforts and results, learning to accept who their offspring is and what kinds of life choices he or she selects. Different families deal with the shadows from the past (biological or experiential) in different ways. Some families attempt to deny and cut off earlier experiences, whereas others become more accepting of variables over which they have no control. Cutoffs and connections, an important theme in any family, are particularly poignant in adoptive families. If the adoptive parents are threatened by the child's biological past, the child may protect them by denying or burying his or her curiosity, concern, or longing for connection to the past. Adoptive parents who have been insecure about their adoptive status may fear that once their primary caretaking is no longer needed, they will be cast aside by their child, particularly if search and reunion has occurred. There is likely to be a fear that biological connection is stronger than the caretaking history.

One issue that some adoptive parents report is envy about their adoptive children's capacity to reproduce. They do not have a genealogical linkage to prospective grandchildren, which reminds them of their own infertility pain. But most adoptive parents would rather cope with the special issues that adoption presents compared to having gone through their life cycle childless. Like any family, parents of adult children are renegotiating relationships, dealing with generativity, and adapting to their changing circumstances.

*   *   *

We see that adoption is a lifetime adjustment for all members of the adoption triangle. All three parties experience feelings of loss that will affect their futures. Whether these losses are the traumas that Lifton (1994) suggests, whether there is truly a higher rate of suicidality and psychopathology among adopted people than among nonadopted people is not really clear, given census and sampling difficulties. However, the powerful experience of adoption touches upon universal human themes of abandonment, parenthood, sexuality, identity, and the sense of belonging. And we are only just beginning to understand the impact of social stigmatization on adjustment to adoption. As adoption practices change, the experiences of the adoption triangle parties will also change as will their interrelationships. And as societal attitudes about biological and psychological bonding change, adoption will better serve the interests of the child.

FOUR

Treatment Issues
Pertaining to Adoption

The Johnson family, consisting of Dad, 49, Mom, 42, and two adopted children, Tom, 19, and Becky, 17, were referred to family therapy by Becky's individual therapist. Becky had been briefly hospitalized
for depression midway through her senior year in high school and
was finding it difficult to return to school and live at home. Tom
had quit college after one semester and was living with friends in a
nearby town. Mr. and Mrs. Johnson were upset, concerned, and confused. During the preliminary family history taking of this initial family therapy session, the therapist discovered that Tom and Becky were
adopted. She announced that "Becky's depression was related to the
attachment loss she suffered from adoption and that it was imperative for Tom and Becky to begin to search for their birth mothers."
At this point, Becky ran out of the therapy room and refused to have
anything further to do with family therapy. Tom left soon after, and
Mr. and Mrs. Johnson were stunned and shaken by this turn of
events.

The above scenario was related to me by the Johnson family and by
Becky's individual therapist in a subsequent meeting. The individual
therapist told me later in private that she had made this referral knowing
that the family therapist was a "renowned expert" in adoption issues,
but she had no idea that the matter would be dealt with so dogmati-
cally and insensitively. In fact, when the individual therapist later spoke
to the family therapist, she was told that this family's reaction to the
insistence on search for birth parents was indicative of "severe
pathology."

We can all share horror stories about people in every profession
and line of work. My point in relating this episode is to highlight the
following three points: As clinicians, (1) we must take people at the
point where they are and with the issues they believe bring them to

us; (2) we must be sensitive to contextual as well as special issues in their backgrounds and experiences; and (3) we must be continuously self-aware as to our own "countertransference" issues, particularly around sensitive, controversial subjects.

Thus, not all clients who are members of the adoption triangle bring adoption-related issues into therapy. Some have worked through the adoption-related issues and are now dealing with other kinds of issues; some choose not to deal with them at all. Each client's unique experiences and circumstances require open-minded assessment and treatment formulation. If clients do not talk much about adoption, we cannot assume they are repressing or denying concerns; they may, in fact, have a background of positive reactions around adoption and be concerned about totally separate issues.

The purpose of this chapter is to discuss the clinical implications of working with individuals, couples, and families who have experienced or are currently experiencing the process of adoption. Although the focus of this chapter is on postadoption, I will briefly discuss clinical issues relating to infertility, the decision to adopt, and the birth mother.

It seems to me that a basic premise for clinicians is a two-fold realization. First, life in an adoptive family is different for both the adopted child and the adopted parents than life in a birth family. And second, this does not mean that it is better or worse, merely different. It is important for clinicians to recognize that divorce; physical, sexual, emotional, or substance abuse; desertion; and pathology exist in both birth and adoptive families. If and how adoption is impacted by pathology or impacts pathology is a question to be considered, not an assumption to be made.

INFERTILITY

A generation ago, most couples did not even think about the possibility of infertility. You got married in your early or mid-20s, and you had a baby within the next few years. And when couples did experience infertility, it was not talked about; there was no treatment, and often others did not know about it until after an adoption was announced.

Today, we know that one in six couples is likely to experience infertility. Because many couples are involved in dual careers and postpone childbirth until their 30s, they begin the conception process with some built-in anxiety. Time is growing shorter, and everyone knows many people who have endured years of infertility struggles and disappointments.

But when a couple has tried unsuccessfully to conceive for at least a year and is referred to an "infertility specialist," the first reaction is usually shock. This may, as previously noted, be the first time in their lives that they have not been able to control important aspects of living. The stresses and strains that infertility places on a couple is often what brings them to the attention of a psychotherapist.

Most therapists will assess the strengths and vulnerabilities of the marital relationship while providing information and support. The objective is to help the couple along their course of choices and decision making in a mutually supportive context. Some marriages can tolerate the stresses and strains of infertility and attempted treatments. In fact, some couples report that their relationship becomes stronger as they share the pain and grieving, and work together to resolve their losses. These couples are a therapist's joy! They respond well to supportive and educative strategies and often use therapy sessions to vent in unison their disappointment, pain, and frustration as they consider how much infertility treatment they can afford and tolerate and at what point they will stop. Other couples, however, use their infertility as a wedge, blaming and resenting the partner for disappointments, and even resisting medical assessment or treatment. If the infertility issues succeed in splitting a couple, the marriage is likely to dissolve.

The grieving process for couples is similar to the loss stages elucidated in crisis intervention theory. After the initial shock, which serves as a protective defense as well as an immobilizer, couples begin to protest. This protest phase is a combination of denial and a determination to find an answer to the problem. During this phase, couples may actively seek "expert" opinions and attempt a variety of treatments. As disappointments continue, such as unsuccessful treatment, a kind of despair sets in. It is often during this phase that couples enter therapy. The doubts about one's own value and worth as well as the partner's value and worth exacerbate whatever frailties or vulnerabilities already exist in the marriage.

In order to reach the resolution phase, the therapist must help the couple to acknowledge and research their choices, such as whether to pursue infertility treatment, remain childless, adopt, or attempt some alternative birthing procedure such as surrogacy. Not only is the narcissistic injury of infertility explored, but also the meanings and expectations of "marriage" and "parenting." Part of the resolution is acceptance of the infertility as a permanent part of one's self-concept. This involves clarifying for the couple that infertility is different from sexual adequacy, which, in turn, is different from the ability to reproduce, which, in turn, is different from parenting competence. It also means accepting and managing the ambivalences associated with whatever resolution choices are made.

Gender and cultural differences in coping with infertility need to be acknowledged.

It took 4 years before Ed, 38, would allow a sperm motility test. Janine, 34, had been through every fertility assessment test and procedure possible and no cause other than some mild endometriosis could be discovered. Ed saw this as "her problem." He knew very little about his own body and, because he was so sexually active and ejaculated a great deal of semen, he was sure that he was "virile." The years put a strain on the quality of their sexual relationship as well as on their ability to refrain from a cycle of Janine's complaining and criticizing and Ed's defensive withdrawal and stonewalling. Finally, when the marriage was about to break up, Ed came to couple therapy (at the insistence of Janine's physician) and learned, for the first time, that virility had nothing to do with the ability to reproduce. It turned out that he did have low sperm motility and once this was identified, the couple was helped to conceive through artificial insemination. A genogram indicated that Ed's views of "masculinity" and "emotion" were consistent with those of his constricted family of origin, whereas Janine's more expressive emotionality was not hysteria, but her Lebanese culture's norm.

I have found that infertile couples feel alienated and isolated: Their peers are having babies; their families are continuously asking them when they will. They feel a sense of shame and often find attending christenings or birthday parties for children intolerable. They feel others cannot understand, much less support, their struggles with feelings of guilt, inadequacy, and blame. In addition to couple work, therefore, I suggest group work or a referral to Resolve, a national support organization for infertile couples based in Somerville, Massachusetts. The realization that others are struggling with the same circumstances and issues is educative as well as supportive.

BIRTH PARENTS

As birth mothers are most prevalent, most of this section refers to them. Birth fathers, as we will see, are participating increasingly in the birth mother's pregnancy, birth, and decisions about the baby, but except for the highly publicized cases about those who are seeking custody rather than providing release for adoption, most birth fathers who acknowledge their paternity see their role as providing cooperative support.

The major clinical aspect of working with birth parents is to help them with their decision making during pregnancy. The goal is responsible self-determination by the birth parent(s). Thus, the most important task for the therapist is to advocate for and support the rights of birth parents to make their own decisions about whom to inform of the pregnancy, whether or not to have an abortion, whether or not to keep and raise the baby, whether to keep parental rights but have others raise the baby, or whether to relinquish the baby to either open, semi-open, or closed adoption.

It is important to consider the context of the pregnancy (accidental, due to rape or incest, the result of a casual fling) and the developmental life stage of the woman. For example, adolescent birth mothers may require different decision-making models than do adults, given what we now know about cognitive development. D. E. Gordon (1990) proposes that adolescents who are able to engage in formal reasoning can benefit from abstract discussions, while those who are unable to engage in formal reasoning can profit from concrete decision-making tasks such as actual role playing, babysitting, and so forth.

The major work focuses on helping the birth parent(s) to consider all of the possible options and to hypothesize possible short- and long-term effects of each choice. Assessment of the attitudes and pressures of the client's family can enable the therapist to advocate for the client's self-determination. Each possible choice will involve emotional regrets and loss. Part of the decision making is to enable birth parents to consider multiple perspectives, as well as sociocultural norms, their life experiences, current resources and responsibilities, and what they now consider to be their future goals. These must be weighed against the advantages and disadvantages of relinquishing the baby. I find that imagery, psychodrama, and sculpting are useful techniques to enable clients to consider options. Use of as many perceptual modalities as possible facilitates the decision-making process.

I may ask the client to sit back and close her eyes. After a few suggestions to encourage muscle relaxation and deep breathing, I'll ask her to imagine herself at a road rotary. She should attempt to get in touch with the sights and sounds of this place. Then I ask her to walk down a road gradually, a road that will include her keeping her baby. We elaborate upon the things she should consider, such as daily gratifications and frustrations, what it will mean to her goals and dreams given what I've learned about her circumstances. After about 7 or 8 minutes, we return to the rotary and slowly go down the road of giving the baby up for adoption. We attempt to visualize and feel the specifics of those circumstances. In another 7 or 8 minutes, I ask her to return to the rotary and to just sit with those feelings for a while. Her assignment is to take the next few days to consider what she learned about herself on these two roads. We process it more thoroughly at the next session.

If the decision to relinquish the baby is made, the focus is on (1) the concrete choices regarding adoption—educating about and suggesting resources for private or public agency support, group homes for pregnant mothers, and open adoption agencies that place the pregnant woman for the duration of the pregnancy and birthing; and (2) preparation of the birth parent for issues of attachment and loss throughout the pregnancy.

Many women are surprised by the intensity of their feelings about the fetus growing within them. Nine months of absorption in one's emotional and physical changes set the stage for a massive physical and emotional loss, as well as relief, at birth. Fortunately, today the birthing process is more sensitive and humane than it was a generation ago, and birth mothers are not as likely to be scorned and disdained by the hospital staff during the actual birthing process. But it is important for therapists to help clients anticipate emotional pain and to prepare for this by lining up supports, such as family, friends, or even the prospective adoptive parents. It is also critical that therapists validate clients' feelings and not shy away from exploring the clients' sense of shame and stigmatization.

The therapist's most essential role is to help the birth mother cope with the necessary and legitimate grieving after the relinquishment. If nothing else, the birth mother needs some acknowledgment of biological bonds and validation for the loss of her baby. Just as women vary in their hormonal and physical recovery from childbirth, the process of their emotional realization of the separation also varies on a continuum from alarm to relief. Therapists can help birth parents to accept their sorrow, anger, guilt, and feelings of a loss of self and can provide support for their emotional and verbal venting. They can offer a safe, warm, empathic setting for this grieving and not expect the birth parent to just "pick up and return to school or work." It is natural for birth parents to become preoccupied with thoughts about the baby and the adopted family. Several birth mothers reported secretly shadowing the adoptive family during the first year, always attempting to get a glimpse of their baby and to reassure themselves that this was the best decision for the baby. Many people believe that open adoption, where information is available, helps the grieving process.

The birth parent's worst fear is that the adoptive family will not provide sufficient nurturing care to her baby, that she made a wrong choice or selection, that something terrible will happen and it will be her fault. The therapist can help her understand these guilty recriminations and ruminations and let her know that, with time, they will lessen. The mother may want to begin a search immediately or recant her decision. Most states have time lines in which birth parents can change their minds and therapists can help clients to consider thoughtfully, rather than impulsively or out of emotional reaction, what they really think is best for the child and for themselves. Again, the goal is self-determination by the client, and we, as therapists, must support their choices rather than impose our own views on them.

The goal of this phase of therapy is to help the birth parent accept, not forget, this relinquishment, and move on with her life. I have found that individually designed rituals can be helpful to this process, such as keeping a journal, writing unmailed letters to one's child, selecting 1 day a month or a year to envision the child in his or her imagined surroundings. One Jewish client decided to plant a tree in Israel every year on the birthday of her son. Another client has used the birthday of her son as a time to take a day away from family and work and to seek solitude in nature. A Catholic client, who travels extensively for her business, makes a point of attending church and lighting a candle for her relinquished daughter no matter where in the world she is on that birthday. Over the past 20 years, nothing has interfered with this annual ritual.

The grief and loss are lifelong. Although the painful feelings may recede with time, triggering events and circumstances can bring them back to the foreground at any time. However, these recurrences are likely to lessen in frequency and intensity.

Later Adulthood

It is not uncommon for birth parents to enter therapy years after relinquishment. The presenting issue may not have anything to do with the relinquishment. However, lingering emotional ramifications and incomplete mourning about the relinquishment may come to light during the course of therapy. One's subsequent circumstances of life—family and occupational gratifications or lack thereof—color one's relinquishment experience. The issue for many clients later in life is whether or not to search for their birth child, and whom to tell about their past.

The clinical tasks are similar to those earlier in life: exploration of the birth parents' expectations and ambivalences about search, the objectives of the imagined reunion (reparation, retrieval, or closure), discussion of possible consequences, and advocacy and support for self-determination.

> Marianne, 48, married for 24 years with three grown children, decided to search for the son she had relinquished to a state agency 27 years earlier. With the full support of her husband and children, she sought the services of an adoption listing agency and soon received

the name, address, and telephone number of her adopted son. She insisted to her family that she just wanted to know "he was well and all right" and that she had no intention of an ongoing relationship. Her children were eager and curious and wanted to incorporate "Steve" into their family. When Marianne finally phoned the number she was given, Steve refused to talk to her. His adopted mother empathically provided Marianne with details of Steve's life and, according to Marianne, tried to encourage Steve to talk to her. Marianne became severely depressed (she felt helpless, cried from feelings of rejection and self-blame, could not eat or sleep) and was referred to therapy by her internist. It became clear that Marianne had unfinished grieving, that she was still punishing herself for relinquishing Steve, particularly because she had later been able to provide an affluent life style to her subsequent children.

Marianne was encouraged by her therapist to relive her first pregnancy, decision-making, and relinquishment experiences in the same way we encourage trauma survivors to reexperience their trauma in a safe, empathic setting. She wrote long letters to Steve, which she placed in her safety deposit box in case he should ever want to see them. In these letters, she talked about her feelings, described her life, asked for his forgiveness, and said "Good-bye" to him. Some Gestalt exercises allowing Marianne to dialogue back and forth between her image of Steve's adoptive mother, birth mother Marianne, and the Marianne of her current family prepared Marianne for some family therapy sessions. She realized that her children were getting ready to leave home and she no longer had their needs as a buffer against the repressed pain and shame associated with giving up her baby. She also recognized the connection between the recent death of her critical mother, who had demanded much caretaking from Marianne and insisted on blotting out "that terrible episode," and the flooding of her yearnings to develop an attachment to Steve. The family sessions enabled Marianne to talk about her preoccupation, explain her feelings of disappointment regarding her fantasies of reunion, and then renew her current commitment to her family and community. She acknowledged that she needed to develop a new life plan, now that mothering was no longer going to be her primary role.

Birth parents who enter treatment postrelinquishment may come in for individual, couple, or family therapy. It is likely that all three modalities will be useful at some time in the course of treatment. With Marianne, treatment began with individual therapy, then included her husband and later her children in order to resolve the past and current ramifications of relinquishment. Marianne had to let go of her fantasies about Steve, forgive herself for the relinquishment, and learn that she could survive the trauma of loss.

ASSESSMENT OF ADOPTION ISSUES

When adoption is directly or indirectly brought into the therapy process, the therapist must decide when and how to pursue the topic. That will most likely depend on the circumstances of the therapy. Sometimes, relinquishment or adoption is not mentioned until the therapist takes a history, such as constructing a genogram. And that may not occur in the initial session. And when adoption or relinquishment is mentioned, some clients express surprise at the therapist's interest. This may be a clue to tread slowly and carefully, allowing for the development of a trusting working alliance as a context for discussing controversial or threatening issues.

But at some time, it is important for the clinician to explore the meaning and experience of adoption by all of the members of the family in order to assess the influence of these meanings and experiences on the family functioning. So, even if the client is seeking individual therapy, at least one family session is helpful to gather information necessary for assessment and treatment planning. Some individual clients will not feel comfortable with the idea of a family session until they have developed a positive relationship with the therapist. And, whether or not the family is included in the actual treatment, a therapist can maintain a family systems perspective by carefully considering the family context.

In most situations, there are differing meanings and experiences among the members of the family system. Intertwined with this exploration process is sensitive psychoeducation. This may include bibliotherapy (recommending books for the clients to read) as well as discussion of the salience of adoption in the family's history and current community. The therapist attempts to empower the individual client and the family by educating them about the common misconceptions discussed in Chapter 2.

Family Assessment

The Adoption Story

Asking each member of the family what his or her perception of the adoption story is can help the therapist understand the meaning of adoption to the family as well as provide him or her with an important opportunity to assess the impact of this mythology on the family members. The adoption story answers the questions of (1) where the baby came from, (2) why the baby was available for adoption, (3) who the birth parents were, (4) what the circumstances of the birth were,

(5) how the adoptive parents were chosen and by whom for this particular child, and (6) how and why the adoptive parents wanted to adopt a baby.

This adoption story has been developed over the family life cycle and may be interpreted differently by various family members during repetitive narrations. Hartman and Laird (1990) comment on how this adoption story can be emotionally compelling in fostering empathy for the birth parents who had to relinquish the child and appreciation for the adoptive parents whose yearnings to parent were gratified by this "special child."

In addition to having family members recount their versions of the adoption story and family romance, it can be fun to have them draw separate pictures that they share with each other or to have them take turns directing a family sculpture, whereby they place each family member in a kinetic, but nonverbal, relationship to each other, giving the "show" a name and theme. "Sleeping Beauty," "Cinderella," and "Hansel and Gretel" are frequent themes elaborated by children. Parents often create "Life with Father" or "Leave It to Beaver" scenes, reflecting their desires for an idyllic family. Drawings, role plays, psychodramas, and sculptures help family members as well as the therapist to understand the mythologies that influence family roles and rules.

As previously mentioned, Rosenberg (1992) points out that contemporary research about children's cognitive development indicates that children under the age of 6 or 7 are really not able to comprehend the concept of adoption and may distort in their minds whatever story is being told to them. Therefore, it is important for parents and therapists to pay special attention to how a young child perceives and interprets this story. Likewise, therapists can be sensitive to the adoptive parents' feelings about the adoption story. They can teach parents to tell the story in a gentle, loving way that doesn't pressure the child to feel grateful or obliged to make reparations.

Many adoptive parents, especially those who endured traditional home visits for closed adoptions, feel the need to prove themselves as "perfect parents." They may be particularly vulnerable to harsh self-judgment about the normal ambivalences and lapses of patience and empathic parenting experienced inevitably by all parents. These parents need reassurance and psychoeducation about the realities of parenting as well as the opportunity to learn concrete behavioral and management strategies.

Therapists also need to consider multigenerational and community aspects of the family adoption story. Is the same story told to everyone? How consistent or discrepant is the "story" to the known facts? What are the unspoken "bad seed myths" in the family, the extended family, or the community? In today's era of belief in genetic influences on temperament and behavior, adopted children can be the target of subtle or not so subtle scapegoating, especially if the fear of the past's influence is handled by denial and is cut off from actual data. Some adopted families seem to blame adoption for their problems, as if that absolves them of considering their own responsibility for changing the way their family operates.

Finally, therapists can ascertain the salience of the adoption story in the family functioning. Depending on the parents' attitudes about adoption, there may be too little, enough, or too much talking about adoption. An assessment of this salience and what it means to individual family members' identity and to the identity of the family as a system is critical in helping families cope with the kinds of identity conflicts that adopted children often present.

Family Relations

When assessing a family, therapists observe and evaluate the emotional climate and interactions of the family in order to determine what the rules and roles are, how they came to be, how they may or may not be modified or adapted, what coalitions and triangles exist and for what purposes, how distance and closeness are regulated, and how information is processed. What are the family resources and patterns for adaptation, for a sense of cohesion and family connectedness, for clear, direct communication? Where does the family get stuck and how?

Considering the family backgrounds of the parents offers opportunities to understand what family relational experiences each parent brings into this family system. Integrating these data with the data about the meaning, experience, and impact of adoption on all members of the family allows therapists to design an effective treatment customized to the needs of a particular family.

Ecological Assessment

A careful look at all the interacting systems in which the adoption triangle members are nested is particularly important for variant normative clients who experience the impact of being "different" and "out of the mainstream." The purpose of this assessment is to identify all possible environmental stressors and resources so as to define problems, treatment plans, and interventions most effectively.

The environmental systems particularly relevant to the adoption triangle include government (state and federal) laws and policies; mental health profession policies and practices; health insurance company benefits; educational opportunities and resources; religious, ethnic, and class influences; sociocultural values and beliefs; neighborhood and community influences; friendship and extended family influences; and adoption agency or lawyer/physician broker policies and practices.

The influences from these mutually influencing social systems can range from problematic to supportive, and therapists can only truly understand clients by considering issues of power and influence between the clients and their contexts.

TREATMENT ISSUES

Individual Therapy

While individuals may enter therapy because of their concerns about parenting adopted children, their unresolved feelings about the impact of infertility on their marriage, previous relinquishment, or their own identity as an adoptee, these concerns often underlie other presenting problems. It is not unusual for clients to deny or minimize the possibility that adoption issues are pertinent to their presenting concerns. Therapists' sensitivity to the clients' resistance and ambivalence allows appropriate timing and level of exploration of sensitive issues. In the era of short-term managed health care, it is conceivable that underlying concerns never even get addressed. However, sooner or later, if they are truly part of the problem, they will surface and need to be incorporated into a treatment plan.

As with any individual therapy, a genuine, supportive, and empathic therapeutic relationship can provide a context within which psychoeducation, exploration, cognitive restructuring, and grief work can be integrated in order to foster the client's capacity to translate increased awareness into effective problem-solving and interpersonal behaviors.

Tom, age 25, entered therapy to learn why he had difficulty keeping a job and getting along with his wife. During the second session, while creating a genogram, the facts of his adoption, alcoholism, and troubled relationship with his minister father came to light. Tom really didn't want to discuss these issues and kept bringing the focus back to his wife and bosses, all of whom didn't understand him and mistreated him. The therapist spent several sessions helping Tom repeat over and over troubling scenes at work and at home. He also instructed Tom to begin to keep a written daily journal. Eventually, Tom was able to see that he was contributing to these difficulties. When the therapist felt that Tom was becoming more trusting and relaxed, he was able to steer him into revealing his feelings about being adopted and being a minister's son, and his own and his father's drinking patterns. Once Tom was able to see the connection between his unresolved identity and loyalty issues regarding the family in which he was raised, he was able to regard his drinking and interpersonal eruptions differently and then to take steps for change.

Attending AA meetings and writing letters to his father and his wife expressing his feelings and concerns gradually enabled him to feel comfortable with couple and family sessions. During those latter sessions, he was able to articulate his resentments about his father's strictures and drinking, reveal his "family romance" fantasies, and begin to respond, rather than react, to his wife's requests and perceptions.

Couple Therapy

When couple work focuses on the marital relationship, the emphasis may be on clarifying and improving communication patterns in order to facilitate effective problem solving. This can allow concerns to be aired in a safe place, where the therapist can ensure that each person is being heard accurately and that messages are being sent directly and coherently. Role playing, sculpting, back-to-back Gestalt dialoguing, and other action techniques enhance communications work and further nurturing marital roles. If the environment is empathic and supportive, couples can be helped to mourn their lack of fertility, for example, learning to accept it without shame or blame. This frees them to be aware of the necessity to balance their marital intimacy with their parenting roles. Many adoptive parents overinvest in parenting at the expense of their marital relationship because, after years of disappointment and struggle, they feel more anxious and intense about parenting than do parents who never had to deal with infertility. Often, one parent overinvests in the child and the left-out spouse defends by withdrawing. This imbalance may go on for several years before the over-involved parent acknowledges the marital problem.

The therapist can help the couple to understand their own or their partner's underlying thoughts and feelings about adoption issues and can model support while educating and suggesting new perspectives to consider. For example, one couple was fighting about the wife's drinking. She had been found passed out on the couch when the children came home from elementary school on more than one occasion, and the husband was at his wit's ends with regard to suggesting treatments. The wife refused to acknowledge she had a problem, even after two separate 30-day inpatient stays. Knowing that the wife was adopted from the genogram constructed during the intake, the therapist wondered out loud if alcoholism was a problem in the wife's birth family. The husband then suggested that finding out about her "roots" might relieve whatever was "causing the drinking." The wife was at first resistant, but gradually came to think this would be an interesting endeavor. She began to confront her own resistance even to thinking about her adoption. Finally, she asked her adoptive aunt for information (her adoptive parents had died). She became intrigued by the search process and, much to her surprise, was able to locate her birth mother in a nearby city within a year. Several visits laid the groundwork for a more sustained relationship with the wife's birth mother and her family. The drinking ceased, and the wife expressed amazement that "the adoption stuff" proved to be so important. She found herself feeling more comfortable and at peace with herself as a person, never having fully realized that "there was something missing" for which the alcohol was an attempt to substitute.

Often, couple work focuses on parenting issues. Although some psychoeducation about adoption issues and the parents' own feelings about infertility and adoption is helpful, if the couple is coming for help with their children, they really want to focus on behavioral problem solving. Most couples do not see adoption as the cause of behavior problems, but, rather, see the problem behaviors as impediments to their feeling good about themselves and their children. If the parents are compensating for their feelings of inadequacy or insecurity as parents, they may be inconsistent or overly permissive with their adopted children. They may have unrealistic expectations of their children and of themselves as parents, and they may also lack nurturing parenting skills. Teaching parents the principles and strategies of consistent behavioral management along with nurturing and empathic responsive listening empowers them to view and respond to their children's behaviors more positively and constructively. This teaching can be augmented with attending parents' groups and/or reading selected books.

It is not unusual for couple issues to surface after the children's problem behaviors are reduced and are better controlled by more effective parenting strategies.

Jan and Bob came to therapy in utter despair about their adopted teenage son and daughter. Both children had difficulties in school, were rageful at home, and had been called to the attention of the authorities in the community for delinquent behaviors. The parents fought continuously over the best way to deal with their kids: Bob wanted strict rules and forced compliance, whereas Jan wanted the children to be able "to express themselves." Each of the youngsters was in individual therapy, and Jan and Bob had each been in individual therapy for many years. But no one had ever addressed the day-to-day roles and rules of the household.

The therapist started out with teaching them contingency contracting principles and then instructing them how to develop a contract with each of the youngsters. The parents were amazed to learn that what they had heretofore considered "rights" were indeed "privileges," such as use of the car, television, telephone, and so forth. Within weeks, the children had agreed to collaboratively constructed contracts, and things were more settled than ever before. At this time, Bob began carping at Jan and serious couple issues emerged, mainly his rage at her infertility (which she had told him about prior to marriage) and his ingrained belief that adopted children were inevitably inferior.

The therapist reframed the family situation by telling them that the kids were saving the parents' marriage by being such difficult kids. These two people were more together when worrying about their children's problems and attempting to solve them than when they had to deal with each other and their disappointments and unresolved resentments. Short-term couple therapy moved into focusing on marital issues with occasional check-ins on parenting. At the end of the contracted sessions, Bob and Jan acknowledged that they wanted to stay together until their youngest child finished high school, but that they were not sure if they would last as a couple after that. They agreed to intermittent couple therapy during the next 2 years and said they would consider joining a couples group in the next few months.

It has been reported that adoptive parents who have persistent difficulty with their children, or even experience the trauma of disruption, have a higher divorce rate than adoptive parents who parent more comfortably (Barth & Berry, 1988). Each case is different, and we cannot automatically attribute adoption failures to faulty parenting or to a flawed child. In most cases, every member of the family contributes to the problem, and a lack of social and agency support can exacerbate the difficulties. In the above case, Bob and Jan's marriage had been in serious difficulty from the beginning. The children had kept them together by creating a focus other than the marital rift.

Family Therapy

The primary task of family therapy with adoptive families is to help them to integrate and blend their differences into a cohesive family unit. We want to help family members develop a sense of self at the same time that they form a sense of belonging. As with couple therapy, the family therapy model is more interactionally than intrapsychically based. Today, adoptive families receive more preparation and longer-term support than in the past, and there is every reason to suppose that this will facilitate their transition to becoming a family. Families can be helped to identify and utilize those internal and external resources that will help reduce and manage their stresses. For example, a parents' group may provide competent models for parenting; an adoptive parents' group may provide support for airing concerns about adoption; a sibling group may improve those relationships. The family structure can be realigned by assigning tasks that will promote closeness between people who are experiencing tension or providing more appropriate distance between overly close members. This can not only help alleviate current conflict, but also sets the stage for new and different patterns of relating. Internal and external resources can be identified by direct or indirect questions such as the following: With whom do the family members feel most comfortable? With whom can they feel relaxed in talking about adoption? Who knows? Who doesn't know? What do they want people to think? What do they want people not to think?

A common stress presented by adoptive families is the minimizing or denial of differences due to adoption. In fact, Kirk (1981) has found that a family's acceptance and understanding of differences due to adoption and of the "unconventionality" attributed by society to adoptive families allows them to develop workable relationships that are unencumbered by traditional rules and norms, which are unlikely to work for them anyway. Families who refuse to acknowledge adoption differences are more likely to experience difficulty. A recent longitudinal study of 111 adoptive families by Bohman et al. (1992) confirms the relationship of Kirk's Acknowledgement of Differences theory (1981) to adoptive parents' ongoing empathy and communication with their child's special needs, with respect to traditional, confidential adoptions. Certainly, it is my experience that the adoptive families I see clinically very often have an investment in not acknowledging adoption differences so as to appear like a "normal birth family," whereas the families I interviewed for this study talk more openly and comfortably about their experience of adoption and its meaning for them. However, as noted by Kaye (1990), some families do not need to communicate much about adoption differences or issues because they have not had negative experiences and, therefore, adoption is not an issue: "Perhaps adopted children can suffer from too much acknowledgment of differences as well as too little?" (p. 140).

When working with families, I typically schedule at least one separate meeting with each different subsystem in order to experience them as their own units with rules, roles, and functions. I recently worked with a highly functioning family with low levels of distress. In a session with the sibling subsystem, consisting of two biological children, ages 12 and 14, and an 11-year-old adoptee (the middle child was the defiant "identified patient"), the middle child asked the adoptee if she ever thought about her "real mother." The adoptee responded, "Sometimes, mostly because Mom asks me if I do. I'm not sure what I'm supposed to think about her." Further discussion about the family's adoption story and this youngster's experience of adoption revealed that the middle child was the one who was fantasizing that she was the adopted child and would escape parental limit setting and criticism by being rescued by uncritical, indulgent parents. At this point, adoption was not an issue for the adoptee, who appeared not only to me to be a relaxed, well-adjusted child, but was perceived likewise by her family and teachers. I have also had sibling subsystem sessions where the adoptee(s) was able to talk more openly about fantasies, concerns, or thoughts regarding adoption without the parents present. Adoptees tend to be terribly sensitive to their parents' feelings and do not want to appear to be disloyal.

Many of the adopted families that I have worked with need to acknowledge their disappointments about the discrepancies between their expectations and reality, in addition to acknowledging differences. Just as in many biological families, high achieving parents may have unrealistic expectations about their offspring, often expecting achievement in the same area as the parents' success. If the offspring do not succeed in the same way the parents did, the parents may feel frustrated and disappointed. In adoptive families, this is sometimes attributed to "adoption." In biological families, it is more often attributed to "laziness and rebellion." Learning to value and accept differences and to work through entitlement fantasies can be a focus of family treatment.

One of the most disturbed families I ever treated consisted of a Mennonite physician father and mother and a Caucasian daughter adopted in infancy through a traditional adoption agency, followed by two South American siblings adopted while toddlers, and an African American infant adopted through the state. The family was referred after a physical abuse charge against the mother was filed by the South American daughter. This family lived in a small farm community where they were the only adoptive family as well as the only family with members of color. The mother insisted that her only focus in life was to be "a perfect mother," and any time the children tried to individuate or talk about racial differences, she would talk about her birth pains and elaborate as to how she experienced them as if the adopted children came from her very own body. They were not allowed to use the word "adoption." She was so enmeshed with her "babies" that she had no interaction with her husband and refused to acknowledge his very evident extramarital affairs. A separate sibling system meeting spilled out the family secrets (Dad's affairs, Mom's craziness, and the two sons' confused identities) and also strengthened the siblings' potentially supportive bonds. Of these four children, the two daughters, who openly rebelled until they were extruded from the family (by being sent away to boarding school), were the strongest and healthiest. The mother was eventually hospitalized for a psychotic break and was diagnosed as a schizoid-type personality disorder.

It is probable that both rejection of and insistence on differences between the biological and adoptive processes of becoming a family can impair the developmental course of an adoptive family system. The current trend toward open adoption may facilitate an adaptive acknowledgment of differences, although research is needed to test how adaptation over time to adoption is impacted by openness in adoption.

When adopted children get ready to leave home, there may be a reemergence of vulnerability in the family, due to the particularly sensitive issues of loss and the threat of loss. In some families, such as the one I just described, the only way to leave home is to be so bad or sick that you're ejected. One adopted offspring I talked with, after enduring a difficult engagement and tense wedding, felt so guilty about leaving home to marry someone whom her parents did not believe was "suitable" that she became clinically depressed 3 months after her wedding and left her husband to return home to be the "grateful daughter." Her delighted parents lavished her with material advantages to ensure her gratitude for having been adopted and raised in opulence. It is likely that she will let her parents select her next husband.

Adoption of Older Children

The first issue for clinicians working with families adopting older children is to provide a safe place, where family members can be open and honest without worrying about jeopardizing a placement. Thus, it is usually advisable for the family to consult a therapist who is not associated with the placement process. This therapist needs to understand that the needs of the family to move toward cohesion and closeness are out of sync with the child's developmental needs to differentiate and to work through the loss of previous caretakers.

It seems that therapists working with families who adopt older children focus on the child as a problem, rather than on the adopting family. Therapists often unwittingly add to the confusion by not acknowledging that the information and advice available to adoptive families is inconsistent. Certainly, however, older child adoptions present particular challenges and difficulties. The statistics show that older child adoption results in the largest rate of disruption (Barth & Berry, 1988).

It is critical for the therapist to find out why the parents have entered into this older child adoption. Were they the foster parents? Did they want to provide a sibling for a biological child? Was it because of the age at which they realized they were infertile? The next task is for the therapist to help the parents articulate their expectations for the parent–child relationship. Many parents think that love is all that is necessary to make an older child adoption work, but, as pointed out by Brodzinsky et al. (1992), parents also need a full picture of the medical, behavioral, and emotional background of the child. Without knowing what kinds of relationships a child has had in his or her past, parents will not be able to be realistic in anticipating the kind of relationship the child will be able to have with the adoptive parents. A child who has had many disrupted attachments is likely to be wary of trusting any new attachments. Also, a child who has endured physical, sexual, or emotional abuse or deprivation is likely to manifest this history in behavioral and learning disorders later in life.

The sad reality is that many children who have spent time in institutional or foster care settings may have actually experienced some form of abuse. And if the parents do not know about it, they may be sorely tried when caught unaware by a child who, for example, sexualizes behavior in such a way as to cause conflict between the parents.

A professional couple who had adopted two children as toddlers came for couple therapy because the younger child was behaving in a sexual way in his preschool class. He was inserting his finger in girls' rectums and trying to get them to touch his penis. The school director called the parents in for a conference and suggested that the child had most likely been sexually abused. This led the mother to wonder whether her husband was the abuser.

The stress and strains this placed on the marriage were enormous. Expert consultation with the child could not glean enough information to accuse the father or anyone. The therapist, while open to the possibility that the adoptive father could be an abuser, had no reason to suspect him after several individual and couple sessions. This was supported by an outside expert. After much investigation, the therapist was able to learn informally that one of the day care centers where this child had spent a year had experienced some incidents of sexual abuse by parttime workers. Although this scandal had been hushed and kept from the media, there was reason to suspect that if abuse had occurred, it might have been there or during the first 2 years of the young boy's life. It took many months of couple work to restore faith and trust in this couple system.

As discussed in Chapter 3, adjustment will be more difficult for everyone in older child adoption, because new routines, roles, and rules will be necessary. It is critical that therapists apprise parents of the realities of these difficulties and actively help them find supportive resources.

Another problem for adoptive parents of older children is the child's loyalty to previous caretakers, even to those who are believed to have been abusive. The adoptive parents may need help in order to tolerate the child's memories and past relationships and incorporate them into the present family system. It will take time for the new family system to develop its own history that includes the adoptee. When this occurs, the past memories and loyalties of the adoptee will not dominate the child's sense of self-in-family.

Adoptive parents need to know what birth story the older child has been told, how the child interprets this story, and how close to the truth it is. This can be a problem, in that the current social policy of placing children may encourage social workers to withhold any kind of negative information that may prejudice the family against a child. Many of the older children available for adoption do have special needs. Parents must learn what their limits are, what kinds of problems they will be able to handle. Are they prepared to cope with learning disability? retardation? problematic medical history? posttraumatic stress syndrome or some other psychological disorder? Some states have more rigorous screening procedures for special needs adoptions, realizing that unique attributes are necessary in order for parents to tolerate and cope with these special needs. Although more than 80% of older adoptions are successful, those that do not work out are traumatic for everyone in the family (Fishman, 1992).

There are many foci for therapists working with such families (L. Katz, 1986). These include helping adoptive parents to tolerate their own ambivalence and strong negative reactions to the behaviors of older adoptees, supporting parents' refusal to be rejected by the child even under the most trying circumstances and to delay their needs for gratification as parents, and reframing the child's behavior so as to be able to empathize with the child's underlying fear of the very closeness he or she craves. It is also important for parents to develop flexibility in parental roles and strategies, avoid scapegoating the child or the process of adoption, and foster the capacity to be intrusive and controlling in a caring way so as to protect the child from his or her own destructive behaviors. Therapists can help parents develop humor, self-care, and openness to outside support as well as new ways of interpreting and resolving problems.

An approach that many therapists find useful is teaching adoptive parents of older children to recognize transference and counter-transference situations between parents and children. This can enable the adoptive parents to depersonalize the child's negativity and view it as a testing of parental limits. Because many older adopted children have attachment problems stemming from earlier trauma and/or multiple placements, they may not be able to tolerate the nurturing and love offered by the adoptive parents. In order for the parents to achieve their goal of bonding, the parents need instruction in how to maintain clear boundaries and identify the children's and their own projections so that they can resist becoming discouraged when their children display disruptive behaviors.

Gerri and Joe had adopted Eddie through a public adoption agency 4 years ago, when he was age 4. Their three biological sons ranged in age from 8 to 17 at the time of the adoption and, while they had not intended to have more children, Gerri had become quite fond of Eddie through her volunteer work at a model day care program. Gerri and Joe had been informed that Eddie had endured several placements; the most significant was his first foster home, from which he had been abruptly removed after his foster's father death in an automobile accident. Subsequent placements were short-term. Gerry was drawn to Eddie. His sadness reminded her of her sadness when she was a preschooler and her father was killed in an airplane accident. She convinced Joe and the boys that, with love and physical security, Eddie would flourish in their home. Eddie had not been released for adoption due to his biological father's refusal to sign a release, even though neither biological parent had ever seen him. The release appeared unexpectedly when the biological father was arrested for armed robbery and sentenced to a lengthy jail term.

At first, Eddie seemed to adapt to his adoptive family. However, it later turned out that everyone was so focused on fostering his adaptation that he was not expected to conform to family rules. In other words, whatever he did was excused as a result of his "previous trauma." Acknowledgment of problems did not occur until Eddie entered kindergarten the following year. By the time this family came for treatment (at the suggestion of the elementary school counselor), Eddie was viewed as a disruptive problem in his classroom and this behavior was transferred to his home life. Gerri and Joe were exasperated. They could not understand why Eddie had suddenly become so oppositional and verbally abusive at home. Where had he learned that vocabulary? They showered him with love and found his rage eruptions very disturbing. In fact, their other sons were beginning to complain and express resentment about Eddie's "favored" status. They thought he was a "spoiled brat." It was clear that Eddie had become the "lightning rod" for all the family tensions and developmental difficulties.

After two family meetings (one in the office, the other a home visit), the therapist scheduled several meetings alone with Gerri and Joe. He explained to them how Eddie's fears of abandonment and not belonging were rekindled when he entered school, because he had to enter a new system 1 year after being adopted. In new situations in the past, he had found that temper tantrums and helpless and needy behavior got him necessary attention. Now his teacher was expecting him to behave differently, and Eddie was confused and frustrated. By reframing these difficulties as persistent replications of how Eddie had worked with some success to enter a new system in the past, and by explaining his expectations of "unconditional approval" and treatment as "someone special," the parents were encouraged to teach Eddie new ways to fit in. They were taught to focus on the process of fitting in, rather than the outcome of belonging and bonding. The parents were given specific strategies to encourage Eddie to behave appropriately, by setting and implementing reasonable, appropriate rules, limits, and boundaries. The therapist modeled and taught them to model patience even though they might be experiencing their own internal frustration and anger. Specifically, the therapist used Eddie's current episodes to help the parents detect his sense of helplessness, fear, hopelessness, or confusion. By helping Gerri recognize how she had confused her own feelings of paternal loss with Eddie's and, as a result, was too permissive as a way of compensating, the parents learned not to personalize Eddie's feelings and behaviors. They learned to acknowledge to Eddie that they recognized his feelings, and to decide whether or not it would be a good time to talk to him about it, to hold him, or to set firm guidelines for his behavior. Gerri and Joe drew closer as they worked together to avoid being "hooked" by Eddie's outbursts (the therapist suggested to them that they visualize themselves as fish not swallowing the bait) and to process their own feelings and disappointments alone together after each episode. Gradually, the situation became more manageable and Eddie's and the other family members' anxieties lessened, allowing true feelings of belonging and bonding to develop.

Therapists also need to be aware of agencies that provide educational and support services for families who adopt older children, and should know about books and support groups (see the "Resources" chapter in this book). Support groups provide an opportunity for parents to understand and explore immediate and later adjustment issues with similar kinds of parents while being exposed to new ways of thinking and coping. Older children are thought to require a more structured and controlled environment upon entrance into a new family than the family might provide to an infant. One adoptive mother told me that she was very pleased at her 9-year-old adopted daughter's adjustment to the family and was cautioned by the members of her adoptive parents support group to expect some anxious behaviors later on. When her daughter began to manifest sleep disturbances the following year, this mother felt that her support group had prevented her from overreacting to her daughter's delayed anxieties.

Group counseling can help older adoptees to work out difficulties with siblings and adjustment to their new family (Cordell, Nathan, & Krymow, 1985). Siblings of older adoptees can also benefit from group work. Intermittent individual and family therapy sessions can enable adoptees to grieve the losses of their past and to resolve some of the identity questions related to being adopted as these issues reemerge within different developmental contexts (Berman & Bufferd, 1986). Changes in development and environment can cause "culture shock" (Ward, 1980) for both the parents and the child. There may be differences between the older child adoptee and parents in life style, values, beliefs, manners, speech patterns, behaviors, and prejudices. For example, parents who value academic performance may need to relax those standards and expectations while the adoptee focuses on coping with the changes in his or her life and the adjustment to a new family system, a new neighborhood, community, school, and so forth. These differences require patience and time to resolve.

If the adoption is likely to be disrupted, careful processing and planning are essential. Therapists need to help families to identify, locate, and utilize all possible resources so that the decision and process of disruption can proceed on the least destructive basis. The best interests of each family member must be taken into account, and the goal is for people to feel they made their best effort and, sad as it is, to accept that it couldn't work out. Blame and recriminations are counterproductive. Therapists who, due to their countertransference, cannot refrain from judging the family members may need consultation on disentangling their feelings from their capacity to be helpful.

Divorce and Adopted Children

How adopted children react to the divorce of their adoptive parents will be influenced by their experience of loss of and separation from their biological parent(s), the length of time in an intact adoptive family, and the quality of their adjustment and identity development. The developmental stage of the child and family are also important. As with biological children in divorcing families, the acceptance and resolution of feelings associated with divorce are affected by parental honesty and comfort as well as by discussion and information.

The disruptive nature of divorce can have special ramifications for adoptees. As pointed out by Wallerstein and Kelly (1980), divorce may delay or complicate the adoptee's resolution of anger, grief, guilt, and rejection. Worse still, it can be detrimental to what were earlier resolved conflicts in the adopted child. In other words, with respect to loss, adopted children can regress from a state of resolution to renewed loss and trauma. The feelings of loss associated with divorce resemble those associated with adoption.

> Ruth, adopted at 8 months and now age 32, recalls that when she was 11, her adoptive mother learned that her husband was having an affair with his secretary. In a rage, she packed up and went with Ruth to her parents' home. Ruth and her mother never returned to their previous home. Instead, they resided with Ruth's grandparents until Ruth left for college, at which time her mother moved into an apartment for a few months and then returned to live with her parents. Ruth remembers her mother "crying and staying in bed." But what she was able to recapture during the interview were intense feelings of, "Something is wrong with me. It's happening again." Ruth's grandparents were pretty distant, and she remembers feeling alone and confused. There was no one to talk to and her father just "slipped out of my life."

Obviously, therapists need to be knowledgeable about the processes and associated issues of both adoption and divorce as well as being aware of their own feelings about these two emotionally loaded situations. They need to be able to provide support to the parents and child, taking into consideration the child's age and developmental stage at adoption and at divorce, ethnicity, race, culture, birth order in the adoptive family, and where the child is with respect to resolution of adoption issues. This requires some understanding of cognitive development. For example, in infancy, loss is experienced in a preverbal, primitive way. The effects of divorce on top of adoption would be profound, as the child has a limited ability to understand and express distress. In the toddler/preschool phase of development, children are confused by explanations of adoption and divorce. They tend to see things dualistically (all good or all bad) and still egocentrically think that they caused and can fix things. School-age children struggle to comprehend having four parents and evidence of vacillation and confusion between the dualistic thinking and emerging abstract and hypothetical thought. Later, in adolescence, even though formal reasoning capabilities exist, the disruption of a family can complicate the already confusing ego identity stage. Adolescents waver between their loyalty to birth parents, adoptive parents, and, now, perhaps stepparents. They experience guilt and confusion, regardless of whom they choose to identify with (Samuels, 1990).

Therapists need to find out what was happening in the adoptive family, particularly in the marital relationship, when the adoption occurred and how the entrance of a new child affected the family system. How did the parents deal with adoptive status, and how comfortable and secure are they about their roles as adoptive parents? Because adopted children have already experienced psychological and/or physical abandonment, they require special reassurance that they will be protected and cared for. In other words, because divorce has a different impact for adopted children, these special needs need attention.

So, in addition to the usual help therapists provide to families to facilitate adjustment to divorce, they need to pay particular attention to the sensitive disruption issues of adoptive families. Divorce may precipitate adoptees' implementing a search for birth parents. This usually reflects a yearning for secure attachment, particularly in the period of tension and disruption.

THERAPIST ISSUES

An understanding of family development and the particular issues associated with adoption as well as personal awareness of one's own attitudes, values, and beliefs are essential in order for therapists to facilitate the growth and development of adoptive families. The therapist's internalized attitudes and expectations of families and adoption, what Beck (1976) terms "cognitive schemas," will determine the nature and outcome of treatment.

Several birth mothers reported that they later realized that the mental health professionals involved with their decision making were more concerned with obtaining an adoptable infant than with helping the birth mothers make an autonomous choice. Many members of the adoption triangle reported feeling pressured by mental health and health professionals, receiving unwanted and unwarranted advice or false information, or encountering the omission of important information. Adult adoptees reported defensive stonewalling from adoption workers.

Clinicians are often unaware of their own biases until faced with a particular set of circumstances. When they feel themselves becoming tense or impatient with clients, it's important for them to reflect on their own values, attitudes, and beliefs.

Recently, a couple I had been working with on marital adjustment informed me that they were about to adopt a newborn through a private attorney. I can remember trying to appear supportive while experiencing internal dismay. This couple had only been married 3 years; it was the first marriage for both. The husband was in his early 70s and the wife in her mid-50s. My internal reactions were ageist, and it took several hours of self-reflection before I was able to work through these resistant thoughts. In our next session, we talked about my concerns, and I was relieved and pleased to learn that this couple had acknowledged and discussed this with the brokering lawyer and the birth mother, who had selected them from several candidate couples. In postadoption sessions, when I saw them so attuned to their baby daughter, I cringed, recalling my earlier biased reactions.

Therapists who are participants in the adoption triangle need to be particularly self-aware in order to avoid projecting their own biases and experiences onto clients. One supervisee, an adoptive mother of 20 years, was stunned when we talked about a session she had taped with a birth mother who was in the process of deciding whether or not to keep her baby son. This very talented clinician was unaware how her bias toward relinquishment was playing out in the session until she heard herself suggesting to the birth mother, "Children really do better with two parents who can provide them with emotional and financial security." Her immediate reaction to her countertransferential discovery was to avoid all cases involving adoption; after several individual and group supervisory sessions, she came to realize that she could utilize her personal experiences to heighten her compassion and empathic skills with all of the adoption participants. Avoidance and evasion could create their own difficulties.

Therapists are not blank slates. We all have our own perceptions, experiences, values, and attitudes, and continuing awareness and open discussion are our best protection against unconscious projection onto clients. Issues we think we have worked through or put to rest can reemerge at any time, so awareness and acknowledgment are essential.

*   *   *

Working with the adoption triangle requires sensitivity to the special issues discussed in these chapters. Within the context of an empathic relationship, particular attention to psychoeducation and coordination of resources along with individual, group, couple, and family therapy are important. In addition, direct and indirect empowerment and advocacy interventions can help clients to work for public policy reform, enabling them to feel more hopeful about and influential in their life spheres.

Working with all three parties of the adoption triangle, rather than specializing with one member, can foster sensitivity and openmindedness in clinicians. We can learn to understand the possible effects of adoption on normal developmental transitions and differentiate psychological distress related to or impacted by the adoption experience from that which is unrelated to adoption.

FIVE

About Homosexuality:
The Participants in Context

Over the years, there have been many changes in American ideas about sexual behavior. During the 1960s, people began to experiment more openly with varied sexual behaviors within and without marital relationships. The meaning of sexuality began to shift, becoming more of a function of the way people defined it rather than things they actually did. Rather quickly, with the advent of birth control pills, recreational, casual sex became as prevalent as procreative sex. The societal norm that females would remain virgins until marriage gradually disappeared. As society adapted to a broader range of sexual behaviors, it became evident that a sexual act can have a variety of "meanings." The meaning (i.e., casual, procreative, relational, consensual, exploitative), rather than the act, formed different norms and mores.

Likewise, there have been changes in ideas about sexual orientation. Sexual orientation—whether it be heterosexual, bisexual, or homosexual—refers to identity as well as to sexual acts. Many individuals engage in homosexual actions, but do not identify themselves as homosexual or bisexual; there are also those who identify themselves as homosexual or bisexual, but do not engage in sexual acts. Although to some, the term "homosexual" represents sexual action as sin, illness, or deviance, to an increasing number, it represents life style choices shaped by awareness and acknowledgment of one's attraction to same-gender love objects.

Increasingly, sociologists and anthropologists are contributing to our understanding of sexual orientation as a social construction involving the meaning one makes of feelings, behavioral choices, and self-identity within a particular sociocultural context. Careful consideration of cultural history helps us to see how we have constructed the concepts of homosexuality, bisexuality, and heterosexuality, each as a group and category, with heterosexuality assumed as the "right," "healthy," "normal" orientation. From this vantage point, homosexuality and bisexuality are seen as deviant, which leads to stigmatization. The presumption of heterosexuality as the norm against which other sexual orientations are measured considers sexual orientation as a fact rather than as a social creation.

In late 20th-century American society, male–male and female–female erotic relationships evoke more intense negative and controversial reactions from mainstream society than just about any other form of relationship behavior. While many experience discomfort even around heterosexual erotic behaviors, this discomfort is mild in comparison to the fear and loathing (often expressed in brutal violence) around homosexual erotic behaviors. As clarified by P. Ellis and Murphy (1994), these reactions can be attributed to the dominant culture's heterosexist and homophobic beliefs about sexuality as well as the sexist and misogynistic views toward femininity, for example, that "heterosexual intercourse is the apogee of sexual expression; orgasm through intercourse is the primary sexual goal" (P. Ellis & Murphy, 1994, p. 58). Other heterosexist and homophobic beliefs define procreative sex as the most desired goal of sexual intercourse (as prescribed by biblical traditions), and sexual pleasure, particularly for females, as shameful. Gay males, seen as "feminine," and lesbians, seen as trying to be male, are an affront to a patriarchal society.

But history tells us that homosexuality has existed throughout the world from the beginning of recorded time. It cuts across socioeconomic, ethnic, and racial groups. As we will see later in this chapter, gays and lesbians in this country were largely invisible until the Stonewall Riot just 27 years ago. This revolutionary event, which will be detailed later, marked the time that this "hidden minority" began to "come out of the closet" and make its presence known.

As a concept, "homosexuality" refers to sexual behavior with a same-gender partner. As a term, it applies to both males and females and focuses more on sexuality than on the broader gay life style. In this text, however, the use of the term "homosexual" encompasses the life style and culture as well as sexual relationships of same-gender partners. While the term "gay" as an adjective encompasses a broader male and female life style and culture, typically the term "gay" is used as a noun for males and the term "lesbian" as a noun for females. Today, some are advocating for the term "queer" to encompass the total homosexual population. For the purposes of this text, the term "gay" will be used for males and the term "lesbian" for females. The terms "homosexual" and "gay" will be used as adjectives to depict both gays and lesbians. "Sexual orientation" will be the term used to avoid the connotation of voluntary choice associated with the term "gender preference."

The participants to be described in this chapter are gays and lesbians, their families of origin, and their current homosexual families, including children from heterosexual marriages. Although there is great diversity among and within each of these groups of participants, they share one major trauma: growing up and/or living with real external and inevitably internalized homophobia resulting from the heterosexism of our society.

"Homophobia" refers to conscious and unconscious irrational values, attitudes, and behaviors of fear, hatred, and intolerance of homosexuals and homosexual desires. It is homophobia that underlies the visceral revulsion often felt toward gays and lesbians by heterosexual friends, family, and society as well as by themselves. Reactions may range from physically violent nonacceptance to outright prejudice and bigotry to subtle fear and discomfort. Regardless of the degree, homophobia underlies the values, morality, and culture of modern American society. Whether we turn out to be homosexual, bisexual, or heterosexual, we are all socialized from infancy to believe that same-gender sexual orientation is wrong, immoral, and abnormal. Thus, people who experience same-gender desires grow up with self-loathing, which increases as they unsuccessfully attempt to reject the homoerotic parts of their core self that are causing such distress. This "internalized homophobia" becomes self-directed and can affect psychological development (Smith, 1988). It is essential that therapists understand the cultural and internalized homophobia deeply ingrained in all of us in order to begin to understand the psychology of the people with whom we work.

"Heterosexism" refers to the currently dominant religious, cultural, and societal assumption that heterosexuality is the only natural, normal, acceptable sexual orientation. Parents, for example, assume that their children are heterosexual. They are shocked when they discover this not to be the case. Our language, psychological and educational theories, and social institutions are all heterosexist in that they assume heterosexual development as the healthy norm and homosexual development as deviant. This presumption rules out consideration of other possibilities. How many therapists and physicians routinely ask clients about their sexual orientation during an intake session?

The effects of oppression and marginalization on the identity and self-concept of those who do not conform to heterosexist norms are enormous. Often this impact is manifested in behaviors reflecting shame, self-hatred, and alienation.

The purpose of this chapter is to explore the political, societal, and scientific changes that have accompanied the emergence of gay and lesbian culture in the past 27 years. It also explores new developments regarding the origins, the life style, and the relationship issues that confront gays and lesbians in today's world. Through the voices of interviewees, Chapter 6 will present gay and lesbian identity development in the contexts of their families of origin, the coming-out process, and relationship and life span issues. Chapter 7 will discuss the clinical implications for heterosexual therapists working with gay and lesbian clients and their families of origin as well as their current family systems.

WHO ARE GAYS AND LESBIANS?

Gays and lesbians are a diverse group of men and women who acknowledge their same-gender sexual orientation at different times in their life cycle, in different ways, and to different degrees. Anybody could be gay or lesbian—a relative, the person next door, a classmate, a colleague, your doctor or nurse, an office worker, a store clerk, librarian, lawyer, teacher, shoemaker, garbage collector, the mailman. They may be flamboyant and obvious, or invisible. Unlike most people of color, they may choose whether or not to be visible. Some consider themselves bisexual at different points in their lives, some live in heterosexual relationships and attempt to deny or suppress their homoerotic yearnings. Especially for females, the feelings of same-gender attraction are usually affectional and relational as well as physical. These feelings may be hidden and internalized, or overtly acted on. The effeminate mannerisms and gestures associated with gays and the "tomboy" qualities associated with lesbians are behaviors, not traits, and are thought to be multidetermined (Green, 1987). Although there is much debate in the literature about the nature and meaning of personality traits, we shall see in Chapter 6 that stereotypes are usually inaccurate as generalizations.

Some of the most prevalent misconceptions about homosexuals are as follows:

Myth: Gays are sick, immoral, sinful, wicked, and so forth, and can change their orientation with treatment.

Fact: Gays are not sick, immoral, sinful, and wicked, and their sexual orientation cannot be changed permanently through psychotherapy.

Myth: Homosexuality is a result of family dysfunction, with a dominant, controlling, overprotective mother and a passive, weak, distant father for gays and an abusive father for lesbians.

Fact: While family dysfunction may contribute to the development of a homosexual orientation, it is likely that genetic, hormonal, family, and social factors also contribute interactionally.

Myth: People choose to be homosexual as a form of perverse rebellion against their families and society.

Fact: For most, sexual orientation is not a choice; the choice is having the courage to own, acknowledge, and live with one's core self.

Myth: Gays were sissies as boys and are effeminate as adults, and lesbians were tomboys as girls and are masculine as adults.

Fact: There is much diversity among gays and lesbians.

Myth: Gay and lesbian relationships never last very long, and gays are more promiscuous than heterosexual men.

Fact: Gay and lesbian relationships may be temporary or long-term and permanent. The latter may be as monogamous as some heterosexual relationships.

Myth: Homosexual parents are more likely to molest their same-gender children than heterosexual parents.

Fact: There is no evidence that homosexual child abuse occurs as frequently as heterosexual child abuse.

Myth: Homosexuals are pedophiles.

Fact: The greater number of pedophiles are heterosexual.

Myth: Children of gay and lesbian parents are more likely to become gay adults than are children of heterosexual parents.

Fact: There is no evidence that homosexual parents are more likely to have homosexual children than are heterosexual parents.

Myth: Children living in a gay/lesbian household are more at risk of being infected by the AIDS virus.

Fact: There is no evidence that children living in a gay/lesbian household are more at risk of being infected by AIDS.

Myth: Parents who disclose their homosexuality to their children do inestimable damage to their children's mental health.

Fact: Children of parents who disclose their homosexuality while divorcing are usually more affected by the divorce than by the disclosure of homosexuality, which, with time, becomes accepted and understood. The "how" of disclosure is more significant than the "what."

Myth: Only homosexual mental health professionals can be of help to homosexual clients.

Fact: The conditions of openness, acceptance, empathy, knowledge, understanding, genuineness, positive regard, respect, and warmth are more important than the clinician's sexual orientation.

Myth: The only reason the American Psychiatric Association removed homosexuality as a mental health disorder is because of the increased political power of homosexual psychiatrists.

Fact: Heterosexual scientists were as involved as homosexual scientists in influencing the American Psychiatric Association to remove homosexuality as a mental health disorder.

Myth: Gays and lesbians claim to be 10% of the population, but are really only 1–2%, and, therefore, they do not merit any special consideration.

Fact: It is impossible to estimate accurately the percentage of the population that is homosexual, but it is likely that the actual proportion is higher than previously estimated or acknowledged.

In 1948, the Kinsey Report (Kinsey, Pomeroy, & Martin, 1948) stunned mainstream Americans with the information that a significant number of men and women had engaged in homosexual behavior. Due to the tradition of silence and invisibility, most Americans assumed that homosexuality was a rare anomaly. The Kinsey Report, plus subsequent research (Fassinger, 1991; Kinsey, Pomeroy, Martin, & Gebhard, 1955), indicates that from 10–15% of the total population is predominantly homosexual. Marmor (1980) suggests that 5–10% of adult males and 3–5% of adult females are homosexual.

A controversial 1993 study conducted in New York City ("Sex Survey Reports Low Homosexuality Incidence," 1994) and sponsored by the Battelle Human Affairs Research Center, a conservative organization, disputes these figures, estimating that at most only 1–2% of the population is homosexual. This latter study has been criticized for sampling and methodological flaws, using face-to-face interviews across a random selection of neighborhoods. There is no reason to suppose that people belonging to such a vilified minority (who, in some states, are vulnerable to criminal prosecution for disobeying the antisodomy laws) would disclose their sexual orientation to a stranger. Thus, it would be difficult, if not impossible, to assess accurately the numbers of homosexuals, because so many deny their sexual orientation even to themselves.

In addition to the statistics about the prevalence of homosexuality, Kinsey et al.'s (1948) research resulted in a seven-group rating scale ranging from exclusive heterosexuality to exclusive homosexuality at either end with varying types of bisexuality in between. While this diversity may help us to understand why a homosexual orientation is clearly not a choice for some and may involve some choice for others, it implies static identity. A more recent model by Klein (1990) also utilizes seven dimensions to measure sexual orientation. However, Klein's dimensions are more fluid, ranging from sexual attraction to self-identification to life style. This multidimensional approach considers the impact of homophobia on self-labeling and allows for people changing their sexual orientation, self-labeling, and life style choices over the life span. In addition to the multidimensionality of sexuality, we need also to consider concepts of fluid versus static sexual identity, such as movement from heterosexual to homosexual and back to heterosexual. The middle ranges of bisexuality are less well understood than the areas of heterosexuality and homosexuality.

Along this line, it is helpful to consider the work of Troiden (1988), who differentiates four types of homosexuals: (1) those who are ambiguous and consciously attempt to engage in a bisexual life style; (2) those who engage in situational homosexual behaviors, such as when in prison or the armed services; (3) those who are clandestine and try to appear to lead a heterosexual life style while either denying their homoerotic desires and behaviors or acting on them secretly; and (4) those who are openly committed to their identity as acknowledged gays or lesbians and who live a life style that is congruent with their identity. The first, third, and fourth types are also seen as stages of identity development in some theories, not types. However, given this inclusive definition of who is homosexual, it is easy to see why self-report and self-disclosure would not accurately reflect the numbers of people in all four of these categories.

Diverse gay and lesbian communities have become more visible in the past two decades, particularly in large metropolitan areas, where many choose to live together in particular neighborhoods, to frequent particular bars or coffee houses. A sense of oppression underlies a sense of shared community and mutual support, which, in turn, underlies the effectiveness of the gay liberation movement. Prior to the AIDS epidemic, gays and lesbians generally had separate social spheres. In San Francisco, for example, the gay baths were the locus of gay sexual and social activity. Lesbians met in more private settings. Many gays traditionally focused on sexual interactions, whereas many lesbians were more concerned with emotional relationships. This difference is in accord with traditional male and female socialization whereby females develop along expressive, relational paths and males along instrumental, individuated paths. Today, lesbians and gays frequent their own clubs as well as mixed heterosexual and homosexual clubs and theaters. Within the gay and lesbian communities, there may be groups based on institutional or professional affiliation, class, ethnicity, ideology, social networks, or special interests. Just as the women's movement has fostered shifts in sex roles for both women and men, the gay liberation movement, together with the women's movement, has influenced many gays to become more similar to lesbians by focusing more on the development and expression of nonsexual aspects of their relationships. Gays are formulating relationship models that transcend the stereotypical anonymous sexual encounters thought by the general public to represent homosexual relationships. Gays, lesbians, and bisexuals share the same needs, desires, and objectives as heterosexuals in all areas of human development.

The reciprocally influencing sociocultural and scientific variables all contribute to our knowledge and understanding of sexual orientation and affect our personal and professional understanding and practices.

SCIENTIFIC CONTEXT

As mental health professionals, we must acknowledge and take responsibility for the ways the mental health professions have contributed to the stigmatization and marginalization of the gays, lesbians, and bisexuals who comprise over 10% of our population. Until the early 1970s, the psychiatric profession, which dominated mental health theory and policy, believed that homosexuality was a pathological choice that was malleable and susceptible to reversal. Focus was on the etiology of the "disease" of homosexuality. The origins of homosexuality were thought to be seriously disturbed psychosexual development due to faulty parenting. Gays were presumed to have overbearing, dominant mothers and weak, unavailable fathers resulting in the son's adoption of a feminine role identity. Lesbians were presumed to repudiate their weak, ineffectual mothers to identify with their more powerful fathers. Actually, this is not particularly surprising given that psychiatrists based their theories on the psychoanalyses of patients, where much of any adult's problems was attributed to early impaired parenting.

As reported by Burr (1993), homosexuality was and may still be viewed by traditional psychoanalysts as an aspect of a psychopathic, paranoid, or schizoid personality disorder. The forms of treatment used included electroshock therapy and other aversive procedures, surgical lobotomy, long years of psychoanalysis, and hormone therapy. The goal of treatment was always reversal of sexual orientation. Psychoanalyst Richard Isay (1989), however, learned from his extensive psychoanalytic practice with gay men that reversal of sexual orientation was ego dystonic, if even possible, and that early, difficult relations between mothers and sons appear to be more characteristic of men who are dissatisfied with their sexuality than of gay men in general. A larger proportion of psychoanalytic clients are dissatisfied than satisfied.

Kinsey's research (Kinsey et al., 1948, 1955) began the shift in the mental health professions' views toward homosexuality. This shift was furthered by cross-cultural studies by Ford and Beach (1951), which indicated a variety of forms of homosexuality in different cultures, and by the first in-depth comparison of gay and nongay subjects by Hooker (1957).

In 1956, at an American Psychological Association conference, Evelyn Hooker presented her data on a landmark study sponsored by the National Institute of Mental Health. She had administered Rorschach and other psychological tests to 30 gay men and 30 straight men who had never sought psychiatric help. This was the first time that homosexuals outside a hospital or prison had ever been studied! Three eminent psychologists rated the test results and could not differentiate between homosexuals and heterosexuals. Both populations shared an equal distribution of mental health and pathology (Hooker, 1957).

In the 1960s, heterosexual and homosexual psychiatrists (under the leadership of the American Psychiatric Association president Judd Marmor [1971, 1972, 1980]) began to question conventional psychiatric formulations. They acknowledged that homosexuality really was immutable. Those who appeared to change their sexual orientation had really only changed their behaviors, but they were still utilizing homoerotic fantasies to achieve sexual orgasm with heterosexual partners and they were still struggling with their homoerotic desires. By 1973, the American Psychiatric Association removed homosexuality from its pathology classification.

However, there are still many homophobic mental health professionals who continue to view same-gender sexual orientation as psychopathology (see Socarides & Vamik, 1991, who claim that all obligatory homosexuals suffer from preoedipal disturbances and narcissistic necessities). My clinical experience and professional surveys in the literature (Brown, 1986; Moran, 1992) indicate that a large number of trained professionals continue to view homosexuality as a disorder. Popper (1991) refers to the subtle, unconscious group-think and compulsive belief in heterosexism that remains common in most of our mental health training programs and clinics, noting that the prevailing belief in the moral superiority of heterosexuality is still rampant in our professions.

> Tom, a 42-year-old psychiatrist, reports that when he was an undergraduate at an Ivy League college during the 1970s, he went to the college mental health service because of his doubts about his sexual orientation. The male psychiatrist assumed that Tom should become a heterosexual and prescribed hormone therapy and behavioral aversive therapy, during which Tom received electroshock jolts every time he thought of or was aroused by a homoerotic image. This treatment was so traumatic that, 4 years after graduation, Tom, now comfortable with his sexual orientation, returned to college to take

premedical courses in order to enter the psychiatry profession himself so as to bring about necessary change. Tom notes that it was not safe to reveal his sexual orientation until he completed his residency. Tom's report is retrospective, but the impact of this psychotherapy experience is evident in his professional choices and practice.

Today, there are significant, impressive studies (Bailey & Pillard, 1991; Bailey, Pillard, & Neale, 1993; Isay, 1989; Pillard & Bailey, 1995; Rist, 1992) indicating genetic and intrauterine factors regarding the etiology of homosexuality. LeVay (1991, 1993) found the condition of dimorphism in his autopsies of 19 gay men, 16 presumed heterosexual men, and 6 presumed heterosexual women: the nucleus of the hypothalamus differed in size between homo- and heterosexuals. Pillard (1993) reported on his study with Bailey of male homosexuality comparing 56 pairs of identical twins with 54 pairs of fraternal twins and 57 genetically unrelated adopted brothers. They found a gay:gay concordance rate of 11% among adopted brothers, 22% among fraternal twins, and 52% among identical twins. The results of this study are similar to their (Bailey, Pillard, & Neale, 1993) released study of lesbian twins in which 108 pairs of twins and 45 adopted sisters were compared. The results found 48% gay:gay concordance among identical twins, 16% among fraternal twins, and 6% among unrelated adoptive sisters.

The anatomical differences theory, however, is not conclusive. Nor are studies of hormonal imbalance or faulty chromosomes. Further scientific study is definitely indicated. From sociological and anthropological studies (Richardson, 1987; Troiden, 1979; Weinberg, 1978), there is evidence that sexual orientation must be considered as a sociocultural construction whereby the meanings individuals attribute to their sexual feelings lead to their sexual behaviors. In other words, sexual identity would be embedded in an individual's understanding and personal meaning of their feelings and behaviors, and this understanding and meaning-making is embedded in a larger sociocultural context.

There seem to be different paths of development that can lead to the outcome of gay, lesbian, bisexual, or heterosexual sexual orientation. It is unlikely that there is just one developmental path for homosexuality, bisexuality, or heterosexuality. For some, sexual identity may not be predetermined and may involve choice. For others, there may not be choice. Still others may change their sexual orientation over their life span. Environmental factors may include prenatal, sociocultural, parental behavior, family constellation, and so forth.

Developmental psychologists tell us that the range of environmental and biological inputs a developing child receives is both enormous and enormously complex. More representative of contemporary scientific thinking is Burr's (1993) assertion that "Pillard and Bailey's multifactorial model suggests a shaded continuum of sexual orientations and of origins and causes more complex and subtle than a simple either–or model can accommodate and is closer to what may be the quirks and ambiguities of our real lives" (p. 65). It is interesting to compare this assertion with Marmor's (1965) prophetic statement that homosexuality is "multiply determined by psychodynamic, sociocultural, biological, and situational factors" (p. 5).

The concept and extent of bisexuality has been largely ignored and needs to be explored in order for us to further our understanding about the development of homosexuality and heterosexuality. Stein (1993) notes that "we have only begun to appreciate the richness and diversity of this form of development" (p. 19). It is possible that bisexuality is the natural middle ground between the polarizations of homosexuality and heterosexuality, and that there can be a natural fluidity of sexual orientation over the life span, if one chooses sexual behaviors that are consistent with sexual feelings (Leland, 1995). This requires consideration of the distinction between emotional orientation and behavior. As with concepts of heterosexuality and homosexuality, we run into definitional difficulties regarding bisexuality: Does it require more than one experience? fantasy and/or action? duration?

There seem to be many forms of bisexuality: a preference for one gender over the other or no preference at all; either simultaneous or sequential relationships with both sexes; transitory, transitional, or enduring same-gender relationships. It has also been suggested that bisexuality may represent a form of denial of homosexuality. M. Nichols (1994) suggests that bisexuality may actually be more prevalent than exclusive homosexuality. People who identify as bisexual do not have the organized support the more dominant homosexual and heterosexual populations do. In fact, they may be stigmatized by both groups. Therefore, they may not self-identify as bisexuals. The current thinking about the etiology of bisexuality, as reported by Zinik (1985), is that it derives either from conflict and confusion about one's sexual preference or as a natural part of the fluidity and flexibility of one's sexual orientation.

Importantly, it is becoming clearer out of the web of complexities revealed by exciting current research that biological factors do play at least some role in determining human sexual orientation. These findings are both positive and negative: positive in that, if sexual orientation is found to not be a choice, perhaps homophobia and oppression will decrease; negative in that, if a gene for homosexuality can be located, abuse may develop in the form of abortion or some other "genetic cleansing." Whether or not sexual orientation is biological, our social construction of heterosexuality being "normal" and homosexuality being "deviant" polarizes and stigmatizes, rather than acknowledging normal variations in sexual orientation.

There are methodological issues in the research about the etiology and development of homosexuality and bisexuality. For one, until all self-identified gays, lesbians, and bisexuals are visible, a truly representative study is impossible. Most of the developmental speculations are based on the study of White, middle-class, urban clinical populations and entail retrospective reports from adult patients about their childhood and adolescent thoughts and feelings. Further, this is a politically charged area of study and is particularly vulnerable to distortion and overgeneralization. Little is known about the gay and lesbian adolescents and we know less about lesbian development than about gay development because most of the research has been conducted with gays. There is great diversity among cultural groups and significant variation within each group.

Despite these recent scientific findings and multidimensional possibilities, many mental health professionals continue to adhere to traditional "faulty parenting" theories. Within the past 3 months, two families, who have each consulted me regarding their offspring's acknowledgment of his and her homosexuality, have reported how other therapists have cited theories of family dysfunction and faulty parenting (primarily distant father–son and overprotective mother–son relationships) as the cause of their offspring's sexual orientation. In addition, several gay and lesbian clients have reported aversive reactions from previously consulted therapists. The therapists in each of these situations have been prominent clinicians within their respective disciplines. As will be seen when we look at the social historical context of homophobia, therapists cannot be immune to homophobia, and current training programs do not give more than lip service, if that, to developing sensitivity to the issues of minorities.

SOCIAL HISTORICAL CONTEXT

For thousands of years, homosexuals have been the target of irrational prejudice, even considering variations attributable to era, culture, and place. Their treatment has included ostracism, verbal condemnation, physical attacks, and even death. In describing the struggle for gay and lesbian equal rights between 1945 and 1990, Marcus (1992) attributes the Western world's pervasive intolerance and oppression of gays and lesbians to religious views that use biblical passages to justify condemnation and persecution. These religious views have shaped our conventional legal codes which have, until recently, prohibited (even though these codes were often ignored) same-gender sexual practices (Atkinson & Hackett, 1988). The legal codes in most states still bar same-gender marriages and discriminate against gays and lesbians in terms of custody, adoption, protection of other family rights, and employment opportunities and security.

Prior to World War II, gays and lesbians went to great lengths to protect themselves from their feelings of difference. Many engaged in heterosexual marriages, sincerely hoping to rid themselves of same-gender erotic feelings and fantasies. The "false self" (Winnicott, 1958) may have been self-convincing as well as other-convincing. Others allowed their authentic natures to be expressed only in secrecy, which may account for the anonymous nature of many such sexual encounters. These people likely experienced tremendous anxiety about the fear of exposure. As did the mental health professionals of the time, most homosexuals viewed themselves as "sick" and "deficient." Work such as Havelock Ellis's *Studies in the Psychology of Sex* (1930), while giving some sense that gay people have personalities and real lives, also contributed greatly to the pathologizing of homosexuality. Exposure could be presumed to result in the loss of friends, family, job, and home, if not in confinement to prison or a mental hospital.

World War II uprooted and dislocated a large segment of our population, exposing them to people, opportunities, and places they may never have known otherwise. For many gays, it was their first contact with diverse people, and gays gradually began to acknowledge their sexual orientation to each other. Thus, after the war, homosexuals began to band together to share information about the nature of homosexuality and how to survive in a hostile world, and to organize secret groups (such as the Mattachine Society, the Daughters of Bilitis, ONE, etc.). It was not until 1969, however, that the Stonewall Riot began the gay rights movement as we know it today. This was a spontaneous protest triggered by a police raid of a gay bar known as The Stonewall in Greenwich Village, New York. Along with the civil rights and women's movements, the gay rights movement has aimed to change legislation and social attitudes. These changes are occurring, but they are slow and not as widespread or significant as some would like to believe.

In the past 10 years, attention to homosexuality and bisexuality has exploded in both the popular media and professional literature. Practically every major periodical has had at least one cover story pertaining to homosexuality; TV and radio talk shows, movies, and plays have featured gay and lesbian concerns, and there has been much publicity about Oregon's and Colorado's passage of gay rights legislation.

This media attention, as well as the public acknowledgment of homosexuality by an increasing number of high profile and typical Americans, is educative, raising the general public's consciousness level. But it has also resulted in a vicious political backlash from more conservative and traditional religious, political, and educational organizations. There are energetic attempts to overturn recently passed liberal legislation in order to thwart the gay rights movement and protect heterosexist norms. This has resulted in more "gay bashing," the physical and verbal assault on gay and lesbian citizens. (This is not unlike the backlash to feminism so aptly described by Faludi, 1991.) This backlash, in turn, causes emotional swings among gays and lesbians: Many become more afraid to reveal themselves in an increasingly hostile environment, while others are motivated to unify and form solidarity in order to fight unfair oppression.

The AIDS epidemic is a major influence on both the increasing visibility and the repudiation of our gay and lesbian population. Many prominent gays have been felled by this disease. Many who might have remained secretive about their sexual orientation have been propelled into the open by this health crisis. Gay and lesbian communities have coalesced among themselves and with heterosexual friends and families of AIDS victims to fight vigorously and with as much publicity as possible for funds and research in order to find a cure for this deadly plague. In fact, gay and lesbian communities have joined forces as never before around AIDS and discrimination. Heretofore, despite variations within each, gay and lesbian communities had focused more on their differences and retained suspicious but respectful separation. The diversity among and within gay and lesbian communities can be attributed to the same variations among and within heterosexual communities: geography, gender, ethnicity, race, class, interests, political views, values, and so forth.

Although the AIDS epidemic has strengthened the political organization of gay and lesbian communities, it has also aided and abetted the rhetoric of conservative political ideology groups and fundamentalist religions, who view the disease as God's punishment for sinful behaviors. This exacerbates the unconscious and conscious homophobia of the general public and leads to further societal intolerance of gays and lesbians. Recent rising unemployment, inaccessibility to health care, and decreasing opportunities for education and upward mobility foster the unconscious displacement of these frustrations and disappointments onto minority target groups. Throughout history, when economic recessions and depressions have occurred, there have been increases in violence against minorities. Because funds for AIDS research and treatment come from shrinking health sources, and because the

general public insists on viewing AIDS as a "gay disease," homophobia is fueled.

Although recent polls do indicate positive shifts in national attitudes toward gays and lesbians (Fassinger, 1991), it is evident from
hate crime statistics and surveys that there is still widespread misunderstanding, disapproval, and stigmatization of homosexuals in our
society. In addition to the political and organizational activism of the
gay and lesbian communities, the courage of increasing numbers to
acknowledge their homosexuality to friends and families is, perhaps,
the most effective way to educate heterosexuals about the realities of
homosexuality. Over time, this can result in increased tolerance and
acceptance. *Outing* (Signorelli, 1994) is the controversial attempt by
some homosexual groups to expose homosexuals who are in positions
of power and who are hypocritically aiding and abetting the oppression of homosexuals. One rationalization for outing is to let Americans know that some of their most respected leaders are indeed
homosexual. Another objective is to hasten the elimination of oppression and marginalization by forcing changes in legislation and social
policy.

Heterophobia is the rejection or denigration of all heterosexuals.
This may still be an issue for some homosexuals, but can result in isolation and alienation. An increasing majority of gays and lesbians, who
work and live in mainstream America, are insisting on the opportunity to feel comfortable functioning openly as gay, lesbian, and/or bisexual in both the homosexual and heterosexual cultures. Aware that
social change can only arise from within mainstream society, not from
separatism, the aims are understanding, equal rights, and inclusion.

THE PARTICIPANTS

Ms. Craig, 54, was shocked and dismayed when her college freshman son, Tom, told her he that he was gay. He seemed to blurt out
this announcement in response to her queries about a girlfriend. Ms.
Craig begged Tom to see a psychiatrist when he returned to college,
sure that this was just a phase and that Tom just had not met the
right girl yet. She later reported to her support group, Parents and
Friends of Lesbians and Gays (PFLAG), that she was aware of the
split inside her head: She wanted to reach out with love and protection to Tom, but, at the same time, was viscerally unable to take in
this dramatic alteration to her view of him and to her hopes and automatic expectations for the kind of adult life style he would have. She
couldn't help asking herself how Tom could not want to have children, what had she done to cause this, how others in her family and

social circle would react. Her first reactions were of protection—of Tom and of the rest of her family—as she begged him not to tell anyone until he had seen a psychiatrist to see if he could change. It took several months before she completed the "mourning" for her assumptions and expectations and was able to feel strong pride in Tom's courage to live his life in an authentic manner.

Mr. Craig, 55, a successful insurance executive, has still not been able to embrace his son Tom's life style. He was always concerned about Tom's indifference to athletics (Mr. Craig had been a college football player), and he did not understand Tom's desire to major in English rather than engineering, business, or science. But, while somewhat emotionally distant, he had always been friendly and attentive. Involved in his career, his wife had been the primary parent in all ways. Despite his study of available literature on homosexuality, Mr. Craig cannot help feeling deeply disappointed and somehow personally wounded. He tells Tom he loves him, but he avoids all references to Tom's life style in discussion with his two daughters, his wife, and Tom. In fact, Mr. Craig has not told anyone about Tom's life, whereas his wife and daughters have been open with their friends and relatives.

Sandra, age 14, was stunned when her mother, Doris, told her that she was divorcing Sandra's father and going to live with her best friend, Norma. Sandra had felt for years that her mother was spending too much time with Norma and neglecting her family. Sandra's mother and Norma taught together in the same elementary school, and Norma was included in most family gatherings and events. Sandra had noticed that her parents rarely spoke to each other and certainly did not share any activities or interests. She felt sorry for her father being left alone all the time. But it had never occurred to her that there might be a divorce. Now she felt rage and shame. How could her mother do this to them all? What would her friends say? Was she going to become a lesbian too? It was the most unspeakable event, and she wanted nothing more than to be away from it all. It was more than 6 months after her mother moved out before Sandra would even talk to her on the telephone, much less have any personal contact with her. And that was only after her older sister returned home from college for the summer and evidenced no difficulty with the new family constellation. It later became known that her sister's college roommate was a lesbian and her sister had learned to feel comfortable with people of different sexual orientations.

Doris, 42, Sandra's mother, had married Robert, Sandra's father, on the rebound from another heterosexual relationship. The marriage was emotionally distant from the beginning. Doris proceeded to have three children and then returned to teaching when Robert was laid off from his sales job. Robert's job instability caused him to withdraw, drink in solitude, and be reluctant to engage with her or anyone else. She found herself craving the intimacy and fun she was developing with her coteacher and friend Norma. After several years, this friendship evolved into a lesbian relationship. This was 3 years prior to Doris's decision to leave her family and live with Norma. During this time, Doris agonized over her feelings and plight, and read everything she could to learn about lesbianism. It was only after her mother died, and with the support of Norma and other heterosexual and lesbian friends, that Doris felt she had the courage to follow the convictions of her heart. She knew what a difficult adjustment this would be for her children, but she believed that her own authenticity was more essential to their well-being in the long run. And "this just felt so right" to her. Doris was amazed at the support she received from her oldest daughter and was very troubled by the impact on Sandra. She kept her door open and hoped that with time Sandra would become more accepting. Doris notes that Robert never undermined her with the children. She thinks he was relieved not to live with the pressure of her unhappiness any longer. He began to go to AA and joined a support group for husbands whose wives had left.

Joanne, a 34-year-old social worker, and Marilyn, a 46-year-old computer systems analyst, had been together as a couple for 6 years. They had been talking for 3 of these 6 years about the possibility of having a baby together, and they had thoroughly researched their options. Joanne was eager to have a biological child. Because of state laws about parenting and custody, Marilyn was anxious about whose baby it really would be: She preferred adoption, which she felt would provide a more equal power base in their relationship. Because they could not agree about this, they ended their relationship, and Joanne became involved with another woman who supported her desire to become pregnant. She became pregnant through artificial insemination, delivered a healthy baby boy, and engaged in a coparenting relationship with her new partner. As of this writing, the state in which this couple lives has just established a legal precedence for homosexual parents to share custody of a biological or adopted child. Joanne and her partner are very excited about this unexpected opportunity.

Justin, a 39-year-old artist, and George, a 29-year-old day care worker, had been together for 3 years when they began to talk about the possibility of becoming parents. Justin was ambivalent at first, but the more he thought about it, the more open he became to the idea. George knew several gay couples who had decided to parent, and he wanted, like his five brothers, to have his own children. Over the past 2 years, this couple had visited many gay and lesbian families, and they had discussed issues and ramifications with whoever would engage in dialogue with them. In fact, they suggest that they probably wore out their welcome with many friends, badgering them to help in their decision making. Eventually, they decided that they would like to have a child. Because Justin was the more financially stable partner, they decided that he would attempt adoption individually through his state social service system. It was likely that the only way he could adopt as a single parent would be to adopt a special needs child. After he passed the screening as a single adoptive parent (keeping his sexual orientation and life style secret), he was approached by a friend who was acting as an intermediary for a woman with an unwanted pregnancy who did not want to keep the baby. A private adoption was arranged, and Justin and George adopted a 10-day-old baby girl. Four years later, this family was awaiting the arrival of a toddler from Central America to complete their family circle. They reported more negative societal reaction to males being primary parents and staying home (they took turns, each freelancing) than to their sexual orientation. They feel fortunate in having a healthy child, their own health, and the support of extended family and friends, in addition to their community of other gay and lesbian parents.

Eric, a 48-year-old Black physician, was walking across town with his lover, Carl, a 24-year-old Italian nurse, when they were physically attacked by a group of Black youths. The verbal taunts as well as the punches and kicks caused Eric to be more ashamed of his race than of his sexual orientation. It was only when Carl felled one of the attackers with a karate chop that the couple managed to get away and escape further harm. Later in the emergency room where Eric was having a dislocated shoulder set, he commented to Carl that being Black, educated professionally, and gay was a triple indemnity and that was why he never took Carl with him to visit his family. Eric was aware of the pain he experienced from having to lead a secret life with regard to his family and the Black community. But he truly believes that his parents and siblings would reject him if he were to be open and honest with them. He comments wryly that the homophobic snickers and jokes in the Black community far outweigh what he's heard in the White community.

Each of these players represents a facet of the current realities faced by gays and lesbians. The common themes are isolation, fear, pain, and secrecy as well as intimacy, love, friendship, acceptance, and happiness. For lesbians and gays, and often for their heterosexual relatives, their lives and relationships exist within the context of both cultural and internalized homophobia. They are denied the basic rights and supports that could help them to confront their confusion, pain, and persecution. Given this pervasive context of marginalization, it is not surprising that large numbers of gays and lesbians are entering mental health professions and that a large proportion of gays and lesbians (particularly Caucasian lesbians) utilize psychotherapy services.

As of 1989, it was estimated that there were well over 1.5 million lesbian mothers and between 1 and 3 million gay fathers in the United States (Schwartz-Gottman, 1989; Turner, Scadden, & Harris, 1990). Patterson (1992) estimates that the number of children being raised by gay and lesbian parents ranges from 6 to 14 million. She believes that 1 to 5 million households are headed by lesbian mothers and 1 to 3 million by gay fathers. The number of gay- and lesbian-headed families is increasing rapidly. Within this population, there are many variations: men and women living in heterosexual families while also having some degree of a homosexual life outside, men and women who left heterosexual marriages to live a homosexual life style and either have custody of their children or are trying to maintain a relationship with them, gays and lesbians who come into a relationship with children from a former marriage, gay and lesbian couples who decide to have children together. Across these variations, individuals make different decisions about "coming out" or remaining "closeted" to some degree.

Today, in addition to childless gay and lesbian couples, we find a spectrum of family arrangements within gay and lesbian communities: (1) gay and lesbian stepfamilies including children from former heterosexual relationships or marriages and a current live-in partner; (2) single gay- or lesbian-headed households with children from a former heterosexual relationship or marriage; (3) single gay or lesbian parents of adopted or biological children; (4) lesbian couples who have adopted or had biological children; (5) gay couples who have adopted or had biological children through the insemination of surrogate mothers; and (6) gay and lesbian couples who live in separate domiciles but share to some agreed-upon degree the rearing of biological children. These families may also be interracial or have interracial children. Many refer to this as the "lesbian baby boom" and the "gay baby boom." Laird (1993b) points out that the issue is *choice*. Just as many heterosexual couples are choosing not to have children, gays and lesbians want the choice of parenting.

In the past, most gay and lesbian parents kept their sexual orientation secret because of the valid, well-grounded fear of losing their children. Increasingly, gays and lesbians are openly claiming the same parenting and family membership opportunities and rights that are available to heterosexuals. Gays and lesbians want to be open, to be accepted and valued as members of their families of origin; they want their couple relationships acknowledged and respected; and they want the rights to parent, work, and serve our society (such as in the military).

My interviews have included 12 lesbian couples, 14 gay couples, 10 individual gays, 12 individual lesbians, 18 sets of parents and 4 siblings of gays and lesbians. In these interviews as well as in my clinical and personal experiences, I have been struck by how many gays reported that their sexual orientation was not a choice, compared to the number of lesbians who reported that it was more choice than compulsion. Whether one feels sexual orientation is or is not a choice does not seem to be as relevant as acknowledging the possibility of different pathways and identity fluidity over the life span.

Gays and lesbians, raised in heterosexual families in a heterosexist world, have few role models or transgenerational histories as guides for the formation and development of gay and lesbian families. Fortunately, more information than ever before is emerging to provide guidance and fill the gaps of role models and history.

All our family therapy theories and practices are based on a two-parent heterosexual family model, ignoring until very recently the existence and viability of alternative family forms. Gays and lesbians are struggling to determine which aspects of heterosexist models they wish to retain, which they wish to discard, and which they wish to alter.

While gay and lesbian clients who are dealing with their relationships with both their parents and their children have many of the same issues as heterosexual clients, these issues must be actively considered in the contexts of isolation, prejudice, discrimination, and invisibility engendered by a hostile sociocultural environment.

Some of the discrimination and prejudice comes from segments of the larger gay culture itself. Choosing to have children has been viewed by many gay activists as a "sellout" to heterosexist values. As Dennis Altman states, "Straight is to gay, as family is to no family" (Weston, 1991). It is likely that some lesbian communities have been more open to childrearing than some gay communities, due both to women's socialization as nurturing caretakers and to biological yearnings. Until recently, many gay and lesbian couples report that they felt isolated and unsupported by gay communities because they wanted to parent.

John and Dennis, a gay couple in their mid-30s who lived 60 miles from a midwestern metropolitan area, found that the gay couples in their social network denigrated any notion that resembled a heterosexual family model. When they had the opportunity to adopt a 3-year-old boy from Central America, they chose to move back to John's parent's farm community. While they missed their gay cohorts, they found family support and involvement to be essential to their desire and what they termed their "need" to coparent. They visited friends in a gay community once or twice a month for a weekend so as not to be totally cut off from the gay culture and began to find support from lesbian parents with whom they could identify. They commented that their friends never asked about their son nor showed any interest. They hope that, with time, things will change.

Caught in this in-between world, gay and lesbian parents have often identified more with heterosexual families with children as well as with supportive extended family. Like John and Dennis, many who became parents as a gay couple have found support from and connectedness more with lesbians than with gays. As in the heterosexual culture, fatherhood has not been valued. However, in the past decade, there have been considerable changes in sexual practices and relationship arrangements in both the hetero- and homosexual worlds. It appears that the gay ethos rejecting fatherhood has been modified accordingly. Today, both gay and lesbian parents are finding more acceptance and tolerance within their own communities. Unfortunately, although Cavaliere (1995, p. 51) declares in the *APA Monitor* that "gay and lesbian couples who are or who would like to be parents can look forward to an increasingly welcome society that won't view a mother's or father's sexual orientation as a flash point of controversy," the recent resurgence of the conservative political right may be refueling a backlash against homosexual families.

COMPARISON OF HETEROSEXUAL
AND HOMOSEXUAL COUPLES

Although there are dangers in comparing gay and lesbian couples to heterosexual couples because of the implication that heterosexual norms are the reference point and same-gender relationships are deficient, ignoring or minimizing differences and commonalities can lead to ineffective treatment. Many straight therapists believe that the only difference between these types of couples is the gender of the sexual partner and that couple therapy is "business as usual." There really is no agreement about what constitutes a gay or lesbian relationship. Must they engage in genital sex, love each other, acknowledge that their relationship is homosexual? Must they share physical living space? How overt or long-lasting must their acknowledgment or commitment be? Clinicians must be sensitive to the couple's definition of their relationship and not attempt to impose any preconceived model on them.

Because until recently the only model available for couple relationships was heterosexist, and because individuals in both heterosexual and homosexual relationships share the same heterosexist background, they usually have some common expectations. For example, typical heterosexual, gay, and lesbian couples expect couple relationships to provide emotional gratification and security, companionship, intellectual stimulation, sexual partnership, and mutual financial benefits. They all have to negotiate relationships and boundaries with each other, their families of origin, the communities within which they live, their friends, and other social networks. Boundaries between work, family, friends, community involvement, and so forth require continuous adaptive renegotiation. There are issues that all couples struggle with: money, sex, intimacy, division of labor, problem solving, conflict resolution, dependence, independence, distance regulation, how to spend time, and so forth.

Recent literature (Berzon, 1988; Bozett, 1987; Bozett & Sussman, 1990; L. Brown & Zimmer, 1986; Kurdek, 1988; Laird, 1993b; Weston, 1991) about gay and lesbian relationships depicts the struggle of gay and lesbian couples to forge innovative relationship rules and roles that work for them. Conformance to the familiar heterosexual rules and roles with which everyone was raised may or may not be considered.

Some of the differences between heterosexual and homosexual relationships are fairly obvious. Gay and lesbian couples do not have the same supports, institutionalized social sanctions, and acceptability as do heterosexual couples. There is an absence of religious or legal bonds and rituals (such as formal engagement) for gay couples. Only within the past couple of years have some companies and local governments extended fringe benefits to gay and lesbian partners. Limited psychological, financial, and social resources can strain any couple relationship.

There are no guidelines for the division of labor and power and for role assignment in same-gender relationships (Blumstein & Schwartz, 1983). While the lack of models or typical patterns and rules for gay and lesbian relationship behavior can expand options, it can also pose problems. Partners may have different interpretations of what constitutes desirable behavior. For example, there is often not a situation of one partner being financially dependent in gay couples; therefore, there may be no functional reason or motivating force for one partner to act subserviently. The gender differences of heterosexual couples may engender role-stimulating complementarity. Because gays and lesbians share the same gender socialization as their partner, they may consciously or unconsciously find themselves attracted to partners of a different ethnicity or class background, which creates qualitative psychological effects of difference similar to those of gender. In more than half of the gay couples I interviewed, partners had class, racial, or ethnic background differences reflected in their current differences in occupational and social status, whereas the partners of the majority of lesbian couples I interviewed had similar current occupational and social status even if they came from different backgrounds. This complementarity in gay couples may alleviate gendered competitiveness. There may also be role complementarity in that individual partners may be at different points in terms of their self-identity as a gay or lesbian and with relation to their family of origin. Several couples I interviewed expressed conflict over the fact that one partner is "out" to his or her family and the other isn't. The out partner resents having to act as just a "friend" when visiting the family of the partner who is not out, and if one partner pressures the other to disclose, tensions in the relationship can ensue. These issues of identity will be elaborated in Chapter 6.

Prior to the changes wrought by the AIDS epidemic, gay couples have not traditionally seemed to form committed relationships as often as have nongay couples (Moses & Hawkins, 1982). This was attributed to the absence of religious or legal bonds (marriage) and rituals (such as formal engagement) for gay couples. Berzon (1988) points out that the lack of gender role guidelines and role models and of legal and social supports has contributed to the tradition of failure of gay relationships. She notes that success seems to be based on the same expectations and criteria as those of heterosexual couples. This can create a self-fulfilling prophecy of nonpermanent relationships for gays and lesbians. Other research demonstrates that, despite lack of societal sanctions, more than half of gay and lesbian relationships are indeed enduring (R. Barret & Robinson, 1990; Bigner & Jacobsen, 1989; Laird, 1993b; Stein, 1988, 1993).

Some researchers are attempting to assess the impact of the AIDS epidemic on the permanence of gay and lesbian relationships. There is speculation that this epidemic fosters longer-term relationships and curtails promiscuity, although younger gays in their teens and early 20s do not seem to be as concerned about safe sex as are their older compatriots who have been more directly and dramatically affected by the losses of the AIDS epidemic. However, as mentioned earlier, I think that the women's movement has had a significant effect on the sex roles and relationships of heterosexual and homosexual males and females. We are transcending rigidly stereotypical gender roles and moving in a direction of "both–and" rather than "either–or" in terms of expressiveness and instrumentality. However, whether or not the specter of AIDS affects the permanence of gay relationships, it certainly impacts the children, wives, and extended families of gays, who are living with vulnerability and anxiety about their gay family members' health and mortality. There is increased stigmatization and ostracization for family members when they are actually struggling with HIV and AIDS.

Another area of difference for gay and lesbian couples involves the differences in the use of social, leisure, and private time. In non-gay couples, there is cultural permission for spending time with others of the same gender in gender-specific, nonsexual activities, such as "boys' or girls' night out." Gay couples, being of the same gender, might find this kind of separation from their partner more threatening. Gay and lesbian couples often spend their social time exclusively with other gay and lesbian couples. Within the gay and lesbian community, they feel free to act and behave outwardly as couples without facing any potential harassment from nongays. There may appear to be little justification or reason to socialize with separate friends. Gay and lesbian friends are also potential sex partners, and when one partner chooses to socialize with same-sex friends without the other, this can create feelings of jealousy and insecurity in the relationship. Moses and Hawkins (1982) speculate that how a person reacts to the threat of a partner's expression of independence seems to be characteristic of one's gender role socialization as opposed to one's sexual orientation. Assertiveness, competitiveness, and enmeshment are shaped by sociocultural values affecting socialization processes.

COMPARISON OF GAY
AND LESBIAN RELATIONSHIPS

The differences between gay and lesbian development and relationships are just beginning to be studied. This is not surprising, given that only in the past 20 years has heterosexual female development been found to differ from heterosexual male development (Chodorow, 1978; Gilligan, 1982; J. B. Miller, 1976). Lesbians have to contend with misogyny (the hatred of women) and sexism (the valuing of one gender, usually male, over the other), in addition to homophobia and heterosexism (P. Ellis & Murphy, 1994).

One of the most frequently mentioned differences between gay and lesbian couples involves that of distance and closeness in relationship. Because we now know that the female path of development is based more on a relational trajectory than the male developmental path, it is not surprising that the emotional intensity of lesbian relationships differs from that of gay relationships. As Pearlman (1989) points out, relationship merger may be prolonged in lesbian relationships. She suggests that this may be due to the intensity of attunement and emotional connectedness in relationships between women, the difficulty many women have with physical and emotional separation when involved with someone romantically, and societal pressures. Women's sex-role socialization fosters dependency and subordination of self to partner.

But at the same time, this gender socialization enables women to have mutually supportive, nurturing, interdependent relationships whether they be friendships or love affairs. Women's relationships are less likely to be based on power struggles than relationships between women and men.

Thus, lesbian couples may be more prone to intense as well as prolonged merging because of women's gender-related capacity for intimacy and empathy, their lesser willingness to put limits on emotional closeness, and their seemingly lower fear of attachment (Mencher, 1990). This merger or fusion may be further intensified because of feelings of alienation from the larger society (Krestan & Bepko, 1980), particularly if the lesbian couple does not have access to a supportive community. As a lesbian relationship continues to develop, a phase involving conflicts over power and control will inevitably occur. It is during this phase, as partners attempt to reestablish individuality and the couple's solidarity is tested, that many lesbian couples seek therapy. The intensity of bonding makes this lessening of merger difficult and painful, and the adjustment and/or transition to a less "bonded" phase of relationship can be stressful. All couples struggle with a balance of individuation and togetherness; gender socialization prescribes different tasks in this struggle for heterosexual and homosexual males and females.

Lesbian and gay relationships may be monogamous, nonmonogamous, or communal. And the meaning and practice of sex may differ considerably. Contrary to heterosexual couples, lesbian and gay couples are typically open about their affairs. However, lesbian affairs tend to be more consistent and ongoing than the more casual sexual affairs of gay couples (Kassof, 1989). As previously mentioned, a major myth involving gays is that they do not form long-lasting relationships. Although gays may have trouble maintaining relationships during their younger years, this is also true for heterosexual men. Many gays in their 20s and 30s are just beginning to experience couple relationships in their coming-out process. Their dating patterns are similar to those of adolescent heterosexual males who are testing out their relational capacities and sexual identities.

Many of the gay couples I interviewed or have worked or socialized with have been together longer than 10 years, supporting current research findings (Berzon, 1988; Laird, 1993a, 1993b; Stein, 1993). The focus of these relationships is a deep emotional attachment with or without sexual activity. Gays expect mutual emotional dependability with their partners, and relationship fidelity is viewed in terms of emotional fidelity as opposed to sexual exclusivity (McWhirter & Mattison, 1984). Gays who seek sex outside of their primary relationship do so for a number of reasons: needs are not met by a partner; the partner may be emotionally and/or intellectually gratifying, but not sexually so; there is a desire for variety and adventure as well as for novelty; sexual behavior may defend against feelings such as anger and fear. Sexual fidelity and monogamy may be a heterosexist, capitalist ideal, and the gay and lesbian culture may be developing different values and norms. Research indicates that more heterosexual males engage in extramarital affairs than do heterosexual females; the same holds true for gays and lesbians. The overarching variable seems to be gender socialization, not sexual orientation.

Stereotypical "butch–femme" roles and gay "husband–wife" roles may be more a function of generation or socioeconomic class than of the homosexual culture miming heterosexual roles. Older gay and lesbian couples are more likely to have adopted traditional roles because of their upbringing in a traditional society. Certainly the same can be said for heterosexual couples; today, more women are working and are invested in careers than was so in their mothers' generation.

GAY AND LESBIAN PARENTING

Gay and lesbian parents and families typically encounter all or nearly all of the issues of heterosexual parents and families in addition to those that are the unique by-products of their specific sexual orientation and living and parenting arrangements. Because almost all gays and lesbians were raised in traditional heterosexual, nuclear families (Harris & Turner, 1985–1986), as parents they are at a disadvantage because of the absence of relevant gay and lesbian parent role models. Each, therefore, must navigate new territory without benefit of the familiar signposts that aid heterosexual families. Homophobic attitudes classify gays and lesbians as inferior, even dangerous, parents. Falk (1994) and Barrett and Robinson (1994) document the gap between empirical research and societal assumptions in gay and lesbian custody cases. In 1994, there was a controversial case in Virginia in which custody of a child was given to the maternal grandmother solely on the judge's belief that a lesbian mother could not be a competent parent. In the same year, a Massachusetts court allowed a lesbian to adopt her lover's biological daughter.

Irrational fears about homosexual parents include concern that a child will be sexually molested by a same-gender parent (even though the data reveal that most sexual abuse is heterosexual), that gender and sexual identity formation will somehow be deviant among children of homosexuals, and that children of gays and lesbians will be subjected to continuous harassment by their peers and, therefore, will experience a general social ostracism. Popular mythology also holds that lesbians lack a maternal instinct and, therefore, are not suited to parent. Gays are considered the least fit parents of all. Fear also exists, to some extent that children of gays will be at higher risk for contracting HIV (Harris & Turner, 1985–1986).

It is clear that gay and lesbian families lack standard social supports, rights, and financial benefits and that these lacks can exert a deleterious effect upon family cohesion and longevity. Gay and lesbian parents who had their children in a previous heterosexual union commonly live in a state of dread that they will lose custody or visitation rights should the courts discover their sexual orientation. The secrecy this realistic dread exerts upon the social adjustment of family members can debilitate individual and family development. Also, extended family members often disown gay and lesbian relatives, leaving the homosexual family without a crucial source of support (Baptiste, 1987). Against such a menacing and deeply rooted backdrop of fear, ignorance, and hatred, it would appear that social stigmatization, ostracism, and stereotyping present formidable external roadblocks to gay and lesbian parents and families.

Gay and lesbian parents coming out of heterosexual marriages may need to work through their coming-out process prior to realizing a harmonious gay or lesbian parent identity. That is assuming that they are allowed visitation or coparenting opportunities, because they are rarely allowed custody if their sexual orientation becomes known. They may have difficulty in forming a new couple relationship, as do any blended or reconstituted families. But for someone coming out of a heterosexual marriage, the inexperience in and novelty of having a same-gender couple relationship, the guilt and self-doubts around divorce, along with internalized and societal homophobia create more intense vulnerability for a homosexual blended family than for a heterosexual blended family.

Most of the literature about the psychological issues of homosexual parenting focuses on lesbian parenting. As pointed out by Schwartz-Gottman (1989), fathers tend to be relegated to the shadows compared to mothers, and gays are often stereotyped as antifamily. The research on lesbian parents asserts that lesbian women are not more likely than heterosexual women to be mentally ill; in fact, the results of various studies indicate that lesbian women are more self-confident, independent, composed, and self-sufficient than heterosexual women (Baumrind, 1995; Falk, 1989; Patterson, 1994; Turner et al., 1990). This would have a positive impact on their parenting. Other comparative studies (Patterson, 1992) suggest that there are no substantial differences between the maternal attitudes and caregiving behaviors of lesbian and heterosexual mothers. And, as reported by P. J. Falk (1989), considering all of the obstacles that lesbians face, a woman who is willing to overcome these difficulties in order to parent is likely to be a highly motivated and very committed parent. The same can be said for gay fathers. Because of their own struggles with marginalization, both gay and lesbian parents are likely to be particularly sensitive to diversity. They tend to foster the development of tolerance in their children (American Psychological Association, 1995).

The complexity of gay and lesbian family concerns increases dramatically with the homosexual couple's choice to have children, as will be seen in Chapter 6. And, as with heterosexual couples, the decision to have children can place strains upon the couple relationship. Gay and lesbian couples have added issues, such as the method of becoming parents, and which parent will have the biological input, in addition to legal and financial constraints.

IMPACT OF GAY AND LESBIAN PARENTING ON CHILDREN'S DEVELOPMENT

In the past few years, considerable attention and research efforts have focused on the psychosocial development of children of homosexual parents. Concerns about the emotional development, sexual orientation, and day-to-day psychological well-being of these children come from all sides, both from those who have the power to decide custody and parenting rights and may be influenced by overt or masked homophobia, heterosexism, and ignorance; and from those who are determined to find results supporting the parenting rights of gays and lesbians. Most of the studies are based on children born within heterosexual marriages. The samples are further limited because many gays and lesbians remain in heterosexual marriages, hiding their homosexuality from their families, and are obviously not available for study.

The phenomenon of gay and lesbian couples choosing to have and raise children solely within the gay or lesbian family structure is too recent to provide sufficient samples to study. In the first statistical study of gays who chose to parent, Sbordone (1993) studied 78 gay fathers who chose to parent as gay couples or as single gay men via adoption or by contracting with a surrogate mother, and compared these men to a group of 83 gays choosing not to parent. Compared to gays who chose not to parent, those choosing to parent displayed higher levels of self-esteem and lower levels of internalized homophobia, although both groups had similar perceptions about intimacy and autonomy in their families of origin during childhood. This is one of the few studies about gays who became parents as gay men. Scallen (1993) also studied gay fathers, finding them less traditional in parental attitudes, with a higher psychological investment in their roles as fathers than as economic providers.

The existing studies of lesbians who became parents as lesbians (Green, Mandel, Hotvedt, Gray, & Smith, 1986; Harris & Turner, 1985–1986; Kirkpatrick, 1987; McCandlish, 1987; Patterson, 1992; Steckel, 1987) found the children to be as healthy as those in heterosexual families. The children of lesbians reported more stress due to homophobia as well as having a greater sense of well-being and feeling more sensitive, lovable, and emotionally responsive than did the children of heterosexual mothers. Patterson (1992) also found that lesbian mothers are more diligent in creating opportunities for their children to have relationships with adult males than are heterosexual single mothers. Golombok, Spencer, and Rutter (1983) found that lesbian mothers arranged for their children to have more contact with their fathers than did heterosexual single or divorced mothers. R. L. Barret and Robinson (1994, pp. 168–169) found children of gay fathers to be (1) like all kids, some with problems, some well adjusted, some doing well in just about all activities; (2) living in unique family situations requiring the development of coping strategies; (3) needing help sorting out their feelings about homosexuality and their anxieties (shared by most youth) about their own sexual orientation; (4) possibly isolated and angry and perhaps having poor relationships with their gay fathers; (5) in little danger of sexual abuse and unlikely to "catch" homosexuality; (6) mostly adjusting well to their family situation and using the family as a means to develop greater tolerance of diversity; (7) advocates of human and gay rights; and (8) having the potential for greater honesty and openness in their relationships with their fathers.

As previously mentioned, the majority of the research is limited to assessing sexual identity formation, including gender identity, sex role identity, sex-typed behavior, and sexual orientation. The methods by which "normality" versus "abnormality" are assessed vary from one study to another, but are consensually agreed to be resistant to any form of objective measurement, such as the available, valid, and reliable standard personality assessment batteries. Thus, the research must be considered within its political context. The research on both gay and lesbian parents, such as it is, is in virtually unanimous agreement that there are no significant differences thus far assessed between the children of homosexual and heterosexual parents on any dimension of personality functioning or personal development, issues of separation and individuation, self-concept, and locus of control (American Psychological Association, 1995; Barret & Robinson, 1994; Falk, 1994; Gibbs, 1989; Golombok et al., 1983; Harris & Turner, 1985–1986; Hoeffer, 1981; Kirkpatrick, Smith, & Roy, 1981; Martin, 1993; Patterson, 1992, 1994; Riddle, 1978). The parental attitudes, behaviors, and childrearing practices of gays and lesbians have been found to be essentially the same as those of their heterosexual counterparts. The focus of the research has been more on children's welfare than on parents' relationships.

The literature does acknowledge the impact on children of the pervasive pressure for secrecy, noting consideration of geographic location. Living in San Francisco as the child of gay or lesbian parents would be a different experience than living in Wichita, Kansas. The degree of acceptance of diversity is influenced by geographical exposure, values, and norms. Thus, it appears that fear of exposure and increased social isolation may burden at least some children of homosexual parents. Research on the impact of homophobia on children and adolescents is sketchy at best.

It is difficult to assess how many of these children are raised solely within a single-sex culture and how many parents consciously attempt to expose their children to opposite-gender role models, as suggested in the previously mentioned studies. Considerable social learning results, however, from extrafamilial models, such as television, school, peer groups, books, movies, clubs, and other community resources. The degree of the parents' heterophobia and comfort with diversity, their identity and coming-out experiences, and their current life experiences all influence their children's perceptions and interpretations of their experiences.

It is noteworthy that the general literature focuses on problems and limitations and minimizes or ignores strengths and assets. Laird (1993a) suggests consideration of resiliency, which can develop from the experience of being marginalized and marching to the tune of a different drummer. Phenomenological studies and informal dialogues indicate that psychological benefits might include increased acceptance of one's sexuality, increased tolerance and empathy, increased willingness to come forward and talk about problems, and increased androgyny.

Another major research problem is that of comparison. Are the groups against which gays and lesbians are compared based solely on sexual orientation, on single parenting, on matched financial and occupational levels? Do we not minimize the cultural diversity as well as the different age cohorts by dichotomizing between two groups and reductionistically exaggerating differences rather than minimizing differences and acknowledging multifactorial complexity?

FAMILIES OF ORIGIN OF GAYS AND LESBIANS

As they gradually come to terms with their different sexual orientation, gays and lesbians have already experienced separation from others for many years because of their "different" identity. Their families of origin may experience the same pain of separation and loss when the disclosure occurs. For the homosexual who is hoping for acceptance from his or her family of origin, the disclosure of what usually has been a secret may lead to an even more pronounced distancing, separation, and loss as the family of origin progresses through its own stages of understanding and of coming to terms with family members' own homophobia. The family's process of coming out and integration has been likened to Kübler-Ross's (1969) stages of grief because of the strong feelings of loss that family members experience at the "death of their heterosexual fantasy" for their child. There are the potential loss of grandchildren and the loss of acceptance and safety for their child. There is the loss of their own identity as good parents because of society's view that somehow their child is pathological or weird.

Some of the literature from PFLAG indicates that lesbians have received more rejection from their families of origin than gays (1990). This may be due to their reproductive capabilities and the subsequent assumption that they will not provide grandchildren. Little research has been conducted about the impact on the family of origin, but there is much folklore about rejection, shame, and guilt. The AIDS epidemic has served to reunite families as well as further the rejection and distance. There is no way of estimating what percentage of families are supportive and what the gender, ethnic, class, and family dynamic issues are that contribute to mutually supportive resolution of this shock to the family-of-origin system. The growing membership of PFLAG across the nation indicates that more and more families are eager to understand and support their homosexual family members.

*   *   *

Individuals and families encountering homosexuality on a personal level face the major obstacle of homophobia as they try to come to terms with integrating a homosexual identity into a heterosexist society. So it is encumbent upon mental health professionals to consider the sociocultural context of homophobia when evaluating developmental problems and psychopathology within the individual and family. Whatever individual developmental issues and/or psychopathology one might have, they are bound to be exacerbated by the effects of oppression and marginalization. Thus, within a social construction frame work, one cannot conclude that homosexuals are "sicker" than heterosexuals, but that they continually contend with extraordinary pressures that heterosexuals do not experience.

As we gain more understanding of the multiple factors likely to contribute to heterosexuality and homosexuality—psychological, social, biological, cultural—and as the gay liberation movement continues to educate the general public, many of the prevailing misconceptions hopefully will lessen.

SIX

Homosexuality over the Life Span

"You can't love me without understanding that I'm gay. My being gay is central to the person you pretend to care about. I won't accept anything less than that. I don't want to be tolerated."
—From interview with Tony Kushner in *The New Yorker* (Lubow, 1992, p. 60)

"When Tom left that letter on our bed, the one telling us he is gay, I died a million deaths. I felt such pain, such confusion. How could this be? How did he know? Surely, this was a phase. It felt to me as if everything I had worked for, the development of a close, OK family, was suddenly ripped away. There was no one to talk to. I felt so ashamed. Now I'm ashamed of those feelings. My pain is around the anguish and isolation he must have felt all those years growing up in our family. How could I not have sensed this or known?"—Janet, 49, mother of Tom, 27

"When my partner, Elaine, and I went to pick up Jessica from kindergarten the 2nd month of school, we were stunned that she introduced us to her friends as 'Mom' and 'Aunt Elaine.' We don't know where or how she got that, because at home she calls us 'Mom' and 'Mommie.' She didn't seem to be uneasy in any way, just as natural as can be. We got the biggest kick out of this!"
—Jane, 36, lesbian biological mother

Discovering and accepting homosexuality are two distinct processes. They are processes rather than events in that they occur over time in individual, family, and sociocultural contexts. These passages are fraught with turbulent thoughts and feelings for gays, lesbians, and their families. Resolution is required in order that the typical adulthood passages can progress, with expected frustrations, disappointments, and gratifications.

In this chapter, I will describe the processes of identity development for gay and lesbian individuals and for their families of origin as well as the developmental issues of gay and lesbian couples and families. Again, the voices of interviewees will depict these processes and concomitant issues. Clinicians need to develop understanding and familiarity with homosexual developmental issues in order to help clients predict and normalize the different stages and aspects of this development. The issues that gays, lesbians, and their families typically confront are the coming-out process (disclosure to self and others), life style choices (including geographical sites, career options, interpersonal and sexual concerns), usual life span concerns, and the impact of AIDS on their sexual practices, their relationships, and society—all within a virulent homophobic sociocultural context.

LESBIAN AND GAY IDENTITY FORMATION

Although many adult gays and lesbians retrospectively recall homoerotic fantasies and feelings of being different in childhood, it is usually not until adolescence that many of them become consciously aware of homosexual inclinations. Statistics reveal that this group is at high risk for adolescent suicide. For many others, this conscious awareness does not occur until early, middle, or later adulthood. The differences in the timing of conscious awareness may be attributable to geographical, gender, ethnic, and sociocultural variables as well as the concept of fluid sexual identity. Certainly, in the 1990s, it is somewhat safer for adolescents to allow themselves to consider privately their differentness than it has been heretofore, due to the slowly increasing awareness and tolerance of differentness in at least some parts of the country.

Regardless of when one begins to question one's sexual orientation, there are some common assumptions with which one must contend: the presumption of heterosexuality by individuals, their families, and society; the presumption that being different is wrong and bad; the recognition of stigmatization and its implications; and the assumption that all gays and lesbians are alike, are homogeneous (Herdt, 1989).

> Joe, now 26, reports that when he was in sixth grade, he knew he was different because he was more comfortable and friendlier with girls than with boys. He felt that he had more in common with the sensitivity, noncompetitive values, and interests of girls, and he was put off by what he now terms "the machoism" of the boys. But he figured this was something that would change with time. He also believed that his fantasies and dreams about boys was another stage, because lots of the boys at summer camp fooled around in the shower and bunk. He wanted very much to be liked by the kids and he

shuddered when they teased a sissy classmate as being a "faggot." Joe says that he went out of his way to blend in and not appear to be different both at home and school. His family did not seem to notice anything different about him, although they noted his sensitivity vis-à-vis his older brother's athletic prowess.

Diane, 19, reports that she had been considered a tomboy in elementary and junior high school. She enjoyed being the first to be picked for an athletic team and others did not dare tease her because of her ability to fight, but she was troubled by her inability to relate to the girls' interests and her feelings of comradeship with the boys. At home, her mother kept nagging her to wear dresses and not to roughhouse so much. By the time she entered high school, she had made efforts to conform to stereotypically feminine gender role behaviors. It wasn't until her first year in college that she allowed herself to acknowledge that her intense emotional attachments to "older women" were more than a passing adolescent phase.

Thus, we see that awareness of a preference for behaviors associated with the other gender may (but not necessarily) develop into awareness of same-gender attraction in fantasy, dreams, and reality. The stirring of this awareness elicits feelings of "differentness" and "wrongness." There are confusion, rejection, and denial of these forbidden thoughts and feelings; fear; and often self-contempt. For adolescents who are naturally struggling with identity development, these emotionally laden feelings can't help but burden their still developing personalities as well as their relationships with family and friends.

Consider how likely it is that disturbed behaviors and symptoms are derived or at the very least exacerbated by a youth's experience of being different and atypical. As Stein (1993) points out, it is amazing that so many homosexuals are able to come through adolescent development with an intact self-concept and identity, given all of the stigmatization, social stereotyping, and categorization associated with homosexuality. We really do not know what the resiliency factors are that allow some to come to terms with their homosexuality without the manifestation of serious psychological disturbance. We can suspect that ego strength, perhaps evolving from secure family attachment experiences, raises tolerance of internalized homophobia.

Fred, age 28, had vague feelings of being different while in high school. But he attributed these differences to his "artistic creativity and sensitivity." Being involved with theatre and hanging out with the arty crowd made him feel less different. Fred was very popular, had lots of girlfriends and boyfriends, and participated actively in the mainstream activities of high school. He felt confident and secure in his academic achievement and social popularity, and he reports no unusual tensions or struggles at home. When Fred went to college, he wondered about his attraction to his roommate. But he continued to date women and just assumed he was heterosexual, not having yet met the "right person" to whom he would feel some sexual attraction. It was not until he was out of college 2 years, floundering around with notions of graduate school, but unclear about a specific direction, that he began to wonder if he was gay. He listened carefully to what others (both gay and straight) said, read whatever popular literature he could about homosexuality, and finally shared his concerns with a close friend. He also went through a period of intense heterosexual activity, attempting to prove to himself that he was just a late bloomer. Fred is grateful that he did not consciously contend with his homosexuality while in high school. He felt much more confident and sure of himself as an adult and believes that his gay identity development was less tumultuous than it would have been while in the throes of adolescence.

Ted, now a 35-year-old day care worker, is in a long-term gay relationship. He and his partner have a 4-year-old son. Ted experienced a tortured adolescence. Although he did not realize he was gay, he did recognize that others considered him a "nerd" and that he was different from the other guys. While he joined them in their derogatory comments about "faggots" and "queers," he felt isolated, harassed, and rejected by his peers. He resorted to drinking and other substance abuse forays, finding this the only way to achieve any social connection to other kids. In his senior year, he overdosed. He remembers wanting to be dead, to get away from the pain of being different, the shame of his sexual attraction to males, the fear of destroying his recently widowed mother. But he claims that he did not intend to commit suicide; he just stopped caring. When he awoke in the hospital, his first feeling was of disappointment that he had not, in fact, died. It was in the detox hospital, with the help of a counselor, that he first began to contend with his sexual orientation.

In the several theoretical models of gay and lesbian identity development referred to in the literature, there seems to be some overlapping between identity development and the coming-out process. Many of the models are prescriptive and pathologize directly or indirectly the gay or lesbian who does not come out all the way and/or become actively affiliated with the gay and lesbian cultures. There is also concern that these models, like other psychological theoretical paradigms, are narrow and restrictive in their linear orientation and their apparent insensitivity to gender difference and cultural diversity. Given the data on the fluidity and ranges of sexual orientations between the extremes of heterosexuality and homosexuality, one must consider these theories of identity development with some caution. There may be some people who never go through all of the stages because they are bisexual. Also, it is important to consider that an individual has several simultaneous identities—all of which influence personality but any one of which may have more salience at a particular time or under particular circumstances. For example, gays and lesbians of color must integrate both their racial identity development and their sexual identity development. Which has salience may depend on many factors. As with any theory of development, one must not overgeneralize; there are always exceptions, variations, and differences. The importance of these models, however, is to provide guidelines to help clinicians assess the level of identity development and facilitate the process with gay and lesbian individuals and their families.

E. Coleman (1982), for example, describes a five-stage coming-out process as a linear, progressive model of identity formation. Each stage requires the accomplishment of developmental tasks in order to be able to progress to the next stage. The first stage is the pre-coming-out stage, where there is vague recognition of being different and of same-gender sexual attraction feelings. Typically, these individuals defend against these feelings, often acting out through behavior problems, psychosomatic illnesses, suicide attempts, or substance abuse. The second stage is coming out to one's self by acknowledging homoerotic thoughts, fantasies, or feelings. The third stage is exploration of homosexual feelings and relationships. Isay (1989) differentiates the sexual activity of gay adolescents from the homosexual explorations of heterosexual boys. Gay adolescents' sexual activities have a strong affective element, whereas their experimental heterosexual activities, as in the above example of Fred, are similar to the experimental homosexual activities of heterosexual adolescents. Coleman's fourth stage progresses to the first homosexual relationships, similar to the first heterosexual relationships of adolescents, and his fifth stage consists of identity integration, the acceptance of homosexuality along with management of its associated stigma.

Cass's (1979, 1984) six-stage, nonlinear, interactive process between the person and environment model focuses more on one's changing perceptions of self and actions than on the occurrence of specific events. Her model delineates accompanying behaviors and is the model most often cited in current literature.

The first stage consists of identity confusion, the beginnings of conscious awareness and questioning regarding one's sexual orientation. The turmoil one experiences at this time is usually responded to by inhibition of these thoughts, personal innocence, or information seeking about what this may mean. Secrecy is a major component of this stage as the individual struggles with the question, "What is wrong with me?" and the fear that somehow it shows and everyone will "know."

The second stage is identity comparison, where one accepts the possibility that one might be gay or lesbian. One begins struggling with feelings of alienation, being different, not belonging, and isolation. If one is in a supportive environment, there might be relief at understanding the vague stirrings previously felt. Or one may accept the homosexual definition of one's behavior, but not of one's self-concept. This is when one may either think of oneself as a special case, going through a stage that will pass when the right circumstances arise, or think of oneself as bisexual. Another response to this stage may be to accept one's self and behavior as gay, but also to accept society's devaluation of homosexuality. This can result in the inhibition of overt gay behavior and the development of self-contempt and internalized homophobia.

In the third stage, identity tolerance, one accepts the probability of one's homosexuality and recognizes one's sexual, social, and emotional needs. At this point, one begins to make contact with other homosexual persons, while still struggling with the feeling that there is something wrong. This is a particularly painful stage, as one may be living two separate lives: one part conforming to society's norms and the other trying to meet one's own needs. During this stage, one might accentuate one's differences from the heterosexual culture, engaging in heterophobic behaviors. This polarization is an unconscious attempt to reduce internal dissonance, creating an identification with the "us" against "them."

Identity acceptance occurs in the fourth stage, when one has continuing and increased contact with the gay and lesbian subcultures. This is a time when the individual can begin to feel a normalcy with a homosexual identity. This is usually when one begins to want to share the homosexual identity with others as a way of validating one's life, perhaps for the first time.

The fifth stage is identity pride. Most come out to nongays during this stage. There is acknowledgment of the incongruity between the individual's acceptance of his or her identity and society's rejection of it, which can lead to further devaluation of the heterosexual culture. One may become more actively immersed in the gay and lesbian subcultures and have even less to do with heterosexuals. In fact, there may be a great deal of anger and resentment expressed against the heterosexual world, including one's family of origin. This stage can be particularly painful for the family of origin, who may feel as if they have lost their child to a different culture.

The sixth stage, identity synthesis, involves the merging of personal and public sexual identities, the integration of the homosexual identity with other aspects of self, and the capacity to understand and accept both the homosexual and heterosexual cultures. Thus, the dichotomy between heterosexuality and homosexuality from the previous stage becomes resolved by integration. It is at this point that the individual has come out to those persons she or he deems appropriate and the gay or lesbian has more of an ability to view sexual orientation as a continuum rather than the dichotomy portrayed by society.

All stage theories are descriptive and explanatory, ignoring cultural, social, and historical contexts (including geographical, generational, and community elements). Nevertheless, an open developmental conceptual framework allows individuals and their families to understand the fluidity of development, which offers hope for progression. The work of Boxer and Cohler (1989) emphasizes that culture-bound stage theories not only ignore contexts, but also ignore the significance of the way gays and lesbians make meaning out of the discontinuities, adaptations, and changes they experience throughout the life span. Continued longitudinal research is necessary in order to validate these theories within changing sociocultural contexts.

In attempting to explore the influences of parent–child relationships on homosexual identity development, I asked the 38 gay males I interviewed about their early relationships with their parents. Of the 32 raised in two-parent families, 23 reported closeness to their mothers, who were traditional stay-at-home primary parents and emotional distance from their fathers. However, those with heterosexual brothers did not believe that their brothers experienced any different relationship with parents during childhood. Several of these men did report that, as they entered preadolescence, it appeared as if their fathers favored their more competitive, athletic brothers. These brothers perhaps were more "like" the fathers.

These findings both support and yet go beyond the findings of Isay (1989) who, based on his 40 gay psychoanalytic patients, describes gay males' early relationships with their fathers as detached and hostile, a state that he attributes both to the son's need to distort the memory of an early erotic attachment to the father and to the father's actual withdrawal from a son who is different from what he had envisioned. Isay describes gay males' closeness to women as derived from the son's alliance and identification with his mother to win the father's attention. He acknowledges that this different developmental pathway is influenced by constitutional factors as well as by family constellation; in other words, the different relationships gay children and adolescents may experience with their fathers vis-à-vis their heterosexual brothers may be the outcome rather than the cause of their being different.

Recent studies of lesbian identity development (Browning, Reynolds, & Dworkin, 1991; Cass, 1984; Falco, 1991; Herbert, 1992) indicate that some aspects of homosexual identity development differ between gays and lesbians. Awareness of one's homosexuality, life style, and the nature of one's relationships are all influenced by socialized gender differences. As previously mentioned, because women have been socialized to please others and define themselves in relation to others, their sexual orientation identity is more likely to be based on emotional relationships than men's, who, socialized to be independent and competitive, are more likely to focus on sexual activity.

As pointed out in Chapter 5, all women in our culture contend with sexism and misogyny. For lesbians, these are added to homophobia and heterosexism. The women's movement, directly attacking sexism and misogyny and indeed bringing about social change, has helped to create a more supportive environment for lesbians. However, homophobia within the women's movement has motivated lesbian feminists to form their own movements within the larger women's movement. (There is no comparable movement for men.) In recent times, the AIDS epidemic has fostered, both from within and without gay communities, a more supportive environment for gays.

In the 1990s, there are multiple, diverse groups of self-identified lesbians and gays, including those whose ideological view is that homosexuality is politically correct; those who discover or choose this sexual orientation and are determined to live openly and congruently; those who become involved in a significant homosexual relationship and, despite their chagrin or discomfort over this discovery about themselves, find this relationship to be more important than their previous self-identity; those who waver in their identity acceptance and life style choices; those who live a secret homosexual life; those who make every effort to conform to mainstream values and repress their homoerotic inclinations; and so forth.

Studies by Saghir and Robins (1973), Chapman and Brannock (1987), and Bell, Weinberg, and Hammersmith (1981) claim that boys are able to recognize and acknowledge their sexual differentness as homosexuals earlier than girls, although Boxer, Cook, and Herdt (1991) suggest that the ages of first homosexual attractions and fantasies are quite similar for both males and females, occurring typically at ages 10–12 years. The indication that lesbians become sexually active at a later time than gays (Saghir & Robins, 1973) is no different from the heterosexual population. The Boxer, Cook, and Herdt (1989) study of 200 racially and ethnically diverse gays and lesbians from Chicago found that more lesbians than gays had experienced heterosexual intercourse by their adult years. Again, this is not surprising, given that women can engage in intercourse without necessarily being biologically aroused and that social factors encourage women to meet the needs of others.

As noted, the importance of relationships for female development places different pressures on lesbians. Their fear of rejection by peers and family is more intense than that of males, and thus they conceal their homosexuality more, attempt to conform to heterosexual gender roles, and experience increased isolation. In our society, women perceived as masculine (in their attire as well as mannerisms) are not as cruelly derided as men perceived as "sissy" or "effeminate." The negative messages females receive about individuation and separation along with their strong need for connection may well underlie lesbians' later identity development. There is some evidence (Mencher, 1990; Slater & Mencher, 1991; Zitter, 1987) that lesbians are more vulnerable to maternal rejection than gays. The mother–daughter, same-gender identification, as elaborated by Chodorow (1978), is so powerful and intense that mothers and daughters both have anxiety about the separation that comes from being "not like me." As women become more aware of the larger feminist culture, they are able to seek support from and connection to lesbian communities. This positive context can encourage and facilitate lesbians' identity development and alleviate the pain from loss of identification with the mother. Male children may have an intense relationship with their mothers, usually the primary caretakers, but the different gender identification may allow mothers to view their gay sons as more like them than different.

Another gender difference may be the fluidity of gender orientation referred to in Chapter 5. Women apparently represent a greater proportion of bisexuals (Isay, 1989; M. Nichols, 1994), and choice of sexual orientation may be more possible for them than for men, given anatomical differences, political and social motivations for power within a male-dominant culture, and their relational rather than sexual priorities for intimacy. Thus, the importance of emotional relationship in women's development cannot be underestimated.

> Linda, 35, is now married with two children. During her freshman year at a liberal college with a politically activist student body, she became active in the women's movement and, out of political conviction, chose a lesbian partner and life style. During her senior year, she came out to her parents who, although disappointed, were supportive. This lesbian relationship lasted 3 years after college. It was followed by two less intense lesbian relationships. In her late 20s, Linda became disenchanted with both the women's movement and the lesbian community, and she chose to date men. She was consciously aware of wanting the security and stability of a more traditional life style. Again, her parents were supportive. Eventually, she

married and had two children. Although Linda does not find her marital relationship as gratifying as her lesbian relationships, she enjoys her mothering and her life style. When asked why she could not have chosen to have children within a lesbian relationship, she replied that she honestly did not believe she possesses the stamina and energy to commit to an alternative life style.

It is clear that sex-role socialization, generation (there is a marked contrast in the social attitudes experienced by different age cohorts), region, class, and racial and ethnic factors impact homosexual identity development. There is diversity of homosexuality and as pointed out by Falco (1991), both homosexuality and heterosexuality are intertwined with social and psychological spheres of life.

THE COMING-OUT PROCESS

The coming-out process consists of disclosure to self and others of differentness in one's sexual orientation or in one's family. There are some similarities and differences in the way individual gays and lesbians and their families experience this process.

Lesbian and Gay Coming Out

There are many variables that significantly influence the coming-out process. According to Hanley-Hackenback (1988), individual variables are related to "personality or characterological makeup, age at first awareness of being different, overall psychological functioning, family rigidity — especially regarding sexuality — religious upbringing, and negative or traumatic experiences regarding sexual orientation — especially in childhood" (p. 30). Other important variables are "gender, race or ethnic group, location — especially urban versus rural — and the values and attitudes of the society at that particular time in history" (p. 30).

Other than themselves, the first person that gays and lesbians usually come out to are their first same-gender sexual and/or romantic partners. During this exploratory part of the identity process, they may be tentative in their self-labeling, even protesting that they are really heterosexual, just "trying something out." A gay and lesbian coming-out cliché is, "I'm not gay. I'm just attracted to you." In general, however, the first other people that they usually disclose to are other gays or lesbians.

The fears of harassment and rejection by peers and family are very real. By the time gays and lesbians, whatever their age, are ready to come out to nongay peers and family, they are well along in their process of identity development. And they have most likely come out to other gays or lesbians. The time lag varies; some take months, some years. Many enter therapy in order to prepare for coming out to nongay friends and family.

> John, 24, reports that he began to wonder if he was gay during his sophomore year in college. At that time, he thought he was in love with a woman on his dormitory floor. He dated her steadily, but could not feel sexual attraction, even though he engaged in sexual play with her. Because he cared so deeply for her, he began to think about his homoerotic fantasies and thoughts. When he told her he thought he might be gay, she was crushed but supportive and urged him to go to the university counseling service. After 12 weeks of counseling, he realized that, while he was not attracted to any particular males at the time, he was gay. For the next 2 years, he maintained a close friendship with this woman and led a monastic life, burying himself in his scientific studies. In graduate school, he had his first homosexual couplings. He found he really did not have a strong sexual drive, maintains his friendship with his college woman friend (subsequently married with children), and has developed some strong friendships, albeit nonsexual, with other gay graduate students. In his own quiet, unobtrusive way, John accepts himself as a gay man with low sexual drive. While he has not come out to his midwestern family, from whom he fears rejection and alienation, he is comfortable coming out quietly to selected nongay friends and colleagues.

> Lisa, 26, first suspected she was a lesbian when she was in high school. She kept having crushes on women teachers and older female students, in contrast to her peers' preoccupation with boys. Her first sexual relationship was with a girl in her neighborhood who went to another high school. Throughout high school, they kept their relationship secret. When Lisa went to work after graduation, she began to have other relationships and gradually found a network of lesbian friends. Lisa was very nervous about coming out, although most of her partners had already done so and they pressured her to do so too. With the encouragement of a therapist, she first came out via e-mail at work to other lesbian workers (whom she had heard about through the grapevine). Several months later, she told a nongay coworker in her department. That was a milestone event, and, when she received a positive, supportive response, she was able to begin to plan to come out to her sister. Lisa believes her mother and sister have known for years, but that the family message is to not talk about it. At this time, she does not think she will ever be able to disclose to her mother, and she is still very anxious about her sister. Lisa's working-class family is open about its homophobia, expressing cruel and derogatory remarks whenever the occasion allows.

Savin-Williams (1989) found that, in general, 44% of gay and 32% of lesbian youth are more likely to come out to mothers than to fathers. If the gay or lesbian offspring reports general satisfaction and contact with the parent(s), if the parents are still married (rather than divorced), and if the parents are young rather than older, coming out to parents seems to be easier. A higher proportion of lesbians than gays among my interviewees and in my clinical practice have evaded coming out to their families. The gender role socialization, and the stronger needs of women to remain connected to their families of origin, particularly their mothers, may account for women's intense fear of separation and rejection. Another difference that I've noticed is that it is easier for women to camouflage their secret lives from their families, introducing and including their partner as a "best friend" or a "roommate." Affectionate behavior between women is more accepted by society than such behavior between men. And, furthermore, men do not exhibit the same close, intimate same-gender friendships.

Family Coming Out

Ted, now 32, revealed to his parents that he was gay about 10 years ago. His parents were understandably shocked and dismayed, but did not ask many questions or want to know much about him or his life. At first, they tried to pretend that nothing had changed. Gradually, he became aware of their distancing — they called less, did not include him in family functions as much as they previously had, and silently pressured him to pretend nothing was different when he did attend a wedding or christening. If he invited them to his apartment for dinner, he had to hide any evidence of his homosexuality and not include his partner. His sister was the only one in the family who openly embraced him, although she too believes that homosexuality is immoral and unhealthy. When Ted was diagnosed as HIV positive last year, he told his sister, who told their parents. To date, his sister has been the only one in the family who has demonstrated concern and caring even though she acknowledges her discomfort with Ted's homosexuality.

Unfortunately, distancing and rejection from families is commonplace. It occurs across all socioeconomic classes, regardless of educational level. There is evidence that some ethnic groups are even more likely to repudiate a homosexual member. Several of my Black and Latino clients and interviewees reported that they feel they have to choose between family relations and open gay or lesbian identity. There can be enormous intrapsychic conflict between racial identity and sexual identity. However, many families — particularly those who, prior to the disclosure, experienced close affiliation, tolerance, and acceptance for members' individuation—do respond supportively, and, as family members go through their own process of identity development, they achieve pride and become more affirming (often politicized) than they may ever have thought possible.

> Ms. Frances, age 54, was dismayed when her 22-year-old son came out to her. At first, she begged him not to tell his father, as it would "kill him"; he has high blood pressure. Mr. Frances had struggled as an accountant to overcome a working-class background, and middle-class acceptance was a high priority. A traditional housewife who had never really been involved outside her home except with social acquaintances, Ms. Frances could not bear her pain. When she discovered indirectly that her son had shared his sexual orientation with his sister and brother, she turned to them for support. Her daughter-in-law introduced her to PFLAG and, as reported by Ms. Frances, that "changed my entire life." After attending meetings for several months, and learning that all kinds of "nice" families had gay and lesbian children, she was able, with the support of all three of her children, to facilitate her son's coming out to his father. At this time, she had the self-confidence to help Mr. Frances with his difficulties understanding homosexuality. Although he never became as active as she in PFLAG, he has not opposed her involvement in any way. It is almost as if he detours his supportiveness through her. At this writing, Ms. Frances is an active leader in her regional PFLAG group. She volunteers in many activities and has made this her "vocation." Actually, her son teases her as being a "professional PFLAG mother"! It does seem as if this has given her an important identity, a sense of purpose and meaning in her life.

When a family member discloses homosexuality to his or her family, it can be a narcissistic injury that is traumatic for all members. The homosexual member wants acceptance from the family for something that he or she may not yet have been able to accept him- or herself, even though the homosexual member may protest that the family's reaction "doesn't matter." The family members feel their core selves— their beliefs, identity, and expectations—to be directly assaulted.

It is critical for clinicians to understand that the families experience their own process of coming out and must come to integrate at some level their child's and their family's new identity (Ritter & O'Neil, 1989). Furthermore, even if some members of the family have suspected something may be different about the homosexual individual, they have not been through the stages of recognizing and acknowledging this difference as has the homosexual family member. So the news can't help but be a shock and may at first (or, for some families, permanently) lead to a more pronounced separation, loss, or abrupt cut-off. If the offspring is an adolescent or young adult, the family is already in the throes of experiencing separation and change as it traverses the launching stage. The disclosure will have a major impact on this developmental passage. It is not as easy to cut off a younger person still living at home.

Families of gays and lesbians experience their own grief process as they struggle with the loss or "death" of their heterosexual assumptions and their fantasies of who their offspring is. Every family with whom I've talked reports that the first internal reactions to the disclosure include pain about the loss of grandchildren (a heterosexist assumption at best, given the increasing number of gays and lesbians choosing to raise children), and fear for the social acceptance, safety, and health of their child. The family grief process has been likened to that described by Kübler-Ross (1969), including stages of shock, denial, bargaining, working through until gradual acceptance, and finally pride. Again, not all families progress through all of these stages, which explains why some families are unable to reach resolution.

Parents, particularly the mother, who is typically the primary parent, lose their identities as "good parents." They know that society will blame them, and they blame themselves. In fact, even today, many mental health professionals still assume that the mother has been overly controlling and intrusive. Mother blaming may be more underground than in the past, but it is still prevalent. Sauerman (1984) suggests the following six stages of understanding that families experience:

The first stage, as mentioned, is one of shock. "Oh, no!" is often the first phrase spoken, even if they have suspected for years. Often parents voice the thought that they have lost their child. One gay son reminded his parents that "I'm the same person now that I've always been and you've always loved me." The pain that family members experience during this phase cannot be underestimated. After the initial shock wears off, the family moves into a period of denial, which is manifested in remarks such as, "Are you sure you are gay?" "Couldn't it just be the people you hang around with?" "Did anyone molest you when you were younger?" There is a desperate attempt to find a blameful cause, to fix it, to restore the family to its previous level of homeostasis. One father reported trying to console his wife by saying, "Look, this isn't the worst thing in the world. He is bright, happy, and well liked. We could have a kid with AIDS, cancer, schizophrenia, and so forth. Let's put this in proper perspective."

When the family is no longer able to maintain their denial, they move into the guilt stage. This is where members of the family will ask what they did wrong or blame one another for this perceived trage-

dy. One couple I had worked with several years ago on marital conflict came back recently in shock, just having learned of their son's
homosexuality. In between the first and second sessions, an article had
appeared in their local newspaper reporting the homosexual gene to
be carried by the mother. The belief that "what you read in the
newspaper is true" furnished the husband with ammunition to carry
on his long-standing beratement of his wife. Now there was "proof"
that this was all her fault!

Guilt leads into the next stage, expressed by anger and a kind of
pleading bargaining. When blaming doesn't work, the parents may use
tactics such as, "If you really loved us, you wouldn't do this to us."
"What will people say?" "You don't know how you are ruining our
whole family." This can be a painful time for everyone. The shame
the homosexual has experienced in his or her own integration process
will once again be experienced and exacerbated within the family context. The family members are feeling intense pain and shame. What
must they do to avoid public ridicule and shame? One couple told me
that they never realized how many homophobic jokes and slurs occurred within their own social groups until they were in this stage and
oversensitized to every little remark or gesture. They continuously felt
as if they had to change the subject or distance themselves from others
and wondered if they'd ever feel relaxed and comfortable with other
people again.

The burden of secrecy and shame on the family can be overwhelming. As with the gay or lesbian offspring, it takes time to work through
these processes. It is often a long while, if ever, before everyone in
the immediate family is openly informed. Then comes the issue of whom
to tell and whom to avoid telling within the extended family, the friendship network, and the community. Many pressures are put on the gay
or lesbian offspring to "disappear" or to "act normal." It is a desolat-
ing time for the family as they deal with their feelings of being cheated
out of their heterosexual expectations. It is also a time when family
members have to face their own homophobia and misconceptions. And
until recently, there have not been many sources of information to help
family members overcome their ignorance about gay and lesbian development. The sources that do exist today are specialized books and
articles. There is no inclusion of homosexual development in the general
popular and professional child and adolescent development books.

Ideally, families will progress into the final two stages of understanding. In the fifth stage, there can be different responses: (1) a beginning of acceptance and a continuation of love for the child, (2) an
acceptance as long as no one speaks about it, or (3) warfare and isolation. In the final, sixth stage, which many families never reach, there

is true acceptance of the child's core identity, and there is an acknowledgment by the parents that they will need to contend with a
homophobic society that makes their lives and the life of their child
frightening and difficult.

Certainly, it is understandable that families struggle with their own
coming-out process. They are a part of a society that values confor-
mity and heterosexuality. It is also not surprising that parents worry
about the consequences of a gay or lesbian life style for their child,
including concerns about physical and verbal assault, AIDS, unemployment, and other types of ostracization. Families are naturally concerned and protective, and their feelings of helplessness in the face of
such social ostracism can be overwhelming.

The ways in which gays and lesbians relate to their families and
how their families relate to them affect both the offspring's gay or lesbian identity and the family's identity. Identity can be spoiled by guilt
and self-denial, just as it can be enhanced by love and understanding.
There seems to be a continuum of family acceptance, ranging from
all embracing, to arm's length, to "Let's pretend you don't exist," to
"We suspect but we really don't want to know," to being totally in
the dark, to the other extreme, violent rejection. The nature or degree
of acceptance can, to be sure, change over the life span, and it is likely
to be influenced by sociocultural exposure and acceptance.

Impact of Coming Out on Heterosexual Spouses and Children

When a parent comes out to his or her family as a gay or lesbian, there
are special issues that the spouses and children experience. The spouse
is likely to progress through the same stages of shock, denial, guilt,
anger, then possible acceptance as does the family of origin. There is
mourning of the marital relationship, of the image of the heterosexual spouse. Much of the spouse's reaction will depend on whether or
not the spouse believes he or she was deceived at the time of the marriage. Many of the gays and lesbians I have known and worked with
did not realize they were gay at the time of their marriages. They were
able to deny their confusion, and they yearned for the "straight, middle-
class life with all the trimmings." This goal had always been the personal and societal expectation. Thus, it never occurred to them to think
about possible harm to spouse or future children, because they truly
believed that marriage would make everything "all right." As a couple
therapist, I must say that I have found this same belief in the magic
of marriage to resolve personal difficulties to be rampant in the heterosexual population. On the other hand, research (R. Barret & Robin-

son, 1990; Wyers, 1987) shows that there are also gays who do in fact marry and have children either to hide their homosexuality or to suppress it.

Auerback and Moser (1987, p. 322) found that 20% of their sample of heterosexual wives clung to the belief that their husbands would "come to their senses," abandon the gay life style, and return to their traditional families. Although many couples separate or divorce after disclosure, others choose to maintain a platonic marriage, focusing on nonsexual marital satisfactions, outside interests, children, and jobs, with all sexual contacts occurring outside the marriage. Still others may choose a "double standard" marriage, where sexual contact occurs both within and outside the marriage. And then there is the rarity that Ross (1989, p. 45) terms the "innovative marriage," characterized by "frequent heterosexual relations as well as homosexual relations, all quite openly."

Whereas some researchers (Hatterer, 1974) claim that women who marry homosexuals display a number of personality disturbances, other studies have not identified common personality traits that would make heterosexual wives more susceptible to choosing spouses with confused sexual orientation. Those who know of their intended spouse's uncertainty about his sexual orientation may be naive in their persistent conviction that, with time, everything will work out.

However, whether or not they knew of their spouse's confusions, these wives are likely to feel intense betrayal and abandonment that is often manifested in hurtful rage. They are feeling the pain of separating physically and emotionally from a husband for whom positive feelings still exist. They also are experiencing frustration in being rejected for something over which they had no control. Many attempt to "rescue" their spouses, facilitating the gay spouse's adjustment by being nurturing and supportive and subordinating their own hurts and concerns. When this doesn't work, they feel the pain of sexual rejection, which undermines their self-esteem and confidence. They feel undesirable, unfeminine, and lacking in sexual attractiveness.

Nora, age 41, was devastated when her husband, Cliff, told her that he could no longer deny his sexual attraction to men. He loved her and the children, but could not stay in the marriage any longer. Nora reports that she ranted and raved, screaming that he could have his flings as long as he stayed with her. She would not make any sexual demands on him. They could pretend. Cliff tried to be gentle as he prepared to move out. Nora's concerns about the effects on the children were similar to his own. Surprisingly, when both Nora and Cliff sat down to tell their preadolescent daughter and son about the pending separation and the reasons for it, the children handled it better than expected. Cliff had always been close to his children, and, while Nora found it easier to discuss the separation with the children than did Cliff, his relationship with the children did not seem to be altered. With the support of family, friends, and a therapist, it took Nora close to 2 years to come to terms with this situation. Her genuine devotion to her children and her caring for Cliff enabled her to develop empathy and return to her previous high level of functioning.

In a review of the sparse literature about once-married lesbians, Bridges and Croteau (1994) noted that many of these women were also unaware of their homosexuality at the time of marriage; others may have married due to heterosexual conditioning, a desire for economic security, or a belief that they would feel differently after marriage. Most of the women studied by researchers married for the same reasons the general population marries—for love of their spouse, and a desire for marriage and children. A study by Charbonneau and Lander (1991) of 30 women who did not become lesbian until midlife, after marriage and children, noted two paths for this sexual orientation shift: (1) those committed to the idea of nuclear family and motherhood but not very involved in the sexual aspects of heterosexuality who discovered new feelings and relationships later in life, and (2) those identifying with feminist politics who chose to embrace a lesbian identity and life style. There have been no studies of differences in the experiences of male and female heterosexual spouses. One might assume that male privilege would afford male spouses more recourse in terms of financial security and the ability to get on with one's life, whereas heterosexual female spouses might have an easier time of obtaining custody of the children.

Children who grow up within heterosexual families that change their identities after a parent comes out as gay or lesbian differ from kids who grow up in families where the parents are gay or lesbian from the beginning. Gottman (1990) reports that children's initial reaction to the news that their father is homosexual depends on the child's age. If children were informed of their father's homosexuality while in their teens, as opposed to earlier, they were less likely to respond positively to the disclosure. During this stage of adolescence, children do not like to be "different" and they yearn for peer approval and acceptance. The gay parent may thus become the target of an exacerbated adolescent rebellion. Patterson (1992) confirms that positive responses are most likely during earlier childhood years.

One 15-year-old son whom I interviewed reported that his first thought was, "Does this mean that I'm gay too?" He was reluctant to talk about this with his parents or anyone and felt that he was "sharing the closet" with his parents. It would not be OK if anyone knew. Whereas he used to invite friends over after school, he no longer felt able to do so. It was a year before he even told his best friend, and he was so anxious thinking about it that he was sick to his stomach. When his friend responded, "Oh yeah?," he almost fainted with relief.

Positive responses to a parent's homosexuality increase when children are informed during postteen years. However, although disclosure during teen years was the most unsettling, the chance for resolution and feeling closer to their gay or bisexual father was greater than childhood exposure or postteen disclosure. It could be that the sharing of sexual identity crises could lead to eventual rapprochement. In general, Bigner and Bozett (1989) note that

> gay fathers tend to teach their children to be accepting of variations in human behavior. It is improbable that children of gay fathers would begin to perceive their fathers in a negative manner so abruptly after having a long history of loving experiences with them. The disclosure may help to relieve family tensions in these homes since the children would be less likely after the disclosure to blame themselves for their parents' marital difficulties. (p. 161)

The biggest fear for children of gays and lesbians is stigmatization and ostracization by their peers. Thus, they feel pressured to keep what's going on in their family secret, to be careful and cautious about coming out as the offspring of a gay or lesbian. The burden of secrecy can have profound effects on their behavior and academic achievement as well as their emotional and social functioning. At the same time, some youngsters report feeling proud of their parents for challenging societal rules and standing up for their beliefs (P. J. Falk, 1989). The parents' self-esteem and comfort with their sexual identity will provide the context for a positive outcome of disclosure.

These children also feel strong concern and protectiveness for the heterosexual parent, and they worry about whether the homosexual parent will lose a job and visitation or custody rights. Custody is a major issue for lesbian mothers, who are frequently the targets of discriminatory legislation and judicial practices (Falk, 1994; Ussher, 1990, 1991). In retrospect, many youngsters report that their parents' divorce is actually more problematic for them than a parent's sexual orientation. They have the same difficulty accepting a gay or lesbian parental partner as they would a heterosexual parental partner.

It seems clear that, if the gay or lesbian parent continues to place his or her highest priority on parenting, and the other parent, despite his or her pain, is able to support the children with the gay or lesbian parent, children's adjustment will be smoother than if secrecy and anger surround the family. The same has been found to be true of heterosexual divorced families, wherein parents who collaborate on coparenting, and who keep their marital conflict separate from their parenting roles, enhance their children's acceptance and adjustment.

GAY AND LESBIAN COUPLES

There is diversity and variability in all couple systems, regardless of class, race, ethnicity, age, and gender orientation. Gay and lesbian couples, however, must contend with the lack of gay and lesbian relationship models. Because gays and lesbians as well as heterosexuals were socialized in the same heterosexual culture, we all, including gay and lesbian partners, attempt to overlay stereotyped gender roles on same-sex couples. These heterosexist assumptions are clearly inaccurate and unhelpful when applied to same-sex couples. They ignore the reality that some gay males are male-identified in their self-concept, while others identify more with being female; and still others are more androgynous. Likewise, some lesbians are super-feminine, some more male-identified, and some more androgynous.

> "As hard as it is for straight people to meet partners, it's that much harder for gays. I'm not screwed up like a lot of these guys. I know what I'm looking for in a lover and, believe me, even here in New York City, it's hard to find another guy who's had an equivalent educational background, similar interests, and is not messed up about being gay." — 32-year-old gay man

One of the major problems that gays and lesbians in young adulthood report is their difficulty in finding potential partners. This is especially so for those who are still in the early stages of coming out. We must remember that most of the public places for socialization, such as coffee houses, bars, and clubs, cater to heterosexuals. However, in metropolitan areas, there are now more opportunities for gays and lesbians to meet and socialize with each other. And a few progressive high schools in metropolitan areas even have gay and lesbian organizations. In more rural areas, the social isolation can be intense. Many gays and lesbians travel to metropolitan areas for socialization purposes whenever possible.

In addition to different meeting and dating opportunities for gays and lesbians, there are none of the social (such as acceptance of pub-

lic affection) and legal supports (such as insurance), rituals, and marker events (such as engagement ceremonies and weddings) for gay and
lesbian couple relationships that heterosexuals take for granted. Furthermore, gay and lesbian couples have to contend with the myth and
expectation that their relationships are temporary and unimportant
(Berzon, 1988).

A stage model of homosexual couple development from the combined works of Mattison and McWhirter (1987), who studied gay couples, and Clunis and Green (1988), who studied lesbian couples,
delineates six stages through which homosexual couples progress. In
addition to the universal couple tasks proposed by Haley (1963) in
his heterosexual couple development model, it pinpoints those tasks
and issues particularly relevant to same-gender couples.

Stage One is the first year of blending. It is a time of getting to
know the partner better and the period in which the couple moves in
together for the first time. Gay and lesbian couples tend to be quicker
at moving in together. Murphy (1993) suggests that this may serve
as a marker event to solidify their couple relationship. During this stage,
couples tend to overlook their differences and discrepancies, putting
their energy into avoiding conflict and differences. They are helped
by what McWhirter and Mattison (1984) call "limerence" (a Jungian
term), an intense type of high-energy romantic love that is all-absorbing.
Many gay and lesbian couples in this stage isolate themselves from
family and friends, focusing solely on their new-found couplehood.
How couples merge and share is influenced not only by gender socialization, but also by their intimacy experiences in their family of origin
and previous relationships. The tasks of Stage One include getting to
know one another; negotiating differences in stages of identity development and coming-out process as well as of age, ethnicity, race, class,
background, values, and goals; balancing the pace of the relationship
with outside relationships and interests; developing trust and communication; negotiating sex and determining whether the relationship will
be sexually exclusive or sexually nonexclusive; coping with jealousy
and envy; determining roles, that is, complementarity or symmetry;
and sharing power. There is some caution during this stage; many
couples do not trust enough to combine income and possessions, mostly
from their fear about whether or not the relationships will really last.
And certainly the AIDS epidemic has impacted the gay male sexual
relationships.

Tom, 26, and Dan, 29, were aglow. They had met a few months
earlier at a soccer match, developed an instant attraction for each
other, and decided to move in together after 2 months. Each claimed

to have "found my other half." Although there were obvious differences in their backgrounds and occupational levels, they were both floating on the buoyancy of having "finally found the right one." They spent every spare minute together, talked several times a day, and sidestepped any possible disagreements. They reported sexual compatibility, although Dan preferred sleeping in his own bed, whereas Tom wanted them to sleep together. The possibility of infidelity was out of the question for them at this time. Dan had lost a previous lover to AIDS, and, while he believed he was ready and eager for a new permanent relationship, his anxiety about attachment and possible loss was apparent to his close friends even though Tom seemed to be unaware of it. Eventually, Tom and Dan broke up. Tom could not cope with Dan's anxieties. He wanted to be more relaxed and to have more emotional closeness.

With regard to monogamous versus nonmonogamous relationships, an interesting study by Kurdek (1988) indicates that 35 of the 65 gay couples he interviewed allowed for sex outside the relationship, whereas none of the 45 lesbian couples interviewed would allow infidelity.

Stage Two focuses on the nesting that occurs in the second and third years of the relationship. During this stage, the couple may rent or purchase a home together, moving into a new place (not the former home of one of the partners) to show to themselves and the community that they are committed and creating a home together. As the honeymoon limerence fades, partners begin to see each other as they really are, with flaws and imperfections. If homosexual couples are not able to understand and accept this loss and change, they may begin to distance themselves from each other and refuse to compromise and negotiate as necessary for the development of any couple relationship. Gay couples may become more restless sexually, and lesbian couples may exhibit less sexual interest but more need for emotional affection and attachment. It is during this stage that the greater number of homosexual relationships may end. (Interestingly, it is during this phase of heterosexual relationships that couples often have children, perhaps as an unconscious way of avoiding dealing with differences, and resulting in perpetuating the couple structure.) Several couples I've worked with ended their relationship because of the discrepancies in their homosexual identity development and their consequent willingness or lack thereof to be politically active in the gay and lesbian culture.

Thus, the Stage Two tasks include developing emotional as well as sexual intimacy; enriching loyalty; improving communication, conflict, and decision-making skills; and furthering companionship. In addition, each couple needs to find a way to handle discrepancies (in age, background, race, class, values, and interests) and to establish some relationship complementarity. This complementarity may be based on gender role identification, occupational attainment, pragmatic role assignment, or interests and activities. Couples having a repertoire of characteristics usually associated with the opposite sex can strengthen these characteristics to maximize couple complementarity (McWhirter & Mattison, 1984). Role complementarity does not necessarily imply a power differential. If the role complementarity is chosen rather than imposed, there can still be egalitarian power.

> Tim, 34, and Chris, 29, have been together 4 years. Tim is a high school teacher, and Chris waits tables in a restaurant. Tim provides the steady income and the physical amenities. Chris provides the creative cooking, entertaining, and socializing opportunities. They are satisfied with their role assignments, although they do bicker over the spending of money and Tim's messiness. They believe that they share power. Tim reports that he is more passive sexually, that he prefers to be penetrated rather than to be the penetrator, and that both he and Chris are satisfied with their sex roles and relationship. Tim believes they will stay together; Chris would like to, but believes that in the future he might like to have some other sexual relationships. Because each has lost previous partners to AIDS, this is a delicate subject, one that is consciously put on the shelf for future discussion. Chris does not think that any outside sexual relationship would affect his feelings for Tim and his commitment to the relationship.

Stage Three, during the fourth and fifth years, is about maintenance. Contrary to heterosexual couple development, there is increasing attention to individual autonomy within the couple context. In other words, healthy distancing occurs as the balance between individuation and togetherness becomes more comfortable within the security of a stable couple relationship. At this stage, having successfully avoided major conflict for several years and building a higher trust level, the couple engages more in risk taking, particularly in the area of separation. Often, this is when gay couples decide to stay together, but to accept sexual nonexclusivity. Lesbian couples may feel more comfortable pursuing separate interests and friendships while still feeling that their relationship is the core of their emotional life. This may be the stage when the couple is more public in affirming their commitment to each other, such as having a commitment ceremony.

Stage Four, from years 6 to 10, focuses on building. The independence of each partner increases, and the result can be an equality of couple relating in which the couple moves together without smother-

ing individuality. There is a risk that the surge of energy toward independence will result in separation rather than adding a new dimension of productivity to the couple. During this phase, there is more
combining of assets and possessions. The emotional task is the shift
from other to self at the same time there is dependency on the partner
to always be there. This means that partners can accept and deal with
one another's independent changes without holding them back.

Stage Five, releasing, occurs from years 11 through 20. At this
stage, the couple begins to accept things as they are, to let go of their
fantasies of the ideal partner and relationship. The emphasis is on the
established friendship rather than the limerence. A final process of merging occurs. Similar to Stage One, which was an intimate merging, merging in Stage Five is of possessions and money. This can be a conflictual
process for men, especially those accultured to equate money with power, independence, and the ability to care for oneself.

Stages Four and Five usually occur in middle age, when gays and
lesbians are dealing with the same midlife issues as are heterosexuals.
Those who do not have children may find mentoring younger gays
and lesbians to be generative. They may become more involved with
nieces, nephews, or neighborhood youngsters, and they may be more
consciously aware of how they balance love, work, and play. They
may fear the loss of their partner, not wanting to put energy into the
dating scene, and, furthermore, they may be confused about the rapid
changes in the gay and lesbian world and the pressures for political
action. Because many who are in midlife today had different experiences
in their identity development and coming-out process than younger
gays and lesbians, they may be struggling with their identification and
assimilation into both the heterosexual and the gay and lesbian cultures. Remember, they made early adulthood career and life style
choices long before gay pride came into existence.

Stage Six is about renewing. This stage brings with it a shift in
focus and perspective that can either pull couples closer together or
distance them. Health concerns, growing old, retirement, and fears
of death may be thought about and shared between the partners similar to the experience of heterosexual partners. Despite these concerns,
the relationship and the feelings of security are strongest now, while
a heightened dependency develops. Security is not only financially established, but is also generalized to the personal and relationship realms.
The couple begins to remember and reminisce, telling story after story. These stories may provide rejuvenation for the couple as they relive and become energized by earlier events. The couple may seek out
younger couples willing to listen to their stories while providing a mentoring or modeling role. But the relationship may also be taken for
granted, which can cause unresolved conflicts to resurface.

Vince, 64, and Wally, 61, have been a couple for over 30 years. Early on, they had other sexual relationships, but in the past 10 years, they have become close, faithful friends. Like many older couples, they believe that they are settled and satisfied with their life together. They have been through a lot together, having lost friends to AIDS, and they have watched from afar, with both envy and sadness, the development of the gay movement. Vince and Wally have gay friends, but they are equally comfortable with their heterosexual friends, and they vacation with Vince's family every summer. While Vince, an antiques importer, is the primary breadwinner, Wally has, over the years, developed an exclusive catering business. They travel together and apart. They care for each other when aging ailments prevail; they seem to have their own gestures and language and they radiate comfort and ease. Their biggest concern is who will be there for the one who survives. Most of their contemporary gay friends have either died or are no longer in stable relationships, so they already are beginning to experience the loneliness and isolation of not having a readily available peer group. In fact, they believe that they are gravitating more to former heterosexual friends and relatives, as they find seeking friends of the same age more comforting than homosexual companions.

Obviously, gays and lesbians have retirement, estate planning, caretaking, and health concerns as they age. Many report being disregarded by younger gays and lesbians as "too establishment." Facilities and community resources (such as nursing homes) for the elderly homosexual population do not exist at this time, forcing many to go back "into the closet" in order to obtain necessary services. Because fewer gay males have children and many have not maintained relationships with nieces and nephews, they have valid fears about their aging, about who will care for them during illness and senescence. Lesbians may have maintained generative relationships with kin and friends, but, in addition, they have to contend with society's devaluation of aging women and the likelihood that they will be less well off financially than their male counterparts.

Although not a linear formula, these stages provide a conceptual framework for understanding the developmental tasks and issues pertinent to homosexual relationships. As with heterosexual relationships, if the partners are out of sync with each other's stages of identity development, if the influences of their families of origin are conflictual rather than merely discrepant, or when they are in transition between stages, any couple relationship is particularly vulnerable to conflict. For gay and lesbian couples, the added challenges of heterosexism and homophobia affecting individual gay and lesbian identity can intensify their relationship vulnerability. And, without the legal commitment of marriage, there may be a tendency on the part of gays and lesbians to "give up" and "quit the relationship" without attempting to work through typical couple conflicts.

GAY AND LESBIAN FAMILIES

Gay and lesbian families come in many shapes and sizes. They can have a single parent, either a gay or a lesbian. They can be coparented by gay or lesbian couples, consisting of a biological, adoptive, or foster parent and the partner. The families can be mixed, where each partner has come into the relationship with children. And an added dimension to this form occurs when the couple decides to have one of the partners participate in artificial insemination or adoption.

Clunis and Green (1988) have developed three homosexual family classifications that follow the forms just mentioned: first, the "nuclear family," which describes the parenting of a mutually gained child as a shared experience; second is the "blended family," in which one partner has children from a previous relationship, with the new partner entering into the already established family; third is the "extra blended family," in which both partners come into the relationship with children from prior relationships (these could be either homosexual or heterosexual). There is little research about the "nuclear family," the newest form. Surveys indicate that lesbian women are more likely than gay men to leave their heterosexual marriages in search of a committed relationship with a woman (Wyers, 1987).

Frequently, the definition of the family is determined by societal pressures. For example, lesbians or gays from a heterosexual divorce may decide to raise their children as single parents to avoid possible custody disputes. If the mother or father does decide to cohabitate with a lover, she or he may decide to maintain secrecy about their sexuality, and define the relationship as "friendship" or "roommates."

Natalie, 24, was 8 when her parents divorced. Her mother, a social worker, did not self-identify as lesbian until Natalie was 10. A year later, Natalie and her mother moved in with her mother's lesbian partner. That relationship lasted 14 years. Natalie describes her mother's lover as distant. She says her mother's partner never really parented her, but did enforce house rules. Natalie did not know about her mother's lesbianism until well into her teens. This was because her mother feared a custody dispute. Natalie saw her father and stepmother regularly and even as a child was aware that she could never talk about "Nan." Years later, Natalie believes that the secrecy and her mother's tension contributed to the breakup of the relationship between her mother and Nan.

One of the most difficult decisions a gay or lesbian couple makes is the decision to become parents. The decisions center around who the adopter and donor will be, who will be the biological parent, and what the other partner's role definition will be. In several couples with whom I have worked, the relationship has fallen apart due to one partner's not wanting to participate actively in parenting. Because of the lack of legal support or role definition for either the nonbiological or the nonlegal parent, a great deal of commitment and energy is required to sustain parent status.

All of the gay and lesbian couples I have worked with or interviewed report that at least one partner knew earlier in his or her life that they wanted to parent. For most, this was an open criterion in selecting a partner. However, when the time to decide and plan actually occurs, previous ambivalences may emerge. The impact of the parenting focus on the couple system itself is similar to that in heterosexual couples. And, because many gay or lesbian couples are older when they make this decision, they may encounter their own infertility as well as legal and societal impediments to adoption.

> Jan, 34, and Betty, 36, decided that Jan would become pregnant by artificial insemination. They would each attempt to work part-time, sharing parental responsibilities. When Jan proved to have endometriosis that impeded her ability to conceive, after much agonizing, they decided that Betty, too, would try to conceive by artificial insemination. Betty was able to become pregnant within months. In her 6th month, Jan was able to become pregnant with *in vitro* fertilization. This family ended up with a son and daughter 6 months apart. Now, they think this was an ideal arrangement, though it occurred accidentally. They coparent, there is no competition, and they feel that this bond has strengthened their couple relationship.

> Matt, 36, always knew he wanted to parent, even when he realized he was gay during college. His partner, Rick, 37 and HIV positive, was the logical adoptive parent, given his occupational and financial status. Through an alliance for single parent adoption, he found a 3-year-old Vietnamese child. Rick comments that he thinks the social worker may have suspected his sexual orientation, but the issue of HIV never arose. Today, this couple lives in farm country where their child is the only non-Caucasian and where they find themselves totally accepted as a family, even though their homosexuality is never mentioned. Rick's health is stable as of this writing. They report that the HIV status has more of an impact on their couple relationship than the child. Actually, the impact of the child is positive in that there is less processing of the relationship, with more focus on parenting as a common goal or interest. The issue of joint custody, particularly in light of Rick's HIV condition is their overarching concern.

Although it has become a bit easier for gays and lesbians to adopt, it is still very difficult. Gay and lesbian couples often are willing to take difficult-to-place children, such as those who are multiracial or who have special needs or medical conditions. Increasingly, gays and lesbians are choosing to have biological children. Lesbians who get pregnant may choose a relative of the nonbiological-parent partner to be the donor in order to have a biological tie, may take turns in bearing children, or may choose a gay man as the donor. The specter of AIDS has become a problem in the general population with regard to sperm donors. Gays often use an anonymous surrogate mother or make an arrangement with a lesbian friend.

> Tony, 41, and Sam, 38, had been unsuccessful in their attempts to adopt. Gail, 35, is a highly successful businesswoman who travels internationally 60% of the year and works long hours the rest of the time. She was enthusiastic about Tony and Sam's desire to parent and offered to be a surrogate parent. Tony and Sam both decided to contribute their semen for artificial insemination (this way, they had an equal chance of becoming the biological father). After Gail delivered the baby girl, Tony adopted her and he and Sam became the primary parents. Gail is the godmother, visiting when she can and acting like the favorite aunt. Five years later, this arrangement seems to be working out well. With the help of a gay parents support group, Tony and Sam are planning to disclose the nature of their unusual family to their daughter before she enters kindergarten. They are not sure what this will mean to her, given that she is growing up in a secure family, feels attached to both parents and to Gail, and has been exposed to playmates in both gay and straight families. Tony's extended family is also involved in their lives, residing nearby, whereas Sam's family is visited once every year or two.

Whether a birth comes through artificial insemination or heterosexual activity for the purpose of conception, the parents will need to make decisions about when and how to explain this to their children. Artificial insemination and *in vitro* fertilization are expensive, as can be adoption. Furthermore, there are only five sperm banks in the country and some of them discriminate against lesbians. There are also issues about health insurance and parental leave, as well as day care, should both parents work. And, most important, are the legal issues about how to ensure that if one dies, the other will be given custody, or if a separation occurs, there will be some kind of continued parenting rights or visitation for the nonlegal or nonbiological parent (Pies, 1989).

The gay and lesbian families that I interviewed chose to live in tolerant communities. The factors that seem to affect their well-being

include their security with their sexual identity, with the couple relationship, and with parenting and the availability of support systems.
Studies by Klinger (1992) and Tasker and Golombok (1995) on
lesbian mothers and Sbordone (1993) and Bigner and Jacobsen (1992)
on gay fathers indicate that gay and lesbian parenting is healthy and
can be a positive experience for both children and parents, enhancing
everyone's self-esteem. The major difficulty for these families is not
based on the parents' sexual orientation, but in the societal homophobia
and reaction to it. Gay parents face the added skepticism of society
about male primary parents. Several gay fathers laughingly told me
that, when they were the only male parent in the playground during
the work day or were picking up children at school or day care, they
were aware of more suspicion and distancing from the mothers than
when they, openly gay, were in heterosexual company.

I was only able to interview two international adoptees of lesbian couples now in adulthood. Both are experiencing difficulties in adult
adjustment that they attribute more to their adoption and racial differences while growing up in the 1970s and 1980s than to growing up
in lesbian households. However, one young woman has always had
a conflictual relationship with her adoptive lesbian mother. When she
was 3, her mother moved in with her partner. She was closer to her
mother's partner, her stepmother, than to her adoptive mother.
However, her stepmother left when she was 14 and her adoptive mother
forbade any contact. This was a significant loss and exacerbated conflict with the adoptive mother. The other young woman enjoyed a secure family upbringing with her lesbian parents, although she
remembers feeling ashamed and secretive about her family's differentness throughout her school years. She's not sure whether she really
was ostracized in school or imagined it. This woman is now married
with two of her own children, and, in today's political context, she
has nothing but admiration and respect for the courageous choices her
"moms" made in their life style. But she does mention that she feels
pressure to appear "healthy and happy all the time" in order to prove
to the world that it's OK to grow up in a lesbian family.

It is clear that gay and lesbian couples and families are an increasing
portion of our society. Certainly, we need new laws and policies in
every state that allow joint adoption by same-sex couples (second parent
adoption), as well as access to employee benefits, parental leave, and
health insurance. As of November 1995, the only states that allow second parent adoption are Alaska, California, Minnesota, New York,
Oregon, Vermont, Washington, District of Columbia, and Massachusetts. A recent appeals court ruling has cleared the way for New
Jersey to be added to this list (Bruni, 1995). We also need social serv-

ices and mental health services sensitized to the experiences of these families, to their unique strengths, and to the difficulties they encounter. George, a 46-year-old teacher, commented:

> "I don't think too much about being a gay father, since I'm challenged enough by just being the dad of two adolescent kids (privately adopted in infancy). I chose freely to be a father. . . . It's a higher priority than my career attainment (something my own father doesn't understand!). . . . I've learned more about myself from parenting than I have any other way. My kids are great, my partner feels the same way about them as I do, and I wish for them the opportunity to be who they truly are and to have the courage and strength to stand up for their convictions. We've been luckier than most, having supportive straight and gay friends and extended family."

George suspects that one of his kids may be questioning her sexual orientation, but the other is definitely heterosexual. Importantly, he does not believe, as do any of my other interviewees, that his parenting style or strategies differ from those of heterosexual parents, noting the diversity and variety among and within families of any orientation.

*   *   *

There is as much diversity and variation among lesbian and gay families as among heterosexual families. There is loving kindness and skillful parenting as well as meanness, abuse, and illness. Some parents are sensitive to the concerns of their children; others are preoccupied with their own needs. We cannot focus only on problems and differentness; we need to value the unique strengths, courage, and resilience to be found in gay and lesbian families and communities.

The difficulties that gay and lesbian families experience cannot be considered outside of a homophobic and heterosexist context. Both homosexual and heterosexual family structures and communication processes are automatically impacted by sociocultural variables, such as economic security, cultural acceptance, and peer stress. The additional impact of homophobia on gay and lesbian families can result in overwhelming stress. The research increases our recognition, however, that children being raised in gay and lesbian households are adjusting and developing as well as their peers being raised in heterosexual households.

SEVEN

Treatment Issues Pertaining to Homosexuality

The Lipson family, Mark, 42, John, 39, and Mike, Mark's 15-year-old son from a previous heterosexual marriage, sought family therapy due to the conflict and tensions developing between Mark and John around Mike's increasingly provocative behaviors. Mike was not performing his assigned household chores, was messy in the kitchen and bathroom, and had become rude to John. This was new behavior, following 3 years of relatively smooth family functioning. When John would complain to Mark, Mark always said he would "take care of it," but it seemed to John as if nothing ever happened. Mark and John have been together for 5 years. Mark left his wife after a 12-year marriage (when Mike was 10 years old), because, after meeting John, he could no longer deny and repress his yearnings for a same-gender love relationship. The divorce was painful, but amicable. Mike came to live with Mark and John 3 years ago, because his mother's job promotion involved more international travel and because she, Mike, and Mark all felt this would be the best arrangement for everyone. It had only been since Mike entered high school last fall, that the day-to-day conflicts and tensions had reached the point where they tested everyone's tolerance and patience.

Several issues emerged in the first assessment session:

1. Mike was beginning to resent his weekend visits to his mother's home in a neighboring community because they interfered with his sports and peer relations.
2. While in junior high school, Mike had adapted to sharing with a few close friends his "different kind" of family, but in the new high school environment, he was experiencing some anxiety about being teased and shunned by other kids if he were open about his dad's "special friend."

3. The arguments with Mike about messiness, laziness, unrelia-bility, and so forth were forcing Mark and John to confront their differ-ent backgrounds and expectations about adolescents and family life in a way that had been camouflaged by "limerence" in this solid, openly gay relationship.

4. Mark, like many parents bringing a child from a previous re-lationship into a reconstituted family, was ambivalent about his ex-pectations for John with regard to parenting responsibilities and de-cision making, and this caused him to operate as placater in the tri-angle.

5. John was increasingly feeling that Mark was more loyal to Mike than to him and, while he really wanted this family to work, he was feeling pushed further and further out.

6. Both John and Mark were reliving some of their own previ-ous adolescent conflicts regarding power struggles and differentiation.

7. As a couple, John and Mark were "out" to their peers and ex-tended families and maintained friendships with both gay and straight couples, but they had little contact with other gay couples who were living with a child, and they depended on straight and lesbian families for support and role modeling.

Many of these issues are typical for reconstituted families. What differs is the lack of role models and societal support for homosexual families as well as Mike's concerns about the effects of both his own homophobia and that of kids at school. This example points out the critical necessity for clinicians, when evaluating and working with homosexual individuals, couples, or families, to consider the very real external sources of stress engendered by homophobia. By talking about these concerns in a supportive, empathic environment; using active tech-niques such as family sculpting and role playing; being introduced to community resources, such as a support group for gay and lesbian par-ents and a separate one for adolescent kids of gay and lesbian parents (where Mark could also deal with his issues of loss regarding his mother); as well as having some helpful reading material, this family was able to move through this troubled passage without further ex-acerbation.

When the Lipsons returned for a consultation around Mike's go-ing off to college 2 years later, they commented that their earlier ex-perience in therapy was the first place where they had felt acknowledged as a "valid family" unit by a straight member of the "establishment." The school and other community organizations seemed to accept them, but any reference to or verbal acknowledgment of their homosexuali-ty was avoided. When Mark and John would come to school for conferences or events, for example, teachers addressed their comments to Mark, nodding to John as Mark's "friend."

In order to provide affirming, empowering therapy, clinicians need to (1) acknowledge and be open to continuous understanding of their own unconscious and conscious homophobia; (2) consider the impact of cultural and societal homophobia on socialized roles and expectations, and the psychological development and well-being of individuals, couples, and families; (3) keep abreast of developing scientific knowledge about homosexuality and concomitant issues (such as health and antigay violence) as well as with emerging life style models; (4) study the most current literature about clinical issues (see Bozett, 1989; L. Brown, 1989; Cabaj, 1988; Falco, 1991; Krestan, 1988; Kurdek, 1988; Laird, 1993b; Levy, 1992; Ricketts & Achtenburg, 1989; Roth, 1989; Roth & Murphy, 1986; Sanders, 1993; Slater & Mencher, 1991; Weston, 1991); and (5) be familiar with local, state, and federal laws, as well as community and psychoeducative resources. Advocacy is an important part of clinical work.

I begin this chapter with a discussion of therapists' biases and attitudes in a heterosexist world. I will then explore the treatment issues associated with (1) an individual's lesbian or gay identity development, (2) the family of origin as the lesbian or gay member discloses his or her homosexuality and as family members reconstruct their own identities, (3) varying lesbian and gay couples and families, and (4) individuals who are HIV positive or who have AIDS and their families.

THERAPISTS' HOMOPHOBIA

Although many contemporary therapists have attempted to adopt the "politically correct" position of being nonhomophobic, heterosexism, the ingrained belief that heterosexuality is the "normal" model for romantic and sexual relationships, still prevails in both clinical theory and practice. A recent study by Carney, Werth, and Emanuelson (1994) found a continued trend of negative attitudes among graduate counseling students toward homosexuals. The following are examples of these attitudes reported by my interviewees:

"When I went to the university counseling center to talk about my lesbianism, the therapist (whom I later discovered to be a lesbian herself!) never asked me about my lover or my relationship."—Sandra, 22

"We were in couple therapy for 4 months and he seemed uncomfortable whenever we wanted to talk about sex."—Tom, 31, and Henry, 48

"The cotherapists we saw around adopting a baby praised us too much. We felt like we were their token prize. But along with their bending over backwards to be "liberal," we felt like they still viewed us as being somehow deficient and deviant. It was just a feeling . . . can't point to anything particular that was said." — Marianne, 29, and Tabitha, 39

Much of the heterosexism experienced in therapy is subtle and unconscious, causing doubt and confusion about the validity of one's feelings and experiences in the therapist–client context. Some of my clients have reported that previous therapists ignored their sexual orientation, insisting that all couple relationships were similar in their communication and structural problems. Others report that previous therapists glorified the couple's homosexual relationship, by reframing everything positively, minimizing and ignoring overt and underlying problems and difficulties. These clients felt as if they had to pretend to fit the therapist's idea of them. Again, these feelings were confusing and unclear.

Tony, 42, and Bill, 38, reminisced about an early couple therapy they underwent over 10 years ago during the first year of their living together. Tony had not yet "come out," and he was passing Bill off as his "roommate" to everyone. Bill was more comfortable with his gay identity and trying to be patient and tolerant of Tony's reticence to declare himself gay. Their reason for entering therapy was their "bickering," and Tony had selected the therapist through his network at work. There was definite collusion between Tony and the therapist to ignore the homosexuality, to act as if it was not part of the problem. Bill realizes that he, too, colluded, afraid to rock the boat. They now laugh as they describe how, without discussing it, they reduced their bickering in order to pretend they were complying with the therapist's behavioral strategies and gain his approval. Now they realize that they just wanted to "finish therapy" as quickly as possible without having to face any of the real issues in their relationship.

L. Brown and Zimmer (1986) identify four potential manifestations of internalized homophobia in therapists: (1) a lack of valuing the couple's relationship and commitment, (2) an overattachment to longevity as opposed to quality of the relationship, (3) a lack of serious attention to substance abuse in homosexual relationships, and (4) overglamorizing the homosexual relationship. Other manifestations that I have noted include a therapist's denial or lack of attention to power abuse within couples, whether in the form of physical, emotional, or sexual behaviors. Women can be mean and violent despite the cultural stereotype of them as nurturing and empathic, and male and female therapists need to be aware of that. M. B. Barrett (1990) affirms that lesbian breakups can be as bitter and abusive as many heterosexual divorces. Of course gender stereotypes can impair work with heterosexual couples too. I have also seen a lack of serious attention to sexual compulsivity, addictive behaviors (such as gambling), and eating disorders, all too often defensive reactions of gays and lesbians.

Therapists who assume that straight, gay, and lesbian couple issues are the same and, who, as a result, avoid distinguishing between gay, straight, and lesbian couple relationships may be motivated by wanting to be nonjudgmental. However, their avoidance of the impact of a homophobic and heterosexist context on a couple relationship can't help but distort their assessment and treatment. And this distortion can deprive clients of the opportunity to work through their problems and develop the full potential of their relationships. For example, therapists may not appreciate fully the legal difficulties surrounding custody battles and adoption by gays and lesbians, the risks and advantages associated with coming out (both to the family and at work), the sense of isolation imposed on a family who is in secrecy, the fears of rejection from extended family, and the fears of rejection from the communities in which they live and work.

What can clinicians do to acknowledge and transcend their own homophobia? The literature (L. Brown & Zimmer, 1986; Dahleimer & Feigal, 1991; Iasenza, 1989; Markowitz, 1991; M. P. Nichols & Schwartz, 1991; Siegel, 1987) has many suggestions.

Therapists need to be aware of their own heterosexist or homophobic biases in order to create a genuine therapeutic relationship, one that is based on acceptance, warmth, empathy, and positive regard. Personally, clinicians can begin to examine their own ideas, feelings, thoughts, fantasies, and stereotypes about all aspects of sexuality and intimate relationships. If they are not comfortable with their own sexual fantasies (which may be both heterosexual and homosexual), sexuality, and intimate relationships, it is unlikely that they will be comfortable with their clients' sexuality and relationships, whether heterosexual or homosexual. In fact, I have learned from my supervisees that clinicians who are uncomfortable with their own homoerotic fantasies and images seem to experience the most aversion to working with gay and lesbian couples.

Clinicians can make a concerted effort to educate themselves by their own personal psychotherapy, by reading professional and popular literature, by dialoguing with their gay and lesbian colleagues and clients, by attending workshops and conferences, and by becoming more politically aware of sociocultural institutionalized biases and discrimination. It is an opportunity for continuous learning.

   Professionally, therapists can demand and support funding for more research about gender identity, sex role orientation, and sexual orientation. We desperately need accurate, unbiased, empirical as well as phenomenological and clinical research on issues concerning homosexuality, such as identity development and maintenance, the impact of violence and oppression, aging, health, career, parenting, and coupling. Clinicians can also demand and support attention to homosexuality in the training programs of all mental health professionals. Exposure in formal training curricula to an ecological perspective—the consideration of individuals within contexts of their family of origin and current family, community, gender, class, racial, ethnic, work, school, religious, and larger sociocultural environments—would enable trainees to examine and assess sociocultural assumptions and values and their influences on social and organizational structures. I believe that understanding the reciprocal influences of these different contexts is essential for accurate assessment of clients and their problems.

   There is some disagreement in the literature about how politically active clinicians and clients should be. Some politically active clinicians and writers (Ballou & Grabalek, 1985; Murphy, 1992) believe that political activism should be a goal of therapy for the client and that a truly congruent clinician will model active advocacy. Certainly, empowerment involves both the therapist and client(s) taking action in private as well as public arenas. However, I think we need to be careful not to impose our own ideologies on our clients. Although some of the models of homosexual identity development include political activism in the gay and lesbian communities as an outcome of higher levels of development, many gays and lesbians, who feel comfortable with their identities, do not choose to be highly visible or active. This choice could be related to age, personality, class, religion, race, geographical location, and/or occupation. It does not necessarily indicate psychopathology or a lower level of identity development. I might point out that there is a parallel concern about activism in feminist therapy. Some feminist writers disdain female therapists who do not insist on client activism and demonstrate public advocacy.

Bess, 49, and Jean, 34, have lived together for 8 years. They live in the same town as Jean's family and spend much time with them. Bess, a migrant from the Southwest, is a professional public relations agent. Jean is a nurse. They are open about their lesbianism to family, friends, and colleagues. They entered counseling for help with deciding how to become parents. They had previously been in therapy with a lesbian therapist who insisted that they become more involved with the lesbian community. Neither one wishes to do that. Bess says that, due to her generation and the geographical part of the country where she lived until her late 30s, she has always affiliated primarily with straight friends and colleagues. Jean is very involved with her family and their friends and has no desire to change that. They both resisted the current therapist's attempts to explore their involvement with Jean's family and their feelings about participating more actively in the lesbian community. While the therapist thought these were important avenues to pursue, she followed a client-centered approach and hoped that, perhaps in the future, they would be more open to further exploration.

If the partners were discrepant in their values regarding their affiliation with the larger lesbian community, there would be a relationship conflict. However, Bess and Jean are in agreement about their life style choice, regardless of the underlying dynamics involved. It's important not to pathologize clients' choices or resistances. I think that clinicians who impose their own agendas on clients are limited in the kind of therapeutic help they can provide. Developmental models offer guidelines and signposts rather than dogma. There is so much diversity within groups (both of clients and clinicians) that we must be sensitive to and respectful of varying choices, as long as they are not harmful to oneself or others. As pointed out by Falco (1991), lesbians (and I believe this applies to gays too) may cope with their homosexuality by quiet assimilation into mainstream society, by open confrontation with mainstream society, by ghettoization with other gays or lesbians, or by specialization as "the token" with special rules and roles in a heterosexual group. It's helpful and encouraging to note that increasing numbers of gays and lesbians are openly entering mainstream professions and services in order to be providers to their own community. (The American Psychiatric Association elected its first openly gay president a few years ago.) Many of them feel comfortable working with both homosexual and heterosexual populations.

Likewise, there are many clinicians who are active politically—both in professional organizations and in the community. Others choose different levels of involvement, perhaps providing emotional and/or financial support or writing letters to influential representatives. Still others influence via their teaching, supervision, and consultation (training and as custody legal experts). The point is to be aware of the necessity for constructive social change and the importance of political strategizing, and to respond to opportunities for indirect and direct activity. There are many ways in which clinicians can advocate for clients.

SPECIAL CONCERNS
REGARDING THERAPISTS' ETHICS

If a clinician is uninformed about the special issues and needs of any population, he or she needs either to learn about them while obtaining consultation and supervision, or to refer to a clinician who is experienced with that population. I think it is important for clinicians to be up front with clients about their feelings and experiences. When gay and lesbian clients first come to see me, I query them as to whether they would feel more comfortable with a gay or lesbian therapist. They usually have clear reasons for having sought out a heterosexual therapist, such as, "My health care plan only gave me three names from which to choose," "I'm not sure I'm really gay and I don't want a therapist with a political agenda," or "Experience in family therapy is more important to me than your sexual orientation." There have been many times when I have worked with an individual and then referred the individual and his or her partner to a gay or lesbian couple therapist.

There is one disturbing issue I have heard from clients that my gay and lesbian colleagues talk about privately, but rarely write about. That concerns therapeutic boundaries. Within the gay and lesbian communities, people can't help but commingle. It is awkward to run into your therapist at a health club or a dance. The network of gossip in any small community can also be troublesome. Another problem is that there are instances of a therapist's abuse of power by engaging in a sexual relationship with a client. This is a known fact in the heterosexual therapeutic world, but is perhaps lesser known in the gay and lesbian therapeutic world. Nevertheless, having been consulted by several subsequent therapists of clients who had been inappropriately sexually involved with their previous same-gender therapists, I am aware that these clients are particularly reluctant to report to members of their own community state boards or professional associations. After all, the clients know the problems associated with belonging to a hated, marginalized minority. The confusion about loyalty and boundaries can be very troubling for clients and can heighten their psychological stress. Ethical codes prohibit sexual involvement with clients, regardless of gender. Boundary violations representing abuse of power are just as harmful for same-gender clients as for opposite-gender clients.

GAY AND LESBIAN IDENTITY DEVELOPMENT

Persons questioning their sexual orientation may enter therapy directly wanting to explore fully their feelings and thoughts about this question or the question may arise indirectly through the manifestation of other problems.

> Evie, 42, had been divorced for 2 years. Although she had two intense friendships with women during and since college, she never questioned her sexual orientation until recently when she found herself attracted to a lesbian coworker. She returned to the therapist she had consulted prior to her divorce to work on these questions.

> Don, 26, had seen therapists on and off since he was 12. He had been involved with drugs and "the wrong crowd," and had barely scraped through high school. In his sophomore year at high school, he had attempted suicide and ended up in an in-patient unit for 6 weeks. At that time, he was diagnosed as schizophrenic. After high school, he worked at a gas station for a year, engaged in frantic heterosexual promiscuity, and then went to the local community college. He was still living at home, unsettled in his own life and continuing to disrupt his family. It was during his second year at college that he began to talk about homosexuality with his therapist. It was a tremendous relief to Don and his family when that turned out to be "the reason" for all his problems.

It is not unusual for clients to resist a therapist's introduction of the possibility of homosexuality. By creating a safe, accepting therapeutic environment, clinicians can open the door and wait for clients' readiness for exploration. But this does not mean that therapists should accept clients' self-definitions without questions and exploration. Some clinicians just pass off clients' self-questioning with reassurances such as, "All adolescents go through that phase; you'll outgrow it," or "If you think it, then it must be so."

It is likely that individuals struggling with sexual orientation have learned over a long while to feel different and that these feelings have led to lack of awareness and distrust of one's feelings. This can result in behaviors that elicit negative reactions, including attacks on one's character and ability. Don, for example, knew that he was different, not just from the other kids but also from what his parents and teachers expected from him. His troubling behaviors, while getting him negative attention, also labeled him as the "bad," "sick" kid. His feelings of depression, substance abuse, and adolescent suicide attempt may very well have been motivated by his wish to dull the pain of confusion and differentness.

If clinicians understand the pain and confusion that anyone would feel when they begin to wonder or suspect if they are part of this socially vilified group, they can better join with clients to gain self-understanding and eventual self-acceptance. The kinds of questions that clinicians can explore with clients might include the following:

1. How long have you been thinking about this?
2. How and when did you first begin to think about it?
3. What kinds of sexual experiences have you had?
4. Have you tried to be involved with the opposite sex? If so, what happened? What did you think and feel?
5. Can you think of any reasons why you might feel this way?
6. What would being gay or lesbian mean to you?
7. Have you talked to anyone about this? Do you have any gay or lesbian friends?
8. Do you think you might ever want to have children?
9. How do you feel talking about this with me?
10. If you had a magic wand, what would you change about yourself or your life?

This last question may raise some eyebrows. There are some people who are seeking a therapist who will help them to change their homosexual leanings. If, after exploration, clients want to try that avenue, the ethical responsibility of the clinician is to make a referral to someone experienced in that area. There are conflicting data about the possibility of such change in the professional literature and I would inform clients of these conflicting data in as neutral a manner as possible. I would also leave the door open so that if clients attempt "reparative therapy" and do not find that it works, they can return to a more affirmative type of therapy. Some clients crave information about homosexual development in order to lessen their confusion. When they reach the stage of identity comparison, they may rely heavily on the therapist for support and acceptance. It is during this period in therapy that the therapist can use his or her self as a vehicle for therapeutic change. The therapist may become the object of a strong positive transference, perhaps representing the client's wish for a loving, accepting, tolerant parent. This can foster the client's development of self-tolerance and acceptance. During this phase of therapy, the therapist can support the client's ventures into the gay and lesbian community and help prepare the client for the coming-out process.

As clients disclose, usually first to gay or lesbian peers and then, perhaps, to straight friends, they can process their own and others' reactions with their therapist. Discussions about the realities of homophobia and heterosexism, both external and internal, are part of the therapeutic process. In order to learn awareness and trust of one's feelings and perceptions, people require validation from others.

So if the therapist can engage the client in this kind of processing, gradually the client will become more skillful in self-processing.

Disclosure to one's family of origin is certainly a desirable objective. However, not all gays and lesbians can attain this objective, and it may not necessarily be due to their faulty identity development. There are some families that simply cannot tolerate their offspring's nonconformance to the family's image. And if the offspring truly believes that the only way he or she can remain connected in any way to the family of origin is by retaining secrecy, that is the client's choice. In these cases, the therapist can support the client's choice and focus on helping the client to develop stronger internalized warm self-acceptance.

> Peter, 28, left his rural farming community in Tennessee when he was 18 to enter the air force. He knew he was gay, but kept it hidden for the 4 years it took him to get the vocational training that he figured was his "ticket out of there." He hated the military, but managed to scrape through. As an airplane mechanic, he was able to land a decent job in a large metropolitan area, where he settled into the gay community. Twice a year he visits his family, for Christmas and Easter. They ask no questions about his life and he volunteers no information. He feels good about his vocational and social life and has no desire for anything to change. He bears no ill will toward his family, just accepts them for who they are.

> Donna, 29, has been talking about coming out to her family for years. Her lover, Edie, is totally out and Donna feels very accepted by Edie's family. Donna is close to her sister and her mother. Every time she gets up the nerve to give her sister a clue about her real relationship with Edie, she finds some excuse and backs down. Donna and Edie entered couple therapy because of this discrepancy in their identity development and coming-out process. The therapist is helping them focus on Donna's readiness preparation and consideration of what's gone on and is going on in Donna's family to cause her reticence.

In order to maximize the possibility for a positive outcome, preparation is required prior to one's coming out to the family of origin. Firstly, gay and lesbian individuals need to clarify their feelings and why they are going to disclose at this particular time. One lesbian client told me she needed to disclose to her family before her cousin's wedding the next spring, because she wanted to be able to dance with her lover at the wedding. A gay client wanted to disclose to his family before he left home to go to graduate school (he had gone to college in town, living at home.) This client was fearful that his disclosure would be the final blow to his parents' already fragile marriage, and he wanted to be sure that he left his parents in "the therapist's capable hands."

Clients need to prepare for all types of possible outcomes, including losing their family's financial support. Clients' available resources, their general relationship with their family in the past and present, and their perceptions of their family's views about homosexuality are necessary topics of discussion prior to disclosure to the family.

I try to help clients focus on the positive as well as the negative reasons for disclosing. We talk about which members of the family should be approached first. Often, a sibling is the first choice for disclosure. The sibling is a barometer for how and when to approach the parents and may also be an important positive support. Marshalling as much support as possible within and without the family is important. We anticipate the family members' possible reactions after discussing the likely emotional climate at home. One of the first questions family members may ask is "Are you sure?" followed by "How do you know?" If the gay or lesbian is truly comfortable with his or her sexual orientation and sexuality, he or she can practice in therapy to sharpen articulation of this comfort to family members.

A critical component of this preparation is helping clients understand that they need to be just as patient and tolerant of their family's reaction to what will be a crisis for the family as the clients want their family to be with them. The gay or lesbian client has lived with these feelings and the eventual knowledge for a long while. Although some family members may have entertained suspicion, this announcement will be a shock. And assimilating the information will take time. That is why the timing and nature of disclosing can influence significantly the family's reaction.

The therapist can help the client assemble appropriate reading material and information about PFLAG for the family. In some locations, there may be other family support groups available as well. And the therapist and client can role play verbal disclosures or review letters of disclosure. They can also discuss whether or not and how the therapist can be of help. The important point is for the client to operate at his or her own pace.

At the same time that therapists are helping clients with the process of disclosing to family and others, attention needs to be paid to the accumulated deleterious effects on one's self-concept and psychological functioning of secrecy and multiple losses. From the beginning of awareness of difference, gays and lesbians struggle with both the fears and, often, the actuality of loss of family and community support and acceptance. Because we live in a culture that values (perhaps overvalues) blood ties, if family acceptance is not forthcoming, one is faced with the choice of secrecy or cut-off. Either of these options bears a psychological cost.

WORKING WITH THE CLIENT
AND FAMILY OF ORIGIN

Coming Out to the Family

Sometimes the family self-refers after a member has disclosed his or her homosexuality. They may return to a previous therapist or seek someone through their own network. The family is likely to be in shock and require crisis intervention. By this, I mean immediate support, opportunities for venting and exploration of feelings, and heavy doses of information. At the same time, it's important to ascertain the meaning of homosexuality and its presence within the family to family members as well as the extent of familial strengths and resources. By careful observation and the use of a genogram, clinicians can assess the family's natural role and boundary structures, communication patterns, meaning making, stage of family development, and coalitions. How the family has coped with change and differentiation in the past, and their relationships to their kin, friends, neighbors, and work and home communities is important information to gather.

Sometimes, the disclosure can bring opposite results than expected. In one family I worked with, the couple was considering separation after 25 years of marriage. When their son came out, I thought that this would surely cinch their decision to separate. To my and the gay son's surprise, after initial periods of blaming and recriminations, the son's special status actually served to unite the couple. This was particularly touching because their son found out he was HIV positive soon afterwards and this, too, became a crisis that enhanced the strengths, rather than the weaknesses, of the family. Another family needed only a few sessions of supportive psychoeducation:

> The Brown family sought a family therapy consultation at the urging of their oldest daughter after their middle daughter, 19, blurted out her lesbianism while driving her mother to her job at a bank. Just before Ms. Brown got out of the car, Lauren stammered that she wanted her mother to know that she was a lesbian and that her roommate, Jill, was her lover, and then she drove off, leaving her mother gasping on the street. Mr. and Ms. Brown were beside themselves. They had never known anyone who was homosexual and just didn't know what to make of it. Their older daughter, Joanne, had just completed her psychiatry rotation as a nursing student and suggested that the entire family seek help.

In this case, the timing and method of disclosure were unfortunate. Lauren had not prepared herself or her parents for disclosure and her impulsivity caused much consternation. It is often helpful to have an individual session with the gay or lesbian member, particularly if the clinician has never met this individual prior to the family session. During the individual session, the clinician can assess the client's level of identity development and coming out and provide support and encouragement. With the Brown family, the individual session revealed that Lauren was self-acceptant of her lesbianism, but rather immature for her age in terms of her self-absorption and impulsivity.

Families need time to adjust. Some do it easily, others have great difficulty. Some eventually learn to become accepting and tolerant, others accept as long as there is an unspoken agreement not to talk about "it," and still others completely reject and cut off (emotionally and geographically) from their lesbian or gay family member. The reactions can range from reasonable thoughtfulness to blame, anger, sadness, and punitive withdrawal. Those who blame and try to induce guilt—"How can you do this to us?"—are in great pain and, despite the vociferousness of their reaction, may still come around with time.

If the family expects the clinician to "fix" the gay or lesbian member and restore the family to its predisclosure status, the therapist can gently but firmly set about educating the family and facilitating their passage through the identity process. Again, bibliotherapy can be of enormous help, and I always have reading material and community resource information on my table to offer to family members. After three sessions, the Brown family moved on to a community PFLAG group.

Therapists can help families through the identity process. They need to talk about whom to tell, when, and how. How do they respond to family and friends' well-meaning "Does she have a boyfriend?" or " . . . when he gets married and has children" comments and questions? How do they become aware of their own internalized homophobia and heterosexism and learn to contend with these in their family, friends, and community? If they maintain secrecy, they need to contend with isolation and cognitive dissonance. The families who seek consultation or therapy are usually those who want desperately to understand and accept, who care deeply and want to stay connected to their gay or lesbian kin. They want to talk about how to treat the "lover" or "significant other" of their family member. So language, the use of a term for the lesbian or gay member and the partner, is an important therapeutic topic.

> Ms. Stone called the therapist in distress. Her son, Jim, 29, was bringing home "his friend" for Thanksgiving. She felt uncomfortable having the two young men sleep in the same room. But she had managed her discomfort when her daughter came home with her boyfriend,

and she had allowed them to sleep together. What should she do now? Mr. Stone was no help. He merely shrugged his shoulders and said it was up to her. A few minutes of phone ventilation and discussion of Ms. Stone's feelings led her to decide that she would have to learn to tolerate and accept their sleeping together in her house. She "knew they lived together" in Chicago, so "what really was the difference?"

Dealing with AIDS

Family members of AIDS patients experience the same social isolation, stigmatization, helplessness, and grieving as the patient and his or her partner. Some families learn about the AIDS diagnosis at the same time they learn about their member's homosexuality. This can be a double whammy, resulting in a numbing immobilization. They are terrified, not only about losing their family member, but of losing support and acceptance in the world as they have known it. This crisis, like any, can either split families apart or bring them closer together.

Family therapy can be effective when the AIDS patient and the family are willing and available to participate. The first order of business for the clinician is medical education: to educate them about the nature and course of the disease and to assure the family that they are unlikely to contract the disease through their contact with the sick member. As with cancer patients, AIDS patients experience a roller coaster effect in that sometimes they can be quite ill and at other times they are in remission. According to the research of Frierson, Lippmann, and Johnson (1987), families also experience a roller coaster effect, functioning poorly when the patient is not showing symptoms, but rallying together during periods of illness.

If the AIDS patient concurs, clinicians can work with the family to discuss what information to disclose about the illness to whom. Families can expect feelings of isolation and some morbid preoccupation. They also need to plan for future caretaking. The strengths, rather than the problems, of the family can be reiterated. An important goal is to maintain boundary flexibility and to help the family restore at least some of the equilibrium that has been disrupted.

As noted by Tiblier, Walker, and Rolland (1989, p. 82), families need help with the following issues:

1. Adjusting to the life-threatening diagnosis.
2. Dealing with fears of contagion.
3. Accepting the sexual orientations of family members.
4. Coping with discrimination and stigma.
5. Managing conflict among family members and significant others.

6. Confronting a time-limited push for reconciliation.
7. Preparing for loss and bereavement.
8. Shifting family roles.
9. Providing necessary care and negotiating with external systems.

Concrete, action-oriented problem-solving interventions are necessary in conjunction with discussions about grief and loss.

Clinicians need to understand these issues in the context of where the family is in their development and how they have handled other illnesses. They also need to consider race, ethnicity, religion, and social class in terms of the above issues, and the utilization and meaning of outside services. Many people of color and members of immigrant groups think that only White gays get this disease. They may be resistant to information propagated by mainstream society, suspecting further oppression and stigmatization. Thus, they may be reluctant to acknowledge the possibility of AIDS occurring within their community or culture. Furthermore, even if they do acknowledge its existence, they may be suspicious of Western medicine and avoid diagnosis and treatment until much too late. These factors will play a role in determining (1) their response to members with AIDS and to issues regarding who will care for the sick person, (2) the type of health care and insurance available, (3) access to community resources, (4) the meaning attached to AIDS and those behaviors that may have led to infection, (5) the ways a family handles illnesses and death, and (6) the nature of the bereavement period and reorganization processes that follow the death of a family member.

In addition to problem-solving and grief-processing interventions, circular questioning can help family members understand and explore their own and each other's perspectives and concerns. For example, one might ask the family members questions such as, "Who in this family has been the designated caretaker in the past? Who is likely to be the caretaker in the future? Is there anybody who does not agree? Who will have the most difficulty in dealing with this illness?" As the clinician uses family members' answers to develop further questions, the family may discover their own solutions. The clinician then has the opportunity to use positive reframing to highlight their strengths and likely successes.

These same techniques can be used with AIDS patients reluctant to inform their families of their illness. Careful exploration of the reasons underlying this reluctance as well as open discussion about the illness representing a last opportunity for the patient and family to be close and supportive and work through past difficulties may broaden the options the patient perceives. Circular questioning can help the client not only to identify potentially supportive members within the family (e.g., "Who in your family is most likely to be supportive? Who is the next most likely to be supportive?") but also to identify possible supportive members within extended family, or others with positive influence on the family. Using circular questioning, I was able to help one client with AIDS identify as a possible support a great uncle who had been his father's favorite uncle. My client was able to disclose his illness to this person (learning, to his surprise, that his homosexuality was known to most family members), and this great uncle secured at least some emotional support from my client's parents. Throughout this process, this client became closer to his great uncle's immediate family and spent his last few weeks in their home.

If therapists focus on helping the AIDS patient to identify family strengths, perhaps by evoking memories of past good times, both the therapist and client will find it easier to avoid gross negative judgments. Obviously, there are many families who refuse acknowledgment of or contact with family members with AIDS. Despite the clients' feelings of anger and sadness, therapists can help these clients come to peace with their family members internally, if not in reality.

Support groups for families concerned with the AIDS patient have proven to be invaluable (Kates, 1992; Walker, 1987). They help families deal with their guilt, shame, blame, anger, betrayal, fear, helplessness, and impotence. They allow members to exchange resources and information, to gain support and overcome social isolation, to express feelings regarding the illness, to practice telling friends and family of the diagnosis, to discuss quality-of-life issues, and to problem solve (Kates, 1992). Whenever possible, it is helpful for the therapist to help the family to locate such a group.

Clinicians who work with AIDS patients are dealing continuously with loss and grief. They are continuously seeking a balance between closeness and distance. They need to assess their boundaries so as to be able to provide humane, caregiving support without personal intrusion. A balanced personal life, the availability of colleague and supervisor consultation, understanding of their professional roles and responsibilities, and the policies and practices of their agencies are some of the factors that help clinicians avoid overinvolvement and emotional fatigue and retain the capacity to provide effective emotional support.

COUPLE THERAPY

Lesbian and gay couples enter therapy with the same kinds of intimacy and sexuality issues as heterosexual couples. But these issues differ in that they can only be understood in the context of homophobia and heterosexism.

Common presenting concerns include permanent versus temporary relationships; separation versus connection, especially within the context of gender role socialization; power equality versus complementarity, often manifested in money, interracial, or class struggles; sexuality concerns, including sexual monogamy versus infidelity; lack of family-of-origin and societal support for the relationship and lack of mentoring role models; identity stage discrepancy; decisions about whether or not to parent; and AIDS.

Permanent versus Temporary Relationships

Berzon (1988, p. 15) refers to the gay and lesbian national anthem as "Why don't we just break up?," meaning that gays and lesbians too quickly accept dissolution as a solution to relationship problems. As discussed in Chapter 5, this mindset evolves from one's early heterosexist socialization, and the internalized homophobia that influences and affects the quality of adult gay and lesbian relationships. There are few visible role models from whom gay and lesbian couples can learn about long-term, permanent relationships. Thus, they may be expecting relationship failure. They may socially isolate themselves and put a preponderance of their time and energy into their couple relationship in order to defend against what they assume to be the fragility of their relationship. These defensive strategies may prove to be adaptive for a period of time, but eventually they can become the source of relationship problems.

Therapists can challenge these couples' assumptions and their expectations for relationship failure. By encouraging clients to question heterosexist models of couple relationships, clients can more freely create alternate models. If they learn to expect conflict over the course of a committed relationship, they are motivated to learn negotiating and problem-solving skills. One useful technique for reframing expectations is to draw a lifeline with each individual and then transpose a couple lifeline on the two individual lifelines. This lifeline will include all the significant milestone events and decisions from birth to the present and project those desired into the future. This creates a context of openness, options, and choice. The goal is to empower clients to design and create more opportunities for developing and maintaining gratifying relationships. At the same time, the goal is to help clients develop realistic expectations about relationships. As with heterosexual couples, they need to expect differences, conflicts, and tensions, perhaps more in some areas of their relationship than in others. In other words, they need to learn to agree to disagree, to experience anger and conflict while staying connected.

Separation versus Connection

Feminist psychologists have made us aware of the male, heterosexist bias that values separation over connectedness. With females, who are socialized to be empathic and nurturing with permeable ego boundaries, an intimate same-gender relationship may appear to be enmeshed. Fused or merged relationships, where there are unclear boundaries between the partners and no sense of self apart from the relationship, are pathologized in psychological theory, and many clinicians have consciously or unconsciously applied heterosexist criteria to lesbian relationships. Obviously merger exists at the beginning of any couple relationship—one idealizes the partner, avoids disagreements or conflicts, and feels bereft away from the relationship. But, over time in any couple relationship, individuation to some degree becomes essential and the goal for couples is to find ways at different stages of the relationship to balance individuation and togetherness adaptively. Slater and Mencher (1991) suggest that lesbian couples use fusion to strengthen their boundaries and to challenge the culture's claim that they're not valid families. This is in line with the relational models of women's development postulated by the Stone Center (Miller, 1976).

Although therapists can certainly help couples with this balance, they need to remember that merger is only a problem when it is fixed and rigid. They can teach couples about appropriate interdependency and appropriate individuation, normalizing the ebbs and flows of distance regulation. As suggested by L. Brown and Zimmer (1986), therapists need to help couples see attempts to establish some boundaries or autonomy in the relationship as healthy, rather than as indications that the relationship is flawed or will fail.

Because males have been socialized to be aggressive, competitive, independent, and unemotional, developing and maintaining an emotionally intimate relationship is new territory for many gay couples. In the heterosexual world, women are the primary relationship caretakers, tending to the emotional work and communication required in intimate relationships. Collaboration is a major component of successful couple relationships, and males have not been taught to collaborate as easily as females. Thus, men in couple relationships with men have to work extra hard to relinquish their ingrained assumptions about rigidly stereotypical masculine roles and to develop the collaborative communication and negotiating skills required for relationship maintenance.

Until the past decade, the gay culture tended to be more centered around a singles life style than around couples. The AIDS epidemic has surely been one of the major influences on the visible shifting from singledom to couple relationships. Gay couples may experience their power struggles within the sexual arena of their relationship. Men are socialized to take an active, ready, willing, and able role in sex. If men expect this of themselves and/or their partners, this may lead to feelings of anxiety about sexual desire and performance. This anxiety may, in turn, lead to sexual performance problems that can perpetuate the feelings of insecurity with regard to masculinity. The power struggles that gay male partners act out sexually can lead to intense, competitive conflict (George & Behrendt, 1987). These sexual struggles mask underlying control and dependency struggles. Even those couples who seem to fare well with complementarity may find the balance of power shifting over time, and this can disrupt the homeostasis of the relationship and result in symptoms of distress. L. Brown and Zimmer (1986) suggest that clinicians explain these socialization and relationship dynamics to the gay couple experiencing these problems in order to help them to normalize and remove blame from their struggles.

Jealousy and envy may be manifestations of distance regulation problems. One partner may feel threatened by the other partner's earlier and current relationships with others of the same gender, always feeling the possibility of betrayal. Even heterosexual friendships may arouse a partner's jealousy and envy, rekindling the internalized homophobia, which can cause feelings of inadequacy and not belonging. Clinicians can help couples understand the nature and effects of jealousy and envy as natural feelings in intimate relationships that do not have to be acted on with controlling behaviors. Therapists can also help couples, via a family-of-origin genogram, to connect excessive jealousy and envy with experiences and fears of abandonment or engulfment in earlier significant relationships.

Stage Discrepancy

Homosexual couples may be at different stages in terms of their identity development and their experience with homosexual relationships. Clinicians can reframe the couple's conflicts as developmental discrepancy, which alleviates the blaming and guilt. There are times when the discrepancy is less disruptive because of the more experienced partner's patience and tolerance. In other cases, the more experienced partner may become impatient and frustrated at the partner's seeming "prolonged adolescence," and decide to look for a partner at a more similar stage of development. As noted by L. Brown and Zimmer (1986, p. 460), "a couple with the same chronological ages may have very different ages in gay life."

Social, Racial, and Ethnic Incompatibility

The heterosexual culture has always believed in homogamy, that is, the pairing of individuals with like characteristics. This norm has changed rather dramatically in the past two decades, and interclass, interracial, and interethnic pairings are quite common in the gay and lesbian communities. If the discrepancies and incompatibilities are not acknowledged and negotiated so as to be acceptable and tolerable to both partners, the conflicts around them may result in a breakup.

Clinicians can reframe these differences and incompatibilities positively, pointing out how differences can be enriching, rather than a source of shame. Genograms can elicit commonalities and the focus on values and interests can be strengthened. There are times, however, when an unconscious element in the choice of a partner from a different race or culture is a rebellious act, perhaps to punish the parents or as a gesture of defiance of the "establishment." If this is the case, careful exploration will enable the partners to process whether or not they can get beyond that.

> Jeff, 26, came from a Caucasian, arch-conservative family. He grew up listening to his father's homophobic and racist remarks. As the only child, he always felt a lot of pressure to be whom his parents wanted him to be. Outwardly, he complied. But when he entered college, he began to lead a secret double life as he began to acknowledge his homosexuality. In his junior year, he became involved in an intimate relationship with a Black student from another university. Although he came out to his parents a year after he graduated from college, he kept this relationship secret. Eventually, the secret became a wedge in the couple relationship and they sought treatment with the therapist who had worked with the family around Jeff's disclosure. After six sessions, Jeff was helped to realize that, while his original motivation was defiance against his father's racism, the relationship had grown to be mutually gratifying, and defiance was no longer the underlying motive. The work of the therapy proceeded on to helping Jeff find a way to introduce his partner to his father, expecting an onslaught of racial epithets. However, what actually happened is that the father, with a couple of years' struggle to adapt to his son's homosexuality, had shifted enough internally to be able to refrain from the expected overt attack when first introduced to his son's Black lover. His subsequent behavior was grudgingly accepting.

Sexuality

Obviously, males and females have been socialized differently with regard to sex. The heterosexual system is based on complementarity.

Typically, men sexualize intimate relationships and take the role of initiator, whereas females value the emotional components at least as highly if not more highly than the physical components. So, sexual desire and performance mean different things to males and females, and there is much diversity within each gender.

Some of the sexual issues that gay and lesbian couples encounter are similar to those of heterosexual couples with regards to frequency, discrepancies in partners' level of sexual desire, performance preferences, and monogamy. Again, the differences lie in the disapproving, oppressive social context for homosexual behaviors. Gay and lesbian clients are often caught in the heterosexist trap of gendered sexual practices, such as male dominance and female submission, and certain positions and routines. As clinicians encourage clients to broaden their views and enjoy more variety in their sexual practices, they can educate clients about the constrictions of stereotyped roles and practices. Clinicians who feel repulsed by certain sexual practices, such as anal penetration, fellatio, or cunnilingus, and by their own homoerotic images of their clients, will either avoid or have a difficult time helping clients to talk about their sexual relationship and devising behavioral and cognitive strategies (often adaptations of the Masters and Johnson [1970] techniques used with heterosexual couples) to improve gay and lesbian sexual functioning. Desensitization to their aversions can come about with introspection, reading, and viewing videotapes, as well as by having open dialogue with colleagues and supervisors. These same techniques can be used with clients.

> Mary Beth, 33, and Dottie, 31, had been together for 2 years. Mary Beth was further along in her lesbian development, engaging and outgoing, and quite active in the lesbian community. She was always on the go, and was not as interested in genital sex as Dottie, who was more introverted and self-contained. The power struggle around sex was that, while Dottie wanted more genital sex and Mary Beth preferred cuddling, Dottie insisted on sleeping in her own bed in a separate room and Mary Beth felt rejected and abandoned. So Mary Beth would become more involved in her social activities, and Dottie would sulk and remain closeted in her room. This couple did not have very effective communication skills, and it was a surprise to Dottie to learn in therapy that Mary Beth was anorgasmic and, furthermore, that she had been sexually abused by an older male cousin when she was 5 years old. Although this particular relationship did not survive, the couple work, focusing on the development of empathic, responsive listening skills and psychoeducation about female sexuality, enabled each partner to develop more self-awareness about relationships and sexuality, which resulted in positive future relationships.

With regard to monogamy, clinicians can explore nonjudgmentally with each partner in joint sessions the meaning and expectations of monogamy and infidelity. The goal is to facilitate the couple's negotiation of an agreement that is acceptable to both partners, rather than a win–lose situation. The AIDS epidemic has heightened concern about exogamous casual sex, and it is important that both partners talk about the risks and agree to safe sex rules. This is particularly important for gay couples, given that the incidence of AIDS is so high in that group. Lesbians are less likely to be exposed to the transmission of AIDS unless they are intravenous drug users or engage in sexual relations with men or lesbian partners who are sexually involved with men.

A situation that often arises with gay and lesbian couples is the matter of current relationships with former lovers. While many gays and in particular lesbians seem to maintain close platonic relationships with former lovers, that is by no means always the case. So, again, we can help clients to explore the meaning of past relationships, to consider the context of the gay or lesbian community, as well as the different gender socialization influences concerning relationship development and maintenance. In small communities, everyone seems to cross paths and maintaining friendly relations is a positive attribute, rather than the kind of bitter cutoffs we see resulting from adversarial heterosexual divorces.

As with heterosexual singles and couples, in today's world it is ethically imperative that clinicians address the issue of safe sex directly with all sexually active clients. It is rare today to find a gay male who has not been personally touched by the AIDS epidemic, and, although AIDS is by no means a gay disease, its prevalence in the gay community necessitates heightened awareness and careful attention to this issue. Oral sex and anonymous encounters are strongly discouraged today by the gay and lesbian communities. Health clinics distribute condoms and spermicidal jellies as well as other safety measures.

Impact of AIDS

Although it is beyond the scope of this chapter to deal substantively with the impact of HIV-related illnesses and AIDS, it is important for clinicians to consider carefully the terrifying impact of this epidemic on gay men's self-concepts, life style choices, and coming-out processes. The particular effect on couple relationships is paradoxical: On the one hand, particularly if one has already lost significant others to the epidemic, there is resistance to forming an attachment and fearing another eventual loss; on the other hand, there is an even deeper yearning for the security and safety of a dependable close relationship.

The AIDS epidemic has elicited courageous nurturing and caretaking from both the gay and lesbian communities. But for males, who do not easily or readily assume the emotional and physical caretaking role, this development has been particularly remarkable. Kaupman (1992, cited in Henry, 1992) writes, "AIDS has broken the playboy stereotype and exposed our humanity to the rest of the world, and that has allowed us to touch it better ourselves. We have been seen as more serious people, and we have become more serious people" (p. 35).

Clinicians need to help each partner work through the process of grieving past losses, openly discuss their fears and concerns with each other, and deal responsibly with their own health status. If one of the partners falls anywhere on the continuum from being HIV positive to full-blown AIDS, the couple needs help with their sense of stigma and isolation, with working their way through the experimental options within the medical system, and with quality-of-life decisions. Encouraging clients to join support groups and to become politically involved with AIDS organizations are two strategies that can improve the couple's self-esteem and feeling of being more in control of their lives.

Dworkin and Pincu (1993) poignantly describe the effects on mental health caregivers of working with AIDS patients. They talk about how easy it is for these caregivers to become overwhelmed by feelings of anger, despair, and hopelessness, and to distance themselves from their clients as a defense against pain and loss and to avoid losing their objectivity. These writers stress the importance of follow-through by the clinician, so that the clinician can not only provide support to the patient in his or her terminal phase, but also be available (either continuously or intermittently) to the partner and family. Attending wakes and funerals, participating in AIDS organizations, and joining peer support groups are important ways for clinicians to deal with their own feelings about death and dying and to restore their own depleted energies.

Parenting Decisions

While lesbian and gay culture has not traditionally been child centered, gay and lesbian couples are increasingly choosing to parent the offspring of one or both partners from a previous marriage or to bring a new child into their family. Several of the gay and lesbian couples I interviewed reported that one of the partners was clear he or she would want children and that this was an important consideration in selecting a partner. Others did not consider the issue until after the relationship had been established.

If the children are from a partner's previous marriage, the bio-logical parent must work with the partner to decide that partner's role in parenting and to deal with a coparenting relationship (or lack thereof) with the former spouse. Given the realistic worry about legal custo-dy, the gay or lesbian couple has to agree on their degree of openness with the children and former spouse, as well as their roles, authority, and responsibilities. One of the biggest stressors for these couples is the lack of legitimacy, the stigma, and the societal disapproval for their family system. This costs them the social and legal supports normally available to reconstituted heterosexual families. Support groups, bib-liotherapy, and parent effectiveness training are important resources clinicians can provide. If clinicians understand the unique problems for the partners as a couple, they can normalize the difficulties that these couples will experience. They can help the couple plan how to introduce the parent's partner to the children, and what to tell the chil-dren, the other biological parent, extended family, neighbors, and the teachers at school.

In my clinical experience, I have found that prolonged secrecy can result in couple and family distress. Several of my interviewees report that a previous couple relationship ended as a result of this secrecy. However, I do not think clinicians should add stress to the couple sys-tem by pressuring the partners to disclose to their children. Rather, clinicians can help the partners to understand their fears, help them to find supportive legal resources if they are concerned about custo-dy, and provide supportive as well as pragmatic guidance. They can help the parents to understand that their children may not only feel different from their parent's gay or lesbian sexual orientation, but differ-ent from their peers in heterosexual families. These feelings of differ-ence can lead to youngsters' isolation and, if secrecy within the family prevails, the children do not have any safe haven where they can seek support.

If the gay or lesbian couple is having difficulty deciding whether or not to have a child, if one partner wants one and the other is un-sure, clinicians can help couples to consider carefully their priorities and possible consequences for the relationship in the short and long term. How will the couple cope with disagreements—about parent-ing, homophobia, relationship and family-of-origin issues? How would they raise a child of the opposite gender? Does a child need a parent of the opposite gender? If so, why? What will happen if the couple splits up? or moves? Frank discussions about emotional and financial resources as well as the realities and stresses of parenthood are essen-tial. If the couple decides not to have a child, clinicians can help them to grieve that loss.

Brenda, 36, and Alice, 49, entered therapy due to their conflict about having a child. They have been together 4 years. When their relationship began, Alice had just relocated from the Deep South to an east coast metropolitan area. She had difficulty finding a job comparable to the one she left, due to the economic recession. Brenda was a tenured secondary school teacher, teaching at the same high school she had attended. Brenda had a network of family and long-term friends in which Alice was generously included. At the start of their relationship, Brenda was clear that she wanted to have a child by artificial insemination with an unknown donor. Alice was agreeable, but she wanted to wait until she found a permanent job and felt more settled in. It took 2 years to find that job and, by that time, Brenda was insisting on beginning her artificial insemination attempts. She rightfully was concerned about her fertility chances with increasing age. After the first two unsuccessful insemination attempts (which were very costly and paid for by Brenda's family), Alice began to realize that she didn't want to coparent with Brenda, that the baby would be Brenda's, and that she would always feel like a "fifth wheel." Brenda was outraged by what she perceived as betrayal, and the couple was in crisis. Sensitive attention to the underlying power imbalance—Alice feeling that parenting was a higher priority than the couple relationship for Brenda, and Brenda feeling that Alice was not appreciative enough for all that Brenda and her family had provided—the therapist was able to help them to be clearer about their needs and expectations and to value and build on the strengths, rather than focusing on the problems, of their relationship. Eventually, Brenda did have a baby, and at this writing, Alice is attempting legal adoption, the precedent for which had recently been established in her state.

Gay and lesbian couples who want to have a child within their couple relationship need to plan and make decisions. Clinicians can help them collect the information necessary to decision making, such as possibilities for foster parenting, adoption, artificial insemination from a known or unknown donor (frozen sperm may be better for testing HIV), heterosexual intercourse with a selected person for the sole purpose of insemination, or surrogate parenting. They need legal information about partners' rights and disenfranchisements, about effective strategies for achieving their goal.

There are many obstacles to adoption for homosexual parents. Every lesbian and gay couple I interviewed kept their sexual orientation secret from the adoption system. One gay man was also able to keep his positive HIV status secret. Transracial and special needs adoptions have been the most available to single parents or interracial couples.

Lesbian couples have the option of artificial insemination or sex with a chosen person for the purpose of insemination. These couples may require help and support not only in their decision making but in the implementation of their decisions. For example, they may not be afforded the same opportunities for health care coverage and parental leave as married women. The more exploration and discussion that can occur prior to implementation, the higher the likelihood of success for the couple relationship. In her groundbreaking handbook on lesbian and gay parenting, April Martin (1993), a clinical psychologist, describes her and her partner's simultaneous pregnancies and parenting experiences as she provides important advice and suggestions to prospective gay and lesbian parents. There is much creativity and variety in the ways gay and lesbian couples have managed to become parents and experience the frustrations and gratifications of parenthood.

In the past, lesbian women have often chosen gay friends for the role of biological father, whether it be via artificial insemination or sexual intercourse. However, due to the AIDS epidemic, this option can be problematic as many gay men are HIV positive or not ready to be tested (Pies, 1989). The role of the biological donor, whether known or unknown, needs to be thought about in advance, particularly in the current judicial climate of valuing biological parenthood, no matter what the circumstances, over other forms of parenthood. And the couple cannot begin too early to think about what, when, and how they will eventually tell the child about his or her origins.

Recently, I have heard of sets of gay and lesbian couples agreeing to share a biological child of one of the gay members and one of the lesbian members of the foursome. While the division of labor and economic support must be agreed upon among the four parents, a child can experience loving parenting from four, rather than the usual two, parents. Another innovative proposal from one lesbian couple was utilizing sperm from a close gay friend and the egg of one lesbian partner with the other lesbian partner, carrying the baby. In coming years, there will be many innovative arrangements and only time and experience will indicate the pros and cons of particular configurations of family.

Gay parents who wish to have a biological child have many factors to consider when seeking and selecting a surrogate mother. The clinician can provide an invaluable service by arranging for medical and psychological assessment (interviewing and testing) to ensure a healthy selection. Interpretation and discussion of the results of assessment interventions enable the prospective gay parents to make informed choices. I find it a good idea to have any psychological assessment conducted by another clinician so that findings are not contaminated by my relationship with the couple.

Gay and lesbian couples who choose to parent need to think about creating legal documents to ensure that, if one dies, the other will be given custody. Pies (1989) notes that some are creating legal agreements that dictate arrangements for the children in the event of separation. A. Coleman (1993) advocates naming the partner as an agent in domestic partner affidavits, health care proxies, living wills, powers of attorney, wills, and trusts. Martin (1993) has several examples of such legal documents in the appendices of her handbook.

Clinicians can be invaluable resources for steering couples to support groups and community resources. They can help couples to obtain emotional support from family and friends in the straight, gay, and lesbian communities. Most of their children will be attending schools that are predominantly heterosexual even if the gay or lesbian family lives in a gay or lesbian enclave. Separatism can be more harmful to these children than preparatory experiences with the mainstream culture.

GAY AND LESBIAN FAMILIES

Although the research (E. D. Gibbs, 1988; P. J. Falk, 1989; Hand, 1991; Laird, 1993a; Loulan, 1986; Martin, 1993) does not indicate much difference between heterosexual and homosexual parents in parenting styles and concerns, there may be some differences in terms of motivation to parent. Gay and lesbian parents have had to overcome enormous obstacles to become primary parents, and this may result in their "trying harder" and being more child centered than many heterosexual parents. Gay and lesbian families are always facing the question of their viability, and this can lead to unrealistic expectations of themselves as parents in their desire to prove to the world that they are competent.

In addition to the typical concerns that all families bring to family therapy, the issues of gay and lesbian families include degree and timing of disclosure about their homosexuality; concern about the effects of homophobia (and possible violence) on the children; societal bias against males, much less gay males, as primary parents; lack of support from their own community as well as from mainstream society; lassitude about limit setting and discipline, sort of an unconscious way to "make up" for imposing this vulnerability on their children; and concerns about providing opposite-gender role models for their children.

Within family sessions, clinicians can ferret out by direct and circular questioning what kinds of secrets and mixed messages may be contributing to the problems. I also suggest conducting a kind of ecogram, which will map out all the resources available for support—from the family of origin, the school system, the community in which they live, their work setting, the gay and lesbian communities, neighbors, friends, the medical system, the legal system, religion, and so forth.

Gay and lesbian parents are particularly concerned about the unique problems their children may encounter, such as the responses from the society at large and their peers and teachers in particular. Clinicians need to ascertain how free the children are to express directly negative feelings toward one or both parents without the parents always experiencing it within the framework of homophobia. Psychoeducation about child and adolescent development can be useful. A major topic for the family therapy is if or how the children can disclose their parents' sexual orientation to their friends. Role plays and preparation for a wide variety of consequences can be helpful, but most important of all will be supportive parents. The therapist can nurture the parents' capacities to be supportive by both modeling and assigning tasks, such as special time together between parent and child as a reward for the child's complying with the household rules.

It seems to me, as a clinician, that the level of security the parents have achieved with their sexual identity and their parenting role and how much they are able to utilize available support systems are the principal determinants for creating a supportive home environment for the children. One of my major objectives is to help the parents improve their self-esteem and self-confidence and become more aware of the availability of resources. Family therapy sessions can also be a good place for members to ventilate their feelings, share their thinking, and learn to communicate with each other more directly so that there can be effective decision making and problem solving.

To those ends, I find family projects to be effective action strategies, such as creating a family drawing, role playing, creating genograms of the parents with the children present so that the children can learn more about their parents, and doing psychodrama and family sculpture.

With interracial and interfaith families, it is important for therapists to encourage the family to learn about their different heritages and to incorporate these learnings into their family culture. Being cut off from a significant aspect of one's heritage can impair identity development. To avoid such cut-off, clinicians can expose clients to a multicultural perspective, utilizing rituals (see Imber-Black, Roberts, & Whiting, 1988), genograms, and co-construction of family history narratives.

Henry, 34, and Jack, 29, adopted a 3-month-old Central American boy 5 years ago. While Henry and Jack live in a rural community where they are accepted as a family (although no one ever acknowledges their homosexuality), their son, Enos, is the only non-Caucasian in the community. This poses problems for him, in that the other kids ask him why he looks different. At the therapist's suggestion, Henry and Jack have traveled to the nearest city (125 miles away) at least one weekend per month to socialize with other interracial families, to attend spiritual services in a church that caters predominantly to Hispanic families, and to allow Enos to attend the religious school of this particular church as often as possible. They are attempting to develop cultural pride in their young son, and they are now receiving improved reports from the kindergarten teacher about Enos's social development.

Because the formation of gay and lesbian families with their own children (as opposed to those brought into the family from a previous marriage) is relatively recent, there are no studies about what kinds of clinical issues may present when the children reach adolescence, a stage fraught with vulnerability under any circumstances. Because these adolescents will have a history of coping with differentness, they may not develop problems that are any different from adolescents raised in heterosexual families. In fact, we could speculate that their degree of resilience, tolerance of and sensitivity to differentness, and effective coping strategies may even be better developed.

ECOLOGICAL PERSPECTIVE

An essential component of clinical work with gay and lesbian families (as with other variant normative family structures) is acknowledgment and recognition of the influence of the environment on social, physical, and psychological well-being. Thus, in addition to identifying resources within the gay and lesbian communities, it is incumbent upon clinicians to advocate with school, health, work, and other community systems.

Hal, 16, was referred by his high school guidance counselor for individual therapy due to academic failure, class cutting, and increased disruptive behavior when he did attend class. Prior to this time, Hal had been an average student. He refused to talk to his counselor at school, and his single mother reported that he was difficult to manage at home. After three individual sessions, in which Hal stubbornly answered any questions with monosyllables, he passed the therapist a written note that said, "She's a lesbian." The burden of secrecy and his mother's recent violent breakup with a partner (to whom Hal was quite attached) were the precipitating events of Hal's sudden depression. In addition to mother–son sessions, the clinician went to school with Hal and ascertained that he needed some special help in order to pass the year. The counselor and outside clinician worked hard to get Hal into a community group of youngsters with gay or lesbian parents and arranged for a scholarship at a work–study camp. The major theme was helping Hal come to terms with his own homophobia and guilt. Without the teamwork of helpers in different systems, and an understanding of the interdependence of Hal and all of his surrounding systems, Hal would have been labeled and treated as an individual "client" with "oppositional disorder."

The ecological perspective allowed the clinician to find a better fit between Hal and his environment—school, camp, and family. The group work enabled Hal to understand homosexuality and to feel less threatened by and more tolerant of his mother's sexual orientation. A major thrust was to improve Hal's peer relations and when he was matter of factly able to mention to his best friend the following year that his mother had "a new girlfriend," the high school counselor hastened to phone the outside clinician, delighted with this validation of their collaborative efforts.

Other issues that clinicians need to consider when working with gay and lesbian families include the reality of antigay violence; the distinction between religiosity and spirituality, particularly when so many feel rejected by the homophobic religions in which they were raised; the impact of substance abuse and current and past sexual abuse; domestic violence; infertility; occupational and career issues; access to health care; and the impact of aging (Browning et al., 1991; Shannon & Woods, 1991).

*   *   *

The attitudes and validating, supportive style of the therapist are more important components of effective treatment than any particular technique or strategy. The major job for therapists is to become familiar with their own ingrained assumptions and biases. The next step is for therapists to take active steps to familiarize themselves with the special concerns of the gay and lesbian population while respecting intragroup differences. It is then important for therapists to keep abreast of political, social, scientific, and clinical developments as well as changing and increasing resources.

By so doing, therapists will be better able to become aware of and monitor their own countertransference reactions. The therapist can use her- or himself as an effective vehicle for change. Although we all learn enormously from our clients, remember, it is not the responsibility of clients to educate their therapists. Rather, it is the therapists' responsibility to take the initiative for continued self-awareness and learning.

EIGHT

About Multiraciality: The Participants in Context

In a report released in 1994 ("Interracial Marriages Increase," 1994), the U.S. Bureau of the Census reported that the number of interracial couples in America nearly doubled in the past 12 years and now more than one out of every 50 marriages crosses the boundaries of race. These figures do not even include the large number of families who have become multiracial due to adoption, nor the 1.2 million marriages between Latinos and other ethnic groups.

This interracial marriage trend is rather astounding, given that the United States is one of the most race conscious countries in the world. "Other countries in Europe and the Middle East as well as Central America, South America, and Africa (with the notable exception of South Africa) have never been as race conscious as is the United States" (P. Brown, 1989–1990, p. 27). What does it mean to and for the men and women who choose to cross racial boundaries in an environment with strong taboos against such choices? What does this trend say or not say about the sociocultural changes of the past couple of decades? What do mental health professionals of all races need to understand about such marriages, and the families they create, in order to provide effective help? These are some of the questions we will consider.

Historically, the term "interracial" refers to partners of different racial backgrounds. These partners may also be interfaith and interethnic, due to "differences in ethnic ancestry, customs, and culture" (P. Brown, 1989–1990, p. 26). The children of these partners are known as "biracial" or "multiracial." For the purposes of this text, I will use the terms "biracial" and "multiracial" interchangeably, because as pointed out by Root (1993, 1994), a significant proportion of the American population is indeed of mixed race—about 24% of European Americans have African American ancestry and 75% of African

Americans have White ancestry (Solsberry, 1994). Thus, our monoracial labels, even of people of color, have no scientific validation, because throughout American history, there have been incidents of miscegenation.

In this country, Black–White intermarriages, while comprising the lowest rate among intermarriages (McLemore, 1991; Solsberry, 1994; Tucker & Mitchell-Kernan, 1990), seem to elicit the most racist responses from others, both Black and White. Latinos, Middle Easterners, Asians, and Native Americans do not experience anywhere near the same degree or intensity of racism as do Blacks. Racism has even impacted the practice of transracial adoption, which will be discussed later in this chapter. Mental health professionals need to understand the historical and current impacts of racism on the development and psychological functioning of all Americans, White and of color, in order to provide accurate assessment and intervention for clients of color. They also need to become aware of their own covert and overt racism, conscious and unconscious.

Like gays and lesbians, most interracial couples and multiracial families choose to reside in specific geographical areas, particularly urban areas in the West, Midwest, and Northeast, where they do not "stand out," where they can blend into a multicultural population. They know that their skin color always calls attention to their "differentness." Yet, in the White world, they feel that they have no recognition, as they are neither White nor Black. Certainly they are invisible with regard to official acknowledgment. There has been little attention paid to the unique status and needs of interracial couples and families who are "other," who do not fit into any one category. Consider, for example, that on most official forms, there is no place to check off "multiracial." The five typical category choices are Black, Caucasian, Asian American, Native American, and other. This is an example of institutional racism, how our society denies the existence of multiraciality, lumping people with any amount of color into a specific category of color. It is also an example of how we classify and define people by race, even though there does not seem to be scientific evidence for this definition and classification. And, the term "Black" lumps all Blacks together, failing to distinguish between African Americans, Caribbean peoples, and Africans. Each of these groups has a different heritage and racial identity. Blacks from the West Indies, for example, do not have the same slavery and migration heritage of African Americans. They are currently the dominant culture on their islands, even though most islands were colonized at some point in their history. Other Caribbean Blacks did originally come from West Africa, having been sold as slaves to work on sugar cane plantations. Over the years, due to intermarriage with Indians and Spaniards, they have become much more mixed than their American counterparts, a rainbow racial composition. As Comas-Díaz (1996) points out, in the Caribbean, one drop of White makes you not Black, whereas in the United States, one drop of Black makes you not White. Social class is more important than skin color in the Caribbean.

A purpose of this chapter is to provide a historical context of race relations in this country, to explore the impact of racism today on both the dominant White culture and people of color, to review the scientific controversies about race, to discuss the reasons for intermarriage and transracial adoption, and to present the predominant issues regarding couple relationships, their families of origin, and interracial parenting.

In Chapter 9, multiracial identity development across the life span will be presented through the voices of interviewees. Chapter 10 will discuss the treatment implications for therapists working with multiracial individuals and families, highlighting the effects of gender, race, and class on the therapeutic relationship.

Most of the existing literature on multiracial families focuses on interracial marriage, particularly Black–White partnerships. Other interracial relationships—such as Asian–American; Native American–Black, –Latino, or –White; and Latino–White or other races—are just beginning to be studied. In addition to the increase of interracial marriages since World War II, when many Black American soldiers came home with foreign brides, there has been a steady increase in all kinds of international and domestic intercultural marriages. This is attributed to the increased mobility of people and the weakening of the boundaries that in the past, limited opportunities for out-of-race marriage. And in the past 20 years, as adoption has become more difficult within this country, there has been a surge of transracial adoption. The emerging literature in these areas will be incorporated into our discussion.

Because the focus in this section is on multiracial couples and families, let's consider the prevalent myths of Whites that abound about Black–White intermarriage, family, and adoption. These myths are examples of cultural racism, which will be discussed later in the chapter. Certainly, one can find examples of people who fit the myths; what makes these myths examples of cultural racism is overgeneralization, leading to assumptions that the myths apply to *all* members of each race.

Myth: Blacks believe that interracial marriages will grant them a higher social and economic status.

Fact: Marrying up for monoracial and interracial couples depends more on class and educational and occupational status than on race.

Myth: Black women seek White men who can offer them social mobility.

Fact: There is no evidence that Black women seek interracial marriage to achieve upward social mobility.

Myth: Lower-class White women marry rich Black men in order to gain economic status.

Fact: The effects of racism on interracial couples are stronger than economic benefits, so if lower-class White women want to gain economic status, they would be better off marrying rich White men.

Myth: Intermarriage occurs due to sexual curiosity about people of a different race.

Fact: Racialized masculinity or femininity concepts may fuel attractions but these do not necessarily develop into significant, long-term relationships.

Myth: Black men always lust after White women.

Fact: There are as many intragroup as intergroup proclivities regarding objects of sexual attraction.

Myth: Black women are free sexual beings who would have sexual relations with anybody.

Fact: There is no evidence whatsoever that Black women or Black men are more sexually active or promiscuous than any other group of people.

Myth: White women marry Black men because they are fascinated with their notion of Black men's sexual, animalistic prowess.

Fact: People typically select marital partners who are perceived to conform to the internal models developed during childhood and adolescence; these models are based on early experiences and desires and may require adaptation or result in disappointment when the discrepancy between the fantasy and reality becomes apparent.

Myth: White men marry Black women for sexual relationships.

Fact: Many people marry for sexual relationships regardless of race.

Myth: Blacks and Whites who marry interracially are rebelling against their families and mainstream American values and standards.

Fact: Many people marry interracially because they believe that intermarriage represents true American values of cultural diversity and tolerance.

Myth: White women who marry interracially suffer from an "oppositional defiance disorder."

Fact: American society has always valued nonconformity and individualism; there is no evidence that White women in interracial marriages have a higher incidence of mental disorder.

Myth: Black men choose to date and marry interracially out of revenge against White men.

Fact: People of all races marry for similar reasons: love, companionship, emotional or economic security, procreation, and so forth.

Myth: Biracial children will suffer from their parents' selfish disregard of societal norms.

Fact: In today's multicultural society, biracial children tend to cherish their biculturalism and have no higher incidence of delinquency or disturbance than monoracial children.

Myth: People who adopt transracially must be pretty desperate.

Fact: Many people choose to adopt transracially because of their social values and desire to help less fortunate populations.

Myth: Transracial adoptees, having to contend with the stigmas of race and adoption, can't help but be disturbed.

Fact: There is some evidence that many transracial adoptees fare *better* than same-race adoptees due to American altruistic values.

In these chapters, we will see how these myths perpetuate and are perpetuated by cultural racism. Cultural racism, based on the belief that the dominant White cultural heritage and value systems are superior to any other, impacts the mental health of both the dominant and nondominant groups.

THE PARTICIPANTS

The participants to be described in this chapter fall into three groups: multiracial/biracial couples, multiracial/biracial couples with children, and families with transracial adoptees. Although there is much diversity within and among these groups, these families all share, to some degree, the effects of persistent, systemic, overt, and subtle oppression. This oppression exists for any minority membership within a dominant White culture. People of color differ from the homosexual population in that they cannot hide, due to the evidence of their skin color and physical features. The only way they can attain invisibility is by blending into multiracial neighborhoods.

Of the 22 biracial couples interviewed, 10 were Black–White, 3 were Asian–American, 3 were Native American–Black, 3 were Latino–White, and 3 were Native American–Asian. The Blacks were all African Americans, although many families with Caribbean Blacks offered to be interviewed. Because the history of Blacks in the Caribbean differs dramatically from those in the United States, effort was made to limit the interviews to African American Blacks. In 12 of the biracial situations, 16 members of various families of origin were also interviewed. Fourteen offspring of biracial couples were interviewed, 9 individually and 5 in family interviews. Nine families whose siblings or offspring participated in transracial adoption were also interviewed. The 16 transracial adoptive families interviewed consisted of 5 domestic White–Black families, and 11 international adoptions comprised of 6 White–Asian families, and 5 White–Latino families.

Herb, 42, is an African American college professor who is married to Yvette, 39, a White social worker. They met in Paris on summer break between college years, and, discovering that they were attending colleges in the same city, continued to date when they returned to the States. After 4 years of dating, they married. Currently, they live in a small midwestern college town, have two biological teenage children and one adopted, elementary-school-age African American child. They both work for the college, and, except for trips to visit each family, they claim to feel pretty isolated from racism. They talk about their children's experiences, but do not think the children feel any loyalty conflict or identity confusion.

Tom, 14, is the oldest biracial child of Herb and Yvette. In an individual interview, he confessed to conflicting emotions: (1) feeling "special because he can be the best of two different races," and (2) feeling uncomfortable as one of only two Black males in his regional high school. He wants to protect both of his parents from his confusion, so he puts a lot of effort into appearing to be confident and "well adjusted." He doesn't let them know about his discomfort, and he doesn't tell when he thinks he's being treated unfairly because of his skin color. They have no idea, for instance, that he resents not having any Black teachers. Or that he resents everyone thinking he knows everything there is to know about racial issues when race does come up in class. But, he confides that he is looking forward to attending a large university where he can learn more openly about his African American heritage.

Paul, 59, and Sarah, 57, are the White parents of Diane, 33, who married Hubert, a 34-year-old African American. At first, they were frightened for Diane, fearing for her safety and her unborn children. They tried to dissuade her from this marriage. However, with time, they became truly fond of Hubert and by the time their first granddaughter was born, they were totally accepting. They say that nothing could make them reject their daughter. They acknowledge the shock and disappointment they felt at first, but they worked hard together to learn to be more "open-minded." Interestingly, Paul and Sarah now report that their marriage improved as a result of sharing their concerns about their daughter's intermarriage and being determined to keep their family intact.

Norman, 24, is the biracial son of a White mother and African American father. He is light skinned and, until he went away to college, he never thought much about race as being an issue. He was shocked when he went to college to find that the African American students rejected him, thinking that he was not Black enough. He hung around mostly with Asian Americans, Latinos and other non-Caucasian kids. In his junior year, he became especially interested in African American studies, and he felt confident enough to force himself into the Black student associations, despite the members' cool reception. He is somewhat bitter with his parents for not having prepared him for these racial conflicts. He is also confused about his loyalties. This is because he has always felt closer to his mother than to his father. He is afraid that he will have to "reject" her because of her skin color.

The Thompsons, both Caucasian, adopted a Vietnamese infant daughter after struggling several years with infertility. Throughout her elementary school years, they made a concerted effort to attend meetings of transracial adoptive families and to eat and shop in Asian sections of New York City. Their daughter, Noni, now 11, has never been particularly interested in her heritage and finds her different appearance an attraction to other children. She resists discussions pertaining to her race and ethnicity. The Thompsons hope that she becomes more interested in and aware of her racial heritage when she enters the more racially mixed senior high school. They find it rather ironic that they are so eager to talk to Noni about her adoption and heritage and she's the one who doesn't want to talk about it. But they've been reassured by friends that she will, on her own timetable, be open to these discussions.

Before we discuss the participants' experiences with personal, institutional, and cultural racism, we will review the historical and political background of race relations in this country. We need to gain some contextual understanding of the historical and current realities people of color face in our society so that we neither minimize nor maximize the effects of the realities of racism on all members of our society.

HISTORICAL/POLITICAL BACKGROUND

Throughout early American history, there was racial mixing in terms of sexual connection, most often between White males and Black female slaves (A. Gordon, 1964). Interestingly, Williams (1972) notes that, prior to 1691, "slaves in the colonies were free to consort with whites and intermarry with them. A study of the slavery laws following this date suggests that the concern for intermarriage was a practical and economic one. The proliferation of mulattos from the liaison of black women and white men served as a serious threat to the one means of accounting for the slave population-visibility!" (p. 77). It was in 1691 that the Maryland General Assembly passed a law requiring a free-born White female servant who married a slave to serve her husband's master throughout her slave husband's life. This law also stated that children of this union would be regarded as slaves. This ensured that the slave population would grow, which would enhance the power of White slave owners. Before 1850, mulattos were viewed as neither Black nor White, but as a third class (Williamson, 1980).

The year 1691 also spawned the Virginia Act, which termed interracial marriage an "abomination" and forbade its occurrence. In 1705, the Commonwealth of Massachusetts passed legislation that provided a heavy fine and servitude for any White who married a Negro/Black. This act also fined clergy who officiated at interracial marriages. Similar legislation was passed in North Carolina (1715), Delaware (1721), and Pennsylvania (1780). Penalties could include fines as high as $10,000 and imprisonment.

These laws were based on, as well as being the source of, ignorance and fear. Economically, however, they served to help the dominant White culture to maintain and justify the practice of slavery by depicting Black people as "savage," "dirty," "animalistic," and "less than human." The idea of the "three-fifths" compromise was incorporated into the United States Constitution as a binding way to define Blacks as less than Whites. (Three-fifths meant that Black people were counted as three-fifths of a White person, giving southern states more political clout in the Congress, by allowing them to count each slave as three-fifths of a person.) It's important to realize that in the 19th century, American White society was struggling to reconcile the practice of slavery with more enlightened philosophies about human nature and equality. Viewing Blacks as inferior allowed Whites to deny them the equal rights guaranteed to Whites in the Constitution. Because this country was founded on democratic principles, the dissonance between slavery practices and democracy served to intensify defensive maneuvering on the part of many leaders.

Even after slavery was abolished in 1863, the Jim Crow laws continued to maintain social, cultural, and economic separation between Blacks and Whites (P. Brown, 1989–1990). Miscegenation laws forbade marriage or cohabitation between Blacks and Whites and were strongly enforced. Multiracial offspring of interracial unions were considered Black, according to the prevalent "one drop theory," whereby an individual with just one drop of Black blood was considered legally to be Black and subject to these laws. Note that this "one drop theory" never applied to other races; Asian Americans were never considered Asian because of one drop of Asian blood.

This deeply ingrained racist oppression continued into the 20th century. The Virginia Racial Integrity Law of 1924, for example, required all individuals with any non-Caucasian ancestry to register with the state. This was required in order to prevent further interracial marriages. If, for example, there was any doubt about the ancestry of either partner, the town clerk had the discretion to deny a marriage license. Even if an American married interracially in a foreign country, that marriage was not recognized in Virginia. Interracial couples who resided in North Carolina, Delaware, Maryland, Mississippi, Montana, Tennessee, Texas, or Virginia could be prosecuted if they returned to their residence after having married interracially in a state that allowed such marriages. Most of the laws prohibiting interracial marriage also prohibited sexual intercourse, cohabitation, and concubinage between the races. Although Massachusetts and Vermont were states legally allowing interracial marriage, if residents from states where intermarriage was illegal came to these states to evade their home state laws, their marriage would be voided in these two states as well.

These social and legislative factors served to preserve the notion of a pure White race. Many commentators today recognize that economic exploitation to prevent Blacks from gaining economic parity with Whites was more the rationale for these antimiscegenation laws than was an abhorrence of interracial sex. It is also interesting to note that, while the myth of racial purity for Whites pertained mainly to Black male and White female interrelationships, the relationships between White men and Black women went "unnoticed by law enforcers" (A. Brown, 1994, p. 21). Yet another explanation for why there was and continues to be so much hostility surrounding Black male–White female couples is given by Williams (1972):

> the sexualization of racism. . . . One of the most profoundly distorted and emotionally laden aspects of American racial mythology (including the concept of White supremacy) has to do with the "supersexuality" of the Black man. He is imagined to have endless virility, including an enormous phallus, and in addition, some woman-enslaving, mystical powers. A point, in fact, that can be found in the old superstition, which has its roots in the south, that states, "once a White woman mates with a Black man she will never again be satisfied with a White man." As this superstition suggests, that contact between the White woman and Black man has become hateful to the White man and can lead and has led to explosive confrontation between the White and the Black man. (p. 77)

The "explosiveness" described by Williams was often seen in the violent punishments of Black men caught with White women. These punishments ranged from imprisonment, enslavement, fines, murder through lynchings, and other grotesque, torturous cruelties such as cutting off toes and fingers, burning with hot irons, and cutting off Black men's penises.

Laws forbidding interracial marriages were found in 30 states and were still on the books 13 years after the 1954 decision in *Brown v. the Board of Education,* which ruled that separate education is inherently unequal. It was not until June 12, 1967, that the United States Supreme Court found miscegenation laws to be unconstitutional in the historical *Lovings v. Virginia* case.

Even though laws have been passed to legalize interracial marriages, multiracial families continue to experience individual, institutional, and cultural racism in many forms. We can see that the very concept of race has politically controversial overtones that can't help but impact all aspects of development and well-being for both people of color and the dominant White culture.

Migration

Prior to the 1950s, the Black community was intact, despite their marginal financial status. The majority of Blacks lived in rural southern communities based on an agrarian economy. World War II created enormous social change. Although segregated into separate troops, Black young men were nevertheless drafted, sent to military bases all over the country for basic training, and eventually deployed to both the European and Pacific fronts. While receiving special technical training, they also earned postwar training opportunities.

When these men returned home after the war, their aspirations had changed. A mass migration to northern cities ensued. Blacks sought higher wages, better education, and opportunities for themselves and their families. This mass migration, however, resulted in a fragmentation of the close-knit kinship system within the Black community. It also resulted in a breakdown of the Church and community support systems. It didn't take the Black migrants long to realize that racism persisted up north, even if it was less overt than in the South. Blacks were closed out of the economy, out of anything but the lowest levels of jobs and education.

Thus, the migration of the 1950s rarely resulted in economic improvement while leading to family disruption and community deterioration. Blacks began to express their anger and alienation as the impact of racism on their sense of worth and adequacy exploded into distrust, alienation, and a withdrawal from mainstream institutions.

The civil rights movement of the 1960s, while fighting for equality, also sought to restore power and pride to the Black communities. Today, although many Blacks have achieved success and made it out of the ghetto, there are continued problems between Blacks and Whites despite increased opportunities for social and economic mobility. A lesser problem is the increasing guilt, confusion, and misunderstanding between the Blacks who have succeeded in the dominant White world and those who have not. Migration led to the civil rights movement, which has opened the door for the increase in interracial marriage.

RACE AND RACISM

Race

Traditionally, race has been a scientific/biological classification system differentiating people by their physical characteristics—that is, skin color, facial features, and hair texture. Over the years, different behaviors, aptitudes, attitudes, interests, and values have been attributed to race. However, the reality is that there is a lack of empirical evidence for defining people by race. Today, scientists are beginning to reassess what the term "race" means. Increasingly, they are leaning toward the notion that race is a sociopolitical construction rather than a biological category. This means that racial behavioral differences are attributed more to centuries of differential experiences in a racist society than to genetically determined physical characteristics.

The definition of race has always been a very controversial subject with economic and political overtones. Racial tensions have always existed in many forms. Currently, the changing demographics in our population (where Whites are soon to be the minority) are challenging both the economic and political well-being as well as the values and traditions of the dominant White culture. Thus, race relations are being fueled by political manipulations based on fear and the determination to preserve the current hierarchical status of Whites. Racial tensions not only disrupt our society at its very core, but create high levels of psychological stress for all members of our society.

Racism and Prejudice

The term "racism" refers to a system of racial prejudice and discrimination used to the advantage of one race and the disadvantage of other races. It is based on the power and privilege of the advantaged race. Racist behaviors maintain the opportunities and privileges of the dominant group, while limiting and denying access to these same opportunities and privileges for nondominant groups. These racist and discriminative behaviors are supported by institutional power and authority, such as the laws we have just reviewed. "The critical element which differentiates racism from prejudice and discrimination is the use of institutional power and authority to support prejudices and enforce discriminatory behaviors in systematic ways with far-reaching outcomes and effects" (American Family Therapy Academy, 1993). J. H. Katz (1978) differentiates prejudice, a "preconceived judgment or opinion often based on limited information," from racism. She points out that prejudices are based on various cultural stereotypes, and, even when they have positive connotations (such as, "Blacks are the only truly gifted jazz musicians"), they deny a person's individuality. Prejudices are the faulty, overgeneralized attitudes and beliefs leading to the myths presented earlier. Racism, on the other hand, refers to patterns of behavior by people and institutions with power and privilege.

Interesting questions arise regarding racism and prejudice. Is intragroup discrimination racism or prejudice? I suggest that when Blacks who have attained status and power discriminate against members of their race who have not attained similar levels of status and power, it is prejudice based on class struggle, rather than racism. Likewise, when a group of Black youth attacks a White youth, it is based on prejudice, not power and status. When the group of Black youth attacks an Asian youth or gang, it is still not racism. If Blacks see Asians as having easier access to opportunities, it is not because the Asians have power, but because the dominant White culture allows Asians easier access than Blacks.

In reviewing the history of psychological theories of prejudice, Duckitt (1992) postulates that prejudice is caused by four processes: (1) universal psychological processes underlying an inherent human potential for prejudice; (2) socialized intergroup dynamics, that is, the conditions of intergroup contact and interaction that elaborate this inherent human potential into normative patterns of prejudice; (3) the social transmission of normative influences to individuals in the form of prejudiced attitudes; and (4) individual differences in susceptibility to prejudice. This integrative framework highlights the interactional causality of internal and external factors. It is useful in that it suggests foci for prevention and remediation, such as school and university curriculum reform, mental health diagnostic and treatment criteria reform, and diverse staff in schools and health and community agencies.

However, this well-accepted view is disputed by researchers such as Gaines and Reed (1995), who argue that racism is *not* a universal feature of human psychology, but rather a historically developed process. They assert that racism begins with the exploitation of people and with the psychological consequences to which that exploitation leads. In all areas of social science, views about race, racism, and prejudice are polarized between the social construction view and the inherent biological view.

Although it is not "politically correct" today to acknowledge, much less express, racist thoughts or views, Ponterotto and Pedersen (1993) alert us to the insidious dangers of "modern racism," the more ingrained, covert, subtle racist views underlying people's protestations. Many people who truly believe that they are not racist still manifest unconscious racist behaviors that they do not recognize as racist. An obvious example of modern racism is the belief that people of color have had enough special treatment with respect to affirmative action and that they no longer need special consideration. Modern racism exists in the training and practice of mental health practitioners. The training ignores the significance of racial identity on the psychological development and functioning of Whites and people of color, and cross-racial therapist–client dyads minimize or ignore racial issues. Less obvious examples include a clinical supervisor's differential treatment and standards for trainees of color, or a clinician's avoidance of sensitive material with Black male clients because of fear of the client's "rage."

Members of all races often share the same prejudices, but these prejudices emanate from the attitudes of the dominant White culture, which alone has the social and legal power necessary to reinforce and institutionalize these prejudices into racism. This point cannot be overemphasized. The dominant White male, patriarchal society has been born into power and privilege. A fraction of this power and privilege may be attained by others with perseverance, luck, and hard work. The dominant White male culture has had the automatic privilege to determine the rules, roles, and structures that have shaped the fabric of our society and livelihoods. This leads to what is known as the doctrine of White supremacism, an entitlement of Whites to privilege. Thus, Whiteness is the central norm of our society. All differences are measured against this central norm. This system of White advantage and privilege clearly operates to benefit the White race economically, politically, and socially, as indicated in our review of slavery and miscegenation laws. And, in order to maintain this power, the dominant White culture must perpetuate stereotypical images of people of color as lesser in all ways. These images allow Whites to justify their racism and keep minorities "in their place." The theories of psychology and psychotherapy are also based on patriarchal White norms. It is only in recent years that feminist and minority theorists have challenged the supremacy of these traditional theories and practices.

A recent example of this kind of racism is the controversial book *The Bell Curve* by Herrnstein and Murray (1994). These authors claim that Blacks' intelligence is genetically inferior to that of Whites. They narrowly define intelligence by White measures and norms and totally ignore the influences of historical and social contexts on personality development and psychological functioning. This is but one example of what D. W. Sue (1990) cites as the use of science to suppress minorities or demonstrate why minorities are inherently inferior. Research is still used to perpetuate or justify racism.

When minority members, raised and socialized in a dominant White culture, internalize the dominant racial and gender stereotypes (such as that White males are the most desirable, valued human beings and that White females are the most beautiful, pure, and desirable love objects), they develop their own cultural racism, just as homosexuals internalize cultural homophobia and, therefore, become homophobic. The effects of internalized racism are similar for people of color as are the effects of internalized homophobia on homosexuals. Their own internalized racism affects their self-identity, their racial identity, and their overall psychological development and functioning.

Mention must also be made of the transgenerational effects of racism on all family members. These are manifested in attitudes of despair, hopelessness, and negative expectations. For example, youngsters of color may not expect to have the same access to educational, health, or occupational benefits as White youngsters assume. Many reportedly ask themselves something like, "So what's the point of trying? One can make more money dealing drugs without going to school than many college graduates can earn." These are examples of *racial socialization*. As described by Carter (1995), racial socialization is the process by which personality development and psychological functioning are impacted by the messages one receives primarily from one's family of origin (but also from one's neighborhood, community, church, and school, as well as the media and other social system forces) about one's attributes, characteristics, and qualities and the opportunities or barriers associated with one's racial grouping. One's personality and psychological life are thus shaped by how one interprets and responds to these messages about one's racial group. And this racial socialization process explains the phenomenological differences within racial groups, for families convey varied messages and even members of the same family may perceive and interpret the same messages differently.

Until recently, there have been few role models for Black empowerment and Black definitions of success. Today, minority groups are making steady progress with their assertive demands for inclusion and equality. Likewise, multiracial groups are coalescing in order to demand their own recognition as distinct from White or Black groups. Multiracial people do not want to be another category of classification. They want to be considered "American" just as do other groups. Many consider the classification by race as artificial.

Impact of Racism on Whites

Few writers until now (see Carter, 1995; Helms, 1992, 1994) have discussed the impact of racism on the dominant White culture. It's interesting to note that most Whites, when thinking about race, think of people of color, and do not view themselves as a White race. Within the past decade, developmental models of White racial identity and their relationship to mental health and racism have been proposed. Partly, this theoretical development has been stimulated by the development of racial identity development models for people of color. Despite the controversy over the empirical validity of these models, they do help us to understand the impact of racial identity on personality development and psychological functioning, as well as the dynamics of racial tensions. Because racial tensions underlie much individual, group, and societal distress, we need system-wide programs, for which the race identity models provide a framework, as well as therapeutic interventions to improve race relations and mental health.

The three most popular White identity stage models (Hardiman, 1982; Helms, 1990a, 1990b; Ponterotto, 1988) present development as moving from precontact assumptions that the norms and values of the White culture are universal, to the assumption of a multicultural identity. Whites are usually not cognizant of their own racism until incidents occur that force them to examine and reassess their ingrained core cognitive schemas. There is much controversy about White racial identity development models (Rowe & Atkinson, 1995). One question is whether or not White racial identity development as a process parallels minority identity development (to be explored in Chapter 9). Another question concerns whether or not a description of how Whites develop racial sensitivity really says anything about the development of a White identity. And then there is some question as to whether or not these models have enough cumulativity and directionality to be developmental theories. Frankenberg (1993) argues that we need to view Whiteness as constructed and dominant rather than as the norm. Her research shows convincingly that race is as significant in shaping White identity and experience as it is with people of color.

For example, racism limits Whites' exposure to and experiences with cultural diversity, constricting their understanding and knowledge. Without this exposure, in ignorance, Whites experience unwarranted, irrational anxieties and fears about people of other races. These fears permeate their experience: they avoid eye and physical contact with people of color, anticipating bodily harm; they feel unconscious guilt about being oppressors, so perceive themselves as victims of these "uncivilized" people of color. However, Whites can choose to ignore the realities of racism. People of color cannot.

Tatum (1992) points out three issues that inhibit White students and trainees from learning about race and racism. The first issue is the cultural discomfort Whites experience when talking about race in racially mixed settings. Their discomfort includes feelings of guilt along with a reluctance to acknowledge any personal responsibility for racism. For example, how many Whites speak up when racist comments are made by their family, friends, or colleagues. How many focus attention on their own personal hardships when Blacks try to talk about their experiences of racism? This is a way to avoid the topic and minimize Blacks' everyday experience of being non-White.

The second issue concerns Whites' ingrained, culturally socialized belief that the United States is a "just" society, a "meritocracy where individual efforts are fairly rewarded" (Tatum, 1992, p. 6). Blacks know better than to buy into that one! According to this myth, everyone is supposed to be able to achieve success if they work hard enough. In our efforts to deny the reality of "class inequality," we blame people who do not achieve, labeling them as being "lazy," "selfish," and "stupid." We live in a society that gives only lip service to fairness and justice. Whites experience cognitive dissonance when they confront the gross discrepancies and injustices that currently exist for minority populations. Their (unconscious) defenses of denial, displacement, and rationalization protect them from the anxieties that are associated with this cognitive dissonance. But they can project these anxieties onto minority targets. The result is scapegoating, blaming others for our own discomfort and then finding ways to justify our rejection.

Tatum's third issue is Whites' denial of personal connection to racism ("I'm not racist . . . "). People who do not think racism applies to them are able to avoid those circumstances and activities that might enable them to learn more about minority issues. Reading, workshops, and conferences are for "others, not for me." This is the same group that Ponterotto and Pedersen (1993) refer to as modern racists.

These three issues are commonplace and serve to inhibit race awareness efforts, particularly in schools, agencies, and organizations where they might have much potential for effectiveness. Whites have difficulty realizing their collusion with and perpetuation of racial inequities in our society. Whites, even those with professional training, underestimate the impact that racism and racial tensions have on the class structure of society and the psychological well-being of all individuals, both dominant and nondominant. Most clients present with feelings of hopelessness and helplessness. As clinicians assess what elements of these feelings emanate from internal factors and what elements are externally created, they must formulate treatment plans that include culture-sensitive reframing and empowerment.

In a stunning article depicting the elements of unearned White privilege, McIntosh (1989) identifies 26 daily effects of this privilege in her life. Some of them include being able to live wherever she wants, socialize with members of her race when she wishes, go shopping without being followed or harassed, learn about her history and culture readily, assure that her children receive good public education, have no difficulty with financial credit, always be treated as a bona fide cultural insider, take a job without suspicion of having been hired to meet affirmative action quotas, choose public accommodations without fearing mistreatment, and so forth. In other words, most Whites take these privileges for granted, never realizing how problematic they are for others. The White spouses of Blacks whom I interviewed all expressed their shock and amazement when they encountered those racist situations that disallowed these automatic privileges, such as getting a hotel room, being shown an apartment, or getting a table at a restaurant. Their Black spouses barely noticed these slights, being so accustomed to them.

There is research that supports Tatum's third issue. J. Miller (1989) points out that studies show underlying racism even in Whites who believe they are not racist. Whites have been socially conditioned, despite their good intentions, "to routinely and subconsciously denigrate the competence of minority people and respond differentially to them when norms aren't clear" (p.91). This maintains the existing institutional barriers. White people often are unaware of their own racism. Again, the White spouses I interviewed were stunned by evidences of their own racism. One White woman was shocked to hear herself suggesting to her Black stepdaughter that she "do something about her frizzy hair to make herself more attractive."

My interviewees of color report everyday experiences of racial slurs, taunts, and gestures; being ignored by salesclerks and waitresses; vandalism on their cars and homes; taxis refusing to pick them up; and landlords and realtors finding excuses not to show apartments and houses upon seeing the minority person. People of color cannot hide as can gays and lesbians. From the moment of birth, they are subject to personal prejudice, to institutional and cultural racism.

Personal Prejudice

Personal prejudice differs from racism in that it is comprised of attitudes and beliefs that are not necessarily acted out behaviorally.
Prejudice is a personal issue, not based on power or privilege. The
prejudiced person is not likely to have real power over the target's life
situation, although personal prejudice is hurtful and cruel. People of
color experience prejudice in many forms. It can be overt or subtle,
such as the avoidance of eye contact, someone moving away from having to sit close on a bus, being called a name, or just being excluded
from social conversation. The confusing thing about racial prejudice
is that one does not know if one is being judged solely on the basis
of color of skin or on some other personality characteristic.

Children of interracial couples may experience personal prejudice
from the racial groups of both parents: they may be labeled "oreos,"
"zebras," "hybrids," or other offensive terms connoting that they are
not one or the other. On the other hand, they may be viewed as "exotic," as some unique, special kind of "object." Whatever, these reactions are based on their physical appearance, not on their personhood.
They are repeatedly asked, "What are you?" Early in life, they realize
that they do not fit in with either race. How they experience this and
what kind of family support they receive will determine their personal
and racial identities.

Individual Racism

Individual racism, as opposed to personal prejudice, can take many
behavioral forms. It involves the harmful behavior of one or several
individuals, such as tokenism, which can force employers or teachers
to give favored or discriminatory attention to the one Black employee
or pupil. The individual does not know if he or she has received a promotion or a slight based on performance or on filling a quota. A child
can find that she has many playmates at school but is never invited
into the homes of her classmates. A person may be the object of suspicion and/or harassment by people in authority positions whenever a
mishap occurs just on the basis of racial appearance (consider the well-
publicized Charles Stuart case, the Susan Smith case, and numerous
times when a perpetrator has been erroneously described as a Black
male by White victims). One lone Black student in a White school
reported that whenever something disappeared from a high school locker, he felt that the kids and staff automatically considered him a prime

suspect. Was this his own paranoia, or did, in fact, these thoughts occur automatically to the White students and teachers?

Cultural Racism

Cultural racism is based on the assumption that White is the norm,
that people of color are inherently inferior, less intelligent, and lacking in impulse control and sexual constraint. They are viewed as uncivilized, emotionally labile, and prone to violence. If people of color
do not attain the status and benefits automatically enjoyed by Whites,
it is because they are "lazy," "less intelligent," and enjoying victimiza-
tion, as "evidenced" by their disproportionate utilization of welfare
programs and other poverty programs. Cultural racism focuses on
minority populations as "problems," in order to avoid acknowledgment of the societal flaws rooted in historical inequities and long-
standing cultural stereotypes. Remember, it is the dominant White culture that defines norms, morality, health, goodness, and American-
ism, and others must adapt and conform to these dominant standards.

People of color who manage to achieve upward mobility are seen
as exceptions and are accepted by the dominant White culture as "You're
OK, you're different." They are viewed as being like Whites, and little
effort is made by Whites to understand their Black experience. This
impacts their psychological well-being, as beautifully illustrated in
Lawrence-Lightfoot's *I've Known Rivers* (1994), a study of six extremely
successful Black men and women. A common theme running through
the lives of these six people as they achieve more and more success
and acceptance by the dominant White culture is their increasing rage
about others' assumptions that they share the views and values of Whites
more than of Blacks. They rage against current racial injustices, such
as the Rodney King verdict; they anguish about the Clarence
Thomas–Anita Hill controversy; they cringe over O. J. Simpson; and
they resent the covert or overt racism they live with within their professions and the institutions with which they are affiliated. They have
to deal with the ugly distortions of tokenism, guilt, ambivalence, insecurity, and divided allegiances, and with the challenges of privilege.
Lawrence-Lightfoot applauds the hope, creativity, and purpose that
underlie their determination to make a difference in the world while
enduring the pain of knowing that their privilege distances them from
their Black brethren.

Another work, by Cose (1992), explores the many injustices
middle-class Blacks experience—rudeness of shopkeepers and service
people, lack of professional advancement, discrimination by landlords
and realtors, and so forth. Black professionals and executives are also

exposed to ignorant, racist comments by their colleagues, based on the automatic assumption that Blacks want to be like Whites and share the dominant culture's views and values. White racism, obviously, extends far beyond the ghetto.

Gender

Cultural racism includes sexist caricatures of people of color. Although both genders were brought to this country involuntarily as property rather than as human beings, Black women had no rights to their children (who were often taken away from them and sold), were forced to have sexual relations with slave owners, and were viewed by White males and females as promiscuous and evil (Greene, 1993). Black men were seen as animalistic rapists. These negative images linger as Black men continue to be viewed as weak, unreliable, violent, and unstable. Black women today are still depicted as matriarchal, emasculating, and sexually promiscuous. In addition to these stereotypes, even the standards of desirable physical appearance, particularly that of females, are based on White values, such as straight hair, lighter skin, and Caucasian physical features.

These sexist stereotypes are often internalized by people of color, and, therefore, standards and values of the dominant White culture become the standards by which nondominant cultures evaluate themselves. For years, Black women have had their hair straightened and tried to conform to these White norms. Obviously this leads to their personal devaluation and its concomitant psychological distress. Cultural gender stereotypes still lead White and Black females to perceive Black males as weak and ineffective, as needing protection. White females perceive Black men as dangerous and untrustworthy. Black and White men still see Black females as being too controlling and manipulative (using sexuality as a mechanism for control). Sometimes it's hard to disentangle the racism from sexism.

Unfortunately, this gender split creates a self-fulfilling prophecy. Black females are gaining higher status employment (reminiscent of their house slave higher status as opposed to Black males' outdoor, fieldhand lower status), and Black males are experiencing more unemployment and becoming more and more identified with gangs and disenfranchised populations, such as criminals, the mentally ill, and the homeless. This is borne out by the fact that Black females are much more likely to complete high school and college than are Black males. As the gender gap widens, inequities increase. These gender stereotypes about Black women's potential for upward mobility are often cited as one of the reasons Black males are more likely to marry out of their race than Black females (Kalmijn, 1993; Kouri & Lasswell, 1993; Solsberry, 1994; Tucker & Mitchell-Kernan, 1990). If there is unequal social and occupational achievement, with Black males lower than Black females, the power differential can be problematic for intimate relationships between Black men and Black women.

Class

Cultural racism attributes differences more to race than to class struggle. This partly results from the American myth that we are a classless society and that anyone can attain status and power if they work hard enough. It is likely that there will always be class differentiations within the larger society as well as within racial groups. While accomplishing much in the areas of culture and gender sensitivity, psychological theory has still not given adequate weight to the power differentials of socioeconomic class. The codetermination of class, race, ethnicity, and gender is complicated and needs to be considered from a broad perspective in order to understand fully the nature and impact of cultural racism. Many of the myths cited earlier in this chapter are based more on perceptions of class struggle than on racial differences.

Ethnicity

People of color and Whites belong to different ethnic groups distinct from their racial identities. For example, Whites may be of Jewish, Irish, Scandinavian, or Russian extraction, which will influence their development and cultural heritage. Likewise, Blacks may be, for example, of Haitian, Cape Verdean, or Nigerian extraction. Although racial identity is usually salient, given that people are classified by the color of their skin, ethnicity shapes differential values, beliefs, and attitudes.

Institutional Racism

Cultural racism supports and is simultaneously supported by institutional racism. Institutional racism is represented by the double standards and differential treatment inherent in our justice, education, medical, government, housing and other social systems. For example, the media will put crimes against Whites on Page 1, ignoring the same crimes committed against Blacks. Whites have greater access to health care, education, justice, housing, and government responsiveness than do people of color. This occurs because of privilege and institutional supports for Whites and discrimination against Blacks. Admission quotas and school and college segregation were overtly rampant until a few years ago and still exist covertly, despite affirmative action practices. And, currently, there is a political push to eliminate affirmative action or at least base it more on need than on race. The politics of race and racism are overriding factors with regard to policy making and enforcement.

Institutional racism exists in our schools, many of which automatically expect children of color to perform less well on academic tasks, tracking them in lower levels and creating a self-fulfilling slow learning prophecy; in industries, which hire Blacks to meet affirmative action quotas, but put them on display in less powerful positions; in the military, which makes Blacks overcome more hurdles for success and promotion than Whites; and so forth.

Within the mental health system, theories and practice are based on Eurocentric assumptions, ignoring the essential impact of race, ethnicity, and gender on psychological development. In fact, theories and practices exist as if they are not embedded in a sociopolitical context. Race, ethnicity, and gender have, until very recently, been viewed as "difference," "inferiority," and "deprivation." These views strongly influence assessment and treatment practices. For example, many agencies utilize standardized psychological tests without consideration of the relevance, reliability, and validity of these tests for diverse cultural and racial groups. Clinicians who do not consider race, gender, class, ethnicity, and culture when assessing and treating clients often blame the client for not fitting into dominant culture norms and attempt to fit him or her into the dominant culture without respectful appreciation of the client's own cultural norms.

Institutional racism puts the burden on minorities (just by labeling them as minority) to earn access or privilege whereby Whites are automatically granted access or privilege by virtue of the color of their skin. There is rarely any attempt by those in the dominant culture to learn about the norms, values, and standards of other populations and to assimilate them or merge them with the dominant culture. Rather, the goal is to include and integrate minorities into the dominant culture. Thus, educational curricula perpetuate the dominant cultural views and resist or create as separate the histories and cultures of other populations and societies.

One theme that came up over and over again in my interviews with biracial couples is that the Black partner, having been raised in a dominant White culture, was intimately acquainted with the norms, attitudes, values, and life style of this culture, whereas the White partner, also having been raised in a dominant White culture, was a stranger to and had to become acculturated to the Black culture. Thus, the minority person, whether a female, a homosexual, or a person of color, has been raised in a dominant culture where familiarity and knowledge is part of the socialization process. The White male, however, can choose whether or not he wishes to learn about female cultures, just as the heterosexual can choose whether to become familiar with homosexual cultures, and Whites can choose whether or not to become familiar with cultures of people of color. The issue of biculturalism, as opposed to monoculturalism, is an important aspect of parenting in multiracial families, as will be discussed later.

Biculturalism is the outcome of dual culture socialization. Rather than being absorbed into mainstream culture, the bicultural individual has no serious conflict about either culture, does not favor one over the other, and has positive affect toward both cultures. In other words, there is cultural flexibility, rather than denial of one culture. This individual has two social personae and identities and can easily switch from one to the other or expand to multiracial cultures.

Many theories have been hypothesized about why people marry interracially. As mentioned before, there is less racism toward Asian–American, Native American–other race, or Latino–other race unions than toward Black–White relationships. Most of the research focuses on Black–White relationships.

SOCIAL SCIENCE THEORIES
ABOUT INTERRACIAL MARRIAGE

The social science research about interracial marriage is limited and not without methodological flaws. For example, because multivariate methodologies are rarely utilized, the conclusions to date are questionable in terms of generalizability, even though they do provide interesting informational trends. Mate selection in general is a complex subject, and no one theoretical view is sufficient to explain either intra- or intergroup marriage. Furthermore, we need to consider why social scientists even perceive a need to explain interracial marriage. There seems to be an assumption of deviance that can't help but contaminate findings. Perhaps we need to focus more on why interracial marriage doesn't occur more often than why it occurs at all.

The biracial couples whom I interviewed had, for the most part, the same reasons for marrying as their generational peers within a same racial group. These include love, companionship, a gain in financial security and socioeconomic status, common interests, sexual attraction, compatibility, shared values and commitments, and a desire to make the world a better place by raising "good" children. Those over the age of 45 reflected on how much harder interracial marriage was for them than for today's young couples. They received no social support or approval whatsoever, and they were isolated from their family, their friends, and other interracial couples. Many never knew other interracial couples until after they had been married for some time. There is no question but that the sociocultural changes of the past 20 years have created the possibility for interracial couples to find a more favorable climate.

There seem to be two broad categories of theoretical explanations of interracial marriages: the contemporaneous structural theory and the traditional racial motivation theory. Structural theory emphasizes the factors that facilitate interracial marriage, whereas racial motivation theory suggests that interracial marriages occur *because* of racial differences rather than instead of or despite them.

Racial Motivation Theory

This theoretical viewpoint (Davidson, 1992; Davidson & Schneider, 1992; Wade, 1991), based on conventional psychodynamic theories, attributes the motivations for interracial marriage to unconscious intrapsychic factors. These include the need to be unconventional and nonconforming, the need to rebel against one's family or culture, the impulse to act out aggressively, or the need to prove some kind of superiority or inferiority. Another perspective of racial motivation theory would be one's conscious or unconscious attraction to aspects or practices of a particular race, such as spirituality, sexuality, musicality, social status, physical attractiveness, and so forth. Davidson (1992, p. 151) points out that, even today, "such theorizing about pathology continues." It should be noted that most of this research is based on the views of White males about Black male–White female couples.

Jeanie, age 29, came from a working-class White family where there was little affection and a great deal of strife, due to her father's alcoholism and chronic unemployment. Her mother worked long hours and was rarely available to the children. As the oldest of three children, Jeanie found herself parentified from an early age. Her best friend from elementary school through junior high school was Melanie, from a Black working-class family several blocks away. When Jeanie did not have to be at home, she loved being at Melanie's house, where aunts and uncles, grandparents, cousins, parents, and siblings were in and out, providing an abundance of warmth and attention. When Melanie and her family moved away, Jeanie felt a deep loss. She retained her images of family life based on Melanie's family, and when she met Will, a Black coworker, she found herself gravitating to him because of his warm, extended family life. After her marriage, she claimed that she finally had "the family she'd always been looking for."

These reasons for marriage may be healthy or unhealthy, just as the reasons mates of the same race select each other can be healthy or unhealthy. Two of my White interviewees claim they were always attracted to Black men, viewing them as "more genuine" than the White men they had dated. One White woman reported that, as the daughter of two civil rights activists, it was natural for her to date Black men, and neither she nor her parents were surprised when she decided to marry one. One White man confessed to marrying an Asian whom he met while in the service because of his belief that Asian women were more subservient than those "cocky, feminist American women."

Structural Theory

This approach to understanding the reasons for interracial marriage focuses on the changing community sanctions over the past 20 years. With desegregation, all races now have more access to higher educational and occupational levels, neighborhoods are less segregated, at least in many parts of the country, and, therefore, the racial gap in income, education, and occupation has narrowed considerably. "Blacks who have achieved higher socio-economic status find more White partners in their pool of eligibles and, as a result of their higher status, Blacks come to be viewed more favorably and hence as more suitable partners by a growing number of White partners" (Kouri & Lasswell, 1993, p. 242).

While slow, there appears to have been a steady decline in racial prejudice since the 1960s. However, as pointed out by Kalmijn (1993), the economic countertrends of the past 10 years may cause the issue of social boundaries to remain an open question. Racism seems to increase during times of economic recession as competition for jobs and available resources intensifies. But surveys do reveal some general societal trends, which appear to be particularly evident in the majority of interracial marriages: (1) an increasing delay in getting married; (2) the increased educational level of interracial couples; and (3) an increase in previous marriage for at least one member of the interracial couple (Kalmijn, 1993). The previous marriage was usually an intraracial one.

In the interracial couples I interviewed, the Black male had at least the same, if not higher, socioeconomic status as the White female, although the White woman may have come from a family with higher socioeconomic status than the family of the Black man. This is somewhat consistent with recent research (Cottrell, 1990; Ho, 1990; Kalmijn, 1993; Tucker & Mitchell-Kernan, 1990). However, it seems that, because of greater occupational opportunities for women, financial security or status is no longer a prevalent reason for marriage.

The sociological work of Cottrell (1990) is particularly interesting. She has identified six types of people who intermarry culturally, ethnically, and/or racially. Two are those who are "rebellious" and "detached," similar to those described in the racial motivation theory, suggesting alienation from or rejection of their culture of origin. Another two are described as "emancipated" and "adventurous," people who move beyond their culture of origin without rejecting it. The final two are the "embracers," those positively drawn to another race or culture, and the "multicultural," those already belonging to a multicultural family or being raised in a multicultural environment. These types depict graphically the differences among people who choose to intermarry.

These people may be psychologically, culturally, or socially outside of mainstream culture. The question for us is whether being outside of the mainstream culture is a manifestation of pathology or of courage. We need to look at the reasons people make choices and be open to a variety of perspectives, so that we can acknowledge pathology when it exists but not automatically assume that it accompanies different choices.

It seems to me that the greatest advantage of the structural theory research is the focus on environmental context. This may help us understand Cottrell's six types of intermarriers. Tucker and Mitchell-Kernan (1990) note that interracial partners are likely not only to have been born in areas of the country that were tolerant of interracial relationships, but that these people were also raised in permissive environments, where possibilities for interracial contact existed. They suggest that Blacks who intermarry often live as adults in a different geographical area than their families of origin, which supports their self-differentiation. The point is that the role of one's birth place, one's current residence, and the social control inherent in one's environment are important influences on patterns of mate selection.

Certainly, environment provides opportunities for meeting people as well as offering helpful supports for or limiting impediments to these relationships. It is not surprising that most interracial dating today occurs on college or university campuses. However, as previously noted, the research shows that actual interracial marriages usually occur between middle-class individuals who are "somewhat older, who have been married previously, and who live or work in integrated environments" (Solsberry, 1994, p. 309). We also need to remember that, just as with intraracial marriages, interracial marriages sometimes occur because of pregnancy or as an attempt to solve individual problems.

Gender is another factor raised in the literature. Because most of the research agrees that Black males outmarry at greater rates than Black females, we need more research to study the different interracial marital behaviors of Black and White males and females. How do these gender differences resemble or differ from gendered marital behaviors of partners within the same racial group? How much of the gender stereotyping is due to depictions by the media? And are there gender differences in other interracial groups?

What is important for mental health professionals to consider is the wide variety of reasons people marry, whether intra- or interracially. Again, I suggest that interracial couples may be courageous in their nonconformance to mainstream mores rather than psychologically flawed. This does not mean that some of the people who choose to marry interracially do not do so for unhealthy reasons and are not in psychological difficulty. It does mean that we cannot assume that interracial couples are automatically at risk with regard to psychological health. We must consider the enormous pressures and strains that racism will inflict on their relationship and family. There is no question but that there is a high failure rate of interracial marriages (J. A. Brown, 1987). Of my biracial interviewees, 80% had to contend with their parents' divorce. In order to sustain an interracial marriage, couples must have the strength and adaptability to address and cope with the issues and challenges of race in their social and personal relationships. The success or failure of the interracial marriage is impacted by the couple's acknowledgment of and responses to the stresses of their own internalized racism and the cultural and institutional racism of society.

ISSUES CONFRONTING BIRACIAL COUPLES

As visible targets of racist bigotry, biracial couples are likely to experience problems with their families of origin, relatives, and friends, as well as with employment and housing. The extent of difficulty these couples face is likely to depend on their economic level and status, their geographical location, and the races of the partners. The higher their socioeconomic status, the better able the couple is going to be to protect themselves from negative public attitudes. It's important to remember that while these relationships can create vulnerability, they can also "present the couple with an opportunity to gain a type of personal and interpersonal maturity that they would probably never have known separately" (Solsberry, 1994, p. 310). And, as mentioned before, the problems emanating from racism are only compounded by individual personality difficulties.

Betrayal of One's Own Race

Many White families view interracial marriage as a betrayal of racial purity (P. Brown 1989–1990; Davidson & Schneider, 1992). Thus, Whites, particularly White females, may face disapproval and even rejection from their families of origin. With the aid of media stereotypes, White families and friends fear for White females married to Black males, expecting the White wife to end up as a statistic like Nicole Brown Simpson.

> Vera, age 31, recalled the dismay of her White family 5 years ago when she told them that she was going to marry Denny, a Black coworker. Her mother was "hysterical," and could not believe that Vera "would do this to her and the family." She regaled Vera with tales of racial hatred and physical harm, revealing what Vera now recognizes as genuine fear and concern. But she threatened to have nothing to do with Vera if she didn't stop seeing Denny immediately. Vera's dad professed more tolerance, claiming to have some special Black buddies at work. But he confessed to Vera that he felt caught between her and her mother, and he didn't want to take sides. Vera's two brothers remained neutral, caught up in their own lives. Vera and Denny eloped, and she did not see her mother for 3½ years, until her son was 1 year old. During that time, however, she would meet her dad for lunch, and she and Denny socialized with her brothers and their girlfriends. It was the birth of her only grandchild that brought Vera's mother around, and she seems to have conveniently forgotten her opposition to this marriage, having become totally enchanted with her grandson.

Many Black families also view interracial marriage as a betrayal, a rejection of the Black race. Some Black families view the Black partner as a traitor or sell-out (P. Brown, 1989–1990). Like White families, they are afraid, remembering the cultural heritage of punitive reactions to Black men who engaged in social or sexual intercourse with White women.

Interestingly, however, the research shows that Black families have been more accepting than White families of these interracial unions. This is confirmed by the recent work of Rosenblatt, Karis, and Powell (1995). It may be that this is due to the multiraciality of many American Blacks. Because biracial children have always been viewed as Black, once a child is born, the Black extended family is likely to be more tolerant and accepting than the White extended family. Also, the Black extended family may not be comprised solely of biological relatives, but often includes other kin (godparents, close family friends, informal adoptees) in the community. Another trend is that the female's family seems to be more distressed than the male's family. This is likely to be related to the gendered cultural tendency of all families to feel more protective about daughters than sons.

The White and Black families of origin that I interviewed suggested that similarity of educational and occupational levels between the two families of origin led to a greater likelihood of acceptance, as did similarity of educational and occupational level between the opposite race partner and the family of origin or higher educational and occupational level of the Black spouse than the White family of origin.

Unmet Expectations

Another source of tension in an interracial marriage may involve expectations that are not met. There may have been certain assumptions at the time of marriage. Later, spouses may feel disillusioned or betrayed if these unspoken "marital contracts" prove to be unrealistic or are broken by one spouse. For example, a Black woman who marries a White man thinking that he is going to provide financial security, only to find him a victim of underemployment, may feel cheated. Or, one spouse may view his or her race or culture as superior and may subtly use this as leverage in a dispute. The spouse whose race or culture is being devalued may be reluctant to express his or her views, fearing that they will be labeled as primitive or backward. This conflict can be underground and not recognized as related to racism. Or the racial and cultural differences may be used to camouflage other problems and avoid dealing with them. They may also be used to distance and avoid intimacy. Many of the interracial couples I've seen in therapy have hidden behind racial differences, and often it's when I've brought in a Black cotherapist that we've been able to get through this barrier.

The family structure can be another area of concern. For example, ideas about how connected one should be to extended family, who is included in the family, what the familial boundaries are, and where the obligations and commitments lie may differ for partners from different cultures. When the couple has children, there may be differences in their ideas about expected relationships between parent and child and between and among siblings. There may be cultural discrepancies about favoritism for male children or for the oldest child, about expectations of housework and child care from older children, about demonstration of respect for parents, about compliance with parental authority, and about values regarding education and work.

Many issues may derive from cultural differences. Another area that can be problematic involves patterns of emotional expression and communication. There may be differences due to ethnicity and race in the style of communication that go beyond typical gender differences. For example, some cultures value verbal communication; some value rational, dramatic, or expressive forms of communication. And, depending on the power structure, conflict may be handled physically, or by withdrawal, teasing, direct confrontation, or indirect responses. Attitudes toward intimacy and dependence may differ, ranging from fearful and withholding to assertive and demanding. How do partners determine if their partner is expressing love, how do they need or want to express love? What do romance and intimacy mean to each partner? There may also be different attitudes and customs for dealing with grief and sadness. Some cultures value stoicism, others value expressive mourning, while still others emphasize denial or anger.

Several of the Black–White interracial couples I interviewed talked about their religious differences. For many, this issue was more significant than race. Although they intellectually discussed religious differences prior to becoming parents, most did not make final decisions. One couple, consisting of a White Jewish male and a Black Baptist female decided to raise their children as Jews. The Black wife laughingly reported that she is the object of more astonishment when she attends religious services in a synagogue than at any other place. She has converted to Judaism and she remembers the beginning weeks of her conversion class as the most difficult weeks of her married life. But, she added that, by the end of the class, she felt that not only had she become a Jew, but her White classmates became much more aware of their own racism and to this day are among her closest friends. Although her in-laws still have difficulty accepting her, her own parents have exhibited full support of her conversion, attending her conversion ceremony and even planning a party for her and her classmates. This same woman commented on her grandmother-in-law's funeral and the subsequent sitting of shiva, which was so much more solemn than the Baptist wakes to which she had been accustomed.

Obviously, all of these issues need to be considered within the context of racism. Other issues that may be present include a sense of guilt about one's choice of mate, a sense of isolation and alienation, and anger about the effects of racism. If only one partner is experiencing these feelings, it will affect the couple relationship in that the other partner may not offer sufficient understanding and emotional support.

Ethnic and Gender Differences

There have been some studies of college students' attitudes towards interracial marriage that indicate an ethnic and gender gap (Aldridge, 1978; Bartelson, 1993; Paset & Taylor, 1991; Todd, McKinney, Harris, Chadderton, & Small, 1992). In general, White females seem to be somewhat more tolerant of interracial marriages than Black females. This is thought to be due to the high mortality rate among Black males, and the fact that for every 10 Black women, there are 7 Black men (Bartelson, 1993). In her best-selling novel, *Waiting to Exhale,* Terry McMillan (1992) depicts Black women as resenting the "weakness" of Black men that leads them to outmarry. Several of my Black women friends and colleagues were thrilled to have this book published, "saying it like it is!" The resentment of Black women toward Black male–White female marriages pertains to the supply and demand for Black men of the same educational and occupational level as Black women, as well as to other factors such as historical relations between the races, the need for children in order to have strong cultural identity, and racial survival. Another striking study of 400 individuals (Todd et al., 1992) in southern California found that both Black and White men had more favorable views about interracial romantic relationships than did Black and White women, that younger Whites and Blacks were more tolerant than older Blacks and Whites, and that Whites, in general, were more tolerant than Blacks. These findings need to be considered within the contexts of geographical, sociocultural, and economic factors.

The greater the discrepancy between partners' gendered cultural beliefs and experiences, the greater the possibility for gender conflict. For example, there may be potential conflict with regard to male–female sex roles, depending on how flexible or rigid they are. There may also be issues of power distribution, such as who decides about money, sex, parenting, and social activities; how problems are resolved; and so forth. If, for example, the Black partner came from a stereotypical matriarchal family and the White partner from a stereotypical patriarchal family, there may be some ingrained conflict with regard to gendered power.

It is clear that individual, couple, familial, and environmental variables reciprocally influence each other with particular force for interracial and intercultural couples. All of these variables need to be given equal weight when assessing clients.

CHILDREN OF INTERRACIAL MARRIAGES

The position of biracial children is one of the first issues raised by family and friends of interracial couples. "But what about your children?

Is this fair to them?" The myth, as clearly articulated by Funderburg (1994)—"Children of interracial unions are born into a racial nether-world, the conventional wisdom continues, destined to be confused, maladjusted 'tragic mulattoes,' the perpetual victims of a racially polarized society" (p. 10)—is typical of common thinking.

However, Funderburg and other authors (Hiraga, Cauce, Mason, & Ordonez 1993; Johnson, 1992; J. M. Jones, 1988; R. Miller & Miller, 1990; Rosenblatt et al., 1995; Root, 1996) point out that, while biracial children experience different stresses than their parents, if they are raised in a loving, secure family, they are likely to emerge with ego strength and resilience. Biracial offspring can never recreate their family of origin, and neither parent can provide the empathic understanding or role modeling helpful to the development of a biracial identity, because neither parent is biracial. Their issues with racial identity, which will be explored in Chapter 9, are unique, given that they are classified as Black but have a White parent. For example, there are societal pressures to choose one parent over the other, which is tantamount to identifying with one parent and not the other. Many biracial children refuse to choose, indicating a dualistic preference toward biculturalism. Or, as pointed out by U. P. Brown (1995), they may compartmentalize into a private interracial identity and a public Black one as a coping mechanism for dealing with the societal pressure to negate White roots.

As previously mentioned, 80% of the biracial offspring I interviewed had experienced the divorce of their parents. This attests to the higher incidence of divorce in interracial marriages than in monoracial marriages. If the children resided with the White parent, they experienced more ambivalence and confusion about their identity and loyalties than if they resided with the Black parent. A child with any color is not considered to be White. All of these offspring expressed bitterness about their parents' divorce. They were unsure how much race contributed to it, but they felt the divorce exacerbated their racial identity dilemma. However, these feelings may not be very different from the feelings of offspring of divorced intraracial couples.

The 20% who were not from divorced homes reported less intense racial identity conflict. All of the biracial interviewees acknowledge struggling to come to terms with their racial identity. This is part of any adolescent's identity struggle. Those who perceived their families to be cohesive and open seem to have experienced less confusion. These findings are similar to those of Kirk (1984) about adoptees; those who came from families who acknowledged differences showed higher levels of self-esteem and adjustment than those who came from families who ignored or denied differences.

In addition to personal and racial identity confusion, biracial children may receive mixed messages from their parents, who, themselves, may be unclear about their racial identities and possible life goals. Thus, biracial children may feel a need to behave differently with each parent. This may further anxiety and confusion as they attempt to please both parents. Reddy (1994), a White mother of two biracial children, poignantly describes her continuous struggle to help her children develop a biracial identity in a racist society. She points out how futile and frustrating it is for a White parent to try to teach her child of color how to be a person of color. It is frustrating and enraging to feel so helpless while a loved one is coping with these realities. On the other hand, she comments about her amazement at her strong feelings of protectiveness.

However, accounts such as Reddy's and those of the interracial parents I interviewed also highlight the strengths and advantages of multiracial families. Interracial couples typically have put more consideration and effort into their preparation for marriage and parenting. As a result, they may have a greater degree of commitment. Their differences may result in a greater sense of self–other differentiation, with less fusion, and this can create greater self-awareness on the part of both partners. Ho (1990) found that the women in interracial and intercultural marriages were more differentiated and assertive than women in more conventional marriages. These strengths can provide broader opportunities for compassion, empathic understanding, and tolerance of all family members, particularly the children. These children may be more adventurous, active, and vital because of these differences.

> Some biracial people see their own identity as an object lesson on the possibilities of integration and racial harmony. They are a living model of a barrier-free world. Others, having found their way with no one's help, expect their children will have to do the same. Still others have found, from their own lives, reason to uphold convention . . . a clear, hard, fast line between races. (Funderburg, 1994, p. 348)

Children of multiracial couples differ from children of biracial couples in that at least one parent is multiracial and can provide empathic understanding and role modeling based on their own direct experience. Depending on their physical appearance, they may have more latitude in their acceptance by different racial groups, but, at the same time, they deal with the same racial identity issues as biracial youth. Because of their multiracial kin, they appear to be more secure in terms of the support and modeling they receive for multiracial identity development. In other words, they are not caught in a dualistic netherworld, neither Black nor White.

Tim, 14, and Karen, 12, are the offspring of a Native American–Black father and a Latino–Black mother. Reared in a geographical region dominated by Native American–Blacks, they have achieved security in their multiracial identity and, if anything, feel lucky and at an advantage to any monoracial group. They feel they have the best of all worlds in this era of "political correctness" and appreciate the favoritism they receive in terms of government affirmative action. Their families receive employment advantages, and they are the recipients of educational advantages. They intend to remain in their rural geographical location and do not expect to have to contend with discrimination or prejudice. Their lives have been advantaged, and their self-concepts and multicultural identities are positive.

TRANSRACIAL ADOPTION

Transracial adoption has a relatively short (beginning in the 1960s) but extremely controversial history. The term "transracial" is used in the literature more so than interracial when applied to adoption. Simply put, transracial adoption is the placement of a child of one race into the family of another race. Domestically, it typically involves White parents adopting Black, Latino, or Native American children. Intercountry adoption began at the end of World War II with small-scale adoption of orphaned European children usually by relatives or others of the same ethnicity. By the 1970s, due to the controversy surrounding domestic transracial adoptions, many couples seeking children discovered advantages (lower cost, less time, fewer health issues) of foreign-born adoptions, particularly from underdeveloped countries experiencing overpopulation and poverty. It has been estimated by Simon and Alstein (1991) that approximately 10,000 intercountry adoptions have been occurring annually since the 1980s, although now they are becoming as controversial as domestic transracial adoptions.

Domestic Controversy

As early as the 1960s, Black children were overrepresented in the foster care system. White children were more often placed for adoption or in institutional care (McRoy, 1989). The low adoption placement rate of Black children was exacerbated by the common adoption agency practice of "matching," whereby children were matched with potential adoptive parents on as many physical, emotional, and cultural characteristics as possible. By one estimate, "During the first six months of 1972, an average of 119 White homes were approved as acceptable for adopting a child per 100 White children available for adoption, whereas 50 non-White homes were approved per 100 non-White children available" (McRoy, 1989). But, when the availability of White children decreased, and the dominant White culture became more aware of the problems of the Black community, due to the civil rights movement, a dramatic increase in the adoption of Black and Native American children by White families began. By 1970, more than one-third of adopted Black children were placed in White homes (C. E. Jones & Else, 1979).

Given the reality that segregation laws and miscegenation laws had only been removed from the statutes in the 1950s for the former and the late 1960s for the latter, no wonder neither the Black nor White communities would readily accept this type of family integration! This trend of interracial adoption would most likely have continued were it not for the vehement protest by the National Association of Black Social Workers who passed a resolution against transracial adoption at their third annual conference in 1972. A much quoted excerpt reads as follows:

> Black children should be placed only with Black families whether in foster care or for adoption. Black Children belong physically, psychologically, and culturally in Black families in order that they receive the total sense of themselves and develop a sound projection of their future. Human beings are products of their environments and develop their sense of values, attitudes, and self concept within their family structures. Black children in White homes are cut off from the healthy development of themselves as Black people. (cited in Ladner, 1977, p. 75)

This opposition from Black professionals, based on fears of "cultural genocide" (Ladner, 1977, p. 87) and concern for children's racial identity, slowed considerably the number of domestic transracial adoptions. Prospective White parents protested that the needs of individual children were being overlooked. They insisted that the destructive effects of multiple placements and institutional care were less desirable alternatives than a White home. However, the number of these domestic transracial adoptions declined from 35.3% of all adoptions involving Blacks in 1970 to 19.6% in 1974 (Feigelman & Silverman, 1983). Subsequently, laws were also passed forbidding the adoption of Native American children by non-Native Americans. In 1975, the federal government stopped collecting data on the number of adoptions, resulting in a dearth of reliable statistics on all types of adoption. There are estimates that, currently, close to 25% of Black adoptions are by White parents. In fact, in 1994, after an emotional debate, Congress approved the Multiethnic Placement Act, preventing child welfare agencies from discriminating against prospective parents solely on the basis of race, color, or national origin.

Longitudinal transracial adoption studies in Minnesota (Scarr, 1993) indicate that racially relevant variables do affect the IQ and adjustment ratings of Black adoptees in White families. However, the quality of the adoption experience, particularly the family's racial identity socialization, along with their racial experiences as minority in a predominantly White community are the most salient determinants of adaptive outcomes with regard to racial identity, self-esteem, and healthy functioning for transracial adoptees.

Recent literature (Pohl & Harris, 1992) indicates that the Black community still opposes transracial adoption. This opposition is based on three main questions: (1) Can White people successfully parent Black children? (2) Will Black adoptees develop positive racial identities? and (3) Will Black adoptees have suitable Black role models and education about their racial heritage? The answers to these questions will be considered in Chapter 9 as we review findings on the adjustment and personal and racial identities of Black and Native American adoptees.

International Controversy

The American culture views intercountry adoptions differently than White–Black adoptions. Interestingly, these children are considered as immigrants and, as such, are not expected or obliged to retain aspects of their cultural and racial background as rigidly as their Black counterparts. A more temperate view of identity formation is tolerated, an orientation wherein a child's two cultures blend.

However, Black professionals are just as opposed to underdeveloped country adoptions as they are to domestic interracial adoptions, viewing these adoptions as the manifestation of White supremacy and White imperialism. Until very recently, when many of the international adoptions became more closely scrutinized and halted, the "supply and demand" mentality of the practice aroused suspicions of corruption and profiteering, of "baby selling."

Again, the controversy focuses on cultural exploitation versus benefits to the children. Opposition, for example, comes from advocates of social change who see intercountry adoption as an impediment to a third world country's needed political and economic reforms, as summarized by Bartholet (1993): "For the poorer classes in these countries, international adoption is said to represent exploitation by their own government; the argument is that by exporting the children of the poor, the government avoids coming to terms with the economic and social needs of its most powerless members" (p. 8).

Issues of Transracial Adoptive Parents

People who adopt transracially have many motives. While many parents adopt transracially because of their altruistic political and social values, the majority do so because of the unavailability of a healthy, White baby. However, there really is no stereotypical transracial parent. In most cases, the decision to adopt across racial lines is made with mixed emotions: sorrow for the impossible (infertility), joy in the possible (adoption), and apprehension in the "what if" (it doesn't work out). People who adopt transracially need to examine their motivations and come to terms with whatever discomforts they may experience contending with the marginality associated with racism. Overall, there are three levels of discomfort:

1. Parents experience conflicted emotions between their need to provide love to and to receive love from a child and their ambivalence about raising a child who does not look like them and will call attention to differentness.
2. Transracial adoptees may become involved in a tug of war between identification with the race and culture of their parents and with their own race and culture.
3. Society is conflicted between commitment to provide each child with a permanent, loving home and the belief that children should be raised by parents of their own race.

Introspection about the meaning of "differentness" and how it might affect parental relationships is required for these adoptive parents that is more intense than in same-race adoption. Numerous questions emerge, according to my interviewees, including, "How will it feel to have a child who doesn't look at all like me?" "Am I capable of handling any problems the child might run into as a minority person at school or elsewhere?" "What if I turn out to be prejudiced against my own child?" "What if the child ends up resenting me because I'm White?"

The emotional impact of these questions intensifies as the couple must select between race, culture, gender, age, physical disabilities, and emotional handicaps. Because most of them are not consciously seeking children with special needs, they rely on agents to help them seek "the best fit," and they often feel guilty about rejecting some children due to their uneasiness about the health, gender, race, or culture of the child.

In addition to the customary evaluation by social workers for suitability as adoptive parents, transracial adoptive parents are also exposed to evaluation for suitability as multicultural parents. Some feel

a great deal of resentment about these evaluations, although they intellectually understand the rationale of the intrusive questioning. For,
once a child of a different race enters the home, all members of the
family become interracial, and White family members need to be prepared for racism, whether it is their own or that of the world around
them. The couples whom I interviewed considered themselves strong
and comfortable with nonconformance. This is consistent with research
such as that of Ringstad (cited in Alstein & Simon, 1991, p. 31), who
found that "people who adopt cross-racially are generally unique persons in their thinking, feeling, and beliefs," and L. L. Falk (1970), who
concluded that transracial adopters live a more independent life style,
are less influenced by the opinions of friends and relatives, and are
more open to interracial relationships.

Some transracial adoptive parents reported unexpected reactions
of opposition or support from their families. With time, most of them
found that the opposers came around. Several couples reported their
perceptions that the grandparents showed subtle favoritism to their
same-race grandchildren, but if their parents were confronted with this
favoritism, they would vehemently deny it.

Every one of the parents I interviewed expressed a lessening of
their own anxiety once they received the child. Because of their efforts
and commitment, they found that "the child quickly became 'their
child.' " They formed an immediate attachment and a strong need to
protect their child. But, at the same time, they experienced the racist
reactions of others, who would stop them in the street with questions
such as, "Is that child yours?" "How come he looks so different?" Often,
well-meaning comments betray an ignorance that can be disconcert-
ing, such as, "I suppose you can learn to love them just like regular
children."

A couple who decides to adopt across racial lines does so with
the express knowledge that their decision will forever be a public one.
The child's "difference" will be apparent to just about everyone the
family encounters. In addition to the stresses that adoption puts on
any family, transracial adoption places even further strain on the system. This pressure begins exerting an influence long before the child
actually arrives, and forever alters the family system.

Issues of Transracial Adoptees

Racial identity and the ability to cope with societal racism are the major
tasks of transracial adoptees, as will be discussed in Chapter 9. The
concern of the Black community is that, as a Black child becomes as-
similated more and more into a White family and the White world,

the racial factor will become less important to the family. Thus, the child's sense of racial identity may not develop, and, ultimately, the transracial adoptee will become marginal in the predominantly White society in which he or she has come to feel comfortable. Obviously, the development of a sense of self is complicated for an adopted child whose parents are of a different race. The child identifies with the parent, and if differences are not discussed, the child may become confused about who he or she is in the larger, race conscious society.

For intercountry adoptees, the issue of cultural identity is changing as the demographics in this country change. Asian and Latino immigration has increased to the point where adoptees of those ethnicities have many models for ethnic identification, and they do not face the intensity of racism that Blacks contend with on a daily basis. Some research (Bagley, Young, & Scully, 1993; Hayes, 1993; Johnson & Nagoshi, 1989) has shown that over time ethnic identification does not seem to have a significant impact on their adjustment. But other research (Hill & Peltzer, 1982; Kim, 1981; Ladner, 1977; McRoy & Hall, 1996) claims that transracial adoptees are more likely to be maladjusted than same-race adoptees. The studies are inconclusive, and, as discussed in Chapter 2, it would be hard to separate adoption variables from interracial variables.

A more serious issue for intercountry adoptees is that they are usually older at the time of adoption, and they may have entered this country with health problems, the effects of poverty, inadequate nutrition, and poor medical care. The research is inconclusive about the impact of these health conditions; some report remediation and others report life-long difficulties such as learning disabilities, weaker health, and posttraumatic stress syndromes. Another issue that can become problematic is the incorrect assessment of chronological age of the child.

One family I worked with adopted a Mexican child off the streets of Mexico, whom they believed to be 7 years old. Two years later, she began to menstruate and became sexually active. After a long, torturous period of delinquency and school problems, the adoption was terminated and it became apparent that the young girl was probably 4 years older than reported.

As with intraracial adoption studies, the research suggests that infant transracial adoptions are the most successful in terms of child and family adjustment (Andujo, 1988; Simon & Alstein, 1991; Singer, Brodzinsky, Ramsay, Steir, & Waters, 1985). The results of studies with older transracial adoptees are not as optimistic. The uncertainty and hardship many experienced in their countries of origin may cause these children to require inordinate amounts of support and reassurance. They may be conflicted over their identity and ambivalent regarding their negative feelings toward their cultural origins (Feigelman & Silverman, 1983; Ladner, 1977). These difficulties often do not emerge until the children reach adolescence. Many are able to work through these difficulties, but a substantial number continue to experience internal conflict and anxiety while maintaining a facade of adjustment.

The problems that transracial adoptees may experience vividly highlight how the intrapsychic, interpersonal, and social factors in a family interrelate to cause increased pressure on the system. Normal adolescent concerns regarding personal identity are compounded by racial identity issues. Societal messages that devalue the child's racial and cultural heritage exacerbate these anxieties and conflicts. And, as the children act out, parental anxiety increases, causing more doubt and uncertainty within the system. Thus, a vicious cycle can emerge that stunts (at least temporarily) the child's ability to adapt successfully to the environment.

*   *   *

We see from the above discussion that racism is a burden for all Americans. Racism not only colors our views of multiracial families, but impacts how White therapists can be of help to individuals, couples, and families of minority groups. Most of the time we are not even aware of how ingrained our racism is.

We need to learn to become open to our own racist assumptions, to learn about the heterogeneity within groups, to differentiate between psychopathology and culture-specific values and behaviors, and to pay particular attention to generational contrasts and geographical variables affecting minorities as well as the dominant culture. This kind of learning will not occur unless we take active steps to engage in the learning process.

We must understand that ethnicity influences one's psychological well-being, that people of color are visible and, therefore, suffer the stigma of inferiority, unequal access to power, and more restricted ranges of opportunity even if they are lighter skinned or are raised in White families. Whites need to learn to question their assumptions of privilege and to experience their personal discomforts associated with their complicity in maintaining the unequal, unfair status quo.

Given the economic and political trends in our society, we appear to be heading more toward economic and cultural chaos than toward the truly multicultural society to which we give lip service. In order to become a truly multicultural society, we need to address the deep, historically based flaws involving inequality and negative stereotyping in our current society. Whites need to be able to tolerate their shame and anger, and a lessening of personal security as they confront these flaws.

The question for mental health professionals is how can we claim to be able to help people who are different, who have different values, norms, and criteria for well-being without examining and assessing critically our theories and treatment interventions to be sure that they are applicable to different populations and cultures? How can we be credible if we do not actively confront our own racism and address institutional and cultural racism whenever possible?

One interviewee, the daughter of a prominent conservative politician, was stunned by her father's reaction to her adoption of a Black infant: "Maybe this is the only way the world can change. You have a lot of courage and I love and admire you." Her reaction to this was, "Gosh, if *he* can change enough to say this, maybe there is hope for the world." All of my interviewees believe they have some kind of a mission to prove to society that a multicultural society is possible. We cannot claim to be helpers unless we share this mission.

The myths about interracial marriages, biracial children, and transracial adoption emanate from centuries of politically and socially constructed racism. There is no empirical validity to them, and they ignore the rich diversity within cultural groups.

NINE

Multiraciality across the Life Span

"I think that the identity process for me has been longer because I was raised as only monocultural and he was bicultural. My culture centered around religion, whereas his centered around busing and desegregation, racism, basically, how to survive in a White world. Privileges that I had taken for granted. Issues that have taken me a long time to see, understand, and deal with. These have been a large factor in my adjustment to, and within this relationship. Learning and experiencing racism as an adult takes a long time to understand and cope with."—Diane, White, 29

"I left home a long time ago. My folks were divorced, there was always a lot of fighting and tensions. I got into the service, then went to college and met her in grad school. I'd been married to a Black woman before, and it didn't work out for many reasons. She's [current White wife] Scandinavian and doesn't understand about all the racism bull in this country. We live on a university campus and socialize with both Black and White families. No big deal."—Edmund, Black, 39

"I had no idea I was different until we moved after my folks split up. We had lived out on Long Island, and there were lots of multiracial families. After my dad [White] died, we moved to my mother's home town into a Black neighborhood. Wow, did I get it! I was just a kid of 11 with lighter skin than any of the other kids, and they taunted me and made my life miserable. I was well into my 20s before I got it all together and I'm still not sure how I can balance both worlds."—Josh, biracial, 29

"My folks were always telling me the adoption story. I loved it growing up. But then when I got into school and I realized I looked different than the other kids, I started to feel bad. It didn't get better. When I reached junior high, I got into drugs and booze and ran around with all the other misfits. My folks didn't understand. They were willing to talk about adoption, but would never talk about race and skin color." — Marie, Hispanic adoptee, 28

"When she told me she was going to marry a Black, I felt such guilt. What had I done wrong? I was so afraid for her. This was her third marriage and his second. What about the children? She lost custody of hers from her first marriage, and all she kept talking about was having more. I even went to a psychiatrist to find out what I had done wrong. He told me it had nothing to do with me." — Katherine, White, 68

"We were determined to raise children who are multicultural and can transcend the ugly racism in this world. We do not want them to have to choose one race or parent over the other, and we are delighted with the results. Both of our kids, now grown, are truly bicultural and one is engaged to a Native American–Asian that she met where we summer every year. This is the only way the world will change. We've seen our marriage through its ups and downs, and we feel terrific about it. We feel blessed in all spheres — good health, wonderful careers, great kids, and friends of all races, as well as support from both families." — Nancy, White, 49, and Don, Black, 52

These vignettes indicate that the most important task facing all members of multiracial families is the integration of their personal and minority identity development. In this chapter, I will use the voices of interviewees to depict their processes of identity formation and the concomitant developmental issues for biracial couples, their families of origin, their children; multiracial families; and transracial adoptive families. Multiraciality impacts the typical boundary, rule, and role negotiations and renegotiations that all couples and families progress through over the life span.

RACIAL IDENTITY THEORIES

Theories of racial identity development emerged from the theories of Erikson (1950, 1968) and Marcia (1980), who outlined the developmental stages and processes White youth go through to commit to an identity status in the areas of occupation, life style, values, gender roles, and intimate relationships. Obviously these models cannot be generalized to all racial, ethnic, and cultural populations. Thus, the attempts by contemporary social scientists (Arce, 1981; Atkinson, Morten, &

Sue, 1989, 1993; Carter, 1995; Cross, 1991; Helms 1984, 1990a, 1990b, 1994; Helms & Piper, 1994; Kim, 1981; Phinney, 1990; D. W. Sue & Sue, 1990; Thomas, 1971) to incorporate race, ethnicity, and minority into models of identity development.

The original theories of racial identity do not consider gender, class, and environmental influences. They are based on assumptions that need further consideration, such as beliefs that aspects of identity are one-dimensional; that there is a linear, rather than circular, progression of development (stage theories); and that there is a parallel identity developmental process between Blacks and Whites.

In her review of the different models of identity formation for people of color, Helms (1990a) consolidates the types of linear stages inherent in the existing models into four stages:

1. The precultural awakening stage, which consists of low esteem for one's self and minority reference group;
2. The transitional stage, characterized by withdrawal, conflicts between self-depreciation and self-appreciation, and cultural reassessment;
3. The immersion–emersion stage, characterized by self-appreciation and by interpersonal relationships limited to one's primary cultural group members; and
4. The transcendental stage, characterized by internalization of one's own cultural identity with improved self-esteem.

These stages typically span the time period from preadolesence to middle adulthood.

The most recent work of Helms and Piper (1994) deemphasizes linearity by utilizing the concept of fluid ego differentiation or status in place of the linear stage. The ego statuses are comprised of attitudes, thoughts, feelings, and behaviors about oneself as a member of a racial group, toward others within the racial group, and toward members of other racial groups (both dominant and nondominant). A person may have several ego identities and one of these may be more salient at any one time, given environmental circumstances.

The traditional theories of racial identity indeed perpetuated the view that biracial individuals suffer from marginalism and, therefore, are impaired in terms of their attitudes toward self and toward each parent's race. These theories implied that biracial youth must choose one or the other race in order to integrate one racial or ethnic identity with a sense of self. Thus, these theories did not acknowledge biculturalism or the fluidity of multiple ethnic identities over the life span. Nor did they acknowledge the reality that some biracial people, who do not experience acceptance by either the minority or the dominant race, find it impossible to ally with one race over the other. Appearances of identification and affiliation are not necessarily congruent with the way biracial people feel about themselves inside. Minorities of all types learn to "play the game," to meld into dominant culture customs and mores as a way of survival. Internally, however, they may be struggling, feeling resentment at having to role play, as well as a myriad of other, hidden emotions. The recent work of Helms and Carter (1991) attempts to address these concerns.

BIRACIAL IDENTITY DEVELOPMENT THEORY

The first attempts to develop a theoretical model of biracial identity (Bernard, 1966; Frazier, 1947; Stonequist, 1937) were based on deficits, comparing Blacks to Whites, and based solely on White norms. These theories did not consider the effects of class, racism, and lack of support on the identity development of biracial individuals.

Only recently have social scientists (Jacobs, 1992; Kich, 1992; Poston, 1990; Root, 1994) paid attention to the unique aspects of biracial identity development. Obviously, the biracial individual is going to encounter unique stress because one of his or her cultures is more valued by society than the other. But, the myths about marginality leading to maladjustment ignore the fact that there is at least as much variability within races as between races (Root, 1994). Recent research indicates that a major developmental task of people of color is to integrate personal identity and racial and ethnic identities. For biracial youth, this is more complicated in that they lack a single racial/ethnic reference point. They both belong and do not belong, and they often need to learn to bridge majority and minority cultures.

If they do not achieve biculturality, the ability to accept and function in both cultures, they are denying a part of themselves. This will make them more vulnerable to racial dissonance and psychological maladjustment. The ideal goal is for each biracial adult to integrate two ethnic identities and two cultural backgrounds into a positive ethnic identity (Bowles, 1993). Carter (1995) argues eloquently that the biracial individual must "(1) evolve a positive internalized Black identity, and (2) embrace and internalize the White side of the biracial identity. . . . Biracial persons do not have much choice in how they are identified. . . . It is imperative that the biracial (Black–White) person have a positive Black identity since he or she is likely to be assigned to that racial group" (pp. 118–119).

The traditional literature suggests uniformly that personal identity is separate from racial group identity, the former depending on family socialization and the latter on community socialization. However, contemporary literature insists that personal identity and racial identity are related (Carter, 1995; Parham & Helms, 1985). High levels of self-esteem are related to consistent comfort with one's racial identity.

Assuming that biracial identity develops within familial, cultural, institutional, and economic contexts and may change because of the influence of events over the life span, let's review a consolidated model of the stages of biracial identity development proposed by Jacobs (1992), Kich (1992), and Poston (1990).

Personal Identity

The first phase of personal identity occurs during the preschool years, when children are constructing their identities ("Who am I?") first by size, then by gender, and finally by race, with some overlapping. Jacobs (1992, p. 200) calls this "pre-color constancy." Children can play with different color dolls, but without a concept of racial classification. Between the ages of 4 and 8, "post-color constancy," children grasp the fact that their skin color will not change, and they usually ask their parents why their skin colors differ. They are beginning to have some awareness that there are implications about racial differences, and they may show some ambivalence in the way they relate to kin of different races. They may even have perceptual distortions, either minimizing or maximizing the color differences.

According to Jacobs (1992), "if the child can maintain ambivalence, his/her development of racial awareness moves forward to the level where discordant elements can be reconciled in a unified identity . . . " (p. 281). The children are trying to make some kind of sense out of having parents and relatives of different colors. They have a sense by this time that society divides people into Black and White categories, and they are trying to reconcile within themselves the societal and racial tensions. In addition to "Who am I?," they are beginning to ask, "Who are we?" and "Who are they?"

Kich (1992, p. 305) states that 3- to 10-year-old biracial children proceed through an "initial awareness of differentness and dissonance between self-perceptions and others' perceptions of them." A secure, predictable family environment helps reduce this racial dissonance.

Lucinda, now age 18, recalls that her parents were loving and warm and that she couldn't ask for a more nurturing family. But, as a little girl, whenever she asked them questions about skin color, they avoided responding and kept telling her she was their "little exotic princess" and by the time she grew up the world would be a place where she would "reign supreme." She was somewhat mollified, but always felt some unease about her questions not being taken seriously.

Jacobs (1992) believes that biracial identity occurs between the ages of 8 and 12, as youngsters begin to realize that racial group membership is determined by lineage and that it is correlated with but not determined by skin color. Gradually, the racial ambivalence diminishes, as these children struggle for acceptance. Spencer (1985) found that children of color's academic achievement in grade school and junior high school had more correlation with their social interactions in the classroom than for White children, whose academic achievement correlated more with personal characteristics. Several of my interviews corroborated this finding.

> Beulah, now age 39, was raised in a White suburb of a midwestern city. The only person of color in her class until high school, she took her White mother's word for it that she was as good as anyone else. Although her reporting is retrospective, Beulah remembers what a "good girl" she was throughout public school, until she went away to college. She always got honor grades, was liked by the teachers, and learned how to be popular by excelling in athletics (she didn't want to be seen just as a bookworm or nerd). She never allowed herself to think about the vague slights or the questions about her skin coloring. Because her Black father traveled a lot on his job, he did not attend many school functions. When he did, Beulah noticed her "friends" and their parents acting differently. She didn't understand it then, but now she sees it as patronizing, and she realizes that her survival depended on her conformance and high achievement.

During adolescence, experiences of racial dissonance are painfully difficult. Individuals often attempt to separate off aspects of themselves both in response to conflicting loyalties toward their parents, often seen as the cause of differentness, and also because of the desire for peer acceptance. Many adolescents overidentify with the parent who seems to be most like them and respond ambivalently to the parent who is most different.

> Josh, 16, a biracial adoptee by White parents, hung around with tough Black peers bussed into his suburban high school. A special needs student, Josh had felt different for years. But in the last couple of years, as he associated more with Black peers, he was getting into all kinds of behavioral trouble at school. He was no longer "the good kid." His parents were very concerned and frustrated. His mother

had nightmares of Josh being hurt by the police because of his skin color and because of the kids he was hanging around with and their activities. "I have to live with the fact that my son could be shot or accused of something in this town just because of the color of his skin. They'll shoot first and ask questions later," she said bitterly. Josh, in the meantime, seemed to be testing the limits of what his being Black means. His feelings about his White parents are the usual adolescent ambivalence compounded by his anger at being placed in this situation. He loves his parents and truly believes they have provided him with a safe, secure upbringing. At the same time, he feels pulls to identify with others of color, and the disloyalty and identity confusion is sometimes overwhelming.

Racial Group Identity

Many biracial adolescents try to avoid choosing between parents and peers by keeping home separate from school and the external world, by essentially living in "two worlds." This is the stage that Poston (1990) calls "choice of group categorization." Adolescents feel pressured by society to choose one race over the other, and this can cause crisis and alienation for the youngsters because such a choice means denying one part of their cultural heritage. Kich (1992) says that most adolescents choose the minority racial identification publicly, but privately still cherish their biracialism. The recent trends in Black Pride make it politically correct for people to choose the minority racial identity, even if this causes them the pain of rejecting and distancing from their White parent. Remember, during adolescence, one is also struggling with uniqueness, acceptance and belonging, physical attractiveness, sexuality, self-esteem, and personal identity. The issue of racial identity affects all of these usual adolescent developmental tasks.

Consider, for example, the importance of dating and the need for peer acceptance. For a biracial youth, skin color and other physical features may be positive or negative to his or her self-concept of physical attractiveness and to how others view him or her. Root (1994) points out that this may be a more salient issue for females, in that they have to contend with both sexism and racism, and, despite more liberated dating practices, males still usually initiate the dating process. Many of my interviewees, both male and female, commented that their racial awareness became heightened when they started to date, and it was clear which Blacks and which Whites, who had previously been accepting and friendly, drew the line at single dating.

Poston (1990) interposes a stage of enmeshment/denial between the adolescent choice of one racial identity over the other and the more advanced stage (both in terms of cognitive and emotional development) which one can more easily choose multiraciality. During this enmesh-ment/denial phase, there are likely to be feelings of disloyalty and guilt over the rejection of one parent. The adolescent may become secre-tive and evasive, and displace his frustration onto his parents. Em-pathic understanding by parents, and peer and community support can facilitate biracial youths' continued racial development.

At some time during this process of racial group identification, whether it be in adolescence or early adulthood, biracial youth, who have been able to survive the painful embarrassments, frustrations, longings, and fear of inferiority, start independently to explore their total heritage. They begin to understand that their parents shared an interracial relationship and that they have the option of choosing a multicultural identity that will integrate the racial heritage of both par-ents. This is what Poston (1990) calls the "appreciation stage."

There are factors that may facilitate or impede the choice of a multicultural identity during adolescence and early adulthood. These factors include status, demographics (ethnicity and class of neighbors, parents' friends, and peers), social supports, parental style and influence, acceptance and participation in various group cultures, acceptance by parents and their relatives, and personal elements, such as physical appearance, individual personality characteristics, knowledge of cul-ture, generation, and political awareness.

Poston's (1990) "integration stage" of racial group identity is similar to Kich's (1992) self-acceptance stage. This lasts from early adulthood to middle age. Through further clarifying and integrating aspects of themselves, fully exploring their histories, and developing mutually reinforcing relationships with biracial peers, the biracial person be-comes less reactive and defensive and more self-expressive. Biracial peo-ple learn when and how they can fit into different racial cultures, when to confront distortions, and how not to depend so much on others' opinions. They are then ready to begin to educate and correct the ra-cist distortions of *both* their White and their Black peers. Bicultural competence maintains an individual's integrity. One cannot be racial-ly neutral. The question raised in particular by Carter's (1995) asser-tions is as follows: Must Black racial identity salience be static throughout the life span or is there fluidity of dominance in racial iden-tities?

The choice of lovers and spouses may be seen as another racial identity litmus test. Events that occur over the life span of biracial peo-ple, such as whom they marry, what careers they choose, where they live and work, what kinds of friendships they develop, the birth of children, the death of parents, and their relationships with siblings and their spouses are only some of the environmental variables that are likely to influence the continued development of their racial identity over the life span. And the influences of the larger political, economic, sociocultural environment will influence and be influenced by an individual's personal events. So racial identity does not stop with the onset of adulthood. It continues fluidly over the life span.

> Ken, 43, son of a White mother and Black father, went through a phase in college where he became a Black militant, rejecting and defying anything having to do with the dominant White culture. He avoided contact with his parents because he couldn't bear his conflicted feelings about his White mother. He used excuses of having to work and take extra courses to avoid returning home for holidays and vacations. His turned a deaf ear to his father's pleas for acceptance of both White and Black heritages. After college, he held temporary jobs, investing most of his energy in political activism. In his late 20s, he began to reflect on what he was doing, and he began to seek out biracial adults who seemed to be at peace with their biracial identities. He also found an area of work that he liked, and he began to focus on his career development. By the time he was 30, he felt more moderate and was able to reconnect with his parents and siblings.
>
> During his 30s, he was married for 2 years to a Black woman, Tess, whom he had known from college. She was cool and distant with his family, who made every effort to embrace and include her in their family unit. Tess had counted on Ken to maintain the same level of Black power activism that he had in his 20s. As they continued to grow apart, Ken really began to learn more about biraciality and decide for himself who he was and what he wanted to do with his life. After the divorce, he retreated from the social scene for a while. One year ago, he met a multiracial (White–Native American–Black) woman at a friend's house, and they are planning to marry within a few months. He feels that he is comfortable now with his own biraciality but that he could not have come to this state if he had not gone through the radical Black years. But he also reminded me that he was slow in developing on many levels of personal identity as well as racial identity. He is turning his Black militant values and experiences into creating a multiracial family and identifying with multiracial communities.

In middle and older age, biracial individuals seem to achieve more comfort with the fluidity of their racial identities and the influence of the larger political and sociocultural contexts, as well as with the gains and losses they have experienced through their life in terms of dreams, expectations, relationships, occupation, and the vicissitudes of life. They can look back on their upbringings with more understanding, and they are more compassionate toward their parents, whom they no longer blame for their own confusions and insecurities.

Frieda, 70, a prominent biracial physician who is just now winding
down her practice, was recently widowed. She and her physician biracial husband had been the only people of color in their neighborhood, although the suburb in which they lived had about a 10% Black
population. Frieda remembers that she and her husband were the only
people of color in their Ivy League medical school. They struggled
with institutional racism throughout their medical training, but, with
mutual support and high achievement, they were able to attain promi-
nence in both clinical and academic circles. Frieda's two daughters
married biracial men, and, therefore, her grandchildren are truly multiracial. Over the years, most of their friends, colleagues, and patients have been White. They really have met with minimal racism,
but they have experienced guilt about their privilege.

   What Frieda finds interesting is that, since her husband's death,
she has become more independent, learning to drive at the age of 68
and venturing to places and into activities that she never had before.
She is much more aware of her Black heritage and has recently volunteered her professional services to a clinic in one of the urban Black
communities. When asked why she had not been interested in her
Black heritage until her husband died, she replied, "I guess everything has been on hold for a long time. Our lives were so blessed.
We were so busy. It just didn't seem relevant. Now, with more time,
I'm thinking more, reading more stuff that is not professional, and
it's just like something is awakening in a very gentle, nonthreatening
manner."

   Not having talked with Frieda when her husband was alive, I'm
not sure how much her emerging racial identity questioning has to do
with being liberated from what sounds like a pretty traditional domestic
marriage (even though their professional status was nontraditional),
with stereotypical gendered roles, rules, and power structure. My point
is that, in later life, while there still might be racial group identification issues, the process can be gentler and less disruptive to one's personal identity. This is particularly so when people are secure in terms
of their socioeconomic status and power.

   As with identity development in general, biracial identity development is facilitated and enriched by intact and openly communicating
families and by a stable socioeconomic status. Enriching factors particularly relevant to biracial identity development include living in an
integrated neighborhood, attending integrated schools, being exposed
to both racial heritages, and experiencing a range of ethnic activities
and role models. The development of a resilient and positive biracial
identity in the face of racism thus depends on a biracial child having
access to secure emotional attachments, being supported while he or
she develops social and physical competencies, and being encouraged

by the parents to differentiate and separate from them at an appropriate time and level. My interviewees report that a multiracial and multiethnic community is a crucial factor.

Factors that may impede biracial identity development may be single-parent families (regardless of the single parent's race), lack of contact with the nonresident parent's family, friends, and racial heritage; the avoidance by the single parent of open discussion about racial issues; and the lack of biracial role models. Those interviewees raised in single-parent homes who had no contact with their other parent felt cut off from the racial heritage of the absent parent and, therefore, cut off from half of their own selves. However, it is difficult for single parents to take on the responsibility of locating and providing access to the other parent's racial group in addition to the usual stresses and strains of single parenthood. And much depends on the reasons and circumstances surrounding the separation of the parents.

MULTIRACIAL IDENTITY DEVELOPMENT

As noted in Chapter 8, children of multiracial couples are different from those of biracial couples in that they are like their parents in terms of mixed raciality. Thus, they have role models for multiculturality. Many multiracial families represent several different races and cultures, and, while they may be identified as people of color, they often do not suffer from the stigma the Black race bears in that they may also have Hispanic, Native American, and Asian ancestors. So their physical appearance may identify them as "different" but not necessarily African American. Depending on the sociocultural and political contexts, children may experiment with different racial identities as they go through the life span.

> Judd, 23, is the son of a Black–Native American father and a Hispanic–White mother. Raised in a farm community with many different races represented, he flirted with learning about the heritage of and identifying with each of the races represented in his parents. During times when the Black Power movement was in the news, he identified himself as Black. He went through his Hispanic stage when he was in high school, mostly because he was interested in a girl of Hispanic heritage. When he was in college, the plight of Native Americans was news, and he became an activist for their cause in reclaiming land. His parents indulged these transitions and were supportive and impartial. It came to him gradually that he could be a "bridge" between many worlds, and it was this realization that motivated him to return to school in order to study law. He is determined to use his own multiraciality to his and others' advantage.

The stages of multiracial identity development are similar to those outlined in the biracial identity development section. But there are some notable differences. For one, these children may not be different from the other members of their family, but their appearances may differ. Some may have darker skin color or different features, and there may be some subtle dissimilarity in attitude and even treatment based on these physical feature variations. Another difference is that, rather than having only two racial heritages to figure out, multiracial children may have several different racial heritages to acknowledge and incorporate into their sense of self. In addition, they may have a variety of kinfolk to relate to and identify with. On the other hand, the more races involved, the more "normal" it may feel. As one multiracial interviewee stated, "There's safety in numbers."

IDENTITY FORMATION OF INTERRACIAL COUPLES

"Before we married, we talked to both families and to friends of both races as to what to expect. We did not know any biracial couples whose marriage had survived, and we were nervous. Tim [Black] was much more sanguine about it than I was. He had just graduated from business college and, because it was the time of affirmative action quotas, he had lots of job possibilities. So we decided to move to a northeastern city where we had no family and where we could find a supportive community and start out fresh. I was stubborn and determined, but also nervous and scared."—Rachel, White, 31, married 4 years to Tim, Black, 29

Biracial couples start out as pioneers, with no role models and no road map. Most people do not grow up expecting to marry someone of another race, so when they make the choice to marry interracially, they have to deal with the dissonance between the expectations from their youth and the reality of their current choice. White spouses often feel overwhelmed and totally unprepared for the experiences of racism. They do not know how to react or what to do with their intense feelings. This is comparable to the way a young child of color feels when first having to confront others' responses to his or her racial difference. The White spouse doesn't understand why he or she is being treated badly when he or she hasn't done anything wrong—except marry the person of choice who happens to be of a different race. It is hard for the White spouse to accept the cruelties meted out to people based solely on the color of their skin. As adults, White partners have not received the benefits of the survival training that Black parents, particularly mothers, build into their parenting from the very beginning. Thus, Whites lack the battle training required for resistance and survival in a racist world.

If the Black partner is patient and understanding, eventually the White partner catches up to his or her adult developmental levels of racism survival. But, sometimes the Black partner is equally confused by the White partner's despair and responds to it with impatience. This further upsets the White spouse and can spill over into couple conflict, which may then be displaced onto another issue. Gender differences can complicate the problem further.

> Jim, age 32, was impatient with his White wife's anxieties about the barriers she suddenly found herself facing. He kept telling her to ignore the slights, not to let them get to her so. Joanne, age 28, needed to talk about the things that were happening to her, and Jim seemed to not really listen. His viewpoint was that the more they dwelled on race issues, the more power they were giving to "them." She wasn't asking him for answers, just a supportive ear. They began to bicker over silly habits, such as who was neater, more reliable, and so forth. When a friend recommended that they read Deborah Tannen's book *You Just Don't Understand* (1990), they developed a new perspective on their different styles, and Jim made conscious efforts to listen more empathically and supportively to Joanne. Joanne says that there were many times in those first few years when she wasn't sure they were going to make it, when her confusion and frustration became jumbled. She credits her friends and her in-laws for their active help.

The above example shows how gender differences can impact the way any couple deals with conflicts. But, gradually, as White partners come to realize that their perspective, their sense of trust and security in a safe world, is changed forever, they are likely to feel a lot of pain and rage. Either these feelings can be projected outward onto other people and events and result in the couple's increased retreat and isolation from the outside, hostile world, or they can be acknowledged and addressed by the couple. If the couple acknowledges and copes with these painful feelings, the feelings can be used as energy to fuel some kind of productive activity, in careers, social life, and/or community.

All of my White spouse interviewees under the age of 40 who lived in urban areas during the first years of their marriage felt closer to and received more emotional support from their Black friends and family than they did from their White friends and family. They did, however, receive support from their White friends who were also in interracial marriages. In general, White spouses depend on Black friends and kin to validate their experiences of racism. They need to learn whether or not they are imagining slights or exaggerating them. Some find it easier to vent to friends than to their spouses, recognizing the difficulties their pain can cause their spouses.

The four biracial couples interviewed who live and work in college or university towns reported fewer racist encounters. They tended to minimize any possible incidents. It seems, as with many same-race couples, as if they are prolonging their protected, ivory-tower life. These couples socialize primarily with their professional colleagues, and the college or university is the center of their life. Although there may be subtle racism within these institutions, biracial couples and families feel "safe" and "accepted" for who they are as people, not as racial oddities.

Couples over the age of 40 had experiences more similar to the academic couples than to the urban couples. They had married during an era of greater intolerance and so they had deliberately established life styles that would make them less visible, either in academia, government service, or a foreign country. A major difference I found between the older and younger couples was the younger couples' sense of shared Black racial pride. They are determined to formulate new norms and criteria for their life style. They strongly oppose acquiescence to White norms and standards. The younger couples openly expressed their anger. The older couples report having felt more fear than anger when they were starting out. They worked hard to fit in with mainstream life styles, wanting acceptance and inclusion. I think this generational difference speaks to the dramatic sociocultural changes that have occurred in the past two decades.

An interracial couple identity model created by an interracial couple (Young-Ware & Ware, 1994), based on their own experience and that of their friends, provides clarification for the differing perspectives of a Black male partner and a White female partner. This model accurately represents the experiences of every one of my Black male/White female couple interviewees. The Black male partner perspective consists of nine stages:

Stage 1: Recognition—He realizes that he has feelings for a person from a different race. He finds that the person of the other race possesses characteristics that he finds attractive despite or because of racial differences.

Stage 2: Pursuance of relationship—He makes the decision to pursue the individual despite inner reservations and fear of rejection. Advances in this stage are more passive/aggressive than aggressive. The desire is to maintain an easy retreat.

Stage 3: Denial—He rejects the idea that the relationship is any different than one with a same-race person.

Stage 4: Isolation—Attention is focused on solidifying the relationship. Outside considerations are continually pushed to the side. This is, again, a form of denial.

Stage 5: Self-evaluation—He evaluates himself and begins to realize some of societal backlashes for this type of relationship. Questioning of self regarding motives for such a relationship given backlashes. Questioning of racial identity.

Stage 6: Anger—He is angry about the fact that certain problems begin to occur in relationship as a result of societal pressures. Anger is translated into arguments with partner, based on concerns regarding the future. It is also possible to overcompensate for "Blackness" in this stage. One begins to need "confirmation" from others that he is still "Black."

Stage 7: Rejection—He rejects negative societal and friendship views. At this stage, he begins to accept the possibility of a future with his partner. This stage cannot be reached if he and his partner are unable to conquer the anger stage.

Stage 8: Fear—He fears what may result from rejection of societal views. Issues of personal safety and comfort level in different environments become vital. Awareness of self and status of relationship in society are prevalent in this stage.

Stage 9: Happy medium—He finds comfort in decision to remain in relationship. However, he is always aware of societal displeasure. There is also an acceptance of the continual struggle to come to terms with this displeasure.

The White female partner's perspective comprises 11 stages:

Stage 1: Initial introduction—She meets person of a different race and finds common interests with this person. She finds herself really liking this person as an individual.

Stage 2: Hypothetical intellectualizing—"What would it be like to be in a romantic relationship with Jim?" How would people in life react and respond? She is intrigued about the person as a man, rather than just as a Black man. Discussions with family and friends about their views. She most likely will experience split reactions or opposition to an interracial relationship from family and friends. She begins to see race differences in new ways. These ways are positive internally, yet negative in terms of consequences with other relationships.

Stage 3: Pursuance of relationship—She makes a choice, based on friendship and qualities of the person, to attempt pursuit of romantic relationship. However, she may feel a lack of confidence that he will reciprocate romantic feelings. During this stage, she begins to recognize her personal stereotypes about Black men and White women.

Stage 4: Shared response—Both partners realize that their feelings have moved beyond a friendship level, and they both decide to pursue a romantic relationship. They both embrace feelings of "not caring what others think, they'll get over it."

Stage 5: Self-doubt and guilt—Family pressures are enormous, resulting in self-doubt and doubt about the partner. She struggles with the possibility of family rejection of self, both alone and as a couple with her partner. She experiences a great deal of internal strife and begins to reject the interracial relationship. This decision to end the relationship results in having to deal with the feelings of anger from the partner. She then feels guilty about this decision, which is based on insecurities, fear, and pressure from others. After many conversations and arguments stimulated by societal pressures, one makes the decision to continue with the interracial relationship no matter what. The thinking is that one can't walk away from a person whom one loves so much because of racial differences. She then makes a firm decision to remain in the relationship, and there are feelings of relief and satisfaction. She actively informs herself of what will be faced in the future. The predominant belief is that love and courage will conquer all!

Stage 6: Immersion and advocacy—She becomes preoccupied with the Black culture and her partner's individual and specific cultural values and beliefs. There is a great deal of excitement associated with learning about the Black culture. She becomes more insightful and attuned to the Black partner. She is enthralled by advocating for cultural and interracial awareness. The Black struggle becomes the White partner's own struggle, and her previous personal causes become secondary to this overriding issue. She begins to recognize and experience racism first hand. She begins to understand the concept of White versus Black and the social, political, and economic differences.

Stage 7: Realization of "White privilege"—She becomes much more aware of what it means to be White and realizes how much she does not know about other cultures. She feels shame, guilt, and anger over the racism that is observed and personally experienced with each new venture as an interracial couple into the public arena. These observations and experiences cause feelings of outrage, focused on White people who exhibit racism. The White partner has to learn to deal with internal anger toward others and toward society as a whole. This anger and hurt are exacerbated by every event of racist oppression observed and/or personally experienced.

Stage 8: Seek equilibrium—She tries to balance her own feelings and beliefs with those of her partner. She begins to process her feelings and thoughts in order to figure out where and how she "fits in." She can begin to feel overwhelmed and anxious about the loss of self, the loss of support and isolation from significant others. These feelings can result in rage and fury about prejudice and racism, about how one's personal life is significantly affected by prejudice and racism. There are feelings of loss—of one's former notion of self, of one's sense of safety and security, and particularly of one's control and capacity to protect one's emotional self from outside hostility.

Stage 9: Depression—She experiences varying degrees of depression brought on by her experiences with others' hostility, which are turned inwards. This depression also stems from the lack of familial support for her choice, experiences of isolation and withdrawal, and the lack of role models to discuss these feelings and issues with. There is a realization that there are no real interracial support systems to lean on.

Stage 10: Cognizance of "reality"—She becomes aware of the realities of being in an interracial relationship, realizing the full impact on self, partner, and life. The White partner realizes that personal experiences since the inception of this relationship are a sliver of what the Black partner has experienced throughout life. She sees the devastation racism causes to personal lives. There is also gradual realization that the adjustment to racism and sexism is not a linear process, but a continuing circular process. One gains more strength and awareness of the issues as an individual and as a partner in the interracial relationship.

Stage 11: Happy medium—She experiences comfort with the decision to remain in an interracial relationship. However, there is always awareness of societal pressures and opinions. But one feels stronger in learning to accept the reality that there will always be racial difficulties to confront.

The authors of this model are committed to helping others understand the impact of racism on both Whites and Blacks. They speculate that these processes are similar regardless of the gender of the Black and White partner. Nowhere in the literature have I come across such a thoughtful presentation of the components of developing an interracial couple relationship and identity. It is this kind of material that is invaluable not only to clinicians working with such couples, but also to couples contemplating or entering such a marriage as well as partners in interracial marriages.

There is no question in my mind but that the decision to enter into and survive an interracial marriage requires strength and courage as well as maturity. These capacities allow one to develop the requisite awareness and coping strategies just outlined. It is important to remember that many of the divorces that do occur with interracial couples are a result of the same kinds of problems that cause intraracial couples to dissolve their marriages. Racial differences certainly compound typical couple difficulties. But, we cannot assume that interracial divorces are solely attributable to racial differences and racism.

In those couples where one member had been previously married, there are often issues to contend with regarding stepparenting and coparenting with the previous spouse. And, if the children and spouse of a former marriage have their own prejudices about a subsequent interrmarriage, these could be an additional strain on the interracial couple relationship.

> Doris, 36, a White nurse, married a previously married Black physician, Will, age 42, with two Black sons, ages 11 and 13. Although the boys were only with their father every other weekend, Doris felt their anger and resentment and just could not get close to them. She assumed they resented their father's divorce, and she felt paranoid about her Whiteness. As a result, she kept as distant as she could on those family weekends, rationalizing that she didn't want to get in the way of the father–sons get-togethers. Will wanted her to be more involved with his boys. He commented that he didn't really understand why Doris couldn't make the adjustment, until a discussion with his sister sensitized him to Doris's feelings of being different and left out. After this discussion, Will was more patient with Doris and encouraged her to join him in activities with the boys. With more open discussion and group activities, these people developed into a gratifying blended family. Doris says that she now realizes that she was projecting her own guilt about taking Will away from his first marriage and family onto the racial issues, and things got all mixed up. Once she disentangled stepfamily and racial issues, she was able to learn survival skills in both areas.

Parenting

Interracial couples often postpone having children until they feel they have stabilized as an interracial couple. Many choose not to have children, because they feel more secure and in control of their lives without adding the complications of a biracial child. In other words, the couples who told me they chose not to have children admitted that they probably would have decided differently if in a same-race marriage. When there are just the two of them as a couple, there is equal responsibility and bonding between two people who have chosen together to cross barriers.

Laura, 38, White, and Lloyd, 37, Black, have been married 9 years. When they first married, they did expect to have children, but when Lloyd was transferred from a midwestern metropolis to a southern city, they became apprehensive about having a biracial child. As a junior high school teacher, Laura is exposed to a variety of people—native Southerners of both races as well as transplants like herself—and, while she finds the racism more open and up front than in the North, she does not feel that they have the same interracial community to provide modeling and support that they did in their former home town. During the two-session interview, however, it became apparent that, as many couples do in their late 30s, they are beginning to rethink the issue before "it is too late." They feel they have a comfortable marriage and life style, and they are nervous about "rocking the boat."

One can do a great deal of preparation for bringing a biracial child into the world, but mothers will tell you, as Reddy (1994) does so beautifully in *Crossing the Color Line,* that you can never truly anticipate or prepare for the realities of raising a biracial child. Just as Chodorow's (1978) work shows how mothers share a particular gender identification with a daughter that differs from their relationship with a son as "other," the White mother, because she can never share her biracial child's experiences as a person of color, experiences her biracial child as "other." Therefore, the White mother cannot prepare her child for survival in a racist society as the Black mother naturally does.

Betty, a White mother of a 9-year-old son, Todd, married to Rick, a Black, talks about her pain and outrage the first time Todd came home from kindergarten in tears because another child called him "Blackie." She and Rick had talked to Todd about his uniqueness, and throughout his years at a Montessori preschool and in the liberal community in which they lived, he had viewed his dark skin as "special," and he, himself, had not seemed even to hear questions asked of his mother (such as, "What is he? He's so cute." "Whose child is he?" "Do you think what you've done is fair to him?"). Now, Betty realized that Rick needed to be the primary role model with regard to Todd's coping with racism and that she would always be "other." Betty and Rick truly believe that they can raise their son biracially, and that, by the time Todd grows up, the world will be more multicultural.

R. Miller and Miller (1990) point to the different socialization goals Black and White parents may have. They cite the special tasks of biracial parents: negating the negative cultural messages of the dominant White society, validating the uniqueness of their offspring, teaching children strategies for emotional and physical survival in confronting racism, and instructing them how to cope with discriminatory practices. Thus, Black and interracial families share the task of integrating the values of three competing systems: the dominant White culture value system; the Black behavioral style that is different from the dominant culture values; and the minority group agenda, which includes recognition of minority status and coping with the competing value systems of each parent. These three value systems are equally critical ingredients to the development of biracial identity.

> Joelle, 42, Black, and Sam, 44, White, have two teenage sons, Arlo, 14, and Tim, 15. Although they live in a predominantly White community so that their sons will have access to top quality education, they have made a concerted effort to expose their children to both racial communities. Every weekend, they visit friends, colleagues, and cousins in an urban Black community, attending church there and then socializing afterwards. The boys attended Sunday School there too, so as to develop friends. The boys have many White friends from school and their neighborhood. Joelle and Sam have also worked hard to find other interracial families so that their boys won't feel so "different." As the boys are getting older, Joelle and Sam together have din-nertime discussions about racism and how to cope with minority status. They instruct their boys to avoid confrontation with the police no matter the circumstances, to walk with their hands out of their pockets, to stay away from trouble spots, and so forth. These tactics are essential for the survival of Black youth, particularly males, in any setting. They cannot afford any of the leeway to make mistakes that White adolescents have. The stakes are much too high as Blacks are much more likely to be shot first and questioned later. Joelle and Sam have seen college-age youth of their interracial couple friends go through the stage of feeling as if they must choose one race (and one parent) over the other, and although they aren't so sure they can prevent their boys from going through that stage, they want to prepare them for what lies ahead. This couple has given a great deal of thought to the special tasks of rearing biracial children. They attend conferences, read, and have formed informal support groups to provide resources, support, and modeling. They make a point of taking vacations in places where Blacks and multiracial families go.

If the couple is unable to resolve their couple conflicts, whether or not these are related to interraciality, their pent-up frustrations may affect the way they treat their children, as in any family. Both parents need to be aware that they may harbor secret wishes for the child to identify more with their own race as a way of playing out competitive power struggles in the couple system. There are potentially many opportunities for interracial couples to displace their aggression, projecting and triangulating a child into the couple conflict.

By the time the children reach adolescence, the interracial couple have usually achieved an established model of family functioning. Adolescence, a time when youngsters are forming their own identity models and values in order to prepare for leaving home, can be a turbulent period in any family system. In multiracial families, natural adolescent rebellion can be compounded by racial and ethnic identity. Depending on the youngster's environment (school, neighborhood, or peer group in particular), he or she may use this time either to attack the parents for putting him or her in a "netherworld," or to identify first with one race and then, perhaps, with the other, as a way of trying out different identities. At the same time, the couple system, the partners' degree of satisfaction, security, and stability, influences and is influenced by the adolescent offsprings' behaviors.

Parents may engage in active or passive parenting strategies with regard to their offsprings' minority status. They may be actively involved in the schools and other social systems in which their children participate. For example, they may actively provide access to Black cultural institutions (e.g., the Church, social clubs). Or, on the other hand, they may disengage, feeling helpless to bring about any system change. They may let their children fend for themselves. Some parents believe their children will develop better survival skills on their own, viewing parental involvement as "overprotection." Parents may need help in learning to distinguish between their children's and their own responsibilities for difficulties and those truly attributable to racism.

What many parents report at the time of adolescence is that they never could have foreseen the way things would go, how complex growing up is even without the uniqueness of biraciality.

> Moira, a White mother age 45, is puzzled and saddened by her college daughter feeling the necessity to identify solely with Blacks. She and her husband, Ralph, age 49, had been determined to raise Pamela with a biracial identity, and throughout high school Pamela had seemed calm and happy with who she was. She was in honors classes, was friendly with both Whites and Blacks, and was invited to parties by both races. She dated both Whites and Blacks, although she never seemed to have a serious relationship. She turned down an Ivy League college for the state university, much to her parents' consternation. At the university, she began to affiliate with the Afro-American Studies Institute, and she became militant and distant. Neither Moira nor Ralph could communicate with her, and they felt hurt and disappointed. Moira, in particular, feared her daughter's

rejection on the basis of her Whiteness and she was mourning the loss of the close relationship they had had. Ralph keeps assuring her that this is "just a phase," that Moira is going through a "delayed adolescence." The tension between the couple is greater than before, but they also describe a greater supportiveness and caring for each other, almost as if they must reassure each other (and themselves) that they are OK and have not done anything wrong.

Middle Age

In middle age, most people reassess their lives to date and reshape or remap their core sources of identity. Midlife is a time, then, for critical self-reflection as one reviews one's expectations, disappointments, losses, and gains. The continuities and discontinuities one has experienced in life become more meaningful. The interracial couple may be more comfortable at this time, understanding that their biracial identity is complex and ever changing. Their perspective about the world they have created for their children is, of necessity, more flexible, as they grapple with how little control they really have over this creation and as they turn the reins of responsibility and power for their children's lives over to these maturing people.

The interracial couples in midlife whom I interviewed felt that they were more equal and balanced than they had been when they began their unique marriages. They both had developed heightened awareness of themselves, their reactions to racism, their attitudes toward both races and to political, economic, and sociocultural influences.

Pat, 52, Black, and Phil, 49, White, told me that these are the "best years ever." They are pleased with their young adult kids, they are pleased with their careers (she's a teacher and he's a secondary school principal), they like their life style, and they feel liberated from the expenses and strains of raising a family in a suburb that is 90% White. Pat has been making more conscious efforts to develop friendships with Black couples, and she feels that her race consciousness and Black pride have developed only recently, partly due to her kids' activism. Phil is supportive of her efforts and says that he's learning that he's been too distant and stand-offish from other people, as if he was protecting himself from any form of racist behavior by burying himself in his work, and his relationships with his wife and children. Now the two of them are venturing out of their safe suburban enclave and reaching out to the Black community in the nearby city. They attribute these changes, not only to their kids, but to their increasing racial awareness in a rapidly changing society. The only way they differ from comparable intraracial couples at this stage of life is that they feel freer to bring more racial balance into their social and personal relationships.

They were, for the most part, open to their children's life style choices, even if they were personally disappointed. They felt less burdened with the responsibility of protecting their children from the pains of racism. Like most couples in middle age who have launched their offspring, biracial couples have the opportunity to put more of their energy into their personal and couple lives.

Older Age

In older age, interracial couples' lives may be intertwined with these of their children and grandchildren. It is in this era that they may feel most multicultural. Because no matter whom their child marries, the marriage and the grandchildren will be multiracial. Obviously, other factors will affect these relationships. If the original couple is still together, that is clearly an opportunity for them to provide their offspring successful role modeling for surviving racism as an intact family. If they are no longer together, much will depend on with which parent and extended family the offspring has more affiliation.

One divorced Black woman told me how surprised she was when she attended the wedding of her biracial son to a White woman. She found on the groom's side of the church a preponderance of Black friends and kinfolk, and only two of her White ex-husband's kin in addition to him. The bride's side was all White. When she queried her son several months later about this, he told his mother that he probably would not have invited his father if his bride had not insisted on it. He never had forgiven his father "for leaving her." He had always felt closer to her side of the family, and he insisted this had nothing to do with race, especially considering that he had married the woman he loves, who just happens to be White. It was a question of people, whom he liked and cared to be with and whom he didn't. He reminded his mother that he'd always been closer to her family and friends than to those of his father. And, he added, he had always felt closer to her than to his father, who was not home much and not available emotionally to either him or his mother.

Families of Origin

The literature does not address the impact of the interracial marriage on the couple's families of origin, although it does discuss the impact of the families of origin on the couple. But these families of origin have to deal with their racial identities once a member of another race is brought into the family. Even if the family totally rejects their child and his or her new family, their identity has been changed.

Shock, dismay, and fear are often the first reactions of both Black and White families. This was not their dream or expectation for their child. Even if they like their child's intended, they are shaken up and worried about issues of safety, future grandchildren, what other people will think, and so forth. No one wants their child to make a choice that is likely to be a lifelong struggle.

What is truly hopeful is that many families are more flexible and resilient than others might expect. And it is difficult to predict which families will be supportive and which will be rejecting—there are always surprises. With time, families often grow to be supportive and to aid the couple actively to create a bicultural familial environment. While the literature indicates that Black families are more accepting early on, how both families will respond also depends on the nature of the relationship between parents and offspring up to the time of this choice. If it's been a strong relationship, it will survive disappointments. If it was fragile to begin with, the intermarriage may provide the leverage that cuts it off. In other words, the previous family dynamics are more significant than race. Some argue that troubled families are more likely to produce offspring who will rebel by marrying someone of another race. That certainly may be so for some, and there are many intermarriers from troubled families who use the survival skills they developed growing up to enable themselves to develop gratifying marriages in difficult contexts.

In-law relationships are strikingly absent from social science study. It's easy to see how race can become the target of what might be tense in-law relationships regardless of race. Sometimes race masks religious, class, or life style choice differences.

> The Gersons, an observant Jewish couple, were devastated when their 28-year-old son married a Black woman. They were more upset by the religious difference than by the racial difference, but they tried everything they could to prevent this marriage from occurring. They begged their rabbi, their doctor, and all of their friends and relatives to dissuade their son. No one wanted to become involved in this way, and the wedding proceeded without their attendance. Because of their rabbi's refusal to dissuade their son, they left the synagogue with which they had been affiliated throughout their married life. Three years later, twins were born to the interracial couple. The Gersons made some overtures in order to have contact with their only grandchildren (to date). When the young couple divorced 2 years later, the Gersons were quite disconcerted because the mother took the twins to another part of the country to live, and their son only saw them in the summer. They were left bereft of the grandchildren they had come to cherish. They were also left with much guilt and confusion about what may have been their contribution to

the breakup of the marriage that they had never approved of in the first place.

RACIAL IDENTITY FOR TRANSRACIAL ADOPTEES AND THEIR FAMILIES

Most of the research on transracial adoptees has been about Black adoptees in White families. In addition to the identity issues that all adoptees face, racial identity issues are charged when neither parent shares even part of the adoptee's race or ethnicity.

Developmentalists agree that secure attachment is necessary for basic trust to develop in the first couple of years. Based on Erikson's (1950) model, this basic trust is the foundation of identity. A recent study by Rosenboom (1993) found that the quality of attachment between adoptive parents and interracial adoptees is lower in the United States, where interracial adoption is viewed as "touchy," than in the Netherlands, where interracial adoption is more accepted. The findings of Steir (1983) and Singer et al. (1985) that interracial mother–child pairs did exhibit a higher incidence of insecure attachment (either overly clinging or indifferent when reunited with the mother) than nonadopted and interracially adopted children may be attributable at least in part to societal attitudes. They also found transracial adoptive mothers to be more anxious and protective, and less comfortable allowing others to care for their babies. This anxiety could also stem from the mothers' awareness of the negativity of society's reactions to transracial families.

A number of studies found no difference between the self-esteem of transracially adopted children and Black children adopted by Black parents. This suggests that positive self-esteem can be effectively generated in a transracial setting (Bagley & Young, 1979; Ladner, 1977; McRoy & Freeman, 1984; McRoy, Zurcher, Lauderdale, & Anderson, 1982; Shireman & Johnson, 1986; Simon & Alstein, 1992). However, significant differences were found between transracial and same-race adoptees regarding their sense of racial identity, confirming the studies that view personal identity and racial identity as operating separately.

In racial identity studies of nonadopted Black children, preschool children evaluate the attractive qualities of Whites more positively than those of Blacks. However, as they develop, this seems to change to a more positive Black identification, especially once they have passed the primary school age. This same transition does not always take place for the transracial adoptee (Simon & Alstein, 1992). The attitude of the adoptive parent about the importance of developing a racial identity greatly impacts the child's positive identification with being Black. Transracial adoptees whose parents acknowledged and discussed race felt more positively about themselves as Black than children raised by parents who minimized the importance of racial difference (McRoy et al., 1982).

How can White parents teach Black children the survival skills to cope in a racist society? Many Black mental health professionals believe that these basic survival skills need to become integrated into ego functions. This can only occur if the Black child has significant Black role models. The greatest fear of the critics of transracial adoption is the same as is present for biracial children, that the child will become marginal to both Black and White worlds and not be able to function in either. For, while the Black adoptee has been socialized by White parents in the White culture, to the rest of the world, this person will always be Black. With idealistic parents, who attempt to transcend race and form a "human identity," Black adoptees are in for major obstacles.

Most experts agree that a Black identity is essential to the well-being of the transracially adopted Black child. There are two critical characteristics of adoptive families most likely to facilitate the healthy development of racially different offspring: (1) openly acknowledging and discussing racial differences, and (2) having extended contact with people of the race of the adoptee by living in a racially mixed neighborhood. Families who through their own ambivalence, guilt, or denial ignore these differences are likely to have confused children.

Children adopted in infancy usually do not question their family relationships until they are old enough to realize that most children look like their parents. Some adoptive parents deal with this realization by stressing similarities, such as hair or eye coloring. As more disturbance is noted, parents need to stress that the child belongs to the family. One adoptive mother told her Hispanic son that "God had made his biological mother smart enough to find me and his dad because that was where he belonged."

It's important for adoptive parents not to attribute all traits of the transracial adoptee to race or ethnicity. There are also factors of the adoptee's heredity and preadoption environment, as seen in Chapters 2 and 3. Transracial adoptive families confront the same adoption issues as intraracial families.

The adoptee may want to search for the biological parents or kinfolk, and the outcomes of the search can be as variable as reported in Chapter 3 for intraracial adoptees. A major difference will be the impact of the search on the adoptee's racial identity. However, search might be difficult in domestic adoptions, as there are fewer birth parents of color registering with the search agencies than White birth parents. With regard to international adoptions, most of the traces have been erased, and it is nearly impossible to achieve success. The adoptee is usually left with whatever information the adoptive parents were given at the time of the adoption, and this information may be incomplete and inaccurate. However, in recent years, as there has been more media attention paid to adoptees' and birth parents' searches, many international adoptees visit their countries of origin when they become adults. They want to learn whatever they can about their culture. Obviously, some of the war-torn countries, such as Cambodia and Guatemala, might be difficult, if not impossible, to visit.

> Maya, now 23, was adopted by missionaries working in El Salvador. Her adoption story informs her that she had been abandoned and was found in an orphanage. As she is contemplating becoming pregnant, she is yearning to fill in the missing information about her background, and she has been attempting to contact another missionary still in El Salvador who had been the person who found her for her adoptive parents. Due to the political situation there, this search has been unsuccessful. But this heightens Maya's determination. She wants at least to visit the country where her parents served for many years, leaving her with relatives while away on their missions. She believes that she will achieve better understanding of her adoptive parents if she can see where they spent most of their missions. She has much ambivalence about her adoptive parents. She loves them and appreciates the opportunities they have provided, but she also resents their aloof, cold style of parenting and the fact that they never talked to her about her racial difference. She always felt different from the kids at school and had a sense of shame about her unusual adoptive circumstances.

There can be perceptions of likenesses as well as differences in a transracial adoptive family. These do not have to depend on race, but on attributes such as habits, interests, and aptitudes. For example, one Hispanic adoptee identifies so closely with her father, a minister, that she has developed an alcohol problem "just like his," and she believes that it is a familial trait. A Black adoptee with seven White biological siblings, when asked how he felt about transracial adoption, replied, "I did pretty well. I went to Yale and Harvard Law School, and I credit my family with enabling me to achieve so much. All of us have gone to excellent colleges and universities and attained the same occupational level as our parents."

Impact on Siblings

White Siblings

The White siblings of Black adoptees, whether adoptees or biological children, experience identity confusion simply because of the fact that their family composition is different from mainstream families. Little attention has been paid in the research to the impact of transracial adoption on White siblings.

> Nancy, now 19, was 6 when her White parents adopted a Black infant, whom they named Todd. She really enjoyed having a baby brother, and her parents were ecstatic. Nancy and her family live in Manhattan, where Nancy attends private school. Until she got into middle school, she accompanied her mother on walks with Todd to the park and up and down the avenues. When other people asked her mother questions such as, "What is he?" "Whose baby is he?," it did not bother her. However, when she entered preadolescence, she began to realize that having a Black baby made her family different. She began to hear racist remarks around her, and she saw how the token Blacks in her elite school were barely tolerated. It was nothing specific, just feelings she picked up. Wanting desperately to be approved of by her peers, she began to distance herself from Todd and from her mother, the primary caretaker. She no longer wanted to invite friends over, fearing that they would be shocked by her having a Black brother, and she no longer wanted to appear in public with her mother and brother. As she began to feel more and more ashamed, she became more irritable at home, and, in order to evade her mother's concerned questions, she withdrew more and more. This lasted until the end of high school, when she could no longer contain her feelings and, in a fit of temper, screamed at her parents how they had "ruined her life" by adopting Todd. Yet, she was conflicted because she truly loved Todd and her parents. Intellectually, she felt transracial.
>
> Three years later and in her second year of college, Nancy has worked through her confusion and is again close to all members of her family. She feels that her parents were so busy preparing Todd and protecting him from racism that they virtually ignored her difficulties, assuming because she was White that she could not be adversely affected. What helped her the most was a new guidance counselor in her senior year who intuitively surmised what was underlying Nancy's moodiness and erratic academic performance. This guidance counselor steered Nancy into an interracial family support group where she could learn about racial issues independent of her family.

Nancy's parents feel the same regrets as do parents of special needs and chronically ill children. In retrospect, they realize that they assumed the sibling was able to cope and survive, and they did not make the effort to reserve some attention and attunement for the child without special needs. The point is that the family's racial identity changes, and this effects every member, regardless of their color. Nancy, as a child, experienced much of the same surprise, unawareness, confusion, and eventual rage that White spouses experience in adulthood when they enter interracial marriages. But interracial spouses typically choose to be in a biracial family and deliberate long and hard before finalizing the decision. White siblings are children, and, although their parents may ask them how they feel about an impending adoption, children can have no understanding of the implications.

On the other hand, some White siblings, while experiencing the same shocks, disappointments, and confusions, are better prepared by their parents, are more personally secure than Nancy, and are able to confront their peers' racism and not let it bother them. They are almost precocious in understanding and supporting their family's new racial identity, and they feel "special" because they participate in this different social constellation.

Black Siblings

Black siblings are strengthened by having another Black adoptee become part of the family constellation. The older sibling can provide support and role modeling to the younger sibling with regards to recognizing and coping with racism. One White adoptive mother talked about how helpless she felt when her older and, at the time, only Black son came home from kindergarten confused by a child calling him "nigger." This mother was able to empathize with him but felt tremendous pain realizing that she had never experienced that level of discrimination, even though she grew up in a community where she was taunted for being Jewish. When she adopted her second Black son, she was relieved that he would have an older brother to be there for him when the same name calling inevitably occurred.

Impact on White Parents

These parents tend to fall into two general groups. One group consists of people who ignore and deny racial differences or who think of their Black adoptees as really being White because the rest of the family is White. In other words, these are the parents who think of their family as White with a Black adoptee. Thus, they do not allow their racial identity to change or develop. They are able somehow to insulate themselves from racial realities, and they minimize racist occurrences. Some families have enough social and economic power that they are able to live in communities that support their White identity.

The second group considers themselves an interracial family and openly engages with families and groups of both heritages, much as multiracial families do. In these families, racial differences and issues are acknowledged, and the family as a whole unites to cope with any incidents of racism. These families were aware of racial issues and the difficulties they would experience as White parents of children of color before the adoption, and they have utilized support groups and whatever resources their adoption agency provides.

> Leila and Jim, White adoptive parents in their 40s, live in a college town where they both teach. Although the college is known to be a fairly liberal institution, there are very few people of color on the faculty or staff and only a small number of minority students. Leila and Jim believe that their biracial daughter, Julia, who happens to be light skinned, would never have had the safe, secure environment she has if she had not been adopted. At the time of her adoption, there were very few eligible Black or biracial couples wishing to adopt, and Leila and Jim felt they were doing the "right thing" by adopting her. Julia, currently a high school sophomore, considers herself just like her friends and families and has, to date, been spared exposure to any incidents of racism. This is a family where the parents and offspring have a White family racial identity. It is inevitable that in the next few years Julia will have to confront the realities of racism, and it is likely that her delayed racial identity development will be particularly painful for her.

Sometimes a particular event is what impels the family to become more aware of their family racial identity.

> Linda and Al live in a midwestern city. They have a White adopted son, 4, and a biracial adopted son, 1. Linda and Al have other friends in their community who have recently transracially adopted, and these families provide support for each other. She was trying to get her older son into a particular preschool for this year and was told there were no spaces available. Linda was amused when one of her friends, also a transracial adoptive parent, suggested she bring her child of color to the orientation meeting. Sure enough, once the preschool director saw the biracial child, her attitude about the older boy's ad-mission changed, and, subsequently, he was admitted. Linda's sud-den insight into the advantage of becoming a multiracial family led her to reconstruct the family identity she had always held. In our in-terview, she laughingly predicted that she'd probably be able to get her older son into the elementary school of choice (school assignment

depends on racial balance) just so that school can have the younger son and increase its minority quota.

Transracial Adoptive Families in Midlife

As with any family, the history of family relations influences adult offspring–parent relationships. If the transracial adoptee has unresolved issues about the adoption and/or identifies primarily with the non-dominant culture, there may be distancing or cutoff. On the other hand, there may continue to be attempts to resolve whatever problems remain.

The families whom I interviewed had a variety of adult family relations. It would be difficult to attribute relationship difficulties to just one issue—race, adoption, or problematic family functioning. In the happiest situations, there was mutual respect, contact, and an embracing of multiculturalism. The adult offspring's life choices—career, life style, marriage, children, and so forth—are a major factor. If these choices are congruent with the family's values, there is likely to be closer contact. If not, distance may be a welcome relief for everyone, despite the concomitant pain and disappointments.

Adult Transracial Adoptees

I find that the political and sociocultural contexts are highly significant factors in how adult transracial adoptees view themselves and their unusual families. If, for example, there is economic competitiveness and they experience more discrimination than they had been prepared for, they may resent the "unreality" of their upbringing and the distance from either the Black or the White community. This feeling of marginality can be expressed in extreme reactions—anger, rejection, antisocial behavior. However, as with biracial families, if there were secure attachments in the adoptive family and racial issues were openly discussed, transracial adoptees may feel confident and competent enough to make proactive, rather than reactive, choices.

Thus, the life style choices the adoptee makes will affect the family racial identity. In some cases, the adoptee immerses him- or herself into the Black community and has distant, if any, relations with the adoptive family. In those circumstances, the adoptive family may revert back to the preadoption family identity. In other cases, where the bonding between the adoptee and the adoptive family continues, the family will continue to develop its multiracial identity.

*   *   *

There are many variables that contribute to the multiracial identity development of individuals, couples, and families. And there is no one timetable or a linear progression of stages that can be applied to all kinds of families. I'm struck by the common themes my interviewees present, but awed by the different impacts of these themes, the wide variety of coping and survival strategies, and the resilience and creativity of these courageous pioneers who do more than give lip service to democratic values and ideals.

Changing sociocultural, political, and economic contexts affect one's life course. Personal events such as health, chance happenings, birth, marriage, divorce, and death all influence personal and racial identity development.

Mental health professionals need to be aware of the typical developmental issues, the factors that can aid or impede development, contextual variables in addition to racism, and available resources so as to facilitate individuals, couples, and families coming to terms with their uniqueness. We need to consider the influence of race on difficulties but not to assume that it is always the cause of people's problems.

TEN

Treatment Issues Pertaining to Interracial Couples and Families

The Jefferson family, Cliff, a 49-year-old Black journalist; Nancy, a 44-year-old White elementary school teacher; Fred, their 14-year-old son; and Marylou, their 12-year-old daughter, were referred to family therapy because of Fred's behavior at school—cutting classes, not turning in homework assignments, and sharply declining academic performance. They presented themselves as a warm, close family. Cliff and Nancy were puzzled by Fred's behaviors, assuming that this was "normal adolescent rebellion" attributable to his entering the regional high school and "falling in with a different group of peers." Both parents are college graduates and place a high value on academic achievement. They have always limited their children's television watching, and strived to expose them to intellectual and cultural activities such as theater, concerts, and museums. When asked about racial issues, they denied any concerns, claiming that the communities in which they reside and work are liberal and multicultural. Cliff was formerly married to a Black woman and has two children from that marriage who periodically come to spend a weekend. Although Nancy was not married previously, she had been in an intense 5-year relationship.

At the first session, the children were pleasant and cooperative, but reticent about participation. Marylou sat close to her mother, looking toward Fred before she answered any questions. Fred seemed skeptical about some of his parents' responses, as evidenced by his raised eyebrows and surprised looks. In the second session, when each family member was asked to draw a picture in response to four questions (Where would you rather be right now? What do you provide to this family? Who hurts the most in this family? What would you like to change about this family?), it emerged that Dad has "temper eruptions" that result in the mother's intimidated physical and emotional withdrawal from everyone in the family. Marylou and Fred have learned to retreat to their respective rooms. Fred then goes to Mom's room to coax her out of her withdrawal. Dad claims that these eruptions are caused by Mom's insensitivity to his needs and to her "overinvolvement" with the children, particularly Marylou. Once he "blows," it's "over" and he doesn't understand "what the big deal is." After Mom, Fred is the next target of Dad's anger. These arguments are always based on Fred's not working hard enough or appreciating the fruits of Dad's labors. Mom and Fred explain these eruptions as "indications of Dad's caring."

The issues that emerged slowly over several assessment sessions included (1) the pseudomutuality of the system, where everyone must pretend to themselves and the outside world that "we are a successful family with no real problems"; (2) persistent denial of racial issues, including lack of acknowledgment and exploration of the meaning of Marylou's light skin color compared to Fred's; (3) a deeply ingrained power struggle within this rigidly authoritarian, patriarchal family (they argue over Mom's childrearing, housekeeping, and spending of money); (4) Fred's emerging racial identity struggles conflicting with his usual role of "the family protector"; (5) Marylou's being Mother's "good girl" as a way of calming the tensions; (6) Mother's overreliance on her widowed mother for what has been unacknowledged financial assistance; and (7) lack of family or couple social relationships, which isolates this family from social support and contact with possible role models for transition into the adolescent phase of family development.

Therapeutic intervention was at a standstill until the therapist's peer supervision group suggested she reframe the couple conflict as a power struggle between Nancy's culturally ingrained assumption that Cliff's power came from his being male and Cliff's culturally ingrained assumption that Nancy's power came from her being White. This reframing created a new balance, which enabled the parents to begin to acknowledge and talk about race. Dad was able to articulate in front of his children that when Nancy didn't hear him or avoided him by siding with the children, he felt he needed to defend himself from the same kind of "pushing around" he had experienced as a Black male until he achieved parity in school and the workplace. He had decided long ago that "no one was ever going to push him around or control his life in any way." Nancy came to see that she was not as powerless as she had perceived, that her "Whiteness" shaped her assumptions of privilege, and that she needed to think carefully about issues of race. As a White woman, the therapist was able to focus on Cliff's need to control so as not to be controlled and his attitudes about White Women, which were displaced onto her (transference), in order to help him become more aware of this defensive need to exert control before he can be controlled. There was a solid caring and level of compatibility between this couple, which motivated them to invest effort and energy into their couple and family treatment.

Watching and listening very carefully, the children were then able to talk about their own concerns and racial pulls. Fred felt caught between Black and White worlds, was afraid of his father while he identified with him, and felt the need to protect his mother and sister. Marylou, closely identified with her mother and yearning for more kind attentiveness from her father, felt confused about her lighter skin and thought maybe this was why her father was angry at her mother. The utilization of genograms and ecosystem maps (a visual mapping out of all the social systems with which this particular family interacts, such as family of origin, neighborhood, community, school system, health system, religion, work, and so forth) facilitated this family's ability to deal with these deeply hidden issues.

They were thus able to understand Fred's acting out in context and disentangle "typical adolescent" behavior from what had heretofore been hidden, underlying family troubles. They also learned to differentiate relationship issues from racial issues. As racial and cultural differences were explored further, common values and goals, such as the importance of family, honesty, and hard work, were emphasized. This focus on commonality is a key strategy when working with interracial and intercultural families. Another focus of the therapist was to explore the barriers the couple used to prevent connection to other couples and families. Their social isolation intensified their feelings of alienation and differentness. They were even given specific homework assignments about initiating contact with potential friends.

This case vignette illustrates the particular attention clinicians need to pay to transference and countertransference issues when working with clients of different racial, gender, or cultural backgrounds. Depending on the past experiences of both the client and the therapist with members of each other's racial and cultural groups, transference and countertransference may play a significant role in the therapeutic relationship. For example, the individual from a minority culture might expect controlling and authoritative behavior from the individual of the majority culture. In addition, there can certainly be a transference process occurring between members of an interracial marriage. Although each member may like to think that he or she is free of bias and prejudices, most of us retain at least minimal stereotypes, which are perpetuated by society. These attitudes may range from totally unconscious to totally conscious. The therapist must be careful not to be an enabler of racism by avoiding areas of discomfort. We need to be cognizant of the social realities others experience. Likewise, we need to be aware of our own experiences and feelings about discrimination, whether they be related to race, religion, gender, or class. If the client is expressing rage about discrimination and that rage taps our own rage about some experience of discrimination, we may overreact to the client's experience, and urge them to more assertive responses than they may desire or be ready for. If we fear a client's anger or suspicion, we may placate and collude rather than challenge and confront. While the effects of transference and countertransference exist in all therapy cases, they may be more insidious in interracial cases, due to deeply ingrained, often unconscious, racist, stereotypical beliefs. These will be explored further in the next section.

Little attention in the literature has been paid to clinical work with interracial and interethnic families, although there has been recent work about multiculturality that includes discussion about multiracial couples and families (see Atkinson et al., 1989; Comas-Díaz, 1996; Comas-Díaz & Greene, 1994; Ho, 1990). The multicultural literature highlights the necessity for clinicians to learn how to adapt and broaden their clinical assessment and treatment approaches to meet the needs of differing cultural orientations. In order to provide effective services, clinicians need to incorporate the following:

1. Become aware of their own attitudes about people of different race and ethnicity and their attitudes toward mixed marriages and families
2. Learn about cultural and experiential differences of clients within a sociopolitical context
3. Develop therapeutic processes and goals that are consistent with and appropriate to the individual differences and cultural orientation of clients
4. Be familiar with available community resources and support groups
5. Understand racial identity development processes
6. Strengthen their capacity for creating a culturally sensitive climate of compassion, empathy, dignity, and respect for differences

In this chapter, I will discuss therapists' racism and the influences of racial transference and countertransference, as well as the treatment issues and the expanding therapist role with regard to interracial couples, multiracial families, and transracial adoptive families.

THERAPISTS' RACISM

As noted in Chapter 8, racism is so deeply ingrained in both Whites and people of color that it is easy for all racial groups to deny its effects. In fact, most writers agree that it is unlikely anyone in our society, regardless of their racial or ethnic origins, is free of some degree and level of racism. White, Eurocentric values provide the norms underlying our socialization. They affect our assumptions, values, attitudes, biases, and stereotypes. These norms perpetuate the racial stereotypes and myths necessary to maintain the dominant White culture.

Professionally, the Eurocentric values that underlie theories and practices of psychotherapy cause us to view people who are different as "troubled" because of their deviance from the mainstream. We assess them from our dominant culture norms.

"When I went to the university counseling service to talk about my interracial relationship, the White counselor told me that I was either 'rebelling or acting out psychological instability' by becoming involved in this kind of relationship."—Dana, 34, White wife

"My sister, a social worker no less, told me that I was an 'Uncle Tom' and more interested in making it as a White by 'crossing' (in response to my announcement of my engagement to a White woman)."—Jeff, 37, Black husband

"The pastoral counselor whom my parents insisted I meet with suggested that my interracial relationship had to be based on my believing that 'Black men were better lovers.' He urged me to have more sexual encounters with White men before I went any further with this relationship."—Maria, 39, White wife

"My high school counselor told me that I'd better not ask any White girls to a school function as the principal would embarrass both of us."—Lloyd, 18, biracial high school senior

"We were told by the White adoption worker that Black adoptees, even when adopted in infancy, would grow up with a greater likelihood of learning disability and psychological disability."—Beth, 32, and Ted, 34, White transracial adoptive parents

Many clinicians think they are helping clients to confront racial "realities" with these kinds of comments. They appear to be unaware that there is no empirical validity to these views, and they overgeneralize rather than attend to individual differences within racial and ethnic groups. Having been trained in a dominant White cultural context, many clinicians have not learned to empathize with the reference norms utilized by clients from diverse cultures. They assume a monocultural stance (a universal set of norms) and are uncomfortable acknowledging their own racist assumptions.

The Asian partner of an interracial marriage, for example, may be very reticent about a collaborative relationship with a therapist, insisting on deference and respectful hierarchy. The White marriage partner may actually value this cultural behavior. Rather than assuming that the Asian partner is low on Bowen's self-differentiation scale and, therefore, is the "problem in the couple system," the clinician needs to respect the different cultural heritages and view whatever the presenting problems are in a bicultural context.

White Identity Model for White Clinicians

Integrating the three White identity models in the counseling literature (Hardiman, 1982; Helms, 1990a, 1990b; Ponterotto, 1988), Sabnani, Ponterotto, and Borodovsky (1991) describe five stages that White clinicians typically pass through on the way to a multicultural identity:

Stage 1: Preexposure/precontact—characterized by a lack of awareness of self as a racial being. White clinicians in this stage have not given thought to their role as part of a dominant White culture, nor have they considered their own racial identity.

Stage 2: Conflict—involving an expansion of knowledge with regard to racial matters. This expansion of knowledge may be stimulated by coursework, conferences, symposia, and independent reading. This new knowledge challenges White clinicians to acknowledge their Whiteness and its concomitant privileges so that they can begin to examine their own cultural values. This stage is characterized by conflict between wanting to conform to mainstream norms while desiring to uphold humanistic, egalitarian values. This cognitive dissonance can cause feelings of confusion, guilt, anxiety, anger, and depression.

Stage 3: Prominority/antiracism—two outlets for White clinicians to utilize in order to deal with the emotional discomfort of the previous stage.

Stage 4: Retreat into White culture—marks another potential response to Stage 2 emotions. At this point, instead of identifying with minority group members, White clinicians may respond to conflict stage emotions by withdrawing from interracial situations. They may also avoid multicultural courses and reading, preferring to work only with White clients.

Stage 5: Redefinition and integration—marks that point when White clinicians achieve a healthy balance with regard to racial identity. In this stage, they acknowledge their Whiteness and their responsibility for contributing to and perpetuating a racist status quo.

This model certainly has implications for training clinicians of all disciplines. In addition, exposure to teachers, supervisors, peers, and clients of diverse backgrounds as well as required formal and informal coursework, reading, and clinical experience should be essential components of any training program. However, knowledge about other cultures is not enough. We need to overcome our own discomfort so as to develop sensitivity to and empathy for the day-to-day struggles that all people of color endure.

Another study, by Pope-Davis and Ottavi (1994), while finding that White racial identity attitudes were predictive of racism, noted gender and age differences. Whites generally seem to hold negative attitudes about Blacks, but White women, perhaps because of their interpersonal orientation and their experiences of sex discrimination, are generally found to understand and appreciate the impact of racial attitudes on ethnic minorities more so than White males. This study also found that older Whites were more likely to be comfortable and accepting of racial differences than younger people. This study, which support the findings of earlier studies, implies that it is necessary for clinicians to address openly Whites' and Blacks' acknowledgment of their own racial identity and ingrained racism.

Awareness of Cultural Traditions

We must recognize that our values are based on our own dominant cultural traditions. In order to deconstruct some of our racist assumptions, the first step is to learn about the cultural traditions of other racial and ethnic groups. Otherwise, even with the best intentions, we are prone to pathologize and devalue behaviors and attitudes that do not fit into our Western value system. This does not mean that pathology does not exist across cultural groups, but that we need to be able to distinguish culture from pathology.

> John, a 34-year-old White Anglo, and Theresa, a 29-year-old Latino of Cuban background, came to therapy because of conflict over whether or not Theresa would return to her professional law career now that their baby is 6 months old. John expects to have an egalitarian dual career marriage, and he believes that Theresa has "broken their agreement," because she is reluctant to return to work. Theresa acknowledges that she had no idea how attached she would become to her baby. Her mother and sister, now living in Puerto Rico, have urged her to put her family first and stay home for a few years, and she has decided that is what she wants to do. John can't understand how she can ignore their plans to save money, build their "dream" home, buy new cars, and so forth.
>
> The therapist, a White male, finds himself siding with John. His

wife works full time and he has little empathy for Theresa's point of view. In supervision, when asked to consider what the cultural value differences might be, he looks stunned and admits that he never thought about that perspective. The therapist's countertransferential reactions impacted the effectiveness of his therapeutic assessment and intervention. His overidentification with John prevented him from understanding and empathizing with Theresa's views.

Without consideration of the cultural context, Theresa and John continue to view this issue as a personal power struggle. Within cultural contexts, they can learn that, even though it appeared as if Theresa had embraced John's cultural values, when it came right down to it, her inner pulls were toward putting child care into a higher priority than professionalism or materialistic acquisitiveness. When a couple can begin to understand the other's frame of reference, they can work more collaboratively to arrive at a mutually agreed-upon solution.

In order to help clinicians become more aware of diverse cultural value systems, let's consider overall value assumptions of the Black, Asian, and Hispanic world views. Robinson and Howard-Hamilton (1994, pp. 338–339) delineate for clinicians the major differences between Afrocentric and Eurocentric value assumptions. Eurocentric values prioritize self-sufficiency, the self as defined by others, autonomy, competition, possessiveness, immediate gratification, productivity, and achievement. These views maintain the status quo, emphasizing the here and now. Afrocentric values, on the other hand, prioritize unity, self-determination through confrontation, collective work, responsibility, cooperative economics, delayed gratification, faith and spirituality through an intergenerational perspective, and creativity. These different value systems shape attitudes and behaviors, and people raised in a Eurocentric culture may consider those influenced by Afrocentric views to be "weak," "irresponsible," or "dependent." Clinicians who do not recognize and respect Blacks' faith and spiritual values, their definition of family as including members who are not blood relatives, and the impact of their historical heritage of racism and migration can't possibly understand their frame of reference.

In the same vein, Berg and Jaya (1993) summarize for clinicians significant Asian cultural values: the importance of form (protocol, respect, forms of address, and procedure) over content; the use of negotiation over direct confrontation; inclusion and unconditional acceptance; family over individual; saving face; respect, dignity and honor; and valuing of the elderly.

Li, a 42-year-old Chinese engineer from mainland China, married Vera, a 34-year-old White woman from the Midwest, 1 year after arriving at graduate school in this country. They lived in the same town as Vera's family and spent considerable time with them. After being married 5 years, Li was able to bring his parents over, and they, too, set up residence in the same small midwestern city. The couple came to therapy in their seventh year of marriage. Vera was furious at Li's "passive dependence." She believed he had been passed over for career advancement because of his laid-back manner, and his refusal to engage with her in discussion led her to vitriolic outbursts. She attacked his parents, feeling that they were not making any efforts to become "Americanized," and one of the presenting issues was her not wanting Li's parents to have much connection with their two small children.

The clinician's first goal was to educate Vera about Chinese values, such as honoring one's parents, avoiding direct confrontation, not wanting to "bother anyone," and to help Li to understand Vera's more emotionally expressive, direct style. After these cultural differences were laid out, the couple could get beyond their disappointments and begin a more mutual collaboration on life style decisions. When family-of-origin sessions were held, it became obvious that Vera's parents were embarrassed by Vera's treatment of her in-laws and wanted to have the grandchildren learn about both cultural and religious traditions. This was quite a surprise to Vera, who thought she was pleasing her parents by conforming to their way of life.

General characteristics of Latino cultures, as summarized by Vasquez (1994), include the importance and value of the family over individual or professional needs, group achievement over individual achievement, and traditional sex roles. A clinician familiar with the Latino culture would be able to empathize with Theresa's conflicts, who wanted to please her husband but, at the same time, follow her natural inclinations about parenting. When a couple is helped to acknowledge and respect both cultural views, the struggle becomes less personal, and compassion and tolerance are likely to be fostered.

Rules concerning endogamy and exogamy vary from culture to culture and, within a culture, according to time, class, and gender. During times when a society wants to create alliances with other groups, exogamy is acceptable, whereas at times when a group wants to maintain boundaries, endogamy is the rule. Likewise, within a culture, exogamy may be acceptable for some classes, but not for others. For example, in Islamic culture, Muslim men are allowed to marry non-Muslims. However, Muslim women are not (Donnan, 1990). And, as pointed out in Chapter 8, while there are no explicit rules regarding interracial marriages today in this country, the U.S. Bureau of the Census (1990) reports that 70% of Black–White marriages involve a Black husband. Perhaps one of the reasons that cultural groups resent their members marrying out, as opposed to earlier times when the American ideal was the "melting pot," is that today's ideal of pluralism encourages each cultural group to preserve its unique ethnic and racial identity. Therefore, intermarriage may be viewed as a threat to a minority group's survival.

Clinicians need also to be aware of a culture's views toward mental health and its treatment. The White spouse may urge the non-White spouse to seek couple or family treatment. The non-White spouse may resist this suggestion, not due to denial, but rather due to a culturally ingrained belief that talking about personal matters with a nonfamily member is taboo. If these cultural attitudes exist, the therapist may be wise to change his or her usual format, perhaps approaching the couple as a focused problem-solving consultant. Some cultures would find experiential techniques suspect; others would perceive a therapist's probing as intrusive and disrespectful.

The area of therapist–client match is understudied. S. Sue's (1995; cited in DeAngelis, 1995) and Rodriguez's (1995; cited in DeAngelis, 1995) research groups found that people who saw therapists from their own ethnic groups stayed in treatment longer. These researchers hypothesize that "the smaller the differences between therapist/client outlooks on probem resolution and treatment goals, the more favorable the outcome" (DeAngelis, 1995, pp. 36–37). My experience indicates that a team consultation model best serves the needs of clients whose ethnicity or race is different than mine. If possible, I invite in a cotherapist or consultant of the client's ethnicity or racial group. I always ask clients at the end of a first session how they feel about working with me, a White female. Do they believe my gender or race will interfere with my understanding them? Are there any specific reasons why they chose to consult me? This checking in must continue throughout treatment. It is my responsibility to learn about clients' ethnic and racial concerns from the literature and my own contacts as well as from them. However, increasingly, with managed health care panels, clients' choices are limited. They may not have the choice of a therapist of their own gender, race, or ethnicity.

Another area that clinicians need to consider is their personal views about acculturation and assimilation. For clinicians to assume that the minority client desires to fit into the dominant culture and be "just like Whites" may be faulty thinking. There must be much open discussion between clinicians and their clients so that treatment goals are in line with the clients' wishes and needs, not the clinician's.

TREATMENT ISSUES WITH BIRACIAL COUPLES

The literature does refer to the potential problems biracial couples may encounter and present in therapy as a result of the stresses associated with intermarriage. Some identify problems particularly noted in biracial couples as related to instability and unhappiness (Ortega, Whitt, & Williams, 1988), proneness to physical violence (Rosenbaum & O'Leary, 1981), and so forth. However, it is hard to draw the conclusion that there is a higher likelihood of these kinds of problems in biracial couples than in other troubled couples. References to case studies and specific treatments are vague, and there is a lack of empirical data and case follow-up.

Assessment

As with any couple, therapists need to consider why and how the couple married, elucidate areas of problems specific to interracial marriage in addition to the problems that any couple may experience, and identify the dysfunctional patterns creating and maintaining these problems. What is usually different for interracial couples is the additional stress they experience due to the cultural racism of the larger, dominant society as well as their own cultural groups. Thus, for intermarried couples, there are likely to be more intense conflicting and competing loyalties among each partner's referent group, family of origin, spouse, and self. For example, each partner's parents may feel threatened, fearing that the very fact of intermarriage will distance their offspring as he or she will likely identify with another cultural group. This can increase their pressures on the couple to reconsider their decision to marry (as seen in the Young-Ware & Ware [1994] model).

In those cases where it seems that one or both partners have unconsciously or deliberately married out for specific reasons, it's important to identify those reasons and the meaning each member of the couple attributes to these reasons. Sometimes, people's stereotyped impressions about the other race lead them to seek each other out. This is likely, as pointed out by Friedman (1982), to result in disappointment. The question for clinicians to consider is whether racial expectations are really any different than the expectations any partner may have.

Possible differences in emotional expression and communication, particularly language difficulties or *meta-communication* (the nonverbal message about the message); expression of physical affection; the beliefs of each partner with regard to male/female sex roles; power distribution; cultural influences on the family structure; views about parenting; and the meaning of love need to be considered in any inter-cultural marriage.

> Willa, a 38-year-old White wife, and her Black husband, Ralph, 38, came for counseling because Ralph felt that Willa allowed her parents to behave rudely to him, and he no longer wanted to go to their home. Ralph interpreted the fact that Willa's parents did not greet him with a hug or kiss as a personal rejection due to the color of his skin. While Willa did receive a cursory kiss on the cheek, she kept trying to tell Ralph that her parents had always been unaffectionate, and she had forced this greeting on them after she left home for college. She pointed out that they never had any physical contact with either of her brothers, their own brothers, or their parents.

Further discussion allowed the marriage counselor to reframe this problem as one of family style differences apart from race. This reframing, supported by genogram work, supported Willa's protestations and encouraged the couple to learn to discuss underlying racial concerns. The counselor focused on the overall style of communication between the couple. This couple tended to debate and argue, and disagreement became a power struggle between each partner's articulation and persistence. When conflict got out of hand and couldn't be debated any longer, Ralph would withdraw and sulk and Willa would try to coax him back into the arena. The goal of therapy was to establish a more effective pattern of communication, which would enable the couple to discuss whether or not incidents that were experienced as problematic had racial overtones. If so, they could work on how to recognize and acknowledge these contributing racial variables so that they could provide support to each other, in other words, how they could stop debating and begin to negotiate toward problem solving rather than problem exacerbation.

The clinician also needs to consider that a problem may reside primarily with one spouse. It is possible that an individual had personal problems prior to the marriage that have been carried over. If one or both partners have experienced previous marital failure, unresolved marital issues may spill over into the second marriage as they might with any couple. Or the stresses of interracial marriage may trigger previous feelings of guilt, an identity crisis, or feelings of alienation and isolation. It is not unlikely that the greater the opposition from one or both sets of parents and/or siblings, the greater the possibility that unconscious guilt about "being bad" and disappointing the parents will be triggered. These feelings of guilt may be further exacerbated for people who were raised in cultures where guilt is used to control behavior, such as Irish Catholic and Jewish cultures.

It is also important to learn how each individual defines his or her racial and cultural identity. In one couple I worked with, a Japanese woman converted to her White husband's faith, Judaism, not because she was interested in becoming Jewish, but because in her culture, a woman merges into the culture and family of her husband. Her husband resented what he called her "overinvolvement" in Jewish traditions, such as sabbath prayers and a reluctance to socialize on Friday evenings. To him, this was viewed as rigidity on her part. However, she was following the lead of her sisters-in-law and her mother-in-law, whom she believed to be the role models she was supposed to follow. Her husband was pleased that she had converted, because it mollified his parents, but he had no interest in such close observation of ritual, particularly if it interfered with his wishes.

Treatment

There really is no clear boundary between assessment and treatment, in that they both intertwine and continue throughout therapy. It seems to me that the overriding objective for the couple therapist is to create a therapeutic context that is empathic, compassionate, dignified, fair, and respectful. Within this context, it is easier to help the partners articulate their personal and cultural values, standards, and expectations. They can be helped to understand and respect the other's culture so as to form a bi- or multicultural family. If one member is supposed to give up his or her cultural beliefs, the cost to that individual's sense of identity can be damaging, and the ensuing couple conflict may be detoured through a child, causing the child to become the "identified patient." Many biracial couples want to acknowledge and honor both racial heritages and identities as they move toward biculturalism. What often happens is that the road to biculturalism is harder to achieve than desired. Societies—both Black and White—have ways of pushing people to choose one identity over the other.

There are a number of specific techniques that are useful to clinicians working with interracial couples. Prior to marriage, it is important to help potential partners check out their assumptions and expectations. They may want to consult with interracial couples in a similar stage of life, so that they develop realistic expectations about what they may experience. They may also want to sound out some family members whom they expect to be accepting about how best to approach those family members from whom they expect resistance. Clinicians can share whatever findings exist in the literature about interracial couples, and identify community resources and other sources of information. They can also role play talking to family members, playing out different expectations and possible outcomes. This gives therapists the opportunity to model effective communication when they play the role of the client, as well as the opportunity to identify possible outcomes when they play the role of different family members.

Cognitive restructuring—a technique that enables clients to identify their underlying assumptions (cognitive schemas), check them out, and modify them in line with their checking-out data—allows people to recognize, reassess, and possibly modify these core beliefs. Clarifying meaning and considering multiple perspectives of meanings are critical components of any therapeutic work.

As noted in previous examples, positive reframing of a couple's conflicts as involving cultural differences, rather than one being "good" or "right" and the other "bad" or "wrong," can enable a couple to see their conflicts as differences having equivalent value. This, in turn, can set a climate that is favorable to negotiation rather than fighting. Positive reframing of a problem can lead to its redefinition.

> Marian, a 48-year-old Black high school teacher, and Will, a 49-year-old White artist, came to therapy because they were locked into conflict over money. Marian was the steady income earner and was viewed by Will as being too "parsimonious." The issue was that Will had the opportunity to invest their savings in a new venture capital scheme if Marian would agree to sell their summer home. To Marian, this was "absolutely unacceptable." In searching for what money and financial management meant to each partner, Will talked about the "man being responsible for overall decision making," and he insisted quite defensively that he actually brought in more money each year than Marian, but it was sporadic and one couldn't know that until tax preparation time. Marian talked about the importance of financial security and conservative investment. Eventually, the therapist was able to elicit enough of each partner's transgenerational issues to enable Marian to articulate that "as the grandchild of sharecroppers, owning property was essential to feeling secure." Within a cultural context, the therapist reframed the money struggle as being about competing cultural and gender values, rather than a power struggle of "right versus wrong" or "bad versus good." This reframing allowed each partner to view the situation as less of a personal threat or assault. They were then able to develop more empathy for each other's view and move into problem solving.

Education leading to greater self- and other awareness can reduce tension and heighten empathy. In a more compassionate context, couples are more open to direct skill building, such as communication, negotiating, and other problem-solving skills. The clinical session can be utilized to model and foster the development of skill building. I often have couples reenact actively (rather than report verbally) their latest go-round, enact how they responded, and then create alternative responses for themselves and their partners.

> Jamie, 37, Black, and Tim, 34, White, were subject to raging verbal battles. The sequence was that Tim would enter the house after work preoccupied with tasks to be done at work, would be irritable and inattentive to Jamie and their two school-age children, and would then complain that "no one appreciates me around here." Jamie would control herself as long as she could, then would erupt verbally, calling him a "lazy White bastard who wanted a slave to pick up after him" and other such comments. The more Tim would ignore her, the angrier and more vitriolic she became. Then, they would not talk for several days. Eventually, the children would find some way to get them to respond to each other. There would be a couple of days of quiet before the next incident. These incidents seemed to occur consistently at the time of Tim's return from work.

The couple was asked to take turns sculpting each one's perception of Tim's homecoming. Tim perceived that Jamie beseiged him with complaints and tasks as soon as he walked through the door and that the children never even looked up from their television watching. He believed that the time he took to change his clothes, go through his brief case, and return a few business calls was perfectly reasonable as long he made it to dinner when Jamie called. Jamie's enactment indicated that her perception was that Tim never came into the kitchen to say "Hi," never asked her how her day was, and never engaged with the kids or did any chores around the house unless she had a "temper tantrum." In the next go-round of enactments, Tim portrayed how he would like the kids to come over to him to say "Hello" (a rule in his family of origin) and would like Jamie to take time from dinner preparation to join him in the bedroom for a few minutes of talk while he changed his clothes and prepared himself for the next day's work. Jamie portrayed how she would like Tim to come into the kitchen and hug her, to pause a few moments and ask what was going on, and then to wait until after dinner to take care of his "business." She wanted him to ask if there was anything he could do around the house instead of assuming that all child care and housework were her responsibility. She also wanted him to express appreciation for her contribution to the family income as a part-time hospital nurse.

Discussion about these enactments focused on each partner's in-grained expectations about sex roles and underlying racial stereotypes. Tim realized that he did expect Jamie to maintain a "low profile" without expectations, as had the Black nanny who raised him. Jamie

realized that she was allowing herself to take on all the tasks and responsibilities because of her ingrained expectation that she should comply
with Tim's maleness and Whiteness. Until the problem was redefined
as a power struggle, Jamie was full of self-loathing for her eruptions
and tumultuous feelings. Once these issues were out on the table, both
Tim and Jamie could use therapy sessions to learn to listen, reflect,
and communicate more clearly and in a more respectful manner.

Within a positive therapeutic relationship, the first phase of any
treatment is problem identification and exploration. The creation of
a genogram for each partner can help determine whether or not there
have been significant life events or crises involving racist overtones that
are unresolved and spilling over into the marriage. Fleshing out the
genogram by asking questions about attitudes, hopes, and expectations can expose any possible hidden agenda. The types of questions
that I ask include the following: "What was it like growing up male
or female in your family?" "What did you perceive your family's views
about the _____ race to be?" "What were your parents' expectations
for you?" "If someone in any generation of this family ever made a
choice that did not conform to your family's values, how was that person treated?" These kinds of questions can bring to the surface suspected patterns of defiance, complicated separation, or cut-off processes
and problems, as well as intimacy patterns and current relationships
within extended families.

While completing the more conventional genogram, clinicians can
also elicit the cultural life story (CLS) of each partner. As conceptual-
ized by McGill (1992), the CLS refers to an ethnic or cultural group's
origin, migration, and identity. This work helps elicit the family of
origin's narrative, beliefs, and meaning so that partners can become
more aware of cultural influences on their present situation. It is important for each partner to learn about the other's cultural history,
such as the impact of slavery and migration on Blacks and the impact
of slave ownership privilege on Whites.

> Eugene, a Black realtor age 46, and Dorothy, a White office manager
> age 46, came to couple therapy because of increased fighting about
> money. They have been married 6 years without children (a second
> marriage for Eugene). Dorothy wants to save for retirement, and Eu-
> gene wants to spend their money now, taking vacations and buying
> new cars. Dorothy is the steady wage earner, as Eugene is on com-
> mission. The process of constructing genograms and CLS brought
> forth information that surprised them. Dorothy learned that she was
> more shaken than she realized by her parents' drastically reduced cir-
> cumstances after their retirement. (They were forced to sell their home
> and live in a trailer park in order to make ends meet.) Eugene real-

ized that materialism represents security to him. His parents' migration from the South caused them to rationalize their loss of community and spiritual values by focusing solely on upward mobility. Eugene began to realize that his drivenness with regard to making and spending money had roots in his cultural history.

The therapist was able to reframe the emotionally loaded issues of money, security, and self-esteem into cultural differences rather than a power struggle for control. With this kind of understanding, she was able to teach them effective negotiating and problem-solving skills.

Many clinicians avoid direct introduction of both racial and sexual matters into assessment and therapy sessions. This may be due to their own discomfort. They must learn to be comfortable raising these issues at an appropriate time in an engaging manner. Racial issues must become the context for any questions or exploration and sexual issues need to be treated more in terms of relationship than race, unless the couple indicates otherwise. Assessing each partner's racial identity level is an important component of open discussion. As with any couple, discussion can include thoughts about having children, raising children, life style, relationships with extended family, the meaning of work and family, and so forth. At some time, the therapist may want to bring into a therapy session each party's family of origin (with the clients' approval and with adequate preparation). The two families may participate either separately or together. The goal is to help the couple check out their perceptions and experiences of family relationships.

An important component of any couple work is a focus on the couple's strengths. Primarily, the clinician must empathize with and give validation to the couple. One Black–White couple told me at the time of termination that I was the first therapist whom they'd ever consulted who defined their interracial marriage as "courageous and admirable." I also characterized this courage as indicating an admirable strength, to be able to make an unpopular choice and withstand adverse reactions. And I truly believe that this capacity to differentiate from one's family and culture is the type of strength that pioneers possess. Only by joining with the couple on their wave length, conveying an attitude of multipartiality (supporting each equally), can we help them to deal with their own racism and work on ways to combat it. We need to identify, acknowledge, and reinforce each partner's strengths and positive attributes.

Another critical treatment strategy is helping couples to locate interracial support groups (including special theme groups such as coping with rejecting family, interracial identity conflicts, and parenting skills), publications, and meetings. Groups may be sponsored by churches, community agencies, national associations, or private individuals. Our job is to foster appreciation, understanding, and improved communication and problem-solving skills, and to empower couples to reach out to possible support and educative resources.

TREATMENT ISSUES WITH BIRACIAL FAMILIES

Working with biracial families presents some unique challenges to clinicians (see Ponterotto, 1991, 1993; Root, 1992). I do not mean to suggest that multiraciality increases the likelihood of psychological maladjustment. However, offspring of biracial couples contend with dual identity development, competing loyalties, and confusing messages from a racist environment.

Assessment

One of the major tasks of clinicians when first meeting with interracial families presenting with a child-focused problem is to differentiate age-appropriate behaviors and concerns from family relationship difficulties. In other words, how much of the presenting problem is attributable to developmental concerns, how much to parenting difficulties or in response to marital conflict, and how much to racial or school variables? In many cases, there will be some attribution to all of these variables. Direct questioning, circular questioning, genograms, role plays, family sculpture, enactments of actual conflicts, and observation of family tasks, such as drawing a family picture together or solving a potential problem, can help in this assessment.

> The Brown family came to therapy because of Sam's aggressive behavior with his classmates in his fourth grade class. Dad, a Black insurance agent of 38, believed that the problems existed because Mom, a White secretary of 36, was too permissive with Sam and his third grade sister, Leslie. Mom believed that Dad wasn't paying enough attention to the children and that when he did, he was always belittling and critical. The therapist, trying to help the parents identify their own racial attitudes and their effect on other family members, asked Leslie (circular questioning) if Sam was the only child of color in his classroom. Leslie replied, "Yes," but that she had one Black and one Indian child in her classroom. The therapist then asked Mom what she thought it was like for Sam to be the only dark-skinned child in the classroom. The Browns were shocked. Their immediate response was to brush racial issues aside. Mom minimized the school

reports, claiming that Sam's behavior was "the way boys his age are," and Dad was angry, at Sam for calling attention to himself in a negative way and at Mom for creating this whole scene. It was clear that there were conflicting messages about "making waves" and "aggressive behaviors" in this family. The children both displayed feelings of discomfort and unease as their parents blamed each other.

The therapist sensitively went on with her assessment, making a note to return gently to racial issues when the family became more comfortable with her. She continued to explore the patterns of family interaction, noting the family's persistent denial and avoidance of racial differences and marital discord. She did not return to racial issues until the third session, when, after asking each family member to draw a picture of the family, she was able to contrast the parents' not coloring in their stick figures with the children's meticulous depiction of the varying skin colors within their family. Further discussion revealed that the mother's protectiveness of Sam was derived from her racist fear that aggressive behavior was a "Black" characteristic and that Dad was reliving his feelings of alienation and rage about being Black in a White society. The goal of therapy then became to help this family learn to discuss openly and comfortably their racial differences so that they could provide mutual support and guidance.

Treatment

Therapists can help families talk about their different physical appearances. Each family member may perceive and experience their own and others' physical appearances differently. They may also perceive differential treatment based on physical appearance. It is important for these perceptions to be identified and explored.

One objective of therapy is to help the family understand their family histories.

The Wilson family, consisting of Mom, a Black nurse; Dad, a White writer; Cynthia, age 17 (light skinned); and Tony, age 14 (darker skinned), was referred to family therapy by the high school guidance counselor. The family was shocked and polarized in response to Cynthia's experiences applying to college. Cynthia's behavior changed drastically, as she turned from being a bubbly, high-achieving, popular high school senior to an avoiding, nonproductive, withdrawing isolate. A top student and National Merit finalist, Cynthia had been led to believe by school personnel and her family that she would have no trouble gaining admission to a top college or university. When she visited the campuses of her two top choices, she was shown around by students. She asked to meet with Black students and was quite open about her racial identity. When one of the Black student guides took her to the Black Students' Association, she was told in no uncertain terms by the group that she was not "Black" enough for these universities, that she had sold out to the Whites by virtue of having a White father, and that these students were only interested in recruiting Black activists. When Cynthia returned home and reported these experiences, the family members began to argue and blame each other for this unexpected happening. Mom, light skinned enough to "pass" (for white), was furious at Cynthia for acknowledging her racial heritage in the first place, Dad was sympathetic, and Tony was derisive at "Miss Perfect" finally having her "comeuppance." The parents began to argue in front of the children, which had never happened before. Cynthia felt as if the rug had been pulled out from under her—her parents had encouraged her to consider herself bicultural, but now her mother was abandoning that, and she was beginning to see her family as not being the secure harbor she had always thought. Her grades began to slip, she skipped school, and she displayed many symptoms of clinical depression.

When the therapist, a White male, learned that Mom's extended family was an integral part of this system, he asked if the grandparents, two uncles, and one aunt could come into a session. The family readily agreed and a double-length session was scheduled. In preparation, the therapist helped the family to construct a large genogram on poster paper, and when the large group met, he asked the extended family members to contribute their narratives to the genogram and CLS.

The grandparents talked about their push for education and upward mobility with their children—each of whom is a successful professional. They talked about skin color, experiences of racism from within their own Black community where many of them resided, and in the White world, where they all worked. It came out that several kinfolk were "passing," visiting only after dark and in hushed silence. From childhood, Cynthia's mother had been conflicted about her racial identity, because so many in her family assumed that she would choose to pass. Her foremost objective was for her children to have every opportunity and advantage. She did not believe they could have that in the Black community, and, while she did not want them to deny their heritage, she wanted them to "play it safe."

Because of their professional status and upward mobility, the grandparents, aunts, and uncles on this side of the family were seen as "uppity" by many of their working-class neighbors. For the first time, Mom and Dad learned about Mom's family's mixed feelings about their marriage, even though they had come to love Dad and supported this young family's quest for biculturalism. It came out from Mom's mother and sister that Mom had experienced painful rejection from her Black high school classmates when she received (25 years earlier) a scholarship to a prestigious nursing college. Mom's anger at Cynthia may have been a projection of her earlier feelings about this. She remembered that she had felt while growing up that her family had focused only on her achievements. To her, they seemed to be unsympathetic to her dismay about her strained peer group relations. Mom surprised herself in this large family session by blurting out that "raising her children in a White community would protect them from this kind of hurt." In turn, her parents acknowledged that they had perhaps been "too unaware" in those times, and they apologized for not being more responsive to her.

This family-of-origin session was powerful, and it enabled the nuclear family to talk more openly with each other in subsequent sessions. The therapist expressed how moved he was by the loving support and wisdom of the extended family. He emphasized the different political and sociocultural contexts of each generation. This facilitated a working alliance that enabled Dad to share with his children how he had always been attracted to Black women and how he had decided consciously to honor this attraction. Dad had been a civil rights activist during the '60s and '70s. In fact, he had marched in Mississippi, where he had met Mom. Idealistically, he had been sure his children would have no problem in the rapidly changing world. Now he was "rocked" by this sudden awareness of the politicization of race. He had never considered that his children might be hurt by Blacks, and had prepared them only for White racism.

The therapist referred Cynthia and Tony to separate groups of biracial adolescents. In the family sessions, he focused on helping the family to share with each other their perceptions, expectations, attitudes, and experiences. At the end of the 10 sessions authorized by the family's health insurance plan, Cynthia had regained her former energy and school involvement and the entire family was more open and responsive to one another.

Three months later, the therapist received a phone call from Cynthia, in which she said that she had been admitted to the two universities where she had been subjected to hostility by the Black students. She came in for one individual session, as she wanted to talk over her choices (she had been accepted by all of the schools to which she had applied). The therapist helped her identify the pros and cons of each school, and they talked about the racial climate and her attitudes about activism and involvement. After much agonizing and discussion with her family members on both sides and her teachers, Cynthia decided to attend her first choice, one of the two places where she had been rejected by members of the Black Students' Association. Her intended goal was to get the best education possible, interact with all races, and decide for herself how politically active she wanted to become.

This case illustrates a multimodal therapy attuned to the specific needs of the client family. The therapist had no preconceived ideas about how he would intervene. The large extended family session just seemed to feel right, and individual and couple sessions in addition to nuclear family sessions allowed for multiple perspectives. The youngsters benefited greatly from their theme-focused groups.

In another clinical situation, the challenges were more complex:

> Norma, a White American, age 36, and Charlie, a Moroccan of color, age 27, were referred to family therapy with their 1-year-old son by the local hospital's emergency room staff. The precipitating event was that Charlie had smashed his hand through a window 2 days earlier. Charlie would only see a woman therapist. He and Norma had married 3 years ago, having met while Charlie was attending an American university on an exchange fellowship. Charlie had difficulty finding a job in his field and worked at different fast food restaurants. Norma, a health care administrator, was the major income provider. The baby was in family day care. They reported that their marital difficulties began after the baby was born. Charlie resented Norma's involvement with the baby, and she resented Charlie's expectations of her to take care of the house, the baby, and him while working full time. In reality, however, Charlie's rage had been building ever since they married. Although the marriage helped him to get a green card, he felt overpowered by Norma on every front. He missed his mother, who had raised him in Morocco as a single parent, his father having died while he was an infant. He was used to strong women taking care of him, and, in his culture, men did not perform domestic or caretaking chores. At the same time, he believed that his race was preventing him from finding a job, and he was shamed by his dependency on Norma. The baby was the conduit of their struggles—they fought constantly over "the right way to raise him." As a result, the baby was difficult, inconsistent in sleeping and feeding and fretful most of his waking time. The pediatrician also reported that the baby was slow in motor development and social responsiveness. This report led to an escalation of the attack–defense cycle in the couple relationship.

The family therapist raised issues of immigration, race, cultural differences, and gender roles in the initial double-length session (due to the emergency room referral), while fostering a working alliance. She also gave them some specific baby handling suggestions, to which they were most responsive. But Charlie displayed physical agitation and seemed to blank out frequently. Determining that there was no substance abuse, the family therapist suggested a psychiatric consultation for pharmacological consideration. At first Charlie was opposed to any suggestion of medication. In the next session, 2 days later, the therapist constructed a genogram and discovered that Charlie's father had committed suicide (a shameful sin in Morocco) and that he most likely had suffered from depression. The therapist did not minimize the cultural, racial, power, and economic issues in this family, but suggested that these issues might be easier to work through if Charlie was feeling better.

The consulting psychiatrist, an African American who had once been stationed in Morocco, diagnosed Charlie with a major depressive episode with some paranoid personality features. After 2 weeks of medication, Charlie's agitation lessened and his clearer thought processes enabled him to engage more readily in family therapy. He met with the psychiatrist once a week for medication monitoring along with individual therapy.

The family sessions focused on parenting and couple work. The baby came to every session, and the therapist, while exploring cultural differences, taught the parents how to collaborate more respectfully and effectively in play and child care by simultaneous in-session play, enactments, and discussion. As Norma became more empathic to Charlie's plight and more aware of the impact of her own cultural assumptions and privilege, she learned to share power more equally, for example, by consulting with Charlie rather than acting on her own unilateral decisions.

Charlie found both his individual and family treatments enormously beneficial. In his individual therapy, he received the kind of attention from a male role model that he had been yearning for all his life. In the family sessions, he was able to engage with more self-confidence and appropriate assertiveness. Once he no longer felt victimized and defensive, his whole mood changed. The baby became more relaxed, with more age-appropriate development.

Collaboration between the family therapist and the individual therapist was crucial, as it always is. In this case, the gender and racial differences of the two therapists (deliberately sought out by the family therapist) provided good gender and racial role models for the client family. In addition, both therapists enjoyed and benefited from their weekly discussions. They respected each other's perspectives and input and felt that their collaboration enriched the total treatment. In this case, techniques and strategies were not as important as the expanded safe, supportive holding environment. Collaboration with other service providers (in school, health, work, and community settings) is an important component of effective treatment, particularly in this era of managed care. And, different people contribute different perspectives and ideas.

With multiracial families, clinicians need to attend to issues of uniqueness, isolation, belonging and acceptance, self-esteem, personal and racial identity, and physical appearance in addition to the more universal developmental issues that all family members contend with in this society. As with any family, identification of subsystems, triangles, and other alliances informs treatment planning. However, interventions are not likely to have lasting effects if there is not a favorable context created by therapists' attitudes and relational skills.

J. T. Gibbs (1989) suggests that therapists attend to biracial adolescents' possible conflicts regarding five major psychosocial tasks: dual racial/ethnic identity, social marginality, sexuality and choice of sexual partners, separation from parents, and educational/career aspirations. She believes that the effects of these conflicts can range from mild anxiety or depression to moderate symptoms such as academic underachievement and peer conflicts to severe symptoms of delinquency, substance abuse, and suicidality. There is no evidence, however, that difficulty with these psychosocial tasks is more prevalent in biracial adolescents than in other adolescents. My point is that, while we need to consider seriously racial and cultural influences on development, we should not assume that multiraciality itself is the cause of adolescent difficulties. Race is a filter that can distort and exacerbate usual adolescent issues.

TREATMENT ISSUES
WITH TRANSRACIAL ADOPTIVE FAMILIES

Probably the most critical issue for clinicians to develop with transracial adoptive families is the encouragement of open discussion of race and racial differences within the family. Equally important is a focus on the meaning of adoption, as discussed in Chapter 4.

Assessment

In the initial session, while getting to know each member of the family and gaining each member's perspective of the presenting problem, the therapist can observe how the family attends to the differences obviated by both adoption and racial and ethnic differences. If the family does not bring up these issues, the therapist can gently probe, by circular questions, such as, "How does everyone in this family feel about your differences in physical appearance?" "How do you think your brother feels about being adopted?" With small children, individual and group paintings, and the use of puppets of different skin color and other tools can be productive.

Obviously, an important task for the therapist is determination of how the presenting problem(s) is or are impacted by adoption and multiraciality. One can't assume that the problems are due to adoption or multiraciality, but one can explore possible influencing factors. Therapists can begin work with these families by expressing admiration for the commitment and determination of the family to overcome the obstacles to transracial adoption. Typically, these families have enormous resiliency in the face of great odds (Rosenthal & Groze, 1992).

Another issue for the therapist to ascertain is the attitudes of extended family and the nature of current kin relationships. Are the attitudes and relationships with families of origin supportive or burdensome? Likewise, the therapist needs to know how the family utilizes available community resources and, particularly, how they interface with the school system. Often, families coming into therapy with a child experiencing school difficulties need help in identifying problems (are they school related? home related? both?), and they need coaching and support as to how to identify school and community resources and then how to obtain assessment and remediation services in an assertive manner.

> The Strum family entered therapy because their 9-year-old adopted Latino daughter was experiencing more and more difficulty keeping up with her classmates in the fourth grade and, as an apparent result of her frustration and her need for acknowledgment, was antagonizing the other children. She no longer was included in other children's play or parties. The adoptive parents acknowledged that these problems had been building up for several years. The therapist was appalled that no testing had been conducted by the school, because it was clear to her, based on initial observation, that there were language processing difficulties. Being familiar with this particular school system, the therapist knew that only the most assertive parents were able to obtain evaluation and special needs services in this era of "cost cutting." Therefore, as part of her assessment, she instructed the parents how to request a core evaluation, and she herself wrote a strong letter to the school advocating for her clients. The therapist maintained continuous follow-up with both the family and the school and attended the core evaluation team meeting. The collection of these data was the first priority in order to address this critical problem. As it turned out, this child had definite learning difficulties that needed specific remediation.

Treatment

Advocacy and psychoeducation are always important elements of family work. Sometimes, families do not know about the availability of services; other times, they are unaware of the meaning and implications of children's manifested behaviors. Although adoptive families usually are better informed than biological families about child and adolescent development, having worked hard in order to achieve the objective of adoption and even harder to achieve transracial adoption, there still may be areas with which they are unfamiliar, such as identification and treatment of special needs or health problems. For example, parents can be helped to reframe their perceptions of a child's problem, to understand the influences of both heredity and environment. Some parents fail to see that the child is learning behavior from the adoptive parents, that the problem behavior is not an inherited trait.

> In the second session with the Burns family, when the parents were reporting how their 6-year-old Black daughter was kicking and biting them when they said "No," the therapist inquired, "How did Jennifer learn that it was OK to hit and bite others?" The parents (both social workers) appeared to be surprised by the question and said they thought it might have something to do with her background (which they later privately revealed included a father incarcerated for armed robbery). In the third session, while describing a family fight at home, Jennifer commented on how her mother screamed at her father and hit him and how her father hit back. The parents looked very embarrassed, and the therapist was able to point out that now she understood where Jennifer had learned to hit. The therapist waited several sessions before she brought this issue up again, using it as an example of how the parents might have minimized the role that environment plays in child rearing. It was important to have formed a working alliance with the parents in order to confront such sensitive material in a way that could promote change.

With families with young children, play therapy, art therapy, or any type of expressive therapy (role playing, story making) can help children to express their feelings about their adoption and race. Another helpful technique is to help children construct a "Life Book," which may help them integrate their personal cultural heritage and their current cultural identity. The parents can also add on to whatever materials (often a scrapbook) they had amassed in order to adopt. The family can then create a "Family Life Book," which can become an ongoing family activity.

In a safe therapeutic environment, family members may talk about their feelings and reactions to the intrusive comments they receive from others. For example, if parents respond angrily in front of the children to outsiders' comments, the young child may believe that he or she is the cause of the parents' anger. Discussing alternative ways of responding to these kinds of questions can alleviate children's anxiety.

Particular attention must be paid to biological siblings. They may harbor jealousy and displace these feelings in ways that appear to be insensitive and cruel. If parents can learn to be more empathic, these typical feelings can be addressed openly.

In one family session, Merle, age 11, a biological child, burst out with anger that ever since David, a Black 6-year-old adoptee, arrived (3 years ago), everyone has paid attention to him, and she feels like she doesn't fit in anymore. She cited how at dinnertime, most of the conversation concerned David, and whenever she tried to talk about her day, her parents replied, "We're talking now, just wait." Merle felt that they never got back to her. Merle's parents were shocked; they perceived that they paid particular attention to Merle, and they began to argue about how "wrong" her perceptions are. The therapist intervened, pointing out that feelings are not right or wrong and that judgment was not the point here. She belabored this point to illustrate to this family the importance of empathic attunement to children's feelings, whether or not you agree with those feelings. She modeled how she might think to herself, "If Merle feels this way, how can I be more careful about paying attention to her so that maybe these feelings will lessen."

Older transracial adoptees have special concerns. The child needs to adjust to the new environment, becoming used to a new culture, to new roles, rules, and expectations. The meaning of "family" to the older adoptee may require careful consideration and adjustment. The older adoptee also needs to acknowledge and grieve the loss of previous racial and ethnic environments as well as separation from previous relationships, regardless of how positive or negative these relationships were. The therapist can help the youngster understand the feelings of anger, sadness, and confusion as part of the grieving process and help the parents become more aware and understanding of the grieving process and its effects on bonding and attachment within the new family. The youngster's identity and separation struggles will take time, and all members of the family need support for coping with the stresses of these struggles. Parents may become frustrated that their attachment is not reciprocated by the adoptee as he or she struggles with grieving. They can be helped to understand that older adoptees may defend against their vulnerability by isolation or angry behavior and that they need to incorporate their past into the present, not deny and cut off from it. Language (verbal and nonverbal) may also be an impediment to bonding and attachment. Learning the nuances and covert messages of a new language takes time.

Many older adoptees, whether from abroad or from this country, have undergone unimaginable betrayals and abuse. The impacts of these past traumas may not become apparent for some time. There is often a honeymoon period at the beginning of a transracial adoption with an older child, which slowly gives way to more overt conflict and struggle.

Henry and Jane, in their mid-40s, adopted Marguerita, age 8, from a Central American agency so that their only son, Tom, age 11, would have a sibling. Reports indicated that Marguerita had been abandoned in infancy and was raised in a convent. When Marguerita first arrived in this country, she was shy and timid and spoke no English. She appeared to be eager to learn and, while she had night fears and sleep difficulties, she seemed to be "adjusting beautifully." Jane stayed home from work (she is a college professor) for one term to help Marguerita adjust. Tom was favorably disposed to his new sibling and forgave her transgressive behaviors, such as her taking things from his room and then denying it. After Jane returned to work, the situations at home and school began to deteriorate. Tom found more of his belongings missing, and Marguerita became increasingly stubborn and angry. When complaints started to come from the school that Marguerita was seen taking things from children's coats in the locker room, Henry and Jane decided to seek help. A cotherapy team, consisting of a male Caucasian and a female Latino, met several times with this family. Gradually, the therapists and family learned from drawings and storytelling that Marguerita had been physically and sexually abused by one of the nuns. She was conflicted about her loyalties—to the nuns who raised her, to her Latino culture, to her new family and country. These startling revelations caused Henry and Jane to question their initial assumptions that "everything really was fine," and when the therapists suggested a more comprehensive medical evaluation, they quickly agreed. They were shocked to learn that Marguerita was most likely 2 years older than reported and that she had been sexually active with peers prior to adoption and relocation. The therapists recommended individual therapy for Marguerita with a Spanish-speaking therapist, and biweekly family sessions to help the family understand and adapt to this new family constellation.

Older international adoptees may be resistant to renaming and different religious customs, whereas at an earlier age they may have been eager for these symbols of absorption into a new family and culture. As the demographics of this country continue to change, youngsters may not be so eager to change their name, given that there are so many different cultures represented in schools and communities.

> Maria, 11, adopted at the age of 9 from Mexico, had no problem with her last name changing. However, having been raised for 8 years in a Catholic institution in Guatemala, she was very uneasy about her adoptive family's Jewish observance. Her parents wanted her to study Hebrew so that she could be bat mitzvahed with her classmates. Maria went to Hebrew class, but refused to study or do her homework. She was afraid to tell her parents that she really felt like she was "sinning" by becoming Jewish because she feared they would "send her back." However, she did share these feelings with a neighbor friend's mother, who reported it to the adoptive parents. They sought out a professional consultation because they didn't know how to respond to this information. The clinician held several family sessions, in which it became clear that racial, ethnic, and religious differences were not being acknowledged and discussed within the family. Once the family learned that they could talk safely about these issues, the well-meaning parents realized that they had assumed that Maria wanted to be "like them" without really considering her feelings and perspectives.

The reality is that older transracial and international adoptees and their families require a great deal of support and reassurance. The youngsters are likely to be conflicted over their identity and ambivalent regarding their negative feelings toward either their cultural origins or the demands of their current culture. Support groups for the parents, youngsters, and entire family afford validation of family members' experiences and feelings as well as opportunities for learning new ways of adapting to and solving problems.

*   *   *

White clinicians working with clients of different race and ethnicity can add to their self-awareness and learning by maintaining relationships with colleagues and peers of different race and ethnicity. It is important to have contact with as wide a variety of people as possible; otherwise, how can one really develop a realistic understanding of intra- and intergroup differences?

Our clinical skills are likely to be more effective if there is genuine congruence between what we think and feel and how we act. The personal and professional influence each other within larger sociocultural, political, and economic contexts. The rules, roles, and expectations we have for others apply equally to ourselves.

Cross-cultural theorists suggest that clinicians learn, in addition to normative values, about effective helping strategies from other cultures. For example, the meditation, imaging, and relaxation techniques adapted from the Asian and Indian cultures can be useful complements to our Western techniques. The therapist who is most effective working with diverse populations is the person who respects and covalues differences.

But most importantly, clinicians need to be familiar and comfortable with community resources both to provide help to client families and to afford families with opportunities for expanding their networks and becoming more acculturated.

ELEVEN

Emerging Families

"I always knew I wanted to be a mother. When I turned 35, I became very anxious. I had devoted my 20s to my career, dated lots of men seeking a permanent relationship, and nothing worked out. A single colleague, who had adopted a baby by herself, suggested I attend a 'Last Call for Mothering for Single Parents' workshop. I did and considered all of the options. It took 3 years for me make the final decision to bear a child. I decided to use an anonymous donor. I considered adoption, but was nervous about the court cases favoring birth parents' rights. . . . What's it been like? Well, my experiences of the past 3 years are totally different from my expectations. I was totally unprepared for the level of physical exhaustion and ambivalence. Women don't tell the truth about mothering enough. But, while I don't think I would do it again, I sure am glad I did, and I adore Naomi. She is the best thing that ever happened in my life. I'm still hoping to find a permanent partner. Actually, I think my relationships with men are more relaxed now that I've already had a child. Do I think about what I'll tell her about her birth? Yes, but it's a long ways off and I put it out of my mind."—Gerry, 43

"My husband retired a year ago and I was all set to join him. We were going to travel around the country, do all the things we never had time or money for before. The kids were all grown and gone, the house is paid up, and now was going to be our time. Then the phone call came. Our daughter, who's had trouble with drugs ever since she was in high school, had just taken off, leaving her two little kids with so-called friends. We thought she was doing better, at least that's what she'd told us on the phone. We never dreamt this would happen, although I guess I always worried about her and those babies. Of course we had no choice. They're our flesh and blood. But I tell you, it's been darned hard. And, while

304 UNDERSTANDING DIVERSE FAMILIES

I love these kids, it's put a strain on my marriage, and made me angry and bitter at *her*. How could she do this to these kids? Where did we go wrong?"—Kathy, 62

"I was raised by my grandparents in a small Canadian town. My mother went to the States to make more money after my little brother was born. She never married my father—I don't know him, but I've seen him once or twice at the county fair while I was growing up. My mother would come home to visit every few years, but I really didn't get to know her until after I married and moved down here. My grandparents were great—now that I'm a mother myself I realize just how great they were. When I was in school, I sometimes resented not having a married mom and dad like the other kids, but I also realized that I was luckier than most kids. My grandparents did everything for us, and they weren't as strict as other kids' folks. Funny, now that I'm living in the same place as my mother, we've become best friends. We do every-thing together—shop, go to the movies, cook. But I still think of my grandmother as my real mom. She's the one who was there for me when I was hurt or sick. I guess I'm pretty lucky."—Sherri, 32

"I really was disturbed when I read that article in *The New York Times* Sunday magazine [Orenstein, 1995]. I mean, my friends and I got through medical school donating sperm every week. Heck, that was 30 years ago! I certainly wouldn't want someone knocking on my door now, expecting some kind of fatherly reac-tion. I mean, I suppose it would be interesting, and I would be curious. But, no, I don't consider jerking off into a test tube mak-ing me a father. There's much more to being a father. I feel sorry for people with infertility problems, but given the way things are now, I'm not so sure I'd recommend anyone donate sperm or eggs."—Henry, 52

Families comprised of never or previously married singles who choose to become parents without a partner and of grandparents who become (more by circumstances than choice) the primary caretakers of their grandchildren are steadily increasing. Single parents by choice, although a small, select population, have more than tripled their numbers since the 1960s, now accounting for more than 1 million families (N. Miller, 1992; Sandefur, 1995). Grandparent-as-parent families have also more than tripled during the same period, now accounting for more than 3.3 million children in this country (de Toledo & Brown, 1995; Wagn-er, 1995).

For our purposes, "single parent by choice" refers to men or (mostly) women who have made a mature, rational decision to become parents and to do so independently, bearing or adopting and raising the child without the benefit of a partner. For biological parents, this decision may have been made prior to pregnancy or upon learning that one has become pregnant accidentally. This group is differentiated from teenage single parents or young adults who bear and raise their children within their family of origin, whether the decision is normative in their culture, and conscious or unconscious.

"Grandparent-as-parent" families, for the purposes of this book, refers to those grandparents who have custody of their grandchildren and are the primary caretakers. This group is distinguished from living-with grandparents, who wish to help out the child's parents with child care and/or financial support, and from day care grandparents, those who care for their grandchildren while the parents are at work, but who relinquish control and care when the parents are not at work. The custodial grandparents have sole responsibility and authority for the raising of their grandchildren. If the biological parents have access to their children, it is under the auspices of the grandparents as legal guardians.

Although perhaps not as controversial as the other family types discussed in this book, these two family types are often subject to societal devaluation for being different, to expectations that children from these families will present with psychological disturbance just because of their alternative family structure. Because these families are fewer in number (which may have something to do with finding them), they receive less attention in research and publicity. Grandparent-as-parent families are more likely to elicit positive reactions from others than are single-parent-by-choice families due to the sympathy grandparents receive as biological relatives, and as altruistic rescuers of children who otherwise might be neglected or abandoned. Single parents by choice, although less stigmatized than they used to be, are still largely viewed as selfish for bringing fatherless (more typical than motherless) children into the world. Dan Quayle's condemnation of the popular television character Murphy Brown in the summer of 1992 attests to this.

I interviewed 12 single mothers and 2 single fathers along with 8 adolescent and young adult offspring. Eleven grandparents as parents and seven adults raised primarily by their grandparent(s) were also studied. Seven sperm donors volunteered to be interviewed. The purpose of this chapter is to consider these types of families within a sociocultural context, to highlight their unique issues so, as clinicians, we can understand the special concerns they pose when they present as clients. I will also raise questions about a unique family structure that is emerging along with the rapid developments in reproductive technology, namely families with a "ghost" in the background, the ghost of a donor providing an egg or a sperm (or both). Increasingly, families who have utilized donor sperm or eggs are experiencing the issues of what, when, and how to tell the children, as well as the impact of an anonymous donor on the couple system. Concerns about information flow and confidentiality are coming into the foreground, posing complicated medical/legal/ethical concerns.

SINGLE PARENTS BY CHOICE

The Participants

The typical single mother by choice is an educated White woman with a successful professional or managerial career (N. Miller, 1992). She is usually in her mid- to late 30s, having devoted her 20s and early 30s to building a career, attempting to seek a gratifying permanent relationship, and consolidating her own identity. The part of her identity that was still in question was that of wife and mother. When her attempts to become a wife without compromising her standards and expectations were not met, the ticking of her biological clock focused her attention more on the "mother" part of her identity. Most of these women assumed as they were growing up that they would get married and have children. While they avidly pursued the careers that the women's movement made more accessible to them, it never occurred to them in their 20s or early 30s that their aspiration of having a family would not fall into place. Everything else had! Becoming a single parent is usually a choice based on circumstances, not part of a woman's original game plan. The place of marriage in our society has shifted, and an increasing number of women who are smart, educated, and successful in their careers are discovering that there aren't enough men who are up to their standards. Rather than lowering their standards for a husband, more of them are choosing the challenge of becoming mothers without being wives.

Two of my interviewees are less representative in that they are successful Black professional women who, while receiving support from their extended families, live independently in predominantly White suburbs. While all of my interviewees would have preferred to have a partner, they place a greater value on parenthood than on marriage. Interestingly, 10 of the 12 single mothers interviewed came from intact families (the other 2 were raised by a divorced parent), but 6 of those 10 reported a tense, conflictual parental marriage. One might speculate that they would be quite careful to seek a partner with whom they could live with more pleasure than their mothers experienced; they may be hypercritical or anxious within their relationships, which, in turn, may be why they either made more selections or had difficulty sustaining intimate relationships.

The two single fathers interviewed were in human service professions (not particularly affluent but able to manage) and had deliberately adopted high-risk, special needs children. They also prioritized parenthood over marriage, but they each enjoy several long-term, close emotional relationships with women who serve as "aunts" to the children. These two men are not interested in marriage at this point in their lives, but they might have been if, in their 20s, "the right person" had come along. When asked to think back to their youth, they recollected that they thought more about having kids than being married, although they both enjoyed romantic relationships. One had been an intermediate foster care parent prior to adoption.

> Fred, age 46, is a special needs elementary school teacher in an urban school. He grew up in the '60s, comes from a farm family with four boys (he was the oldest), and was the first in his family to attend college. Fred's youngest brother was mentally retarded, and Fred, as the oldest, performed a lot of child care. To this day, he is closely involved with his brother's care. Fred loves his work, particularly with difficult children. He had been considering adoption as a single parent for quite a while when a close friend, a social worker with the Department of Social Services, recruited him for a "special" 4-year-old boy. In the 4 years that Fred has been a single parent, he has experienced the same exhaustion and exasperation that all parents face. He has an informal support group of other single dads (most by divorce), and he is fortunate to live close to family and friends. He and Jeff, his son, spend a lot of time hiking and camping with other families. If he had his wish list, it would include enough money to purchase housecleaning and in-home child care when Jeff is unable to attend school. Fred says the most difficult time was the first year he had Jeff. But, he had had enough experience with difficult children to have realistic expectations, and he was very appreciative of all the support and encouragement he received. Today he is a proud father, showing me examples of Jeff's assignments from school and favorable reports from the learning center. The only surprise Fred experienced as a new father was the suspicious attitudes of the mothers at the playground. One even asked him if he was gay, unable to believe that a man would choose primary parenting.

> Delia, now in her early 60s, always knew that she wanted to be a parent. Her fiance was killed in the Korean War, and she never again fell in love with anyone who was available. A college history profes-

sor, Delia took a sabbatical in England in her mid-30s. She had been contemplating single motherhood for some time, but she did not believe she would be eligible for adoption. While in England, she became involved with a married man. He agreed to father a child with her, and they both determined that he would not be involved in any other way. The distance enabled them to achieve this end. They have had intermittent contact over the years, updating each other on their respective lives. So, 28 years ago, (long before this was acceptable) Delia returned to her west coast university in midpregnancy. No one in the university community did more than raise their eyebrows.

After the baby, Dan, was born, Delia moved to a large midwestern university, where she has remained. Within a protected university community, Dan was raised along with all of the other faculty children. When he would ask about his father, he was given a detailed description. When he was 9, he asked his mother why she had not married, and Delia told him about her fiance, her relationship with his father, and how badly she had wanted to have a child to love and cherish. Dan accepted his mother's explanations. Delia claims that she worked very hard to provide other family and male role models for Dan, that she never felt excluded from family activities within her community, and that she was as honest as she could be with Dan. She also commented on what an easy, even-tempered child Dan had been, not presenting any of the difficulties her peers' children did. Delia is content with her life. Dan remained home until graduate school. Now that he is gone, she is venturing into new aspects of research, and she maintains close ties within the academic community. The main foci of her life—Dan and her work—have been extremely gratifying, and she feels very fortunate to have made the decisions she did.

My female interviewees all agreed that the changing roles of women, both in the work place and at home, enabled them to become more financially independent, and that their financial resources were a critical factor in enabling them to consider and successfully meet the requirements of single parenthood. This is a major factor, as the research clearly shows that starting a family with a reduced or low income has a major impact on single parents (Blankenhorn, 1995; McLanahan & Sandefur, 1994; McLeod & Shanahan, 1993; Zill & Nord, 1994). Without adequate financial resources, single parents work longer hours, have less emotional and physical energy available for parenting, and are less involved with their communities. Even with adequate financial resources, they still have less than they would with an income-producing partner.

The fact that there is more acceptance today of alternative life styles has reduced the stigmatization of illegitimacy, and, although many of my interviewees' families were initially resistant to the idea of single parenthood, they all became supportive, some even enthusiastic. One interviewee's mother, for example, relocated to the city where her daughter resides in order to provide day care and other support. Even if the Dan Quayles of the world are scornful, these single parents, because of their socioeconomic status and privilege, are often able to insulate themselves from the negative effects of this discrimination. This does not mean, however, that Quayle's argument about the need for fathers and marriage for children's healthy development does not have merit. This argument applies also to children of divorce. Parental abandonment has different effects, however, than planned single parenthood. And single parents by choice are typically careful to provide alternative role models.

The major motivation for becoming a single parent is the desire to have a child to love and raise. These parents tend to equate autonomy with the creation of attachment, interdependency, and the actualization of what they perceive to be their innate need for motherhood (or fatherhood). Most single parents would prefer marriage and the legitimate and conventional way of childbearing as the ideal way of life, but unable to attain that goal, they decide to choose "second best" and "at least" have a child (Kamerman & Kahn, 1988; Linn, 1991).

There is no evidence to suggest that single parents by choice have more difficulty with intimate relationships than married parents, considering the fact that 50% of marriages end in divorce and that there are far greater numbers of children in single parent families due to family disruption. So clinicians should not jump to the conclusion that clients considering the option of single parenting are "troubled" because they have not found a suitable marital partner. This choice may be a better one than choosing to marry based more on the desire to have a child than on the viability of the couple relationship.

Issues from the Single Parent's Perspective

The primary difficulty reported by all single parents, both in the literature and by my interviewees, is exhaustion. There is no partner helping with night feedings, early morning risings, temper tantrums, and so forth. There is no one with whom to share the frustrations and disappointments, the joys and exhilaration. As one single mother put it, "Would anyone reject a partner? another income?" The single parent, while highly motivated, has four demanding jobs: (1) mom, (2) breadwinner trying to earn the equivalent of two incomes, (3) father, and (4) resource manager (launderer, housekeeper, cook, bill payer, repairer, etc.). The single parent does not have the choices that parent couples have, such as whether or not to work; how much, how, and when to have alone time; and shared decision making and responsibilities.

Single parents struggle to provide a supplementary emotional and financial emergency support system, from friends and relatives, and to find a career that allows them some flexibility with regard to child care, such as when a child is sick or needs car pooling. Child care and flexible careers are their major concerns. They know in advance that without the emotional, logistical, and financial advantages of marriage, they will be constrained with regard to the freedom to travel and participate in the spontaneous romantic relationships they experienced as singles. They also are prepared to contend with their child's queries about and yearnings for a father.

Although this population of single parents is as prone to depression and anxiety as other groups of single parents, their social and financial resources may enable them to call on friends for support, purchase child care assistance, and obtain mental health services so as to contain the negative impact of this psychological stress. By having the resources to minimize daily hassles, they are less prone to becoming overwhelmed than are those single parents struggling with limited social and financial resources. They did not enter into this decision without a great deal of preparation. However, my interviewees report that their most significant stress comes from trying to find sufficient physical and emotional energy for work and child care, leaving their own personal needs as the lowest priority. "Social life? Who has time?" Professional and managerial mothers in marriages, however, report the same time and energy crunch.

Two major worries of single parents are the specter of unemployment and concern about the child in case something happens to the single parent (illness, death, incapacitation of some sort). Identifying legal and custodial guardians, and thinking about contingencies should something happen to one's employment (increasing disability insurance, exploring alternative career options) are immediate concerns. Clinicians should ask about these plans at the outset of contact.

On the positive side, single parents report that they actually have more energy and time to devote to their child than do career women with partners, given that single parents do not have to negotiate or comply with a marital relationship. One study (Groze, 1991a, 1991b) reported that a single adult, unencumbered with the demands of a marital relationship, may be better able to give the kind and amount of involvement and nurturing needed by some children than a married adult. Many single parents yearn for intimate partners, but express dissatisfaction with the relationships available. N. Miller (1992) suggests that single mothers may express their attachment needs in overly independent behaviors and this may lead to disappointment in romantic relationships. On the other hand, as pointed out by Gerry at the beginning of this chapter, it is possible to have more satisfying relationships with romantic partners after experiencing an intimate relationship with a child. Intimacy gratification breeds intimacy and that can far outweigh anxiety and tension.

Single parents generally make a concerted effort to provide same- and opposite-gender role models for their offspring. They're concerned about their children being exposed to a wide range of play activity and sex roles. "Naomi may not have a father, but she has lots of special uncles." Gerry noted that two of these "uncles" have been named legal guardians for Naomi should anything happen to her. Other single parents belong to groups, such as the New York "Single Parent by Choice" group, or create family systems comprised of friends and their families. If they are not close to extended family, they spend holidays and vacations with their "family" of friends. Many report that their chosen families, those comprised of selected friends, are more supportive and loyal than blood relatives. Most single parents found, as do many couples, that their friendship circles changed after they became parents. Childless single friends often resent the attention parents focus on their children. People tend to seek friends in similar circumstances for modeling and sharing.

Although little research has been conducted on single parents by choice, even less considers single fathers by choice. Risman (1986) found that single fathers feel comfortable and competent in their parenting role, but wish they had more role models and peers. My two interviewees found their greatest difficulty to be the balancing of work and family responsibilities. They also commented on how much better off they are compared to their married friends who, no matter how much they involve themselves in child care, never seem able to satisfy their wives' notions of how it's supposed to be done. One expressed the view that his confidence level was high because there was no one "to shoot me down with a volley of criticisms."

Effects on Children

One of the main criticisms leveled against single parents is that children are deprived of seeing a happy couple relationship between the parents and that this deprivation will lead to later intimacy difficulties in relationships. Most single parents would retort that conflicted marriages and divorces have a stronger negative impact on children. While father absence has been deemed a critical factor on child development (McLanahan & Sandefur, 1994), absence from the beginning may be better than abuse, abandonment, or neglect by a known father. As previously noted, most single parents by choice make a concerted effort, out of concern for their children's culturally normal development, to ensure that their children are exposed to conventional families and role models.

As mentioned earlier, research on the effects on children of growing up with a single parent has not been conducted with this select population. There is research on single parent adoption of special needs children (Feigelman & Silverman, 1983; Groze, 1991a, 1991b; Shireman & Johnson, 1985), however, that indicates that the children receive perhaps even more intense, individual attention than do adopted children in couples' homes. The adoption success rate is just as high for single parents as it is for couples. A single parent may have only one child, whereas in couple families there may be sibling adoptions or a combination of birth and adopted children. This may allow single parents to focus more on the one special needs child. On the other hand, the parent–child relationship could become excessively intense, given that there are no siblings or spouse. This could impede a child's development of independence and identity during adolescence.

McLanahan and Sandefur (1994) studied the consequences of single motherhood. They argue that there is a loss of economic, parental, and community resources for families when there are not two parents pooling their resources. Obviously, two incomes are higher than one, regardless of how high any one income is. One parent, filling multiple roles simultaneously is likely to experience high stress levels and, perhaps, anxiety and depression if there is not adequate support. This one parent may not be available for school and community activities. These researchers conclude that the loss of these possible resources affects the social and emotional adjustment, educational attainment, family formation, and labor force participation of children raised in this type of family.

The single parents by choice whom I interviewed would disprove these findings. Because of their commitment to parenting priorities, they formed networks to provide adequate support and, once past the stressful infancy stage, reported that they were as available to their children with regard to community and family functions as any other parent. Most single-parent-by-choice families contain just one or two children. Those with two children reported that the sibling relationship provided extra support to each child. If I compare these single parents by choice with the large number of stressed, dual career families with whom I have worked over the years, I find much more parental availability to children among the single parents. They are less ambivalent and conflicted than their professional couple counterparts. This

may be attributable to their focused, high motivation to parent as well
as their ability to defy societal customs.

But let's hear from Delia's son, Dan, now 28:

> "When I was a kid, I wondered why I didn't have a dad like most
> of the other kids. I had one friend whose father had died and a
> few whose fathers had taken off after divorce. But it really was
> no big deal, because my mom was really great, there were always
> a lot of people in and out of our home, and I really felt like the
> whole university community was my family. I went to the univer-
> sity school through high school. When other people asked me if
> my mom had been married, I sort of shied away from answering.
> All I told kids was that my father was in England. When I was
> in high school, I started thinking about him a lot, wondering what
> he was like. Whenever I was mad at my mom—if I thought she
> was too strict or something—I'd think nasty thoughts about what
> she'd done. But I never said them out loud, because I love her very
> much and never wanted to hurt her. When in college, I found out
> more about him. I thought of looking him up one summer when
> I was traveling with friends, but decided not to, that I wanted
> to keep my image and not have to deal with the reality of him.
> My high school and college friends really liked my mom, liked
> coming to my house. Through their eyes, I began to realize how
> courageous she was. In those days, women just didn't do what
> she did. I think the most important things I've gained are under-
> standing and appreciating people who are different and really ap-
> preciating the importance and power of love. My mom gave me
> so much—intellectual stimulation and exposure, cultural sensi-
> tivity, appreciation of art, and, most of all, the art of loving."

Dan is currently in graduate school studying architecture. Some
would say that he is denying part of himself by not wanting a meeting
with his biological father. Others would say he's the exception to the
rule. What I think is important to note is that not only did he have
a competent, confident parent, but he was raised in an enlightened
community where differences were valued rather than devalued and
where there were many opportunities for close ties, good education,
and exposure to diversity. Had Delia and Dan lived in another context, the outcome might well have been different.

When children are very young, they conceptualize family as being whoever lives in the same house. This is why young children are
so devastated by divorce; when a parent leaves the house, they feel
as if they no longer have a family. They are also confused by the fact

that most of children's books are based on a traditional family with a mother, a father, and kids. If they do not belong to such a family, they begin to wonder what's wrong with them and their family. This can be a trying time for single parents and a time when extended family and friends are important to the child's concept of family. As children grow older, they are better able to understand the concept of biological relatedness, that someone can be your parent or sibling even if they don't live in the same house, and that people not biologically related can be as "close" as members of a traditional family. Many of the child's classmates live in single-parent-by-divorce homes, blended families, or multiracial families, so they are at least aware that others, too, live in circumstances different from the conventional model. During adolescence, youths have the most confusion about their conceptualization of family. This is due to the dissonance between their intellectual awareness of the social construction of family, their emotional yearnings for simultaneous connectedness and autonomy, and their need for peer approval and being "like" rather than "different."

> Jennifer, age 18, knows that her mother moved to a different part of the country when she was born in order to begin a new life. Although nothing was said, Jennifer somehow had created the notion that her mother's boyfriend had been killed in the war and that they would have married if he had returned. It was not until she was 10 years old that she overheard a conversation between her mother and aunt that led her to question her mother more carefully. At that time, her mother told her that she had been in love with her married boss and that when she became pregnant, she decided to move away and have the baby. Jennifer was satisfied with that, and developed a lot of admiration for her mother's strength. But, 1 year ago, upon graduating from high school, Jennifer learned from her mother that her father had wanted her mother to have an abortion and fired her when she refused. Her mother had then moved away. Jennifer's comfortably constructed fantasy of the "couple caught in a tragic web where the husband couldn't leave his legal wife for his true love and child" crumbled. Because there has been no further contact whatsoever between the parents, neither Jennifer nor her mother have any idea of the father's whereabouts.
>
> Jennifer believes she had a good home life. Her mother, a successful writer, has been able to work at home, so she was always available when Jennifer came home from school. Contrary to the mothers of her friends, Jennifer's mother was the prototype of a "stay-at-home" mom. Now, Jennifer is feeling confused and angry with her father for wanting her to be aborted and with her mother for the years of secrecy or deliberate silence. Jennifer sought help at her university counseling center because these feelings were interfering with her abil-

ity to concentrate and study. In just a few sessions, her therapist was able to help her consider different ways of viewing both parents in the context of their generation and work. Once Jennifer got beyond blaming, she regained her feelings of well-being and was able to work with her mother toward better understanding. Jennifer was going through the normal strains of attachment–separation in a mother–daughter relationship at this stage of development, and it was important for the therapist to differentiate that from the added issue of her birth circumstances.

Justin, age 16, is a freshman in high school. Adopted as a special needs 5-year-old by a male social worker, Justin has been in special programs throughout his schooling. Large for his age, Justin has a history of preadoption peer difficulties and aggressive conduct. He is also prone to epileptic seizures. As he looks back on his childhood, he recalls all of the different foster placements, the abuse, the neglect, and all of the pain and anger. When he first went to live with his dad, he didn't trust anyone, and today he expresses amazement that his dad waited it out. Father and son are very close. They camp together, do a lot of construction and woodworking projects, and Justin believes he never would have learned how to read and write if his dad hadn't taught him. Justin's dad aggressively sought out all possible services. Justin struggles with his school work, but he is determined to finish high school and get a decent job (he wants to do something outdoors with his hands).

Justin can't imagine what it would be like to have a mother living with them or anyone, for that matter. He thinks his dad is "the best guy ever," and when Justin gets into trouble, he knows his dad will be able to help him understand what it's all about. His dad is very strict, and Justin has a lot of chores to do around the house. If he doesn't get them done, he's not able to watch TV or go to the movies. Justin doesn't think much about his birth parents or all of the foster parents. He feels lucky to be where he is, and he is fiercely loyal to his dad. "Folks who think dads aren't good parents don't know nothing."

Justin will need special services in order to complete high school, and it is likely he will also require special training and job placement. He is close to his cousins and has two close friends at school. He is beginning to become interested in girls, and this is something he and his dad are devoting a lot of discussion to. Justin was a failure-to-thrive baby; it is amazing to witness his progress. His dad, who has the reputation of being one of the most caring social workers in the state system, has done a fantastic job of parenting this youngster who came to him with a grim prognosis.

Overall, it does not appear as if children born or adopted into single parent families with adequate financial resources fare any worse than their dual parent family counterparts (Groze, 1991a, 1991b; Kamerman & Kahn, 1988; N. Miller, 1992). It seems that family structure is not as significant as poverty and its effects.

Clinical Impliciations

Clinicians need to be familiar with different options and resources in order to help people considering single parenthood in their decision-making process and the implementation of their decision. Most of the treatment with this population occurs during the decision-making period, prior to the formation of the family system.

Decision Making

One of the first tasks of therapy is to help the client understand her or his motivation for single parenting. It will take some time for the client to get in touch with and process the apparent and underlying reasons for this consideration. Sometimes, clinicians may be uneasy about the motivation of the client to parent; it is important to discuss these feelings with the client so as to differentiate between the clinician's issues and those of the client. The following is one of my cases from 5 years ago.

> Linda, now 39, decided to become a single parent when she was 32. She had a history of failed homosexual and heterosexual lover and friend relationships. Her coworkers found her difficult, and I also found her hard to relate to. Linda came from an unstable family — her father had committed suicide when she was 11, and her mother had always been emotionally aloof. An only child, Linda defined herself as a "hippie of the '70s." She had had several abortions in her youth and had been involved in abusive relationships. After her 30th birthday, coming into a trust fund from her grandparents, she decided to have a baby by herself. Because of scar tissue from her abortions, she was unable to conceive by artificial insemination. As part of her *in vitro* fertilization program, she was required to seek counseling. I was troubled by Linda's distorted expectations about having a baby — "Finally she would have someone over whom she had complete control, who would love her and never leave her." Linda was determined to be totally self-sufficient. She didn't want anyone involved with her conception, pregnancy, or subsequent childrearing. Linda remained in treatment reluctantly during her fertilization procedures. She brushed aside all of my concerns and was closed to my suggestions that she read about parenting, talk to other single mothers, or really take a close look at her expectations. It was a very frustrating experience for me. I really did not think Linda was emo-

tionally ready to parent a child or appropriately motivated. She just could not relate to me (or seemingly to anyone, for that matter). Linda used me as a sounding board, focusing solely on her body and its reactions to the fertilization procedures. But she did come in every week, reporting every nuance of her procedure and body. She became pregnant on her third try, but miscarried after 8½ weeks. When she called me from the hospital, I felt her pain and loss, but also felt some relief. After a few sessions of supportive grief work, Linda terminated therapy.

I felt very badly about Linda and my failed treatment with her. I had wanted to help her become more self-aware so that she could view becoming a mother from a broader perspective. I always wondered what happened to her. Imagine my surprise not long ago, when a prospective client said that she was referred by Linda, a colleague. Upon meeting with this new client, I learned that Linda has become a successful computer consultant and seems quite satisfied with her single, childless life. She told her colleague, "Dr. Okun helped me put my life on track."

Once a client has decided to become a single parent, the therapy will focus on the implementation of this decision. The options available to prospective single parents include artificial insemination with either a known or unknown donor, domestic or international adoption, or intercourse with a known donor. Adoption of newborns has only been an option in the past two decades, due to the scarcity of such children. It is much easier for single parents to adopt hard-to-place special needs children than it is for them to adopt newborns. And the cost of adopting older, difficult, or special needs children is the least expensive of all of the options, given that these adoptions usually occur through public agencies. However, in recent years, more and more single parents have adopted transracially, particularly from underdeveloped countries.

In fact, there are very few domestic adoption agencies that will match with single parents, and these agencies are likely to avoid placing with men. There is still a great deal of societal prejudice against men who want to be primary caretakers of infants. These adoption agencies are extremely selective and extremely costly. Several of my interviewees paid close to $40,000 for the adoption (which included birthing costs for the biological mother); the least expensive adoption was $22,000, and that was several years ago. On the other hand, it is only in recent years that health policies provide maternity benefits for single parents. The cost of taking time off from work, artificial insemination, pregnancy, and delivery can come to almost the same as adoption fees. Some states allow adoption costs to be deducted from income taxes as medical costs are.

One interviewee went so far as to endure a home visit from a private adoption agency before she decided to attempt birthing. The money that she would have paid the agency (upwards of $20,000) went towards *in vitro* fertilization. Her reason for opting for childbirth as opposed to adoption was her growing fear, as she attempted to complete all the paperwork for adoption, about protection for the baby and for her parenting. She also watched a close friend cope with six failed matches. Although this particular woman had a difficult pregnancy—she had to remain in bed the last trimester and lost a significant portion of the business clientele she had developed—she is very pleased with her decision. However, she notes that people are much less tolerant of single birth parents than they are of single adoptive parents: Adoption is seen as altruistic and birthing as selfish. "It's OK for single parents to adopt a needy kid who's already here versus going to make a new kid."

Donor sperm is considered for many reasons. The research (McCartney, 1985) points out that women select this option in order to eliminate paternal obligations, emotional entanglements, and custody questions. For those considering donor sperm or donor eggs, the single parent must give advance consideration to how they will explain this to their child. This is complicated and will be discussed further in a later section. Today, more complete genetic and descriptive data are collected about donors, and recipients are able to select a donor from among several based on descriptive profiles.

Adoption consists of two phases, the home study phase, performed by state certified agencies, and the matching phase, which, as described in Chapter 2, may involve several failures. With regard to the home study for single parents, their financial solvency is a major consideration. Because there is only one possible income, the concern with the financial resources and career stability and potential of singles is greater than with couples. Some states require psychological testing of the prospective adoptive parent, as well as a minimum of three references. The adoption agency may require many more references for matching. Tax forms and a criminal offense records investigation are part of the home study phase. Single parents believe that they receive more intense scrutiny than do couples.

Clinicians working with prospective single parents can help them collect and appraise information about which route to take. They can engage in problem solving with their clients in order to consider all of the pros and cons of each option. They can help clients to locate people who have been through each of the experiences to learn about them first hand. It is important that prospective single parents give careful consideration to the demands of childrearing, and the availability of social supports, financial resources, babysitting resources, and health insurance.

Clinicians also can help clients prepare for the steps and likely disappointments that are possible within each option. For example, I have helped prospective adoptive mothers prepare their scrapbook for the birth mother, fill out forms, obtain information, and so forth.

Family Therapy

Often, the single parent enters therapy because the child is presenting symptomatic behaviors. Single parent families need to be evaluated in the context of the extended family and other support networks as well as on a societal level. As noted by Westcot and Dries (1990, p. 370), "it is clear that the family therapist working with single-parent families must first assess the multitude of possible subsystems, maintain flexibility in terms of treatment methods, and allow for the entrance of various extended family members into treatment at appropriate times and for appropriate duration."

> Nell, a single parent of 42, came for therapy with her 5-year-old daughter, Tina, because of tantrum behaviors. These tantrums had begun when Tina was 3 and slowly increased in frequency and duration. Nell was an entertainment lawyer who periodically had to travel. While she was gone, Tina would stay overnight with her great aunt Martha, a surrogate grandmother, who had also been a surrogate mother to Nell. The therapist spoke to Tina's kindergarten teacher, her preschool teacher from the previous year, and to her pediatrician who had made the initial referral. Within the six allotted sessions, the therapist held an initial session with Nell, one observation/interactive session with Nell and Tina and one with Tina and Aunt Martha, one individual session with Tina, and one session that included Nell, Tina, and Aunt Martha. If the therapist had not included Aunt Martha in the sessions, she would never have learned that Aunt Martha, age 72, was really having a difficult time physically keeping up with Tina. As a result, Tina stayed indoors, watched a lot of TV and videos, and was indulged with sweets and whatever else she wanted to keep her quiet. So, when Tina returned to her mother, she was angry about the very different rules and expectations. Aunt Martha truly loved "her girls" and wanted to be of help to them. But Nell had not noticed that Aunt Martha was aging, slowing down physically, and that her failing eyesight prevented her from reading to Tina. In the sixth session with Nell, the therapist helped Nell explore her own anxieties about employment travel, which affected the way she responded to Tina's tantrums. Together, the therapist and Nell brainstormed other options for child care that would

not be problematic for any of the parties. For the interim period, Nell arranged for a high school student to take Tina out in the afternoons after school and to help Aunt Martha through the dinner hour. Behavioral strategies for managing Tina's tantrums were outlined, and Nell was instructed to write out a "policy book" for all of Tina's caretakers. Nell elected to have an extra session with the therapist (for which she paid) in order to review her draft of this policy book.

I tell my clients about the New York City group called Single Mothers by Choice (SMC) described by N. Miller (1992), which provides therapeutic services to single women planning families. Established in 1981, this group supplies information and support through workshops and ongoing support groups. The information shared includes names of fertility specialists, adoption resources, lists of sperm banks, and names of supportive physicians. The organization also provides the members with social and emotional support and assists them in establishing social networks. Generally, mothers remain in the group for 2 years after the birth or adoption of their child. This group can serve as an information resource and model for women in other locations.

Obviously, it is important for the therapist to be accepting, supportive, and nonjudgmental about the notion of elective single parenting. At the same time, it is important for the therapist not to shy away from or evade critical questions. I was struck by the number of my interviewees who acknowledged the dissonance between their expectations and realities. That is why I think it important for therapists to suggest that men and women considering this route talk to others who have done it. In addition, clinicians can share some of their own experiences managing professional and family roles and responsibilities. As with any nontraditional group, clinicians need to examine their own attitudes and biases.

GRANDPARENT FAMILIES

The Participants

In the past, grandparent-headed families have been most prevalent among African American families due to their cultural traditions regarding the nature of extended family and surrogate parenting. But, currently, grandparents raising grandchildren cut across race and class.

The traditional view of grandparents as declining elderly no longer holds true. Today's grandparents may be younger, still employed, and caring for their own elderly parents, and may even have children or adult offspring still living at home. There are a variety of styles, meanings, and types of grandparenting among this varied age group. These grandparenting styles are influenced by age, gender, divorce, family separation, and multicultural family composition.

Today, the major reason grandparents need to become the primary caretakers of their grandchildren is related directly to substance abuse (Burton, 1992; Ehrle & Day, 1994; Jendrek, 1994; Minkler, Roe, & Price, 1992; Minkler, Roe, & Robertson-Beckley, 1994; Seamon, 1992; Shore & Hayslip, 1994; Vardi & Buchholz, 1994). In the past three decades, the use of crack, cocaine, and other hard street drugs, resulting in addiction, has contributed to a rise of criminality, child maltreatment, abuse and neglect, joblessness, divorce, desertion, illness, AIDS, and teenage pregnancy. Unfortunately, these conditions result in many parents being unable or unsuited to take responsibility for raising their own children. Because siblings of these parents are often unavailable (due to their own families or difficulties), it often falls to the grandparents to assume parenting responsibility. The alternative is foster care or adoption, and love, duty, and the bonds of family, as well as what Schwartz (1994) terms the "impulse to care," leave most grandparents feeling "there is no choice." A sense of moral obligation prevails. As always, there are also grandparents who assume parenting responsibility due to accidental death of the parents and/or incapacitation or death by major physical or psychiatric illness.

A common bond among the varied group of grandparents who raise their grandchildren is disappointment regarding this necessity. It is unplanned in all but the most unusual cases. Sometimes, in fact, it is very sudden. Other times, it may be negotiated over time, sometimes beginning with short-term care, often evolving into long-term or permanent care. Still other times it may, due to the parents' troublesome circumstances, be inevitable, awaiting precipitating circumstances or crises.

> Carolee, 61, and Don, 62, middle-class Whites, were eagerly anticipating their retirement. Their dream was to sell their home, purchase a mobile home, drive around the country to visit their family, and settle in Florida. Don had 3 more years of work, and Carolee, who worked part-time, knew she could leave her secretarial job whenever she wanted. Three of their four children were married, lived in other parts of the country, and were emotionally and financially independent. Except for their youngest child, Liza, age 37, they were satisfied with the way their family turned out. Liza had a history of alcohol and drug abuse and disappeared for long periods of time. Eventually, she would resurface and let them know where she was. She was unmarried, and they knew she had a 4-year-old son, Will,

whom they had met once when he was 2. Their son woke them up one night to tell them that he had been contacted by the police. Liza's 4-year-old son had been found on the beach, abandoned with no identification. He was unable to give the police information about whom to contact. Several days later (he had been placed in temporary foster care), Liza's body washed up on the shore. There were questions as to whether her death was an accidental drowning or suicide. When the police finally identified her, they found her brother's name and address in her belongings. The brother was on his way to collect his nephew. Carolee and Don flew out for their daughter's funeral, talked to her friends, and attempted to piece together what kind of life she had led. Their grandson was still in foster care. Evaluation had indicated that he had several special needs. Carolee and Don spent several days poring over options with their other children. "There was never any question in my mind. I knew I had to take him. I wasn't going to let him go to strangers, and I understood why the other kids couldn't take him, although I must admit, that would have been the best solution," said Carolee. Don resisted at first, but when it became clear that Carolee was determined, he acquiesced. "She's not that well. I don't want her to have to keep on working so hard. We had such plans," admitted Don. The family agreed that Carolee and Don would become the custodial guardians, but that the boy would alternate between his three sets of uncles and aunts during the summer.

The first few months were tumultuous. Not only did Carolee, Don, and Will experience the trauma of mourning and grieving about their personal losses, but Will had to adapt to strangers and a totally unfamiliar environment. Carolee and Don provided a structured, stable home life and had the same expectations of Will they had had for their own children. This just couldn't work, and the tensions and conflicts rose. The marriage was affected, Carolee began to somatize her anxieties, and Will suffered from enuresis, temper tantrums, and sleep disorder. After 6 months, they were referred for family treatment. Carolee was directed by the therapist to join a grandmothers' group at the community center. Will was given a complete neuropsychological evaluation and found to be affected by his mother's drug usage. The therapist arranged for a comprehensive psychoeducation plan including medication, individual psychotherapy, special tutoring, and speech therapy. Carolee learned new parenting strategies from her group and, eventually, persuaded Don to join a couples grandparent group. Once a month, Don, Carolee, and Will had a conjoint family session, sometimes including other adult offspring as they visited. By the end of the first year, as Will prepared to enter kindergarten, Carolee and Don had adjusted to their new roles and were both actively involved in a grandparent rights group. "We share the same meaning in our lives now. It's no longer him and his work and me and the kids. This time, despite the fact we're always tired and there's never a day when we don't feel as if a knife has gone through our hearts thinking about Liza, we are really together, like partners. Will is a challenge, but he's also a gift and we've learned that we can learn and can manage," said Carolee.

Marie, age 51, is a never-married Black grandmother who has legal custody of two grandchildren, Lena, 8, and Ralph, 4, each by a different father. Ralph has been diagnosed with attention-deficit/hyperactivity disorder (ADHD) and is being treated successfully with medication. Lena is developmentally delayed and is suffering from unspecified learning disabilities. Both children are suffering from their mother's drug use. Marie's 23-year-old daughter, Marnie, has been abusing drugs since preadolescence. Prior to Marie's obtaining legal custody, Marnie would return home to her mother's periodically, stay a couple of days, steal money, take to the street, be picked up by the police for prostitution or dealing drugs, go to jail or rehab, and then the whole cycle would start over. The kids would be upset for weeks after each visit. Finally, Marie, advised by her welfare worker, threw Marnie out for good and went to court. "That was one of the hardest things I ever had to do. Turn against my own kin. But I had to. I couldn't stand the way she was with her own kids. My heart is broken. I want my little girl back. I don't know what went wrong," says Marie. Marie feels cut off from her friends and relatives. Every minute of her day is focused on getting the kids to school, doctors, special clinics, meeting with social workers. She's always tired; she feels depleted and wonders "where she went wrong." She can't let the kids out of her sight for a minute, given the dangers in the housing project. She worries about "bad influences." The only thing she does for herself is attend church every Sunday. She finds great solace and support from her congregation and pastor, although she feels guilty that she no longer has the time or energy for the choir or sewing group. "It's God's will," she sighs.

Tim, a 27-year-old White man, was raised by his grandfather. His parents were killed in an automobile accident when he was 2. He really doesn't remember much about them other than what he has been told. He does remember his grandmother as a loving surrogate mother, who died suddenly when he was 7. His grandfather became severely depressed when his wife died and began to drink. Tim was shunted from relative to relative and remembers that time as "awful, I was a brat; always getting into trouble. Now I realize I was scared to get close to anyone, cuz they'd die too." When Tim's grandfather, who had been a highly respected store owner, was arrested for drunk driving, he was sentenced to a year-long rehab program. Six months into the program, about a year after widowhood, his grandfather "got his act together" and came to claim Tim.

Those were tough times, because Tim was angry and sullen. Two years later, when Tim got into trouble at school for hurting another kid in a fight, Tim's grandfather took him away for a fishing trip—the first time for either of them. They never talked, they just fished. Tim says the two were "buddies" from then on. He can't explain it, it just happened. His grandfather was strict, made him study and get good grades, but also listened a lot and encouraged him to "try all sorts of things." They did woodwork together, took nature walks, and fly-fished in the mountains. Fishing became their way of communicating and his grandfather's major avocation. His grandfather was not at all social, so Tim never brought kids home and he doesn't remember any company visiting. He doesn't even think his grandfather had any friends, although he knew lots of people. But his grandfather always encouraged Tim to visit other relatives and friends, and Tim says he felt "different but special." Tim recalls that when he asked his grandfather about his parents, his grandfather would get very quiet and couldn't talk. So Tim learned not to ask him. When he went to college, he contacted other relatives and put the pieces together for himself. It was during that time of his life that he began to realize how difficult life had been for his grandfather. His grandfather never complained, but when he referred to Tim as the "darned brat" it was done lovingly and with a special kind of pride as evidenced by the twinkle in his eye. Today, no matter where he is (he's a travelling computer technician), Tim manages to take a week off in the fall to go fishing with his grandfather.

Tim believes that if his grandfather had not taken him in and he had continued to float from relative to relative or ended up in foster care, he would not have turned out as well as he did. When queried, he remembered fantasizing about his parents and wanting "two young parents like everyone else," but as fishing became a more salient part of the grandfather–grandson relationship, those fantasies faded.

Issues from Grandparents' Perspectives

Grandparents who are the sole caretakers of their grandchildren experience unique stress in many areas, even if they are able to adjust to their new role and reap gratification from their relationships with their grandchildren. Their life style is certainly changed and challenged. They are out of sync with their peers, who have completed primary parenting. Whatever expectations and plans they had for their senior years evaporate.

A significant stress comes from the rupture in their relationship with their own offspring, the parent of the grandchild. The normal flow among three generations is now skewed, with the grandparent's concern focused on the grandchild rather than on the offspring. They may experience doubts and role confusion between the roles of parent and grandparent. They yearn for the expected, traditional grandparent role—indulgent and loving without the primary responsibility of total care. When drugs are involved, they may feel compassion and love toward their offspring, but they also experience tremendous pain, anger, shame, and guilt from the loss of their desired expectations for their offspring. This role confusion can be transmitted to the grandchild, who may feel some conflicted loyalties between parent and grandparent.

Grandparents as parents strongly feel their loss of freedom, which affects all of their social and familial relationships. They are isolated from social relationships with their peers who have finished with primary parenting. In addition, due to age difference and circumstances, they can feel distanced from their grandchildren's friends' families as well. This can lead to feelings of loneliness. "I'm stuck with this all by myself. There's no one who understands or can help."

The primary parenting role can also change the nature of their relationships with other grandchildren and adult offspring. One grandmother reported, "I don't get to take my son's kids to the beach anymore, and when they come to visit, I'm always busy with the baby. I feel bad, but what can I do?" They may have to contend with the resentment of their other offspring and grandchildren. There may be ambivalence and conflicting alliances within the extended family.

Financial strain is a big worry. One grandmother had to take a leave of absence from her job as an office worker in order to deal full-time with a troubled youngster. Her husband had just retired from his construction job and had to take a job driving a cab in order to help support this addition to his family. These unexpected changes created some marital strain as well as disruption in their work life. In therapy, it became clear that he blamed her for their daughter's drug addiction, and she blamed him for his lack of involvement as a father. He had looked forward to the time when they wouldn't have to worry so much about money. This grandparent couple learned from their therapist that there might be financial resources available to them for child care from the Department of Social Services. Without legal custody, however, eligibility for financial assistance may be difficult, depending on state regulations. The costs of raising a child today—food, clothing, education, health, recreation—are enormous under any circumstances. People living on fixed incomes from Social Security (and pensions, if they're lucky) are barely able to make ends meet, much less tend to the financial needs of a growing family. They do not have sufficient resources. This financial stress can impact their physical as well as psychological health, exacerbating existing conditions and giving rise to other stress-related disorders. Older people do not have the same likelihood as younger people of increasing their income in the future. The worry and concern are unending.

The emotional toll can be enormous. Many of these grandparents report being on an "emotional roller coaster." They do not have role models, and they are besieged with feelings of grief, anger, guilt, resentment, and being cheated. They wonder if it's all their fault, and they think others are blaming them too. After all, their kids wouldn't be so messed up if they had been OK parents. So how can they do it right now? They're repeating a stressful phase of life they thought they had passed through, and, while many view this as a "second chance," others are baffled by the sociocultural changes in childrearing, to say nothing of the physical, financial, and emotional requirements.

Childrearing practices are new and different. One grandparent told me, "I would have given my kid a crack across the behind for behaving like that, but the social worker tells me I can't do that, I have to give her 'time-outs,' whatever that's supposed to do." This grandparent is overwhelmed by the emotional, behavioral, and psychological difficulties her grandson came to her with. "I feel a lot of resentment toward her [daughter]. . . . She's off doing whatever she wants and it's up to me to pick up the pieces, just like always. I'm the one who has to deal with the courts, the social workers, the tutors, and all." These grandparents want to "do right" by their grandchildren, to provide protection and safety for them, but they're confused about how to do that. They no longer have the physical and emotional resilience of youth, so child care, even under the most optimal circumstances, is more depleting.

As previously mentioned, relationships with their children present other emotional difficulties. Some grandparents take a while to learn that they have, in fact, been "enabling" their offspring's behaviors by acquiescing to their pleas for "one more chance." They may learn the hard way that they need legal leverage to protect their grandchildren from the disruption that can occur when the unstable, troubled parents come back and want to take over for a while. These grandparents are always in the middle unless they have legal custody, and, even in the most dramatic circumstances, the courts are reluctant to turn over custody to anyone but the parents. Grandparents worry constantly that the courts will return their grandchild to an unfit parent. They also worry that their grandchildren will "inherit" their parents' substance abuse or personality disorders. There may be overt or covert competition between the parents and the grandparents for the child's love and loyalty.

"I had to do it. I had to go to court and tell them, and show them my datebook with notations, that Ellie would go off for days, would say she's coming and not come, would bring me that little girl [Martha, age 3] dirty, unchanged, with bruises all over her, just for a few days and that would turn into months. I always believed her, I wanted to. And then something snapped, and I knew I couldn't do it anymore. So I did go to the judge. Now my other kids are pissed at me because, while they don't want Ellie to have Martha, they are telling me I'm not paying enough attention to them. I can't win. I'm so tired, I can barely make it to work on time. But I have to, as we need the money and the health benefits. Thank goodness for the social worker at the community center. She really is always there and I couldn't do it without her."
— Natalie, 45-year-old White divorcee

These grandparents have concerns about the actual raising of their grandchildren. One major concern is worry about what will happen if they become ill or incapacitated or don't live long enough to see these youngsters into adulthood. If they know that other kin will step in and take over, they may at least feel some peace of mind about that issue. Some of the grandparents who become widowed after assuming responsibility for their grandchildren find that their caretaking responsibility assuages their loss. It is as if the grandchild compensates for the loss of a spouse. Another concern for grandparents involves keeping up with the school, social, and physical activities of their grandchildren. School and social activities and customs are different than they were when they were raising their own children, and they don't want their grandchildren to feel isolated or strange. They want to make up to their grandchildren for the pain and loss they have had to endure, and, perhaps, they want to make up for whatever they feel they didn't do right the first time. They also are aware that their grandchildren may have experienced trauma prior to coming to live with them and that their earlier difficulties may require long-term special services and skills. There is a need for respite from these stresses. And, if these grandparents are isolated, they are unlikely to have even minimal relief.

Burton (1992) summarizes the kinds of stressors these grandparents feel as having three levels:

1. Contextual stressors, which involve housing and neighborhood dangers.
2. Family stressors, possibly involving drug dependent spouse, siblings, or children; kin in crisis; frail, elderly kin; coping with

special needs grandchildren and school-age challenges; and a drain on economic and psychosocial family resources.

3. Individual stressors, such as the necessity to balance multiple roles in multiple settings, feelings of "putting my life on hold," and having "no time for myself and feeling guilty about wanting it."

These stressors can be manifested in physical illnesses, alcoholism, increased smoking, depression, and anxiety.

> Martha, 62, and Ben, 64, a biracial couple, experienced all of these stressors in some way. Yet, they found that working together to rear their granddaughter Bessie, age 8, had positive benefits for their relationship and life style. Martha marveled that Ben was so attached to the child (taken in at age 3 when her mother died of cancer) and says she "fell in love" with him all over again as she saw him enjoy this child in a way he had been too busy to do with his own two kids. Martha admitted to physical fatigue, but felt that this child gave them both "a new lease on life." They take turns as much as possible so that they can each get some rest. They report feeling lucky that their extended family is available for intermittent babysitting, so that they don't have to give up completely their social activities, and that they are both healthy and still able to work. Martha has quit her job but is doing family day care in her home, which allows her to stay home and still earn money. "Being around kids keeps you young" is what she tells her friends and relatives who worry about the stresses they see her undergoing.

To summarize, some major themes identified by Vardi and Buchholz (1994) from group therapy sessions with parenting grandparents include the following: authority, control, sibling rivalry, a generation gap, dealing with schools, illness, mortality, isolation, defensiveness, anger, fear of going crazy, guilt, shame, separation, and abandonment.

How grandparents experience these stresses will depend on race, class, and gender. All grandparents do not have equal access to economic and emotional sources of support. The interwoven variables of race, class, and gender pointed out by Dressel and Barnhill (1994) are central organizers of one's "life chances" across the life span. They may mediate the impact of grandparent caregiving as

> the economic need in their families of origin coupled with life-long gender and race discrimination that seriously limited their own educational and economic mobility have carried into late middle and old age. The struggles of these grandmothers to achieve economic equilibrium are less conditioned by their present aging than by life histories of marginalization. (Dressel & Barnhill, 1994, p. 687)

Shore and Hayslip (1994) found that the grandparents' perceptions of grandparenting affected their well-being and satisfaction, and
their expectations about the later phases of their life would affect their
perceptions of grandparenting. For example, middle-class Whites and
Blacks may have expected their retirement years to be focused on the
pursuit of leisure, and the assumption of parenting responsibilities for
grandchildren could result in grave disappointment when their expectations were unmet. On the other hand, working-class Blacks, particularly those living in communities with rampant poverty, violence, and
drug use, may expect lifetime caretaking of some type, so there may
not be a wide gap between their expectations and the realities. Middle-
class Blacks may yearn for leisure time, but, because of their cultural
heritage being more attuned to communal care, they may be more
adaptable when circumstances require them to assume primary caretaking.

But even in the most difficult circumstances, many grandparents
as parents point out the positive outcomes of such caregiving. There
can be a lot of psychological growth for those grandparents able to
realize the energizing, gratifying benefits of having children to love and
raise. They may enjoy the companionship of their grandchild, the support in the form of praise and compliments for the good job they're
doing from friends and others in the community, and the meaning that
is associated with doing something "good and right." One grandmother
reported that she doesn't "have time for worry or depression," and
another commented that "she'd been too busy surviving when she was
raising her own children so this time she's enjoying it more."

The literature is in agreement about the inevitable, complex, and
multiple stresses and strains that these grandparents contend with and
the requirements for specialized social policy and clinical intervention.
Before I discuss the clinical implications, I should note that there is
virtually no literature on the impact of grandparents as parents on the
grandchildren. Most social service personnel would agree, however,
that if reunification with the parents is not desirable, feasible, or possible, living with kin is a better solution than foster care. And grandparents may be the ones with the highest motivation for assuming this
caretaking responsibility.

Clinical Implications for Working
with Grandparents as Parents

A large number of grandparents as parents seek help for their grandchildren from social service agencies. They are reluctant to seek help
for their own distress, and they tend to detour their personal and marital
distress through their grandchildren. They may not seek help until in

crisis, so instrumental crisis intervention may be the first phase of treatment along with individual needs assessment and the provision of empathic emotional support. Workers from social service agencies advocate the availability of community support programs with a wide range of services to assist these families to cope with trauma and loss, to adjust to new roles, and to meet the challenges and demands of this difficult parenting. Survival, problem-solving, and coping skills are the primary objectives.

First off, it is important for clinicians to arrange comprehensive medical and psychological evaluations for the children so that appropriate educational and therapeutic treatment plans can be developed and implemented. Many of these children were born with drug-related problems, and they are legally entitled to early medical, psychological, and educational intervention. The earlier the intervention, the greater the likelihood of positive outcomes. At the same time, grandparents as parents require information about financial, legal, educational, health, and other community resources. Many, for example, do not realize that they may be eligible for certain services or financial aid. It is important to help these grandparents consider all options before making a final decision about assuming this responsibility, as there may be health and other mitigating circumstances that necessitate consideration of alternative child care. Clients also require instruction about the necessity of keeping objective, accurate, and detailed financial, medical and parental contact records in order to obtain necessary services. If grandparents have to go to court, they need to be able to document their offspring's neglect or "unfitness" to parent.

In addition to providing information and helping clients identify and locate resources, individual, couple, and family therapy can help the grandparents come to terms with the circumstances of this unplanned parenting and prepare them for the stresses they are likely to experience. Clinicians need to advocate, to intervene with the schools, courts, and social service agencies. But they also need to provide emotional support and to help the grandparents deal with their raw, intense anger, sadness, and loss. If the parent is still available and in contact, the therapist can encourage the grandparent to keep communications open and attempt to seek intergenerational cooperation despite the validity of the negative feelings.

The grandparent as parent is in a peculiar emotional bind in that he or she wants things to be the way they "should be," with the child living with his or her parents, at the same time that the grandparent dreads losing the child. The clinician needs to balance the needs of the grandparent and the grandchild. It's important that the clinician be aware of countertransference issues, such as overidentification with one of the three generations, leading to contamination of a multipartial stance. The age of the therapist and his or her experience as a grandchild, child, parent, or grandparent may be the source of unconscious bias.

Parenting classes and peer support groups are perhaps even more important than individual, couple, or family therapy. Grandparents need an opportunity to learn about the childrearing goals and practices of current times, such as alternatives to corporal punishment. They also need to learn about today's norms of child and adolescent development, the expectations of school teachers, and the availability of respite care. They need emotional support and constructive psychoeducation from peers in similar roles, as well as "experts," to give them hope, encouragement, and a feeling of self-efficacy.

Depression and anxiety appear to be the most prevalent clinical features of grandparent caregivers. Group therapy formats can provide opportunities for ventilation and validation of these feelings in addition to parenting instruction and skill learning. In individual therapy, clinicians can help the grandparents examine their own role in their caregiving situation. Grandparent caregivers may be revisiting their own childrearing stages of life, old family conflicts, and unresolved parenting issues, all of which need to be explored so that they make different choices in the future. The therapist's sensitivity, acceptance, and empathy may help grandparents develop firmer boundaries and pay more attention to their own needs and issues.

Social policy is a major factor for the welfare of this type of family structure. Wagner (1995) has reported on the outcomes of the White House Mini-Conference on Aging and Grandparents Raising Grandchildren held in March 1995. The many issues facing grandparent-headed households were discussed, and two resolutions were passed to deal with these problems:

> One [resolution] recommends that grandparents have legal surrogate decision-making authority for the care of children in the absence of other responsible persons without having to go to court; the other recommends that a public awareness campaign be launched to educate the public as well as policymakers and professionals about the grandparent-headed household and the very significant contributions the grandparents are making to society. (p. 27)

According to Wagner, these resolutions have made their way into the minds of the delegates to the May 1996 White House Conference on Aging and, hopefully, will remove some of the barriers that grandparents face in gaining access to food stamps and Aid to Families of

Dependent Children. Funding for community-based services is essential for this increasing population.

ADVANCED REPRODUCTIVE TECHNOLOGY

In the past 10 years, the number of families created by means of new reproductive technologies, such as *in vitro* fertilization, gamete intrafallopian transfer, and donor gametes, has increased dramatically, particularly in the United States, Great Britain, and Australia. These new technologies challenge the traditional definition of parenting, pregnancy, motherhood, and fatherhood, and raise important moral, ethical, and legal questions. For whom should these procedures be available and under what circumstances? How long should frozen embryos be kept? Are donors biological parents? These and related questions result in legal quagmires. Our concern in this chapter is about the psychological consequences for these children, who are unrelated to one or both caretaking parents. We are also concerned about the parents themselves, and the family as a whole. The literature is sparse and divided with regard to the impact of donor gametes on the child, the parents, and the family system. Most likely this is because sufficient time has not elapsed to permit evaluation of the long-term outcomes for individuals and for society.

The Participants

Third party reproduction can include as many as six possible participants. As pointed out by Braverman and English (1992, pp. 356–357), Mother A could provide an egg and womb (as birth mother or embryo donor); Mother B could provide the egg (as genetic mother or donor); Mother C could provide the womb (as egg recipient, gestational carrier, or embryo donor); Mother D could be a traditional adoptive mother, a surrogate adoptive mother, or the adoptive mother who is an egg donor with carrier. Father A could provide the sperm (as biological father with partner/wife, with surrogate, with carrier, or with egg donor or egg carrier, or as sperm donor). Father B could be the sperm father or the traditional adoptive father.

Typically, the caretaking parents have been struggling with infertility for several years. These parents are likely to be in their mid-30s to early 50s by the time they actually conceive, having undergone several years of infertility and advanced reproductive technology attempts prior to the successful conception and full-term pregnancy. They also tend to be highly educated and relatively affluent, in order to be able to absorb the enormous costs of such treatments. Increasingly, in this era of cost-contained health care, these expensive treatments are not eligible for insurance reimbursement. In some cases, the parents have successfully reproduced one or two times, experience secondary infertility, and utilize advanced reproductive technologies for an additional child. Or, they may have adopted a child before realizing the possibilities of these new technologies.

Donors of eggs and sperm may perform this function for general altruistic reasons, for financial remuneration, for the narcissistic gratification of knowing that they will be reproducing even though anonymously, or because of a personal relationship with the recipient(s). Heretofore, this has been an anonymous, secretive process. In fact, most artificial insemination donor clinics have not kept long-term records, and the information they collected in the past dealt solely with medical history and physical description. Currently, the record keeping is more detailed and comprehensive, and records are kept indefinitely. Most donors do not seem to have more than a fleeting thought about their genetic offspring, although more and more of those being queried today are admitting to curiosity. Many clinics have a policy of limiting one donor to 8 to 10 conceptions.

Issues of Parents

The first issue that parents must contend with is infertility. Donor sperm insemination is more common than the more recent donor egg procedure. If donor sperm is necessary, that is usually because of male infertility, which seems to be more shame evoking than female infertility. This is most likely related to our cultural association of virility and male fertility. In order for a male to be able to tolerate and accept donor sperm, he must grieve the loss of his fertility. If he is unable to do this, he may experience difficulty in relating to the child of his wife and a sperm donor, and he may be overly anxious about donor anonymity. This anxiety may communicate itself to the child, who yearns for his loving responsiveness and feels some kind of inexplicable estrangement.

Another critical issue for the parents is their marriage. The divorce rate for these families is lower than for conventional families (Amuzu, Laxova, & Shapiro, 1990). However, if there are serious conflicts, the issue of donor sperm (more so than donor eggs because the woman still bears the child) can come up in parenting fights, for example, "He's not really your child, so you don't have the right to. . . . " The couple may also suffer with the secrecy of the nature of their conception. While coping with infertility, they may have enjoyed the support of other infertile couples. Once they achieve pregnancy, couples still struggling with infertility may draw away and the couple may feel uncomfortable sharing their secret even with their obstetrician, much less family and friends. Braverman and English (1992) point out that, once into pregnancy, the implications of using donor gametes may begin to prevail, now that the desperation to achieve a pregnancy has been resolved. There is always concern about genetic abnormality—not just because of donor sperm or egg, but also given the older age of the primipara mother. Many developmental psychologists believe that critical bonding begins prenatally and that excessive anxiety can affect prenatal attachment.

A major concern for the parents is whether or not to tell the child about his or her biological background. The literature attests that disclosure is a complex, multifaceted issue (Amuzu et al., 1990; Blyth, 1990; Braverman & English, 1992; Cook, Golombok, Bish, & Murray, 1995; Golombok, Cook, Bish, & Murray 1995; Karow, 1993; Klock, Jacob, & Maier, 1994; Kovacs, Mushin, Kane, & Baker, 1993; McWhinnie, 1992; Pruett, 1992). Those that advocate for disclosure believe that children have an inherent right to know about their genetic heritage, that secrecy itself creates barriers within family systems, and that children need to know their biological origins in order to develop a full sense of self (American Fertility Society, 1993; Pruett, 1992). Furthermore, if, perchance, someone reveals the secret, the child's basic trust will be impaired.

In fact, Pruett (1992) argues,

> it is my best clinical judgment that we should err on the side of disclosure over secrecy, as it is less damaging to the child's inner emotional world than the gap in the narrative of the self. Knowing the circumstances of one's origins is less psychologically malignant than not knowing, assuming the content of the knowledge is not especially nefarious or emotionally charged for a particular family or parent. By knowing the facts of one's conception, these children have a better chance of feeling and understanding that they were conceived in love (if not in situ), a knowledge reassuring to all young beings pondering the mystery of their origins and its human connection. (p. 316)

This position is similar to that of adoption researchers, who argue that knowledge about genetic origins is important for a clear sense of identity. However, one must remember that adoptive families and donor insemination families differ in that the child in the latter family is typically related genetically to one parent and has always been wanted, whereas the adopted child may not have been wanted by his or her birth parents. Few in mainstream psychology have questioned whether the conventional theories about child development apply to the different culture groups represented in our society. Or whether there are different paths of development for different racial and ethnic groups to experience attachment and achieve a secure sense of self. While there is certainly a need for genetic information regarding medical histories, it is more speculation than proven fact to suggest that a child needs to know the identity of his genetic parent in order to develop a sense of self.

Thus, many professionals support parents' right not to disclose. They argue that there is not yet enough research to support advocating disclosure, that the effects could, therefore, be harmful rather than beneficial, and that stigmatization and lack of sufficient information are real dangers. Parents may fear their child's anger and rejection. One could also argue that each case needs to be assessed individually in its unique contexts, that there is no one right answer about disclosure to be applied across the board. Golombok et al. (1995) recently found that keeping the method of conception secret from the child did not appear to have a negative impact on family relationships. In a study comparing 45 donor insemination families with 55 adoptive and 41 *in vitro* fertilization families, these same researchers (Cook et al., 1995) found that donor insemination parents were concerned about protecting the child, protecting the father, and lacking information about the donor father. They were also confused about when and how to tell their child if they were going to.

Impact on Children

The little research that has been conducted indicates that these children are at no more risk for congenital anomalies or psychological difficulty than are normally conceived children. In fact, some studies show that they actually fare better. For example, the Golombok et al. (1995) study just mentioned compared 45 naturally conceived families with 45 *in vitro* fertilization and donor insemination families and found that the quality of parenting in families with a child conceived by assisted conception was actually superior on several measures. They suggest that the greater commitment to parenting of the assisted reproduction families may be more important than genetic ties. Klock et al. (1994) support the findings of other studies indicating that the majority of donor recipients are psychologically well adjusted, have average marital adjustment, and that their children fare as well as those in naturally conceived families.

Because these families have traditionally been secretive, a truly representative sample has not been available for study. However, since the open adoption movement has gained momentum, there has been a similar movement for open disclosure for donors and the donor insemination families. More families are now agreeing to be studied to help learn what the answers may turn out to be, are requesting that clinics maintain long-term records, and are open to discussing the psychological consequences of donor insemination. Hopefully, when sufficient time has passed for adolescents and young adults to be followed, we will have more data about the pros and cons of disclosure and the effects of donor gametes.

Implications for Clinicians

It is important for clinicians to focus on helping couples work through the losses associated with fertility prior to or during fertility treatment. These losses — of self-esteem, status, self-confidence, security, control, and of a naturally conceived child — can precipitate the onset of depression and couple strain. And, as noted in Chapter 4, the treatments themselves evoke further stresses and strains. Couples may need help in selecting a reputable clinic, sorting through various options, and dealing with their feelings and relationship throughout the procedures. The clinician may be the only person outside of the fertility clinic with whom they can share their feelings and thoughts.

When couples decide on donor insemination, clinicians need to help them begin to think about the implications. Both members may not feel the same way about the use of a donor. It is important for the couple to feel safe about discussing their true feelings.

> Nora, 39, and Jeff, 52, were considering donor sperm insemination. Nora was determined to have a child, and Jeff, who had two children from a previous marriage, was ambivalent. He had consented to attempt to have his vasectomy reversed, and when that proved unsuccessful, Nora pursued aggressively the idea of donor insemination. Jeff felt like "he was over a barrel." He loved Nora and wanted to strengthen their relationship, but did not know if he could make an emotional commitment to a child for whom he was not the biological father. The therapist served as both a sounding board and a multipartial advocate. In this way, she was able to help Jeff focus on his disappointments from his first marriage and his parenting experiences. As he began to gain some understanding about these disappointments, he was able to differentiate this marriage and the possibility for parenting with Nora from his previous experience. She helped Nora to lessen her pressuring and to empathize with Jeff's perspective. The couple agreed to a 6-month moratorium during which time they would explore the possibility of adoption and attempt to

repair Jeff's relationships with his two grown sons before making any further decision about donor insemination. While both felt the pressure of Nora's biological clock, this 6-month "breathing space," as Jeff termed it, allowed them to focus on strengthening their relationship as a foundational context for this decision. Multipartiality was a critical therapeutic element.

Once the decision to utilize donor insemination is made, clinicians can help couples to prepare for the implications. For example, couples can be told that open communication about their continuing reservations is important and helpful. They are likely to fantasize about the donor during the fertility procedures, pregnancy, and even during early childhood. Braverman and English (1992) suggest that the frequency of this fantasizing usually fades as the child asserts his or her own personality. But, it may return during illnesses or special events. Clinicians should encourage couples to talk about these thoughts and fantasies even if they decide not to disclose to their child. But they should be encouraged to think about disclosure at the outset of considering donor insemination.

Because there is so little guidance and information available, couples will rely on the therapist for advice regarding disclosure. I have been asked by four couples within the past year about this. Hence my immersion into the literature. I can only suggest that each case is unique. In one, where there is marital strife detoured into a power struggle over which partner's parenting style is the "best," I've suggested that the couple difficulties be dealt with as couple system issues separate from the parenting issues. So the decision about disclosure has been postponed.

In another situation, where the parents both want the child to know from them the circumstances of her birth, I've suggested that the couple answer the child's questions as honestly as possible. This couple was afraid that a relative or friend who knew might let something slip, and they wanted to be open, honest, but in control of disclosure. Obviously, timing is an important issue but the literature has not yet determined what the appropriate age to disclose is. When discussing possible options, we talked about the trauma that might accompany later disclosure as opposed to the more natural acceptance and internalization of this information if disclosure gradually occurs as the child is able to process it.

If disclosure is decided on, Pruett (1992, p. 317) recommends that the psychological readiness of the child with regard to timing and content of disclosure should be the most relevant factor. He suggests that there are three levels: (1) giving the most basic information in the first

4 to 5 years of life, for example, "Babies are grown in a special place in Mommy's body called the womb or uterus. There is a special place between her legs for the baby to come out of when it is ready to be born"; (2) after the age of 5, letting children know that there are various ways for babies to begin growing, for example, "Seeds and eggs can be put together inside or outside the mommy's body"; (3) "One way to make babies is for a seed to come from another man and be mixed with Mommy's egg (or vice versa) to start growing into you." Along with this statement can come a distinction between a "birth father" and a "life father." During adolescence, more specific data may be provided.

One couple consulted me because of feelings of guilt around withholding information about their fertility procedures from their parents. This couple was in complete agreement with each other that their parents' religious views would precipitate a negative reaction toward the circumstances of their conception. But they were uncomfortable because their parents kept commenting on how different the child looked from his father; there were teasing remarks like, "Whose child is he? The milkman's?" The underlying issue, it turned out, was not the child's paternity, but the couple's guilt about leaving their parents' church. They felt as if they were disloyal. Somehow, they thought they had managed to obfuscate how they spent Sundays and other religious occasions to keep their abandonment of religious observance from their parents. It became apparent that their parents were aware of their lack of religious observance and were very distressed about it.

In this particular situation, where the 11-year-old child and parents were delighted with each other and functioning optimally, the couple decided not to disclose to the child. I shared with them my belief that warm, sensitive, and responsive interactions between spouses and between parents and children are more significant determinants of child development than genetic ties. Disclosure should be for the benefit and welfare of the child and the parents, not to conform to popular thinking of the day.

It is not unusual for families who have waited so long and desperately to have a child to compensate for their anxieties by overly protective or permissive parenting. These families may come into therapy with a symptomatic child. Clinicians can focus on effective parenting skills, such as the setting and implementation of appropriate limits and open communication. These couples may require sensitive exploration and restructuring of their expectations and ideas about parenting. In addition, they may need help in articulating their fears of loss or harm to the child, their feelings about their uniqueness, and the feelings pertaining to the aftermath of their decision making.

Clinicians may have their own biases about reproductive technology and anonymous donor insemination. Because the issues these new technologies present are so complex, they may not even be aware of these biases until confronted with a particular case. They need to keep abreast of the literature and dialogue with others about the legal, ethical, moral, and professional dilemmas presented by these technologies. The questions continue to arise; the answers are much slower in coming.

Conclusions

Most of the brave new family structures covered in this book are both normal and different. Like traditional families, they all encounter a variety of problems over the life span on a continuum ranging from mild to severe. Because norms, services, and social policies have been based on traditional family structures, some of the problems nontraditional families encounter are more in response to societal misunderstanding and devaluation than to family dynamics. Along with these problems and difficulties, however, nontraditional families also can experience a wide range of happiness and satisfaction. They create new pathways of understanding family process.

At this point, there are no data to suggest that living in a variant family structure is inherently disadvantageous to children's development. In fact, there are data to suggest that children's natural resilience may enable them to transcend what society views as "different" and, therefore, "wrong." Furthermore, children in the families described in this book may not even perceive their family as being "different" or "unique" until others point it out to them.

It is my hope that professional associations and training programs can take the lead in broadening and redefining our conceptualization and perspectives of "family," of which variables contribute to optimal family functioning and what impedes development. This means that we cannot base our norms solely on a traditional family form, which is outdated and increasingly outnumbered. This also means that traditional families should not be utilized as the control group in research, against which all other groups are measured. More longitudinal, multivariate, and qualitative methodology will enable us to learn about family resilience in multicultural and multiplistic contexts. The literature does show us that having family interactions based on mutual respect, love, nurturing, empathy, and encouragement along with firm, consistent boundaries and limits is more crucial than whether the family structure is traditional or creative.

Resources

n this section, I will list some the organizations and adult and juvenile readings that my clients have found helpful in learning about and dealing with diverse family formats. Many of the children's books were contributed by David Fassler, M.D., and his associates.

INFERTILITY

Support Organizations

Resolve, Inc., 1310 Broadway, Somerville, MA 02144 (617) 623-0744
Miracle Moms, P.O. Box 42139, Cincinnati, OH 45242
Internet address: Alt.infertility

Recommended Reading

See listings under Single Parents by Choice, Grandparent Families, and Families by Reproductive Technology for further listings about conception.

Berger, G. S. (1989). *The couples' guide to fertility: How new medical advances can help you have a baby.* New York: Doubleday.
Glazer, E. (1992). *The long-awaited stork: A guide for parents after infertility.* New York: Free Press.
Lasker, J., & Borg, S. (1994). *In search of parenthood: Coping with infertility and high-tech conception.* Philadelphia: Temple University Press.
Monach, J. H. (1993). *Childless, no choice: The experience of involuntary childlessness.* London: Routledge.
Salzer, L. (1990). *Surviving infertility: A compassionate guide through the emotional crisis of infertility.* New York: Harper Perennial.
Zoldbrod, A. P. (1993). *Men, women, and infertility.* New York: Lexington Books.

ADOPTION

National Advocacy (and Search Information) Organizations

Adoptee Liberty Movement Association, P.O. Box 154, Washington Bridge
Station, New York, NY 10033 (212) 581-1568
Adoption Information Services, 901-B East Willow Grove Avenue, Wynd-
moor, PA 19118 (215) 233-1380
Adoptive Families of America, Inc., 3333 Highway 100 North, Minneapolis,
MN 55422 (612) 535-4829 or (800) 372-3300
American Adoption Congress, 1000 Connecticut Avenue, N.W., #9, Washing-
ton, DC 20002 (202) 483-3399
Concerned United Birthparents, 2000 Walker Street, Des Moines, IA 50317
(800) 822-2777
Council for Equal Rights in Adoption, 356 East 74 Street, Suite 2, New York,
NY 10021 (212) 988-0110
International Concerns Committee for Children, 911 Cypress Drive, Boul-
der, CO 80303 (no phone)
National Adoption Information Clearinghouse, 1400 I Street, N.W., #600,
Washington, DC 20005
North American Council on Adoptable Children, 970 Raymond Ave., Suite
106, St. Paul, MN 55114 (612) 644-3036

Adoptive Parent Support Groups

Adoptive Families of America, 3333 Highway 100 North, Minneapolis, MN
55422 (612) 535-4829
Families Adopting Children Everywhere, P.O. Box 28058, Baltimore, MD
21239 (410) 488-2656
North American Council on Adoptable Children, 970 Raymond Ave., Suite
106, St. Paul, MN 55114 (612) 644-3036
Open Door Society of Massachusetts, P.O. Box 1158, Westborough, MA
01581 (508) 429-4260

Adult Recommended Readings

Anderson, R. (1992). *Second choice, Growing up adopted.* Chesterfield, MO:
Badger Hill Press.
Benson, P. L., Sharma, A., & Roehlkepratain, E. C. (1994). *Growing up
adopted.* Minneapolis, MN: Search Institute.
Blau, E. (1993). *Stories of adoption,* Portland, OR: New Sage Press.
Brodzinsky, D. M., Schechter, M. D., & Henig, R. M. (1992), *Being adopt-
ed: The lifelong search for self.* New York: Doubleday.
Gediman, J. S., & Brown, L. P. (1989) *Birth bond: Reunion between birth-
parents and adoptees—What happens after.* Far Hills, NJ: New Horizon
Press.
Gilman, L. (1992). *The adoption resource book* (3rd ed.). New York: Harp-
er Perennial.

Lifton, B. J. (1994). *Journey of the adopted self: A quest for wholeness*. New York: Basic Books.

McColm, M. (1993). *Adoption reunions: A book for adoptees, birth parents and adoptive parents*. Toronto: Second Story Press.

McNamara, J., & McNamara, B. (1990). *Adoption and the sexually abused child*. Orono, ME: University of Southern Maine.

Melina, L. R. (1987). *Raising adopted children: A manual for adoptive parents*. New York: Harper Perennial.

Melina, L., & Roszia, S. K. (1993). *The open adoption experience*. New York: Harper Perennial.

Miles, S. G. (1991). *Adoption literature for children and young adults: An annotated bibliography*. New York: Greenwood Press.

Register, C. (1990). *Are those kids yours? American families with children adopted from other countries*. New York: Free Press.

Rosenberg, E. B. (1992). *The adoption life cycle: The children and their families through the years*. New York: Free Press.

Schaefer, C. (1991). *The other mother: A woman's love for the child she gave up for adoption*. New York: Soho Press.

Silber, K., & Dorner, P. M. (1990). *Children of open adoption*. San Antonio, TX: Corona.

Strauss, J. (1994). *Birthright: A guide to search and reunion for adoptees, birthparents, and adoptive parents*. New York: Penguin.

Sullivan, M. R. (1990). *Adopt the baby you want*. New York: Simon & Schuster.

van Gulden, H., & Bartels-Rabb, L. (1993). *Real parents, real children*. New York: Crossroad.

Waldron, J. L. (1995) *Giving away Simone: A memoir*. New York: Times Books.

Watkins, J., & Fischer, S. (1993). *Talking with young children about adoption*. New Haven, CT: Yale University Press.

Juvenile and Young Adult Recommended Reading

Bloom, S. (1992). *A family for Jamie*. New York: Clarkson N. Potter.

Carney, A. (1976). *No more here and there*. Chapel Hill: University of North Carolina Press.

Duprau, J. (1989). *Adoption: The facts, feelings, and issues of a double heritage*. Englewood, NJ: Messner.

Fahlberg, V. (1991). *A child's journey through placement*. Fort Wayne, IN: Perspective Press.

Girard, L. (1986). *Adoption is for always*. Niles, IL: Whitman.

Girard, L. (1989). *We adopted you, Benjamin Koo*, Niles, IL: Whitman.

Gravelle, K., & Fischer, S. (1993). *Where are my birth parents? A guide for teenage adoptees*. New York: Walker.

Krementz, J. (1982). *How it feels to be adopted*. New York: Knopf.

Lifton, B. J. (1994). *Tell me a real adoption story*. New York: Knopf.

Nickman, S. (1985). *The adoption experience*. New York: Messner.

Schilling, S., & Swain, J. (1989). *My name is Jonathan (and I have AIDS)*. Denver: Prickly Pair Publishing.

GAY AND LESBIAN FAMILIES

Support Organizations

Center for Reproductive Alternatives, 727 Via Otono, San Clemente, CA 92672

The Federation of Parents and Friends of Lesbians and Gay Men, Inc. (PFLAG), 1101 4th Street, NW, Suite 1030, Washington, DC 20005 (202) 638-4200 (A national organization with braches in many states. A self-help group, composed of parents and friends of lesbians and gay men, who are trying to help parents and friends to accept their loved one's homosexuality.)

Gay and Lesbian Parents Coalition International, P.O. Box 50360, Washington, DC 20091 (202) 583-8029

Lesbian–Gay Family and Parenting Services, Fenway Community Health Center, 7 Haviland Street, Boston, MA 02115 (617) 267-7766, ext. 570 (Alternative insemination program in addition to providing education, support, and advocacy.)

Lesbian Mothers' National Defense Fund, P.O. Box 21567, Seattle, WA 98111 (206) 325-2643

National Gay/Lesbian Task Force, 80 Fifth Avenue, New York, NY 10011

The Sperm Bank of California, 2115 Milvia, 2nd floor, Berkeley, CA 94704 (510) 841-1858

Surrogate Mothers, Inc., P.O. Box 216, Monrovia, IN 46157 (317) 996-2000

Adult Recommended Reading

Alpert, H. (1988). *We are everywhere: Writings by and about lesbian parents*. Freedom, CA: Crossing Press.

Barrett, M. (1990). *Invisible lives: The truth about millions of women-loving women*. New York: Harper.

Berzon, B. (1984). *Positively gay*. Los Angeles: Mediamix.

Borhek, M. (1983) *Coming out to parents: A two-way survival guide for lesbians and gay men and their parents*. New York: Pilgrim Press.

Bozett, F. W. (Ed.). (1987). *Gay and lesbian parents*. New York: Praeger.

Buxton, A. (1991). *The other side of the closet: The coming out crisis for straight spouses*. Santa Monica, CA: IBS Press.

Corley, R. (1990). *The final closet: The gay parents' guide for coming out to their children*. Miami, FL: Editech Press.

Curry, H., & Clifford, D. (1991). *A legal guide for lesbian and gay couples*. Berkeley, CA: Nolo Press.

Fairchild, B., & Hayward, N. (1989). *Now that you know: What every parent should know about homosexuality.* New York: Harcourt Brace Jovanovich.

Gil de Lamadrid, M. (Ed.). (1991). *Lesbians choosing motherhood: Legal implications of donor insemination and co-parenting.* San Francisco: National Center for Lesbian Rights.

Griffin, C. (1986). *Beyond acceptance: Parents of lesbians and gays talk about their experiences.* New York: St. Martin's Press.

Hanscombe, G. E. (1987). *Rocking the cradle: Lesbian mothers: A challenge in family living.* Boston: Alyson.

Holmes, S. (1988). *Testimonies: A collection of coming out stories.* Boston: Alyson.

Hutchins, L., & Kaahumanu, L. (1991). *Bi any other name: Bisexual people speak out.* Boston: Alyson.

Klein, F. (1993). *The bisexual option.* New York: Harrington Park Press.

Martin, A. (1993). *The lesbian and gay parenting handbook.* New York: Harper Perennial.

MacPike, L. (1989). *There's something I've been meaning to tell you: Lesbian and gay parents come out to their children.* Tallahassee, FL: Naiad.

Muller, A. (1987). *Parents matter: Parents' relationships with lesbian daughters and gay sons.* Tallahassee, FL: Naiad.

Pies, C. (1985). *Considering parenthood: A workbook for lesbians.* San Francisco: Spinsters/Aunt Lute.

Pollack, S., & Vaughn, J. (Eds.). (1987). *Politics of the heart, a lesbian parenting anthology.* Ithaca, NY: Firebrand.

Rafkin, L. (Ed.). (1990). *Different mothers: Sons and daughters of lesbians talk about their lives.* San Francisco: Cleis Press.

Rafkin, L. (Ed.). (1987). *Different daughters: A book by mothers of lesbians.* San Francisco: Cleis Press.

Rich, A. (1986). *Blood, bread, and poetry.* New York: Norton.

Weinberg, M., Williams, C., & Pryor, D. (1994). *Dual attraction: Understanding bisexuality.* New York: Oxford University Press.

Weinrich, J. D. (1987). *Sexual landscapes: Why we are what we are, why we love whom we love.* New York: Scribner's.

Whitlock, K. (1989). *Bridges of respect: Creating support for lesbian and gay youth.* Philadelphia: AFSC.

Juvenile and Young Adult Recommended Reading

Bauer, M. D. (Ed.). (1990). *Am I blue.* New York: HarperCollins.

Bosche, S. (1983). *Jenny lives with Eric and Martin.* London: Guernsey Press.

Brown, F. (1991). *The generous Jefferson Bartleby Jones,* Boston: Alyson.

Elwin, R., & Paulse, M. (1990). *Asha's Mums.* Toronto: Women's Press.

Garden, N. (1984). *Nancy on my mind.* New York: Farrar.

Heron, A. & Maran, M. (1991). *How would you feel if your dad was gay.* Boston: Alyson.

Koertge, R. (1989). *The Arizona kid.* New York: Avon.

Mack, B. (1979). *Jesse's dream skirt*. Chapel Hill, NC: Lollipop Power.
Newman, L. (1991). *Gloria goes to gay pride*. Boston: Alyson.
Newman, L. (1989). *Heather has two mommies*. Boston: Alyson.
Severance, J. (1983). *Lots of mommies*. Chapel Hill, NC: Lollipop Power.
Valentine, J. (1992). *The day they put a tax on rainbows*. Boston: Alyson.
Valentine, J. (1991). *The duke who outlawed jelly beans*. Boston: Alyson.
Vigna, J. (1995). *My two uncles*. Morton Grove, IL: Whitman.
Willhoite, M. (1990). *Daddy's roommate*. Boston: Alyson.
Willhote, M. (1991). *Families: A coloring book*. Boston: Alyson.
Willhoite, M. (1993). *Uncle what-is-it is coming to visit*. Boston: Alyson.
Zolotow, C. (1972). *William's doll*. New York: Harper Trophy.

MULTIRACIAL FAMILIES

Support Organizations

Adoption Resource Center, P.O. Box 383246, Cambridge, MA 02238 (617) 547-0909
Adoptive Families of America, 3333 Highway 100N, Minneapolis, MN 55422 (612) 535-4829 or (800) 372-3300
International Concerns Committee for Children, 911 Cypress Drive, Boulder, CO 80303 (Transracial Adoption) (303) 494-8333
Latin American Adoptive Families, 23 Evangeline Road, Falmouth, MA 02540 (508) 548-1963
New England Alliance of Multiracial Families, P.O. Box 148, West Medford, MA 02156 (617) 965-3287
Open Door Society, P.O. Box 1158, Westborough, MA 01581 (617) 965-3287 (800) 932-3678

Adult Recommended Reading

Comer, J., & Poussaint, A. F. (1992). *Raising black children: Questions and answers for parents and teachers*. New York: Dutton.
Crohn, J. (1995). *Mixed matches: How to create successful interracial, interethnic, and interfaith relationships*. New York: Fawcett Columbine.
Frankenberg, R. (1993). *White women, race matters: The social construction of whiteness*. Minneapolis: University of Minnesota Press.
Funderburg, L. (1994). *Black, white and other*. New York: Morrow.
Grosz, G. (1993, January/February). 1993 guide to best and worst cities for interracial couples, families, and multiracial people to live. *Interrace*, pp. 31–34.
Hearst, M. R. (Ed.). (1993). *Interracial identity: Celebration, conflict, or choice*. Chicago: Biracial Family Network.
Ho, M. K. (1992). *Minority children and adolescents in therapy*. Newbury Park, CA: Sage.
Khanga, Y. (1993). *Soul to soul: The story of a black Russian American family, 1865–1992*. New York: Norton.

Ramirez, G., & Ramirez, J. L. (1994). *Multicultural children's literature.* Albany, NY: Delmar.

Reddy, M. (1994). *Crossing the color line: Race, parenting and culture.* New Brunswick, NJ: Rutgers University Press.

Root, M. P. P. (Ed.). (1992). *Racially mixed people in America.* Newbury Park, CA: Sage.

Scales-Trent, J. (1995). *Notes of a white black woman.* University Park: Pennsylvania State University Press.

Simon, R., Alstein, H., & Melli, M. S. (1994). *The case for transracial adoption.* Washington, DC: American University Press.

Spickard, P. (1989). *Mixed blood: Intermarriage and ethnic identity in twentieth century America.* Madison: University of Wisconsin Press.

Sung, B. L. (1990). *Chinese American intermarriage.* New York: Center for Migration Studies.

Tizard, B., & Phoenix, A. (1993). *Black, white, or mixed? Race and racism in the lives of young people of mixed parentage.* New York: Routledge.

West, C. (1993). *Race matters.* Boston: Beacon.

Williams, G. H. (1995). *Life on the color line: The true story of a white boy who discovered he was black.* New York: Dutton.

Juvenile and Young Adult Recommended Reading

Adoff, A. (1982). *All the colors of the race.* New York: Lothrop, Lee & Shepard.

Adoff, A. (1992). *Black is brown is tan.* New York: Harper.

Angel, Ann, (1988). *Real for sure sister,* Fort Wayne, IN: Perspectives Press.

Banish, R. (1992). *A forever family, A child's story about adoption.* New York: Harper Trophy

Bradman, T. (1988). *Wait and see.* New York: Oxford University Press.

Davol, M. (1993). *Black, white, just right.* Morton Grove, IL: Whitman.

Garland, S. (1992). *Billy and Belle.* New York: Viking.

Keller, H. (1991). *Horace.* New York: Morrow.

Pellegrini, N. (1991). *Families are different,* New York: Holiday House.

Rosenberg, M. (1984). *Being adopted.* New York: Lothrop, Lee & Shepard.

Say, A. (1984). *How my parents learn to eat.* Boston: Houghton Mifflin.

Say, A. (1991). *Tree of cranes.* Boston: Houghton Mifflin.

Simon, N. (1976). *All kinds of families.* Chicago: Whitman.

Turner, A. (1990). *Through moon and stars and night skies.* New York: HarperCollins.

Williams,. G. (1958). *The Rabbit's wedding.* New York: Harper.

SINGLE PARENTS BY CHOICE, GRANDPARENT FAMILIES, AND FAMILIES BY REPRODUCTIVE TECHNOLOGY

Support Organizations

AARP Grandparent Information Center, AARP Headquarters, 601 E Street, N.W., Washington, DC 20049 (202) 434-2277

Grandparents as Parents, P.O. Box 964, Lakewood, CA 90714 (310) 924-3996
Grandparents United for Children's Rights, 137 Larkin Street, Madison, WI 53705 (608) 238-8751
Massachusetts Grandparent Support Group network at the state Office of Elder Affairs, 1 Ashburton Place, 5th floor, Boston, MA 02108 (617) 727-7750
Single Mothers by Choice, P.O. Box 1642, Gracie Square Station, New York, NY 10028 (212) 988-0993

Adult Recommended Reading

Andrews, L. B. (1989). *Between strangers: Surrogate mothers, expectant fathers and brave new babies.* New York: Harper & Row.
Baran, A. (1993). *Lethal secrets: The psychology of donor insemination problems and solutions.* New York: Penguin.
Brill, A. (1990). *Nobody's business: Paradoxes of privacy.* Reading, MA: Addison-Wesley.
de Toledo, S., & Brown, D. (1995). *Grandparents as parents: A survival guide for raising a second family.* New York: Guilford Press
Kornhaber, A. (1995), *Grandparent power!* New York: Crown.
Massachusetts Executive Office of Elder Affairs. (1994). *A resource guide for Massachusetts grandparents raising their grandchildren.* (Available from Office of Edler Affairs, 1 Ashburton Pl., 5th fl., Boston, MA 02108)
Mattes, J. (1994). *Single mothers by choice: A guidebook for single women who are considering or have chosen.* New York: Times Books.
McCuen, G. E. (Ed.). (1990). *Hi-tech babies.* Hudson, WI: G. E. McCuen.
Miller, N. (1992). *Single parents by choice: A growing trend in family life.* New York: Plenum Press.
Pretorius, D. (1994). *Surrogate motherhood: a worldwide view of the issues.* Springfield, IL: Charles C. Thomas.
Saffron, L. (1994). *Challenging conceptions.* London: Cassell.
Truly, T. (1995). *Grandparents' rights with forms.* Clearwater, FL: Sphinx Publications.

Juvenile and Young Adult Recommended Reading

Dolmetsch, P., and Shih, A. (1985). *The kid's book about single parent families.* New York: Doubleday.
Evans, M. (1989). *This is me and my single parent.* New York: Brunner/Mazel.
Gardner, R. (1982). *The boys and girls book about one parent families.* New York: Bantam Books.
Gilbert, S. (1982). *How to live with a single parent.* New York: Lothrop, Lee & Shepard.
Lash, M., Ives, S., & Fassler, D. (1990). *My kind of family.* Burlington, VT: Waterfront Books.
Lindsay, J. W. (1991). *Do I have a daddy?* Buena Park, CA: Morning Glory.
Simon, N. (1983). *I wish I had my father.* Chicago: Whitman.

References

Adoption Assistance and Child Welfare Act. (1980) Pub. L. 96-272.

Aldridge, D. (1978). Interracial marriages: Empirical and theoretical consideration. *Journal of Black Studies, 8*(3), 355–368.

Alstein, H., & Simon, R. J. (1991). *Intercountry adoption: A multinational perspective.* New York: Praeger.

American Family Therapy Academy. (1993). *Resource packet.* Washington, DC: Author

American Fertility Society. (1993). Guidelines for therapeutic donor insemination: Sperm. *Fertility and Sterility, 59,* 1S–9S.

American Psychological Association. (1995). *Lesbian and gay parenting: A resource for psychologists* (A joint report of the Committee on Women in Psychology, the Committee on Lesbian and Gay Concerns, and the Committee on Children, Youth, and Family). Washington, DC: Author.

Amuzu, B., Laxova, R., & Shapiro, S. S. (1990). Pregnancy outcome, health of children, and family adjustment after donor insemination. *Obstetrics and Gynecology, 75*(6), 899–905.

Anderson, S., Piantanida, M., & Anderson, C. (1993). Normal processes in adoptive families. In F. Walsh (Ed.), *Normal family processes* (2nd ed., pp. 254–281). New York: Guilford Press.

Andujo, E. (1988). Ethnic identity of transracially adopted Hispanic adolescents. *Social Work, 33,* 531–534.

Arce, C. A. (1981). A reconsideration of Chicano culture and identity. *Daedalus, 110,* 177–192.

Atkinson, D. R., & Hackett, C. (1988). *Counseling non-ethnic American minorities.* Springfield, IL: Charles C. Thomas.

Atkinson, D. R., Morten, G., & Sue, D. W. (Eds.). (1989). *Counseling American minorities: A cross-cultural approach* (3rd ed.). Dubuque, IA: Wm. Brown.

Atkinson, D. R., Morten, G., & Sue, D. W. (Eds.). (1993). *Counseling American minorities: A cross-cultural perspective* (4th ed.). Dubuque IA: Wm. Brown.

Auerback, S., & Moser, C. (1987). Groups for the wives of gay and bisexual men. *Social Work, 32*(4), 321–325.

Aumend, S. A., & Barrett, M. C. (1984). Self-concept and attitudes toward adoption: A comparison of searching and nonsearching adult adoptees. *Child Welfare, 63*(3), 251–259.

Bagley, C., & Young, L. (1979). The identity adjustment and achievement of transracially adopted children: A review and empirical report. In G. K. Verna & C. Bagley (Eds.), *Race, education and identity* (pp. 192–279). New York: St. Martin's Press.

Bagley, C., Young, L., & Scully, A. (1993). *International and transracial adoptions*. Newcastle, UK: Athenaeum Press.

Bailey, J. M., & Pillard, R. C. (1991). A genetic study of male sexual orientation. *Archives of General Psychiatry, 48*, 1089–1096.

Bailey, J. M., Pillard, R. C., & Neale, M. C. (1993). Heritable factors influence sexual orientation in women. *Archives of General Psychiatry, 50*(3), 217–235.

Ballou, M., & Grabalek, N., with D. Kelly (1985). *A feminist position on mental health*. Springfield, IL: Charles C. Thomas.

Baptiste, D. A. (1987). Psychotherapy with gay/lesbian couples and their children in "stepfamilies": A challenge for marriage and family therapists. *Journal of Homosexuality, 14*(1/2), 223–228.

Barret, M. B. (1990). *Invisible lives*. New York: Harper & Row.

Barret, R. L., & Robinson, B. E. (1990). *Gay fathers*. Toronto: Lexington Books.

Barret, R. L., & Robinson, B. E. (1994). Gay dads. In A. E. Gottfried & A. W. Gottfried (Eds.), *Redefining families: Implications for children's development* (pp. 157–171). New York: Plenum Press.

Bartelson, C. (1993, October). Don't leave romance to chance. *The Atlanta Journal*, p. C3.

Barth, R. P., & Berry, M. (1988). *Adoption and disruption: Rates, risks and response*. New York: Aldine de Gruyter.

Barth, R. P., Berry, M., Carson, M. L., Goodfield, R., & Feinberg, B. (1986). Contributions to disruption and dissolution of older-child adoptions. *Child Welfare, 65*(4), 359–371.

Barth, R. P., Berry, M., Yoshikami, R., Goodfield, R., & Carson, M. L. (1988). Predicting adoption disruption. *Social Work, 33*(3), 227–233.

Bartholet, E. (1993). International adoption: Current status and future prospects. *The Future of Children, 3*(1), 89–104.

Baumrind, D. (1995). Commentary on sexual orientation: Research and social policy implications. *Developmental Psychology, 31*(1), 130–136.

Beck, A. T. (1976). *Cognitive therapy and the emotional disorders*. New York: International Universities Press.

Bell, A. P., Weinberg, M. S., & Hammersmith, S. K. (1981). *Sexual preference: Its development in men and women*. Bloomington, IN: Indiana University Press.

Benson, P. L., Sharma, A., & Roehlkepratain, E. C. (1994). *Growing up adopted*. Minneapolis, MN: Search Institute.

Berg, I. K., & Jaya, A. (1993). Different and same: Family therapy with Asian-American families. *Journal of Marital and Family Therapy, 19*(1), 31–38.

Berman, L. C., & Bufferd, R. K. (1986). Family treatment to address loss in adoptive families. *Social Casework, 67*, 3–11.

Bernard, J. (1966). Note on educational homogamy in Negro–White and

White–Negro marriages, 1960. *Journal of Marriage and the Family, 28,* 274–276.

Berry, M., & Barth, R. P. (1989). Behavior problems of children adopted when older. *Children and Youth Services Review, 11*(3), 221–238.

Berzon, B. (1988). *Permanent partners: Building gay and lesbian relationships that last.* New York: Dutton.

Bigner, J. J., & Bozett, F. W. (1990). Parenting by gay fathers. *Marriage and Family Review, 14*(3/4), 155–175.

Bigner, J. J., & Jacobsen, R. (1989). The value of children to gay and heterosexual fathers. *Homosexuality and the Family, 30*(2), 163–185.

Bigner, J. J., & Jacobsen, R. B. (1992). Adult responses to child behavior and attitudes towards fathering: Gay and nongay fathers. *Journal of Homosexuality, 23,* 99–112.

Blankenhorn, D. (1995). *Fatherless America: Confronting our most urgent social problem.* New York: Basic Books.

Blanton, M. L., & Descher, J. (1990). Biological mothers' grief: The post adoptive experience in open versus confidential adoption. *Child Welfare, 69,* 525–535.

Blumstein, P., & Schwartz, P. (1983). *American couples: Money, work, sex.* New York: Norton.

Blyth, E. (1990). Assisted reproduction: What's in it for children? *Children and Society, 4*(2), 167–182.

Bohman, T. M., McRoy, R. G., & Grotevant, H. D. (1992, October 24). *Acknowledging differences: A confirmatory test of the shared fate theory of parents' adaptation to adoption.* Paper presented at the annual meeting of the Academy for Child and Adolescent Psychiatry, San Francisco, CA.

Bowles, D. D. (1993). Bi-racial identity: Children born to African-American and White couples. *Clinical Social Work Journal, 21,* 417–428.

Boxer, A. M., & Cohler, B. (1989). The life course of gay and lesbian youth: An immodest proposal for the study of lives. *Journal of Homosexuality, 17*(3/4), 315–355.

Boxer, A. M., Cook, J. A., & Herdt, G. (1989, August 24). *First homosexual and urban community.* Paper presented at the annual meeting of the American Sociology Association, San Francisco, CA.

Boxer, A. M., Cook, J. A., & Herdt, G. (1991). Double jeopardy: Identity transitions and parent–child relations among gay and lesbian youth. In K. Pillemer & K. McCartney (Eds.), *Parent–child relationships throughout life* (pp. 59–92). Hillside, NJ: Erlbaum.

Boyd-Franklin, N. (1989). *Black families in therapy: A multisystems approach.* New York: Guilford Press.

Bozett, F. W. (1987). *Gay and lesbian parents.* New York: Praeger.

Bozett, F. W. (Ed.). (1989). *Homosexuality and the family.* New York: Harrington Park Press.

Bozett, F. W. (1993). Gay fathers: A review of the literature. In L. D. Garnets & D. C. Kimmel (Eds.), *Psychological perspectives on lesbian and gay male experiences* (pp. 389–455). New York: Columbia University Press.

Bozett, F. W., & Sussman, M. B. (Eds.). (1990). *Homosexuality and family relations.* New York: Harrington Park Press.

Braverman, A. M., & English, M. E. (1992). Creating brave new families with advanced reproductive technologies. *NAACOG's Clinical Issues, 3*(2), 353–363.

Bridges, K. L., & Croteau, J. M. (1994). Once-married lesbians: Facilitating changing life patterns. *Journal of Counseling and Development, 73*(2), 134–139.

Brodzinsky, D. M. (1990). A stress and coping model of adoption adjustment. In D. M. Brodzinsky & M. D. Schechter (Eds.), *The psychology of adoption* (pp. 3–24). Oxford, UK: Oxford University Press.

Brodzinsky, D. M., & Schechter, M. D. (Eds.). (1990). *The psychology of adoption.* Oxford, UK: Oxford University Press.

Brodzinsky, D. M., Schechter, M. D., & Henig, R. M. (1992). *Being adopted: The lifelong search for self.* New York: Doubleday.

Bronfenbrenner, U. (1979). *The ecology of human development.* Cambridge, MA: Harvard University Press.

Brown v. Board of Education, 1954, 349 U.S. 294.

Brown, A. (1994). Group work with "mixed membership" groups: Issues of race and gender. *Social Work with Groups, 17*(3), 5–21.

Brown, J. A. (1987). Casework contact with Black–White couples. *Social Casework, 68*(1), 24–29.

Brown, L. (1989). Lesbians, gay men, and their families: Common clinical issues. *Journal of Gay and Lesbian Psychotherapy, 1*(1), 65–77.

Brown, L., & Zimmer, D. (1986). An introduction to therapy issues of lesbian and gay male couples. In N. S. Jacobson & A. S. Gurman (Eds.), *Clinical handbook of marital therapy* (pp. 451–470). New York: Guilford Press.

Brown, L. S. (1986). Confronting internalized oppression in sex therapy with lesbians. *Journal of Homosexuality, 12*(3/4), 99–107.

Brown, P. (1989–1990). Black–White interracial marriages: A historical analysis. *Journal of Intergroup Relations, 16*(3 & 4), 26–36.

Brown, U. P. (1995). Black/White interracial young adults: Quest for a racial identity. *American Journal of Orthopsychiatry, 65*(1), 125–130.

Browning, C., Reynolds, A., & Dworkin, S. (1991). Affirmative psychotherapy for lesbian women. *Counseling Psychologist, 19*(2), 177–196.

Bruni, F. (1995, November 5). For gay couples ruling to cheer on adoption. *The New York Times,* p. 41.

Burr, C. (1993, March). Homosexuality and biology. *The Atlantic, 271*(3), 47–65.

Burton, L. M. (1992). Black grandparents rearing children of drug-addicted parents: Stressors, outcomes, and social needs. *Gerontologist, 32*(6), 755–751.

Cabaj, R. (1988). Gay and lesbian couples: Lessons on human intimacy. *Psychiatric Annals, 18*(1), 21–25.

Carney, J., Werth, J. L., & Emanuelson, G. (1994). The relationship between attitudes towards persons who are gay and persons with AIDS, and HIV and AIDS knowledge. *Journal of Counseling and Development, 72*(6), 646–659.

Carter, R. T. (1995). *The influence of race and racial identity in psychotherapy: Toward a racially inclusive model.* New York: Wiley.

Cass, V. (1979). Homosexual identity formation: A theoretical model. *Journal of Homosexuality, 4,* 219–235.

Cass, V. (1984). Homosexual identity formation: Lessons on human intimacy. *Psychiatric Annals, 18*(1), 21–25.

Cavaliere, F. (1995). Society appears more open to gay parents. *APA Monitor, 26*(7), 51.

Chapman, B. E., & Brannock, J. C. (1987). Proposed model of lesbian identity development: An empirical examination. *Journal of Homosexuality, 14,* 69–80.

Chapman, C., Dorner, P., Silber, K. T., & Winterberg, T. S. (1987). Meeting the needs of the adoption triangle through open adoptions: The adoptive parent. *Child and Adolescent Social Work Journal, 4*(1), 3–12.

Charbonneau, C., & Lander, R. S. (1991). Redefining sexuality: Women becoming lesbian in midlife. In B. Sang, J. Warshow, & A. J. Smith (Eds.), *Lesbians at midlife: The creative transition* (pp. 35–43). San Francisco: Spinsters Book.

Chodorow, N. (1978). *The reproduction of mothering: Psychoanalysis and the sociology of gender.* Berkeley: University of California Press.

Clunis, D. M., & Green, G. (1988). Lesbian couples with children. In D. M. Clunis & G. Green (Eds.), *Lesbian couples* (pp. 113–130). Seattle: Seal Press.

Coleman, A. (1993, January 23). *Children: To have or not to have—Ethical, legal, and clinical challenges.* Paper presented at Harvard Medical School Conference on Clinical Issues for Gay and Lesbian Families, Cambridge, MA.

Coleman, E. (1982). Developmental stages of the coming out process. *Journal of Homosexuality, 7*(2/3), 31–43.

Coleman, E. (1989). She married lesbian. *Marriage and Family Review, 14*(3/4), 119–135.

Comas-Díaz, L. (1996). LatiNegra: Mental health issues. In M. P. P. Root (Ed.), *The multicultural experience* (pp. 167–191). Newbury Park, CA: Sage.

Comas-Díaz, L., & Greene, B. (Eds.). (1994). *Women of color: Integrating ethnic and gender identities in psychotherapy.* New York: Guilford Press.

Comer, J., & Poussaint, A. F. (1992). *Raising Black children: Questions and answers for parents and teachers.* New York: Dutton.

Cook, R., Golombok, S., Bish, A., & Murray, C. (1995). Disclosure of donor insemination: Parental attitudes. *American Journal of Orthopsychiatry, 65*(4), 549–559.

Cordell, A. S., Nathan, C., & Krymow, V. P. (1985). Group counseling for children adopted at older ages. *Child Welfare, 44,* 113–121.

Cose, E. (1992). *A nation of strangers: Prejudice, politics, and the populating of America.* New York: Morrow.

Cottrell, A. B. (1990). Cross-national marriage: A review of the literature. *Journal of Comparative Family Studies, 21*(2), 151–169.

Court rules for second parent adoption . . . (1995, November 5) *The New York Times*, p. 14.

Cross, W. E. (1991). *Shades of black: Diversity in African-American identity.* Philadelphia: Temple University Press.

Dahleimer, D., & Feigal, J. (1991). Bridging the gap. *Family Therapy Networker, 15*(1), 44–53.

Daniluk, J. (1991). Strategies for counseling infertile couples. *Journal of Counseling and Development, 69*(4), 317–321.

Daniluk, J. (1994, March). *Infertile women need help accepting inability to conceive.* Paper presented at American Psychological Association Conference on Women's Health, New York City.

Davidson, J. R. (1992). Theories about Black–White interracial marriage: A clinical perspective. *Journal of Multicultural Counseling and Development, 20,* 150–157.

Davidson, J. R., & Schneider, L. J. (1992). Acceptance of Black–White interracial marriage. *Journal of Intergroup Relations, 19*(3), 47–52.

DeAngelis, T. (1995). Ethnic research is more sophisticated. *APA Monitor, 26*(3), 36–37.

Demick, J., & Wapner, S. (1988). Open and closed adoption: A developmental conceptualization. *Family Process, 27,* 229–243.

de Toledo, S., & Brown, D. E. (1995). *Grandparents as parents: A survival guide for raising a second family.* New York: Guilford Press.

Deykin, E. Y., Campbell, L., & Patti, P. (1984). The post-adoption experience of surrendering parents. *American Journal of Orthopsychiatry, 54*(2), 271–280.

Deykin, E. Y., Patti, P., & Ryan, J. (1988). Fathers of adopted children: A study of the impact of child surrender on birthfathers. *American Journal of Orthopsychiatry, 58*(2), 240–248.

Donnan, H. (1990). Mixed marriage in comparative perspective: Gender and power in Northern Ireland and Pakistan. *Journal of Comparative Family Studies, 21*(2), 207–225.

Dressel, P. L., & Barnhill, S. K. (1994). Reframing gerontological thought and practice: The case of grandmothers with daughters in prison. *Gerontologist, 32*(5), 685–691.

Duckitt, J. (1992). *The social psychology of prejudice.* New York: Praeger.

Dworkin, S. H., & Pincu, L. (1993). Counseling in the era of AIDS. *Journal of Counseling and Development, 71*(3), 275–281.

Ehrle, G. M., & Day, H. D. (1994). Adjustment and family functioning of grandmothers rearing their grandchildren. *Contemporary Family Therapy, 16*(1), 67–82.

Ellis, H. (1930). *Studies in the psychology of sex.* New York: Random House.

Ellis, P., & Murphy, B. (1994). The impact of misogyny and homophobia on therapy with women. In M. P. Mirkin (Ed.), *Women in context: Toward a feminist reconstruction of psychotherapy* (pp. 48–76). New York: Guilford Press.

Erikson, E. H. (1950). *Childhood and society.* New York: Norton.

Erikson, E. H. (1968). *Identity: Youth and crisis.* New York: Norton.

Falco, K. C. (1991). *Psychotherapy with lesbian clients: Theory into practice.* New York: Brunner/Mazel.

Falk, L. L. (1970). A comparative study of transracial and inracial adoptions. *Child Welfare, 49*(2), 82–88.

Falk, P. J. (1989). Lesbian mothers: Psychosocial assumptions in family law. *American Psychologist, 44,* 941–947.

Falk, P. J. (1994). The gap between psychological assumptions and empirical research in lesbian-mother child custody cases. In A. E. Gottfried & A. W. Gottfried (Eds.), *Redefining families: Implications for children's development* (pp. 132–152). New York: Plenum Press.

Faludi, S. (1991). *Backlash.* New York: Crown.

Family and Medical Leave Act of 1993, Pub. L. 103-3 107 Stat6 (1993).

Faria, G. (1994). Training for family preservation practice with lesbian families. *Families in Society, 75,* 416–422.

Fassinger, R. E. (1991). The hidden minority: Issues and challenges in working with lesbian women and gay men. *Counseling Psychologist, 19*(2), 156–176.

Feigelman, W., & Silverman, A. (1983). *Chosen children: New patterns of adoptive relationships.* New York: Praeger.

Fishman, K. D. (1992). Problem adoptions. *The Atlantic, 270*(3), 37–69.

Ford, C., & Beach, F. (1951). *Patterns of sexual behavior.* New York: Harper & Brothers.

Frankenberg, R. (1993). *White women, race matters: The social construction of whiteness.* Minneapolis: University of Minnesota Press.

Frazier, E. I. (1947). *The Negro family in the United States.* Chicago: University of Chicago Press.

Friedman, E. H. (1982). The myth of the shiksa. In M. McGoldrick, J. K. Pearce, & J. Giordano (Eds.), *Ethnicity and family therapy* (pp. 499–526). New York: Guilford Press.

Frierson, R., Lippmann, S. B., & Johnson, J. (1987). AIDS: Psychological stresses on the family. *Psychosomatics, 28,* 65–68.

Funderburg, L. (1994). *Black, white and other.* New York: Morrow.

Gaines, S. O., & Reed, E. S. (1995). Prejudice: From Allport to DuBois. *American Psychologist, 50*(2), 96–103.

Gediman, J. S., & Brown, L. P. (1989). *Birthbond: Reunion between birthparents and adoptees—What happens after.* New York: West Horizons Press.

George, K. D., & Behrendt, A. E. (1987). Therapy for male couples experiencing relationship and sexual problems. *Journal of Homosexuality, 14*(1/2), 77–88.

Gergen, K. J. (1985). The social construction movement in psychology. *American Psychologist, 40,* 266–275.

Gibbs, E. D. (1988). Psychosocial development of children raised by lesbian mothers: A review of research. *Women and Therapy, 8,* 55–75.

Gibbs, J. T. (1989). Biracial adolescents. In J. T. Gibbs, L. N. Huang, & Associates (Eds.), *Children of color: Psychological intervention with minority youth* (pp. 322–350). San Francisco: Jossey-Bass.

Gilligan, C. (1982). *In a different voice: Psychological theory and women's development.* Cambridge, MA: Harvard Universities Press.

Golombok, S., Cook, R., Bish, A., & Murray, C. (1995). Families created by the new reproductive technologies: Quality of parenting and social and emotional development of the children. *Child Development, 66,* 285–298.

Golombok, S., Spencer, A., & Rutter, M. (1983). Children in lesbian and single-parent households: Psychosexual and psychiatric appraisal. *Journal of Child Psychology and Psychiatry, 24,* 551–572.

Goodrich, T. J., Rampage, C., Ellman, B., & Halstead, K. (1988). *Feminist family therapy: A casebook.* New York: Norton.

Gordon, A. (1964). *Intermarriage.* Boston: Beacon Press.

Gordon, D. E. (1990). Decision-making about pregnancy and contraception. *American Journal of Orthopsychiatry, 60*(3), 346–357.

Gottfried, A. E., & Gottfried, A. W. (Eds.). (1994). *Redefining families: Implications for children's development.* New York: Plenum Press.

Gottman, J. (1990). Children of gay and lesbian parents. *Marriage and Family Review, 14*(3/4), 177–196.

Green, R. (1987). *The "sissy boy syndrome" and the development of homosexuality.* New Haven: Yale University Press.

Green, R., Mandel, J. B., Hotvedt, M. E., Gray, J., & Smith, L. (1986). Lesbian mothers and their children: A comparison with solo parent heterosexual mothers and their children. *Archives of Sexual Behavior, 15,* 167–184.

Greene, B. (1993). Diversity and difference: Race and feminist psychotherapy. In M. P. Mirkin (Ed.), *Women in context: Toward a feminist reconstruction of psychotherapy* (pp. 333–351). New York: Guilford Press.

Groze, V. (1986). Special-needs adoption. *Children and Youth Services Review, 8*(4), 349–361.

Groze, V. (1991a). Adoption and single parents: A review. *Child Welfare, 70*(3), 321–332.

Groze, V. (1991b). Single parents and their adopted children: A psychosocial analysis. *Families in Society, 72*(2), 67–77.

Haley, J. (1963). *Strategies of psychotherapy.* New York: Grune & Stratton.

Hand, S. (1991). *The lesbian parenting couple.* Unpublished doctoral dissertation, Professional School of Psychology, San Francisco.

Hanley-Hackenbruck, P. (1988). "Coming out" and psychotherapy. *Psychiatric Annals, 18*(1), 29–32.

Hardiman, R. (1982). *White identity development: A process oriented model for describing the racial consciousness of White Americans.* Unpublished doctoral dissertation, University of Massachusetts, Amherst.

Harris, M. B., & Turner, P. H. (1985–1986). Gay and lesbian parents. *Journal of Homosexuality, 12,* 101–113.

Hartman, A., & Laird, J. (1990). Family treatment after adoption: Common themes. In D. H. Brodzynsky & H. D. Schechter (Eds.), *The psychology of adoption* (pp. 221–239). New York: Oxford University Press.

Hatterer, M. (1974). Problems of women married to homosexual men. *American Journal of Psychiatry, 131*(3), 275–278.

Hayes, P. (1993). Transracial adoption: Politics and ideology. *Child Welfare, 72*(3), 301–310.

Helms, J. E. (1984). Toward a theoretical explanation of the effects of race on counseling: A Black and White model. *Counseling Psychologist, 12*(4), 153–161.

Helms, J. E. (1990a, August). *Black and White racial identity theory and professional interracial collaboration.* Symposium presented at the 98th annual convention of the American Psychological Association. Boston, MA.

Helms, J. E. (1990b). *Black and White racial identity: Theory, research and practice.* Westport, CT: Greenwood Press.

Helms, J. E. (1992). *Race is a nice thing to have.* Topeka, KS: Content Communications.

Helms, J. E. (1994). Racial identity and "racial" constructs. In E. J. Trickett, R. Watts, & D. Birman (Eds.), *Human diversity* (pp. 285–311). San Francisco: Jossey-Bass.

Helms, J. E., & Carter, R. T. (1991). Relationships of white and black racial identity attitudes and demographic similarity to counselor preferences. *Journal of Counseling Psychology, 38*(4), 446–457.

Helms, J. E., & Piper, R. E. (1994). Implications of racial identity theory for vocational psychology. *Journal of Vocational Behavior, 44,* 124–138.

Henry, W. A. (1992). An identity forged in flames. *Time, 140*(5), 35.

Herbert, S. E. (1992, October 24). *The lesbian adolescent.* Paper presented at the annual meeting of the American Academy of Child and Adolescent Psychiatry, San Francisco, CA.

Herdt, G. (1989). *Gay and lesbian youth.* New York: Haworth.

Herrnstein, R. J., & Murray, C. (1994). *The bell curve.* New York: Free Press.

Hill, M., & Peltzer, J. (1982). A report of thirteen groups for white parents of black children. *Family Relations, 31*(4), 557–565.

Hiraga, Y., Cauce, A. M., Mason, C., & Ordonez, N. (1993, March 25–28). *Ethnic identity and the social adjustment of biracial youth.* Paper presented at the annual meeting of the Society for Research in Child Development, New Orleans, LA.

Ho, M. K. (1990). *Intermarried couples in therapy.* Springfield, IL: Charles C. Thomas.

Hoeffer, B. (1981). Children's acquisition of sex-role behavior in lesbian-mother families. *American Journal of Orthopsychiatry, 5,* 536–544.

Hoffman-Riem, C. (1990). *The adopted child.* New Brunswick, NJ: Transaction.

Hooker, E. (1957). The adjustment of the male overt homosexual. *Journal of Projective Techniques, 21,* 18–31.

Iasenza, S. (1989). Some challenges of integrating sexual orientations into counselor training and research. *Journal of Counseling and Development, 68*(1), 73–76.

Imber-Black, E., Roberts, J., & Whiting, R. (Eds.). (1988). *Rituals in families and family therapy.* New York: Norton.

Interracial marriages. . . . (1994, May 14). *Boston Globe,* p. 3.

Isay, R. (1989). *Being homosexual: Gay men and their development.* New York: Avon.

Jacobs, J. (1992). Identity development in biracial children. In M. P. P. Root (Ed.), *Racially mixed people in America* (pp. 190–206). Newbury Park, CA: Sage.

Jendrek, M. P. (1994). Grandparents who parent their children: Circumstances and decisions. *Gerontologist, 34*(2), 206–216.

Johnson, R. C. (1992). Offspring of cross-race and cross-ethnic marriages in Hawaii. In M. P. P. Root (Ed.), *Racially mixed people in America* (pp. 239–250). Newbury Park, CA: Sage.

Johnson, R. C., & Nagoshi, C. (1989). The adjustment of offspring of within-group and interracial/intercultural marriages: A comparison of personality factor scores. *Journal of Marriage and the Family, 48,* 279–284.

Jones, C. E., & Else, J. F. (1979). Racial and cultural issues in adoption. *Child Welfare, 58*(6), 373–383.

Jones, J. M. (1988). Racism in Black and White: A bicultural model of reaction and evolution. In J. E. McGrath (Ed.), *The social psychology of time: New perspectives* (pp. 21–38). Newbury Park, CA: Sage.

Jordan, J., Kaplan, A., Miller, J. B., Stiver, I., & Surrey, J. (1991). *Women's growth in connection: Writings from the Stone Center.* New York: Guilford Press.

Kagan, J. (1984). *The nature of the child.* New York: Basic Books.

Kalmijn, M. (1993, September). Trends in Black/White intermarriage. *Social Forces, 72*(1), 119–146.

Kamerman, S. B., & Kahn, J. (1988). What Europe does for single parents. *Public Interest, 93,* 70–86.

Karow, A. M. (1993). Confidentiality and American semen donors. *International Journal of Fertility and Menopausal Studies, 38*(3), 147–151.

Kassoff, E. (1989). Nonmonogamy in the lesbian community. *Women and Therapy, 8,* 167–182.

Kates, T. (1992). *A support group for families of persons with AIDS: A review of the literature and practical applications.* Unpublished paper submitted to graduate class, Northeastern University, Boston, MA.

Katz, L. (1986). Parental stress and factors for success in older child adoption. *Child Welfare, 65*(6), 569–578.

Katz, J. H. (1978). *White awareness: Handbook for anti-racism training.* Norman, OK: University of Oklahoma Press.

Katz, J. H. (1985). The sociopolitical nature of counseling. *Counseling Psychologist, 13,* 615–625.

Kaye, K. (1990). Acknowledgment or rejection of differences. In D. M. Brodzinsky & M. D. Schechter (Eds.), *The psychology of adoption* (pp. 121–143). Oxford, UK: Oxford University Press.

Keeney, B., & Sprenkle, D. (1982). Ecosystemic epistemology: Critical implications for the aesthetics and pragmatics of family therapy. *Family Process, 21,* 1–19.

Kich, G. (1992). The developmental process of asserting a biracial, bicultural identity. In M. P. P. Root (Ed.), *Racially mixed people in America* (pp. 304–317). Newbury Park, CA: Sage.

Kim, J. (1981). *Process of Asian-American identity development: A study of Japanese-American women's perceptions of their struggle to achieve posi-*

tive identities. Unpublished doctoral dissertation, University of Massachusetts, Amherst.

Kinsey, A. C., Pomeroy, W. B., & Martin, C. E. (1948). *Sexual behavior in the human male.* Philadelphia: Saunders.

Kinsey, A. C., Pomeroy, W. B., Martin, C. E., & Gebhard, P. H. (1955). *Sexual behavior in the human female.* Philadelphia: Saunders.

Kirk, H. D. (1981). *Adoptive kinship: A modern institution in need of reforms.* Toronto: Butterworth.

Kirk, H. D. (1984). *Shared fate: A theory and method of adoptive relationships* (rev. ed.). Port Angeles, CA: Ben-Simon.

Kirkpatrick, M. (1987). Clinical implications of lesbian mother studies. *Journal of Homosexuality, 13,* 201–211.

Kirkpatrick, M., Smith, C., & Roy, R. (1981). Lesbian mothers and their children: A comparative survey. *American Journal of Orthopsychiatry, 51,* 545–551.

Klein, F. (1990). The need to view sexual orientation as a multivariable dynamic process: A theoretical perspective. In D. P. McWhirter, S. A. Sanders, & J. M. Renisch (Eds.), *Homosexuality/heterosexuality: Concepts of sexual orientation* (pp. 277–282). New York: Oxford University Press.

Klinger, R. L. (1992, October 24). *Lesbian mothers.* Paper presented at the annual conference of the American Academy of Child and Adolescent Psychiatry, San Francisco, CA.

Klock, S. C., Jacob, M. C., & Maier, D. (1994). A prospective study of donor insemination recipients: Secrecy, privacy, and disclosure. *Fertiity and Sterility, 62*(3), 477–484.

Kouri, K. M., & Lasswell, M. (1993). Black–White marriages: Social change and intergenerational mobility. *Marriage and Family Review, 19*(3–4), 241–235.

Kovacs, G. T., Mushin, D., Kane, H., & Baker, H. W. (1993). A controlled study of the psycho-social development of children conceived following insemination with donor semen. *Human Reproduction, 8*(5), 788–790.

Krestan, J. (1988). Lesbian daughters and lesbian mothers: The crisis of disclosure from a family systems perspective. *Journal of Psychotherapy and the Family, 3*(4), 113–130.

Krestan, J., & Bepko, C. S. (1980). The problem of fusion in the lesbian relationship. *Family Process, 19*(3), 277–289.

Kübler-Ross, E. (1969). *On death and dying.* New York: Macmillan.

Kurdek, L. A. (1988). Relationship quality of gay and lesbian cohabiting couples. *Journal of Homosexuality, 15*(3/4), 93–118.

Ladner, J. (1977). *Mixed families: Adopting across racial boundaries.* Garden City, NY: Anchor Press/Doubleday.

Laird, J. (1988). Women and ritual. In E. Imber-Black, J. Roberts, & R. Whiting (Eds.), *Rituals in families and family therapy* (pp. 331–362). New York: Norton.

Laird, J. (1989). Women and stories: Restorying women's self-constructions. In M. McGoldrick, C. M. Anderson, & F. Walsh (Eds.), *Women in fam-*

ilies: A framework for family therapy (pp. 427–450). New York: Norton.

Laird, J. (1993a, January 23). *Gay and lesbian families: Strengths, resilience, and cultural diversity.* Paper presented at Harvard Medical School conference on Clinical Issues for Gay and Lesbian Families, Cambridge, MA.

Laird, J. (1993b). Lesbian and gay families. In F. Walsh (Ed.), *Normal family processes* (pp. 282–330). New York: Guilford Press.

Lawrence-Lightfoot, S. (1994). *I've known rivers: Lives of loss and liberation.* Reading, MA: Addison-Wesley.

Leland, J. (1995, July 17). Bisexuality. *Newsweek,* pp. 44–48.

LeVay, S. (1991, August). A difference in hypothalmic structure between heterosexual and homosexual men. *Science.*

LeVay, S. (1993). *The sexual brain.* Cambridge, MA: MIT Press.

Levy, E. (1989). Lesbian motherhood: Identity and social support. *Affilia,* 4(4), 40–53.

Lifton, B. J. (1994). *Journey of the adopted self.* New York: Basic Books.

Linn, R. (1991). Mature unwed mothers in Israel: Socio-moral and psychological dilemmas. *Lifestyles,* 12(2), 145–170.

Loulan, J. (1986). Psychotherapy with lesbian mothers. In T. S. Stein & C. H. Cohen (Eds.), *Contemporary perspectives on psychotherapy with lesbians and gay men* (pp. 181–208). New York: Plenum.

Lovings v. Virginia, 388 U.S. 1 (1967).

Lubow, A. (1992, November 30). Tony Kushner's paradise lost. *New Yorker,* pp. 59–64.

Luepnitz, D. A. (1988). *The family interpreted: Feminist theory in clinical practice.* New York: Basic Books.

Marcia, J. E. (1980). Identity in adolescence. In J. Adelson (Ed.), *Handbook of adolescent psychology* (pp. 159–187). New York: Wiley.

Marcus, E. (1992). *Making history: The struggle for gay and lesbian equal rights. 1945–1990. An oral history.* New York: HarperCollins.

Markowitz, L. (1991). Homosexuality: Are we still in the dark? *Family Therapy Networker,* 15(1), 26–36.

Marmor, J. (1965). *Sexual inversion: The multiple roots of homosexuality.* New York: Basic Books.

Marmor, J. (1971). "Normal" and "deviant" sexual behavior. *Journal of the American Medical Association, 217,* 161–170.

Marmor, J. (1972). Homosexuality: mental illness or moral dilemma? *International Journal of Psychiatry, 10,* 114–117.

Marmor, J. (1980). *Homosexual behavior: A modern reappraisal.* New York: Basic Books.

Martin, A. (1993). *Lesbian and gay parenting handbook: Creating and raising our families.* New York: HarperCollins.

Masters, W. H., & Johnson, V. E. (1970). *Human sexual inadequacy.* Boston: Little, Brown.

Mattison, A. M., & McWhirter, D. P. (1987). Stage discrepancy in male couples. *Journal of Homosexuality,* 14(1/2), 89–99.

McCandlish, B. (1987). Against all odds: Lesbian mother family dynamics. In F. Bozett (Ed.), *Gay and lesbian parents* (pp. 23–28). New York: Praeger.

McCartney, C. F. (1985). Decision by single women to conceive by artificial donor insemination. *Journal of Psychosomatic Obstetrics and Gynecology, 4*(4), 321–328.

McGill, D. W. (1992). The cultural story in multicultural family therapy. *Families in Society, 73*(6), 339–349.

McGoldrick, M. (1993). Ethnicity, cultural diversity, and normality. In F. Walsh (Ed.), *Normal family processes* (2nd ed., pp. 331–360). New York: Guilford Press.

McGoldrick, M., Pearce, J. K., & Giordano, J. (Eds.). (1982). *Ethnicity and family therapy.* New York: Guilford Press.

McIntosh, P. (1989). *White privilege: Unpacking the invisible knapsack.* Working paper, Wellesley College Center for Research on Women, Wellesley, MA.

McLanahan, S., & Sandefur, G. (1994). *Growing up with a single parent: What hurts, what helps.* Cambridge, MA: Harvard University Press.

McLemore, S. D. (1991). *Racial and ethnic relations in America* (3rd ed.). Boston: Allyn & Bacon.

McLeod, J. D., & Shanahan, M. J. (1993). Single parenting and children's mental health. *American Sociological Review, 58,* 351–366.

McMillan, T. (1992). *Waiting to exhale.* New York: Viking.

McRoy, R. G. (1989). An organizational dilemma: The case of transracial adoptions. *Journal of Applied Behavioral Science, 25*(2), 145–160.

McRoy, R., & Freeman, E. (1984). Racial identity issues among mixed race children. *Social Work Education, 8,* 164–174.

McRoy, R. G., Grotevant, H., & White, K. (1988). *Openness in adoption.* New York: Praeger.

McRoy, R. G., Grotevant, H. G., & Zurcher, L. A. (1988). *Emotional disturbance in adopted adolescents: Origins and development.* New York: Praeger.

McRoy, R. G., & Hall, C. C. (1996). Transracial adoptions: In whose best interest? In M. P. P. Root (Ed.), *The multiracial experience: Racial borders as the new frontier* (pp. 63–78). Thousand Oaks, CA: Sage.

McRoy, R. G., Zurcher, L. A., Lauderdale, M. L., & Anderson, R. N. (1982). Self-esteem and racial identity development in transracial and inracial adoptees. *Social Work, 27,* 522–526.

McWhinnie, A. M. (1992). Creating children: The medical and social dilemmas of assisted reproduction. *Early Child Development and Care, 81,* 39–54.

McWhirter, D. P., & Mattison, A. M. (1984). *The male couple: How relationships develop.* Englewood Cliffs, NJ: Prentice-Hall.

Mencher, J. (1990). *Intimacy in lesbian relationships: A critical re-examination of fusion* (Work in progress, No. 42). Wellesley, MA: Stone Center Working Paper Series.

Miall, C. (1987). The stigma of adoptive parent status: Perceptions of community attitudes toward adoption and the experience of informal social sanctioning. *Journal of Applied Family and Child Studies, 36*(1), 34–39.

Miller, J. (1989, Spring). A guide for the well-intentioned. *Bryn Mawr Bulletin,* pp. 11–14.

Miller, J. B. (1976). *Toward a new psychology of women.* Boston: Beacon Press.

Miller, N. (1992). *Single parents by choice: A growing trend in family life.* New York: Plenum Press.

Miller, R., & Miller, B. (1990). Mothering the biracial child: Bridging the gaps between African-American and White parenting styles. *Women and Therapy, 10,* 169–180.

Minkler, M., Roe, K. M., & Price, M. (1992). The physical and emotional health of grandmothers raising grandchildren in the crack cocaine epidemic. *Gerontologist, 32*(6), 752–761.

Minkler, M., Roe, K. M., & Robertson-Beckley, R. J. (1994). Raising children from crack-cocaine households: Effects on family and friendship ties of African-American women. *American Journal of Orthopsychiatry, 64*(1), 20–29.

Mirkin, M. P. (Ed.). (1994). *Women in context: Toward a feminist reconstruction of psychotherapy.* New York: Guilford Press.

Moran, M. R. (1992). Effects of orientation similarity and counselor experience level on gay men's and lesbians' perceptions of counselors. *Journal of Counseling Psychology, 39*(2), 247–251.

Moses, A. E., & Hawkins, R. O. (1982). *Counseling lesbian women and gay men.* St. Louis: Mosby.

Multiethnic Placement Act (Howard M. Metzenbaum). Pub. L. 103-382, 108 Stat. 4056, Sections 551–554 (1994).

Murphy, B. (1992). Counseling lesbian couples: Sexism, heterosexism, and homophobia. In S. H. Dworkin & F. G. Gutierrez (Eds.), *Counseling gay men and lesbians: Journey to the end of the rainbow.* Alexandria, VA: AACD Press.

Murphy, B. (1993, January 23). *Therapy with gay and lesbian couples.* Paper presented at Harvard Medical School conference on Clinical Issues for Gay and Lesbian Families, Cambridge, MA.

Nichols, M. (1994). Therapy with bisexual women: Working on the edge of emerging cultural and personal identities. In M. P. Mirkin (Ed.), *Women in context: Toward a reconstruction of feminist therapy* (pp. 149–170). New York: Guilford Press.

Nichols, M. P., & Schwartz, R. C. (1991). *Family therapy: Concepts and methods* (2nd ed.). Boston: Allyn & Bacon.

Nuland, S. (1994). *How we die: Reflections on life's final choices.* New York: Knopf.

Orenstein, P. (1995, June 18). Looking for a donor to call dad. *The New York Times Magazine,* p. 28.

Ortega, S. T., Whitt, H. P., & Williams, A. J., Jr. (1988). Religious homogamy and marital happiness. *Journal of Family Issues, 9*(2), 224–239.

Out-of-wedlock birthrate soared. (1995, June 7). *Boston Globe,* p. 7.

Pannor, R., Baran, A., & Sorosky, A. D. (1978). Birth parents who relinquished babies for adoption revisited. *Family Process, 17,* 329–337.

Parham, T. A., & Helms, J. E. (1985). Relation of racial identity attitudes to self actualization and affective states in Black students. *Journal of Counseling Psychology, 32,* 431–440.

Partridge, P. C. (1991). The particular challenges of being adopted. *Smith College Studies in Social Work, 6*(1/2), 197–208.

Paset, P., & Taylor, R. (1991) Black and White women's attitudes towards interracial marriage. *Psychological Reports, 69,* 753–754.

Patterson, C. (1992). Children of lesbian and gay parents. *Child Development, 63,* 1025–1042.

Patterson, C. (1994). Children of the lesbian baby boom: Behavioral adjustment, self-concepts and sex-role identity. In C. Patterson (Ed.), *Contemporary perspectives of gay and lesbian psychology: Theory, research, and applications* (pp.). Beverly Hills, CA: Sage.

Pearlman, S. (1989). Distancing and connectedness: Impact of couple formation in lesbian relationships. In E. D. Rothblum & E. Cole (Eds.), *Loving boldly: Issues facing lesbians* (pp. 77–88). New York: Huntington Park Press.

PFLAG. (1990). *Why is my child gay?* (Pamphlet available from by the Federation of Parents and Friends of Lesbians and Gays, P.O. Box 27605, Central Station, Washington, DC 20038.)

Phinney, J. S. (1990). Ethnic identity in adolescents and adults: Review of research. *Psychological Bulletin, 108,* 499–514.

Pies, C. A. (1989). Lesbians and the choice to parent. *Marriage and Family Review, 14*(3/4), 137–154.

Pillard, R. C. (1993, January 23). *Genetics and homosexuality: Recent findings.* Paper presented at Harvard Medical School conference on Clinical Issues for Gay and Lesbian Families, Cambridge, MA.

Pillard, R. C., & Bailey, J. M. (1995). A biologic perspective on sexual orientation [Special issue: Clinical sexuality]. *Psychiatric Clinics of North America, 18*(1), 71–84.

Plomin, R. (1993, March 25–28). *Nature, nurture, and psychology.* Paper presented at the 60th annual meeting of the Society for Research in Child Development, New Orleans, LA.

Pohl, C., & Harris, K. (1992). *Transracial adoption: Children and parents speak.* New York: Franklin Watts.

Ponterotto, J. G. (1988). Racial consciousness development among White counselor trainees: A stage model. *Journal of Multicultural Counseling and Development, 16,* 146–156.

Ponterotto, J. G. (1991). The nature of prejudice revisited: Implications for intervention. *Journal of Counseling and Development, 70,* 216–224.

Ponterotto, J. G. (1993). White racial identity. *Counseling Psychologist, 21*(2), 213–217.

Ponterotto, J. G., & Pedersen, P. B. (1993). *Preventing prejudice.* Newbury Park, CA: Sage.

Pope-Davis, D. B., & Ottavi, T. M. (1994). The relationship between racism and racial identity among White Americans: A replication and extension. *Journal of Counseling and Development, 72*(3), 293–297.

Popper, C. W. (1991, October). *Rethinking adolescent homosexuality: Impact on professional education.* Paper presented at the annual meeting of the American Academy of Child and Adolescent Psychiatry, San Francisco, CA.

Poston, W. S. (1990). The biracial identity development model: A needed addition. *Journal of Counseling and Development, 69,* 152–155.

Pruett, K. D. (1992). Strange bedfellows? Reproductive technology and child development. *Infant Mental Health Journal, 13*(4), 312–318.

Reddy, M. (1994). *Crossing the color line: Race, parenting and culture.* New Brunswick, NJ: Rutgers University Press.

Richardson, D. (1987). Recent challenges to traditional assumptions about homosexuality: Some implications for practice. *Journal of Homosexuality, 13*(4), 1–12.

Ricketts, W., & Achtenberg, R. (1989). Adopting and foster parenting for lesbians and gay men: Creating new traditions in family. *Marriage and Family Review, 14*(3–4), 83–118.

Riddle, D. I. (1978). Relating to children: Gays as role models. *Journal of Social Issues, 34*(3), 38–53.

Risman, B. J. (1986). Can men "mother?" Life as a single father. *Family Relations Journal of Applied Family and Child Studies, 35*(1), 95–102.

Rist, P. (1992). *Heartlands: A gay man's odyssey across America.* New York: Dutton.

Ritter, K. Y., & O'Neil, C. W. (1989). Moving through loss: the spiritual journey of gay men and lesbian women. *Journal of Counseling and Development, 68,* 9–15.

Roberts, J. (Ed.). (1993). Honoring and working with diversity in family therapy. In *Resource packet.* Washington, DC: American Family Therapy Academy.

Robinson, T. L., & Howard-Hamilton, M. (1994). An Afrocentric paradigm: Foundation for a healthy self image and healthy interpersonal relationships. *Journal of Mental Health Counseling, 16*(3), 327–339.

Roles, P. (1989). *Saying goodbye to a baby: Vol. 1. The birthparents' guide to loss and grief in adoption.* Washington, DC: Child Welfare League Association.

Root, M. P. P. (Ed.). (1992). *Racially mixed people in America.* Newbury Park, CA: Sage.

Root, M. P. P. (1994). Mixed-race women. In L. Comas-Díaz & B. Greene, (Eds.), *Women of color: Integrating ethnic and gender identities in psychotherapy* (pp. 455–478). New York: Guilford Press.

Root, M. P. P. (Ed.). (1996). *The multiracial experience: Racial borders as the new frontier.* Thousand Oaks, CA: Sage.

Rosenbaum, A., & O'Leary, K. (1981). Marital violence: characteristics of abusive couples. *Journal of Consulting and Clinical Psychology, 49*(1), 63–71.

Rosenberg, E. B. (1992). *The adoption lifecycle: The children and their families through the years.* New York: Free Press.

Rosenberg, E. B., & Horner, T. M. (1991). Birth parent romances and identity formation in adopted children. *American Journal of Orthopsychiatry, 61*(1), 70–77.

Rosenblatt, P. C., Karis, T. A., & Powell, R. D. (1995). *Multiracial couples: Black and white voices.* Thousand Oaks, CA: Sage.

Rosenboom, L. (1993, March 25–28). *Patterns of attachment of interracial adopted children in a Dutch sample compared to an American sample.* Paper presented at the 60th annual meeting of the Society for Research in Child Development, New Orleans, LA.

Rosenthal, J. A., & Groze, V. (1992). *Special needs adoption: A study of intact families.* New York: Praeger.

Rosenthal, J. A., Schmidt, D., & Connor, J. (1988). Predictors of special needs adoption disruption: An exploratory study. *Children and Youth Services Review, 10*(2), 104–117.

Ross, M. W. (1989). Married homosexual men: Prevalance and background. *Marriage and Family Review, 14*(3/4), 35–57.

Roth, S. (1989). Psychotherapy with lesbian couples: Individual issues, female socialization, and the social context. In M. McGoldrick, C. Anderson, & F. Walsh (Eds.), *Women in families* (pp. 286–307). New York: Norton.

Roth, S., & Murphy, B. (1986). Therapeutic work with lesbian clients: A systemic therapy view. In M. Ault-Riche & J. C. Hansen (Eds.), *Women and family therapy* (pp. 78–89). Rockville, MD: Aspen.

Rowe, W., & Atkinson, D. R. (1995). Misrepresentation and interpretation: Critical evaluation of White Racial Identity Development Models. *Counseling Psychologist, 23*(2), 364–367.

Rutter, M., & Rutter, K. (1993). *Developing minds.* New York: International Universities Press.

Rynearson, E. K. (1982). Relinquishment and its maternal complications: A preliminary study. *American Journal of Psychiatry, 139*(3), 338–340.

Sabnani, H. B., Ponterotto, J. C., & Borodovsky, R. G. (1991). White racial identity development and cross cultural counselor training: A stage model. *Counseling Psychologist, 19*, 76–102.

Sachdev, P. (1989). The triangle of fears: Fallacies and facts. *Child Welfare, 67*, 491–503.

Sachdev, P. (1991). Achieving openness in adoption: Some critical issues in policy formation. *American Journal of Orthopsychiatry, 61*(2), 241–249.

Sachdev, P. (1992). Adoption reunion and after: A study of the search process and experience of adoptees. *Child Welfare, 1*, 53–68.

Saghir, M., & Robins, E. (1973). *Male and female homosexuality: A comprehensive investigation.* Baltimore: Williams & Wilkins.

Samuels, S. (1990). *Ideal adoption.* New York: Plenum.

Sandefur, G. D. (1995, June 24). *Whither the family in the 21st century?* Paper presented at the annual meeting of the American Family Therapy Academy, Cambridge, MA.

Sanders, G. (1993). The love that dares not speak its name: From secrecy to openness in gay and lesbian affiliations. In E. Imber-Black (Ed.), *Secrets in families and family therapy* (pp. 215–242). New York: Norton.

Savin-Williams, R. (1989). Parental influences on the self-esteem of gay and lesbian youths: A reflected appraisal model. *Journal of Homosexuality, 15*, 93–109.

Sbordone, A. (1993, July 24). *Gay men choosing fatherhood: Extending the parameters of inclusion.* Paper presented at the 15th National Lesbian and Gay Health Conference and 11th Annual AIDS/HIV Forum, Houston, TX.

Scarr, S. (1993, March 25–28). *The Minnesota twin adoption studies.* Paper presented at the 60th annual meeting of the Society for Research in Child Development, New Orleans, LA.

Scharff, D. E., & Scharff, J. S. (1987). *Object relations family therapy.* Northvale, NJ: Jason Aronson.

Schmidt, D., Rosenthal, J. A., & Bombeck, B. (1988). Parents' views of adoption disruption. *Children and Youth Services Review, 10*(2), 119–130.

Schwartz, L. L. (1994). The challenge of raising one's nonbiological children. *The American Journal of Family Therapy, 22*(3), 195–207.

Schwartz-Gottman, J. (1989). Children of gay and lesbian parents. *Marriage and Family Review, 14*(3/4), 35–57.

Seamon, F. (1992). Intergenerational issues related to the crack cocaine problem. *Family and Community Health, 15*(3), 11–19.

Sex survey reports low homosexuality incidence. (1994, April 15). *The New York Times,* p. 1.

Shannon, J. W., & Woods, W. J. (1991). Affirmative psychotherapy for gay men. *The Counseling Psychologist, 19*(2), 197–215.

Shireman, J. F., & Johnson, P. R. (1986). A longitudinal study of Black adoptions: Single parent, transracial, and traditional. *Social Work, 31,* 172–176.

Shore, R. J., & Hayslip, B. (1994). Custodial grandparenting: Implications for children's development. In A. E. Gottfried & A. W. Gottfried, *Redefining families: Implications for children's development* (pp. 171–213). New York: Plenum Press.

Siegel, R. (1987). Homophobia: Learning to work with lesbian clients. *Women and Therapy, 6*(1/2), 125–133.

Signorelli, M. (1994). *Queer in America: Sex, the media and closets of power.* New York: Random House.

Silverman, P. R., Campbell, L., & Patti, P. (1988). Reunions between adoptees and birth parents: The birth parents' experience. *Social Work, 33,* 523–528.

Simon, R. J., & Alstein, H. (1991). *Intercountry adoption: A multiracial perspective.* New York: Praeger.

Simon, R. J., & Alstein, H. (1992). *Adoption, race and identity: From infancy through adolescence.* New York: Praeger.

Singer, L. M., Brodzinsky, D. M., Ramsay, D., Steir, M., & Waters, E. (1985). Mother–infant attachment in adoptive families. *Child Development, 56,* 1543–1551.

Single parent households rise, (1994, July 20). *Boston Globe,* p. 3.

Slater, S., & Mencher, J. (1991). The lesbian family life cycle. *American Journal of Orthopsychiatry, 61,* 372–382.

Slipp, S. (1984). *Object relations: A dynamic bridge between individual and family treatment.* New York: Jason Aronson.

Smith, J. (1988). Psychopathology and homosexuality and homophobia. *Journal of Homosexuality, 15*(1/2), 57–73.

Socarides, C. W., & Vamik, V. D. (Eds.). (1991). *The homosexualities and the therapeutic process.* Madison, CT: International Universities Press.

Sohol, M. P., & Cardiff, J. (1983). A sociopsychological investigation of adult adoptees' search for birth parents. *Journal of Applied Family and Child Studies, 32*(4), 477–483.

Solsberry, P. W. (1994). Interracial couples in the United States of America: Implications for mental health counseling. *Journal of Mental Health Counseling, 4,* 304–377.

Sorosky, A. D., Baran, A., & Pannor, R. (1976). The effects of the sealed record in adoption. *American Journal of Psychiatry, 133*(8), 900–904.

Sorosky, A. D., Baran, A., & Pannor, R. (1978). *The adoption triangle.* New York: Anchor Press/Doubleday.

Spencer, M. (1985). Cultural cognition and social cognition as correlated with Black children's personal-social development. In M. Spencer, G. Brookins, & W. Allen (Eds.), *Beginnings: The social and affective development of Black children* (pp. 215–230). Hillsdale, NJ: Erlbaum.

Stanley v. Illinois. 1405-U.S. 645 (1972).

Steckel, A. (1987). Psychosocial development of children of lesbian mothers. In F. Bozett (Ed.), *Gay and lesbian parents* (pp. 75–85). New York: Praeger.

Stein, T. S. (1988). Homosexuality and new family forms: Issues in psychotherapy. *Psychiatric Annals, 18*(1), 12–20.

Stein, T. S. (1993). Overview of new developments in understanding homosexuality. In T. S. Stein (Ed.), *Changing perspectives on homosexuality* (pp. 9–39). Washington, DC: American Psychiatric Press.

Steir, M. E. (1983). *Patterns of attachment of adopted infants to their mothers.* Doctoral thesis, Yeshiva University, New York.

Stonequist, E. V. (1937). *The marginal man: A study in personality and culture conflict.* New York: Russell & Russell.

Sue, D. W. (1990, August). *The minority perspective on Whites researching minority issues.* Symposium paper presented at the 98th annual convention of the American Psychological Association, Boston, MA.

Sue, D. W., & Sue, D. (1990). *Counseling the culturally different: Theory and practice.* New York: Wiley.

Tannen, D. (1990). *You just don't understand: Women and men in conversation.* New York: Morrow.

Tasker, F., & Golombok, S. (1995). Adults raised as children in lesbian families. *American Journal of Orthopsychiatry, 65*(2), 203–215.

Tatum, B. D. (1992). Talking about race, learning about racism: The application of racial identity development theory in the classroom. *Harvard Educational Review, 62*(1), 1–24.

Thomas, C. (1971). *Boys no more.* Beverly Hills, CA: Glencoe Press.

Tiblier, K., Walker, B., & Rolland, J. (1989). Therapeutic issues when working with families of persons with AIDS. *Marriage and Family Review, 13,* 81–118.

Todd, J., McKinney, J., Harris, R., Chadderton, R., & Small, L. (1992). Attitudes toward interracial dating: Effects of age, sex, and race. *Journal of Multicultural Counseling and Development, 20,* 202–208.

Troiden, R. R. (1979). Becoming homosexual: A model for gay identity acquisition. *Psychiatry, 42,* 362–373.

Troiden, R. R. (1988). *Gay and lesbian identity: A sociological analysis.* New York: General Hall.

Tucker, M. B., & Mitchell-Kernan, C. (1990). New trends in Black American interracial marriage: The social structural context. *Journal of Marriage and the Family, 52,* 209–218.

Turner, P., Scadden, M., & Harris, M. (1990). Parenting in gay and lesbian families. *Journal of Gay and Lesbian Psychotherapy, 1*(3), 55–65.

U.S. Bureau of the Census. (1990). *Household and family characteristics, March 1989 & 1990* (No. P-20-447). Washington, DC: U.S. Government Printing Office.

U.S. Census report on interracial couples. (1994, May 14). *Boston Globe,* p. 3.

Ussher, J. M. (1990). Couples therapy with gay clients: Issues facing counselors. *Counseling Psychology Quarterly, 3*(1), 109–116.

Ussher, J. M. (1991). Family and couples therapy with gay and lesbian clients: Acknowledging the forgotten minority. *Journal of Family Therapy, 13*(2), 131–148.

Vardi, D. J., & Buchholz, E. S. (1994). Group psychotherapy with inner-city grandmothers raising their grandchildren. *International Journal of Group Psychotherapy, 44*(1), 101–122.

Vasquez, M. J. T. (1994). Latinas. In L. Comas-Díaz & B. Greene (Eds.), *Women of color: Integrating ethnic and gender identities in psychotherapy* (pp. 114–138). New York: Guilford Press.

Virginia Act. (1691). 3 Laws of Virginia, 86-89 (HENING 1823), Virginia Racial Integrity Law (1924), Virginia Acts of Assembly, C3II at 534–535.

Wade, T. J. (1991). Marketplace economy: The evaluation of interracial couples. *Basic and Applied Social Psychology, 12*(4), 405–422.

Wagner, D. L. (1995, July–September). The changing American family: Grandparent-headed households. *Perspective on Aging,* pp. 26–28.

Walker, G. (1987). AIDS and family therapy. *Family Therapy Today, 2,* 4–8.

Wallerstein, J. S., & Kelly, J. B. (1980). *Surviving the breakup: How children and parents cope with divorce.* New York: Basic Books.

Walsh, F. (Ed.). (1993). *Normal family processes* (2nd ed.). New York: Guilford Press.

Walters, M., Carter, B., Papp, P., & Silverstein, O. (1988). *The invisible web: Gender patterns in family relationships.* New York: Guilford Press.

Ward, M. (1980). Culture shock in the adoption of older children. *Social Worker, 48,* 46–49.

Wegar, K. (1996). Adoption and mental health: A theoretical critique of the psychopathological model. *American Journal of Orthopsychiatry, 65*(4), 540–548.

Weinberg, T. (1978). On "doing" and "being" gay: Sexual behavior and homosexual male self-identity. *Journal of Homosexuality, 4,* 143–156.

Westcot, M., & Dries, R. (1990). Has family therapy adapted to the single-parent family? *American Journal of Family Therapy, 18*(4), 363–372.

Weston, K. (1991). *Familes we choose: Lesbians, gays and kinship.* New York: Columbia University Press.

Weyrauch, W. O., Katz, S. N., & Olsen, F. (1994). *Cases and materials on family law: Legal concepts of changing human relations.* St. Paul, MN: West.

Williams, L. (1972). Sex, racism and social work. In A. L. Gochros & L. G. Schultz (Eds.), *Human sexuality and social work* (pp. 75–81). New York: NASW Press.

Williamson, J. (1980). *New people: Miscegnation and mulattos in the U.S.* New York: Free Press.

Winnicott, D. W. (1958). *The maturational processes and the facilitating environment.* New York: International Universities Press.

Wright, M. (1995, August 11–15). *A review of separated twin studies.* Panel discussion at the annual convention of the American Psychological Association, New York, NY.

Wyers, N. (1987). Homosexuality in the family: Lesbian and gay spouses. *Social Work, 32,* 143–148.

Young-Ware, D., & Ware, D. A. (1994). *An interracial identity model.* Unpublished paper prepared for graduate course at Northeastern University, Boston, MA.

Zill, N., & Nord, C. W. (1994). *Running in place: How American families are faring in a changing economy and individualistic society.* Washington, DC: Child Trends.

Zinik, G. (1985). Identity conflict or adaptive flexibility? Bisexuality reconsidered. In F. Kleing & T. J. Wolf (Eds.), *Bixsexualities: Theory and research* (pp. 7–19). New York: Haworth.

Zitter, S. (1987). Coming out to Mom: Theoretical aspects of the mother–daughter process. In Boston Lesbian Psychologies Collective (Eds.), *Lesbian psychologies: Explorations and challenges* (pp. 177–194). Urbana, IL: University of Illinois Press.

Index